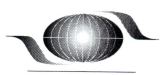

WORLD TOURISM ORGANIZATION
ORGANISATION MONDIALE DU TOURISME
ORGANIZACION MUNDIAL DEL TURISMO
ВСЕМИРНАЯ ТУРИСТСКАЯ ОРГАНИЗАЦИЯ

Compendium of Tourism Statistics

(1996 - 2000)

2002 Edition

TABLE OF CONTENTS

Pages   **Pages**

TABLE OF CONTENTS

Pages

Pages

iv

TABLE OF CONTENTS

COUNTRY TABLES BY GEOGRAPHICAL ORDER

AFRICA – AFRIQUE

East Africa – Afrique orientale – Africa Oriental

Pages

Central Africa – Afrique centrale – Africa Central

North Africa – Afrique du Nord – Africa del Norte

Southern Africa – Afrique australe – Africa Austral

West Africa – Afrique occidentale – Africa Occidental

AMERICAS – AMERIQUES

Caribbean – Caraïbes – El Caribe

TABLE OF CONTENTS

TABLE OF CONTENTS

Pages   **Pages**

INTRODUCTION

The Compendium of Tourism Statistics provides statistical information on tourism in 209 countries and territories around the world. This is the twenty-second in a series which began in 1975 as a biennial publication; it has been issued annually since 1986.

The present edition of the Compendium of Tourism Statistics is edited in English only, with countries classified according to English alphabetical order. For easy reference in Arabic, French, German, Russian and Spanish, the text of the selected indicators and the basic methodological references has been printed in a thin separate pasteboard.

The terminology used in the selected indicators by country corresponds to the new or updated concepts applied in the "Tourism Satellite Account (TSA): Recommended Methodological Framework" approved by the United Nations Statistical Commission in March/April 2000.

The statistical data published are those officially received from national tourism administrations, national statistical offices and international organizations (United Nations, International Monetary Fund and World Bank).

All the data received are subject to different kind of controls:

- comparison with the data provided at a previous moment, but referred to the same period;
- comparison of the total figures with the corresponding breakdown;
- comparison of the same figures with the corresponding breakdown by concepts;
- control for logic consistency between data;
- control for percentage variation to remain acceptable.

Any discrepancies observed are consulted with the informing unit that confirms or rectifies, if necessary, the data previously sent.

Statistical data on individual countries are grouped under:

- Inbound tourism;
- Domestic tourism;
- Outbound tourism;
- Tourism activities;
- Economic aggregates.

Consequently, **the data included in this Compendium have an official character and have been introduced in WTO database as of 18 March 2002.** Therefore, any corrections or changes received after this date will be included in the next edition of the Compendium.

The Compendium is designed to provide a condensed and quick-reference guide on the major tourism statistical indicators in each country. Users who wish to obtain more detailed statistics than those presented here are invited to consult other statistical publications of WTO, or visit WTO website *http://www.world-tourism.org*.

The World Tourism Organization wishes to express its gratitude to the national tourism administrations, national statistical offices of the various countries and territories and the above mentioned international organizations for their valuable co-operation.

Madrid, April 2002

INTRODUCTION

Le Compendium des statistiques du tourisme fournit des informations statistiques sur le tourisme dans 209 pays et territoires du monde entier. Il s'agit de la vingt-deuxième édition d'une publication bisannuelle lancée en 1975, qui est devenue annuelle à partir de 1986.

Cette édition du Compendium des statistiques du tourisme n'est publiée qu'en anglais, avec les pays classés dans l'ordre alphabétique anglais. Pour l'allemand, l'arabe, l'espagnol, le français et le russe, le texte de la sélection d'indicateurs et des références méthodologiques de base figure à part dans un mince fascicule facilement consultable.

La terminologie utilisée dans la sélection d'indicateurs par pays correspond aux concepts, nouveaux ou mis à jour, appliqués dans le document « Compte satellite du tourisme (CST) : recommandations concernant le cadre conceptuel » que la Commission de statistique des Nations Unies a approuvé en mars/avril 2000.

Les données publiées sont celles officiellement reçues des administrations nationales du tourisme, des instituts nationaux de la statistique et d'autres organisations internationales (Nations Unies, Fonds monétaire international et Banque mondiale).

Toutes les données reçues sont soumises à différents types de contrôle:

- comparaison avec les données fournies précédemment pour la même période,
- comparaison des totaux et de leur ventilation,
- comparaison des mêmes chiffres avec la ventilation correspondante par concepts,
- contrôle de la cohérence logique des données,
- contrôle de l'acceptabilité, compte tenu du pourcentage de variation.

Les anomalies éventuellement relevées sont consultées avec l'unité chargée de l'information qui confirme ou, au besoin, rectifie les données envoyées.

Les données statistiques des divers pays sont regroupées sous les rubriques suivantes :

- Tourisme récepteur ;
- Tourisme interne ;
- Tourisme émetteur ;
- Activités touristiques ;
- Agrégats économiques.

En conséquence, **les données figurant dans le présent Compendium ont un caractère officiel et ont été introduites dans la base de données de l'OMT jusqu'à la date limite du 18 mars 2002.** Toute correction ou modification reçue après cette date sera incorporée à la prochaine édition du Compendium.

De par sa conception, le Compendium est un condensé rapidement consultable des principaux indicateurs statistiques du tourisme de chaque pays. Les utilisateurs souhaitant obtenir des statistiques plus détaillées que celles présentées ici sont invités à consulter les autres publications de l'OMT dans le domaine des statistiques ou à visiter le site Internet de l'OMT (*http://www.world-tourism.org*).

L'Organisation mondiale du tourisme tient à exprimer sa gratitude aux administrations nationales du tourisme, aux instituts nationaux de la statistique des divers pays et territoires et aux organisations internationales mentionnées plus haut pour leur précieuse coopération.

Madrid, avril 2002

INTRODUCCION

El Compendio de Estadísticas de Turismo ofrece información estadística sobre el turismo en 209 países y territorios de todo el mundo. Este número es el vigésimo segundo de una serie que comenzó en 1975 como publicación bienal y siguió publicándose desde 1986 anualmente.

La presente edición del Compendio de Estadísticas de Turismo sólo se edita en inglés, con clasificación de los países en el orden alfabético correspondiente a este idioma. Para una fácil referencia en alemán, árabe, español, francés y ruso, el texto de los indicadores seleccionados y las referencias metodológicas básicas han sido impresas sobre cartulina por separado.

La terminología empleada en los indicadores seleccionados por país corresponde a los conceptos nuevos o actualizados aplicados en la "Cuenta Satélite de Turismo (CST): Recomendaciones sobre el marco conceptual" aprobado por la Comisión de Estadística de las Naciones Unidas en marzo/abril de 2000.

Los datos publicados son los remitidos oficialmente por las Administraciones Nacionales de Turismo, los Institutos Nacionales de Estadística y las Organizaciones Internacionales (Naciones Unidas, Fondo Monetario Internacional y Banco Mundial).

Todos los datos recibidos están sujetos a diversos controles:

- comparación con los datos facilitados con anterioridad y referidos al mismo periodo;
- comparación de los totales con el desglose correspondiente;
- comparación de las mismas cifras con el desglose correspondiente por conceptos;
- control de coherencia lógica entre diferentes datos;
- control de mantenimiento de aceptabilidad, cuenta habida del porcentaje de variación.

Se consultan todas las discrepancias con la unidad informante, la cual confirma o rectifica, si es necesario, los datos remitidos.

Los datos estadísticos correspondientes a cada país se agrupan de la siguiente forma:

- Turismo receptor;
- Turismo interno;
- Turismo emisor;
- Actividades turísticas;
- Agregados económicos.

Así pues, **las cifras incluidas en este Compendio tienen carácter oficial y han sido introducidas en la base de datos de la OMT al 18 de marzo de 2002.** Por consiguiente, cualquier corrección o cambio recibido después de esta fecha aparecerá en la próxima edición del Compendio.

El Compendio está concebido como guía resumida y de referencia rápida sobre los principales indicadores estadísticos de turismo de cada país. Los usuarios que deseen obtener estadísticas más detalladas pueden consultar otras publicaciones estadísticas de la OMT o visitar el sitio de Internet *http://www.world-tourism.org*.

La Organización Mundial del Turismo quiere expresar su gratitud a las Administraciones Nacionales de Turismo, a los Institutos Nacionales de Estadística de los diversos países y territorios y a las Organizaciones Internacionales mencionadas anteriormente por su valiosa colaboración.

Madrid, abril de 2002

COUNTRY
TABLES

ALBANIA

Basic Indicators	Units	Code	1996	1997	1998	1999	2000
INBOUND TOURISM							
Arrivals							
Visitors	Thousands	(1.1)	287	119	184	371	317
Tourists (overnight visitors)	Thousands	(1.2)	64	23	22	26	32
Same-day visitors	Thousands	(1.3)	..	..	..	..	..
Cruise passengers	Thousands	(1.4)	..	..	..	..	..
Arrivals by region							
Africa	Thousands	(2.1)	..	..	..	..	..
Americas	Thousands	(2.2)	5	1	1	2	..
Europe	Thousands	(2.3)	29	12	14	19	..
East Asia and the Pacific	Thousands	(2.4)	1	..	1	..	..
South Asia	Thousands	(2.5)	..	..	..	..	..
Middle East	Thousands	(2.6)	4	..	2	3	..
Arrivals by mode of transport							
Air	Thousands	(3.1)	..	..	..	86	72
Rail	Thousands	(3.2)	..	..	..	..	..
Road	Thousands	(3.3)	..	..	..	133	166
Sea	Thousands	(3.4)	..	..	..	152	79
Arrivals by purpose of visit							
Leisure, recreation and holidays	Thousands	(4.1)	14	..	..	3	2
Business and professional	Thousands	(4.2)	39	..	..	11	17
Other	Thousands	(4.3)	11	..	..	12	13
Overnight stays and length of stay							
Overnight stays in H&S	Thousand nights	(5.1)	144	66	73	96	98
Overnight stays in CE	Thousand nights	(5.2)	..	..	..	..	..
ALS of non resident tourists	Nights	(5.5)	..	..	..	..	..
Tourism expenditure in the country of reference	US$ Million	(8.1)	77	27	54	211	389
DOMESTIC TOURISM							
Overnight stays							
Overnight stays in H&S	Thousand nights	(5.3)	250	42	81	119	228
Overnight stays in CE	Thousand nights	(5.4)	..	..	..	..	..
OUTBOUND TOURISM							
Departures	Thousands	(6.1)	16	15	18	..	..
Tourism expenditure in other countries	US$ Million	(8.2)	12	5	5	12	272
TOURISM ACTIVITIES							
Hotels and similar establishments							
Number of rooms	H&S	(7.1)	2,265	2,241	2,241	2,644	2,954
Number of bed-places	H&S	(7.2)	4,361	3,423	3,423	3,575	5,919
Occupancy rate	Percent	(7.3)	34.60	..	..	..	..
Average length of stay	Nights	(5.6)	2.60	3.70	3.20	..	..
ECONOMIC AGGREGATES							
Gross National Product (GNP)	US$ Million	(9.1)	2,745	2,510	2,728	3,137	3,757
Exports (F.O.B.)	US$ Million	(9.2)	208	139	205	264	261
Imports (C.I.F.)	US$ Million	(9.3)	841	649	829	1,140	1,091

Abbreviations used in tables and notes:
H&S: Hotels and similar establishments; **CE:** All types of tourism accommodation establishments; **ALS:** Average length of stay; **THS:** Non-resident tourists staying in H&S; **TCE:** Non-resident tourists staying in CE; **TF:** Arrivals of international (or non-resident) tourists; **VF:** Arrivals of international (or non-resident) visitors; **NHS:** Overnight stays at H&S; **NCE:** Overnight stays at CE.

..	data not available
incl	including
excl	excluding
nra	nationals residing abroad

Notes:
(1.2,2.2-2.6,4.1-4.3) Arrivals in hotels only; (3.1-3.4) VF; (8.1,8.2) International Monetary Fund.

ALGERIA

Basic Indicators	Units	Code	1996	1997	1998	1999	2000
INBOUND TOURISM							
Arrivals							
Visitors	Thousands	(1.1)	605	635	678	749	866
Tourists (overnight visitors)	Thousands	(1.2)	..	..	..	..	..
Same-day visitors	Thousands	(1.3)	..	..	..	..	..
Cruise passengers	Thousands	(1.4)	..	..	..	..	..
Arrivals by region							
Africa	Thousands	(2.1)	35	34	37	51	56
Americas	Thousands	(2.2)	2	2	2	3	3
Europe	Thousands	(2.3)	46	48	57	73	99
East Asia and the Pacific	Thousands	(2.4)	1	1	3	4	5
South Asia	Thousands	(2.5)	..	..	..	..	..
Middle East	Thousands	(2.6)	10	9	8	10	13
Arrivals by mode of transport							
Air	Thousands	(3.1)	370	343	..	..	..
Rail	Thousands	(3.2)	..	..	..	..	..
Road	Thousands	(3.3)	63	184	..	..	..
Sea	Thousands	(3.4)	172	107	..	..	..
Arrivals by purpose of visit							
Leisure, recreation and holidays	Thousands	(4.1)	..	..	..	..	..
Business and professional	Thousands	(4.2)	..	..	..	..	..
Other	Thousands	(4.3)	..	..	..	..	..
Overnight stays and length of stay							
Overnight stays in H&S	Thousand nights	(5.1)	354	85	132	159	..
Overnight stays in CE	Thousand nights	(5.2)	..	..	..	..	..
ALS of non resident tourists	Nights	(5.5)	..	..	..	..	..
Tourism expenditure in the country of reference	US$ Million	(8.1)	24	6	24	..	..
DOMESTIC TOURISM							
Overnight stays							
Overnight stays in H&S	Thousand nights	(5.3)	3,487	3,404	2,775	3,275	..
Overnight stays in CE	Thousand nights	(5.4)	..	..	..	..	..
OUTBOUND TOURISM							
Departures	Thousands	(6.1)	874	827	879	903	1,006
Tourism expenditure in other countries	US$ Million	(8.2)	40	..	..	..	..
TOURISM ACTIVITIES							
Hotels and similar establishments							
Number of rooms	H&S	(7.1)	32,347	32,837	..	..	..
Number of bed-places	H&S	(7.2)	64,695	65,704	70,981	..	..
Occupancy rate	Percent	(7.3)	33.64	40.20	37.00	38.00	..
Average length of stay	Nights	(5.6)	..	..	..	..	..
ECONOMIC AGGREGATES							
Gross National Product (GNP)	US$ Million	(9.1)	43,953	44,460	46,123	46,259	48,325
Exports (F.O.B.)	US$ Million	(9.2)	12,621	..	..	..	..
Imports (C.I.F.)	US$ Million	(9.3)	8,690	..	..	..	..

Abbreviations used in tables and notes:
H&S: Hotels and similar establishments; **CE:** All types of tourism accommodation establishments; **ALS:** Average length of stay; **THS:** Non-resident tourists staying in H&S; **TCE:** Non-resident tourists staying in CE; **TF:** Arrivals of international (or non-resident) tourists; **VF:** Arrivals of international (or non-resident) visitors; **NHS:** Overnight stays at H&S; **NCE:** Overnight stays at CE.

..	data not available
incl	including
excl	excluding
nra	nationals residing abroad

Notes:
(1.1) Including nationals residing abroad; (2.1-2.6) Excluding nationals residing abroad.

Basic Indicators	Units	Code	1996	1997	1998	1999	2000
INBOUND TOURISM							
Arrivals							
Visitors	Thousands	(1.1)	..	..	..	9,422	10,991
Tourists (overnight visitors)	Thousands	(1.2)	..	..	..	2,347	2,949
Same-day visitors	Thousands	(1.3)	..	..	..	7,075	8,042
Cruise passengers	Thousands	(1.4)	..	..	..	..	..
Arrivals by region							
Africa	Thousands	(2.1)	..	..	..	..	..
Americas	Thousands	(2.2)	..	..	..	..	..
Europe	Thousands	(2.3)	..	..	..	..	..
East Asia and the Pacific	Thousands	(2.4)	..	..	..	..	..
South Asia	Thousands	(2.5)	..	..	..	..	..
Middle East	Thousands	(2.6)	..	..	..	..	..
Arrivals by mode of transport							
Air	Thousands	(3.1)	..	..	..	..	..
Rail	Thousands	(3.2)	..	..	..	..	..
Road	Thousands	(3.3)	..	..	..	..	..
Sea	Thousands	(3.4)	..	..	..	..	..
Arrivals by purpose of visit							
Leisure, recreation and holidays	Thousands	(4.1)	..	..	..	..	..
Business and professional	Thousands	(4.2)	..	..	..	..	..
Other	Thousands	(4.3)	..	..	..	..	..
Overnight stays and length of stay							
Overnight stays in H&S	Thousand nights	(5.1)	..	..	..	..	..
Overnight stays in CE	Thousand nights	(5.2)	..	..	..	6,491	8,628
ALS of non resident tourists	Nights	(5.5)	..	..	..	2.77	2.93
Tourism expenditure in the country of reference	US$ Million	(8.1)	..	..	..	..	..
DOMESTIC TOURISM							
Overnight stays							
Overnight stays in H&S	Thousand nights	(5.3)	..	..	..	..	..
Overnight stays in CE	Thousand nights	(5.4)	..	..	..	..	..
OUTBOUND TOURISM							
Departures	Thousands	(6.1)	..	..	..	..	..
Tourism expenditure in other countries	US$ Million	(8.2)	..	..	..	..	..
TOURISM ACTIVITIES							
Hotels and similar establishments							
Number of rooms	H&S	(7.1)	..	..	..	..	..
Number of bed-places	H&S	(7.2)	..	..	..	..	..
Occupancy rate	Percent	(7.3)	..	..	..	..	..
Average length of stay	Nights	(5.6)	..	..	..	..	..
ECONOMIC AGGREGATES							
Gross National Product (GNP)	US$ Million	(9.1)	..	..	..	..	..
Exports (F.O.B.)	US$ Million	(9.2)	..	..	..	..	..
Imports (C.I.F.)	US$ Million	(9.3)	..	..	..	..	..

Abbreviations used in tables and notes:
H&S: Hotels and similar establishments; **CE:** All types of tourism accommodation establishments; **ALS:** Average length of stay; **THS:** Non-resident tourists staying in H&S; **TCE:** Non-resident tourists staying in CE; **TF:** Arrivals of international (or non-resident) tourists; **VF:** Arrivals of international (or non-resident) visitors; **NHS:** Overnight stays at H&S; **NCE:** Overnight stays at CE.

..	data not available
incl	including
excl	excluding
nra	nationals residing abroad

ANGOLA

Basic Indicators	Units	Code	1996	1997	1998	1999	2000
INBOUND TOURISM							
Arrivals							
Visitors	Thousands	(1.1)	..	..	..	..	
Tourists (overnight visitors)	Thousands	(1.2)	21	45	52	45	51
Same-day visitors	Thousands	(1.3)	..	..	..	..	..
Cruise passengers	Thousands	(1.4)	..	..	..	..	..
Arrivals by region							
Africa	Thousands	(2.1)	5	14	7	8	8
Americas	Thousands	(2.2)	2	3	8	6	8
Europe	Thousands	(2.3)	13	27	34	29	31
East Asia and the Pacific	Thousands	(2.4)	1	1	2	2	3
South Asia	Thousands	(2.5)	..	..	..	..	1
Middle East	Thousands	(2.6)	..	..	..	..	..
Arrivals by mode of transport							
Air	Thousands	(3.1)	20	44	51	43	48
Rail	Thousands	(3.2)	..	..	..	..	..
Road	Thousands	(3.3)	1	1	..	2	2
Sea	Thousands	(3.4)	..	..	1	..	..
Arrivals by purpose of visit							
Leisure, recreation and holidays	Thousands	(4.1)	5	5	3	3	6
Business and professional	Thousands	(4.2)	3	6	9	6	5
Other	Thousands	(4.3)	13	34	40	36	40
Overnight stays and length of stay							
Overnight stays in H&S	Thousand nights	(5.1)	..	..	..	..	..
Overnight stays in CE	Thousand nights	(5.2)	33	89	95	48	77
ALS of non resident tourists	Nights	(5.5)	..	..	..	..	..
Tourism expenditure **in the country of reference**	US$ Million	(8.1)	9	9	8	13	18
DOMESTIC TOURISM							
Overnight stays							
Overnight stays in H&S	Thousand nights	(5.3)	..	..	..	..	..
Overnight stays in CE	Thousand nights	(5.4)	9	37	7	24	11
OUTBOUND TOURISM							
Departures	Thousands	(6.1)	3	..	..	..	..
Tourism expenditure in other countries	US$ Million	(8.2)	73	98	75	127	..
TOURISM ACTIVITIES							
Hotels and similar establishments							
Number of rooms	H&S	(7.1)	4,943	6,157	6,157	6,157	6,157
Number of bed-places	H&S	(7.2)	6,783	9,014	9,014	9,013	9,013
Occupancy rate	Percent	(7.3)	44.00	45.00	92.00	68.00	46.00
Average length of stay	Nights	(5.6)	..	..	..	..	..
ECONOMIC AGGREGATES							
Gross National Product (GNP)	US$ Million	(9.1)	3,245	4,133	3,554	2,749	3,079
Exports (F.O.B.)	US$ Million	(9.2)	..	..	..	..	..
Imports (C.I.F.)	US$ Million	(9.3)	..	..	..	..	..

Abbreviations used in tables and notes:
H&S: Hotels and similar establishments; **CE:** All types of tourism accommodation establishments; **ALS:** Average length of stay; **THS:** Non-resident tourists staying in H&S; **TCE:** Non-resident tourists staying in CE; **TF:** Arrivals of international (or non-resident) tourists; **VF:** Arrivals of international (or non-resident) visitors; **NHS:** Overnight stays at H&S; **NCE:** Overnight stays at CE.

..	data not available
incl	including
excl	excluding
nra	nationals residing abroad

Notes:
(8.2) International Monetary Fund.

Basic Indicators	Units	Code	1996	1997	1998	1999	2000
INBOUND TOURISM							
Arrivals							
Visitors							
Tourists (overnight visitors)	Thousands	(1.1)	86	114	114	107	112
Same-day visitors	Thousands	(1.2)	37	43	44	47	44
Cruise passengers	Thousands	(1.3)	49	71	70	60	68
	Thousands	(1.4)	..	..	..	..	..
Arrivals by region							
Africa	Thousands	(2.1)	..	..	..	..	..
Americas	Thousands	(2.2)	34	37	33	33	33
Europe	Thousands	(2.3)	3	5	10	12	9
East Asia and the Pacific	Thousands	(2.4)	..	..	..	..	..
South Asia	Thousands	(2.5)	..	..	..	..	..
Middle East	Thousands	(2.6)	..	..	..	..	..
Arrivals by mode of transport							
Air	Thousands	(3.1)	28	33	29	29	28
Rail	Thousands	(3.2)	..	..	..	..	..
Road	Thousands	(3.3)	..	..	..	..	..
Sea	Thousands	(3.4)	58	81	85	78	84
Arrivals by purpose of visit							
Leisure, recreation and holidays	Thousands	(4.1)	84	111	111	104	109
Business and professional	Thousands	(4.2)	2	3	3	3	3
Other	Thousands	(4.3)	..	..	..	..	..
Overnight stays and length of stay							
Overnight stays in H&S	Thousand nights	(5.1)	..	..	..	..	
Overnight stays in CE	Thousand nights	(5.2)	352	408	404	400	377
ALS of non resident tourists	Nights	(5.5)	9.40	9.50	9.20	8.50	8.60
Tourism expenditure **in the country of reference**	US$ Million	(8.1)	48	57	58	56	55
DOMESTIC TOURISM							
Overnight stays							
Overnight stays in H&S	Thousand nights	(5.3)	..	..	..	..	..
Overnight stays in CE	Thousand nights	(5.4)	..	..	..	..	..
OUTBOUND TOURISM							
Departures	Thousands	(6.1)	..	..	..	..	..
Tourism expenditure in other countries	US$ Million	(8.2)	..	..	..	..	..
TOURISM ACTIVITIES							
Hotels and similar establishments							
Number of rooms	H&S	(7.1)	866	915	1,045	1,120	1,067
Number of bed-places	H&S	(7.2)	..	..	..	..	..
Occupancy rate	Percent	(7.3)	..	..	80.30	..	..
Average length of stay	Nights	(5.6)	..	..	..	..	..
ECONOMIC AGGREGATES							
Gross National Product (GNP)	US$ Million	(9.1)	65	72	78	86	..
Exports (F.O.B.)	US$ Million	(9.2)	2	2	3	3	..
Imports (C.I.F.)	US$ Million	(9.3)	52	62	..	..	..

Abbreviations used in tables and notes:
H&S: Hotels and similar establishments; **CE:** All types of tourism accommodation establishments; **ALS:** Average length of stay; **THS:** Non-resident tourists staying in H&S; **TCE:** Non-resident tourists staying in CE; **TF:** Arrivals of international (or non-resident) tourists; **VF:** Arrivals of international (or non-resident) visitors; **NHS:** Overnight stays at H&S; **NCE:** Overnight stays at CE.

..   data not available
incl   including
excl   excluding
nra   nationals residing abroad

Notes:
(1.1,3.1-4.2) VF; (1.2,2.2-2.3) TF, excl nra; (7.1) Hotels, guest houses, apartments/villas; (7.3) Rooms; (9.1) GDP.

ANTIGUA AND BARBUDA

Basic Indicators	Units	Code	1996	1997	1998	1999	2000
INBOUND TOURISM							
Arrivals							
Visitors	Thousands	(1.1)	522	541	596	589	..
Tourists (overnight visitors)	Thousands	(1.2)	220	232	226	232	..
Same-day visitors	Thousands	(1.3)	..	..			..
Cruise passengers	Thousands	(1.4)	302	309	370	357	..
Arrivals by region							
Africa	Thousands	(2.1)	..	..	..	..	
Americas	Thousands	(2.2)	128	138	134	..	..
Europe	Thousands	(2.3)	88	90	88	..	..
East Asia and the Pacific	Thousands	(2.4)	..	..	..	..	..
South Asia	Thousands	(2.5)	..	..	..	..	..
Middle East	Thousands	(2.6)	..	..	..	..	..
Arrivals by mode of transport							
Air	Thousands	(3.1)	202	211	204	208	207
Rail	Thousands	(3.2)	..	..	..	..	
Road	Thousands	(3.3)	..	..	..	..	..
Sea	Thousands	(3.4)	18	21	22	24	..
Arrivals by purpose of visit							
Leisure, recreation and holidays	Thousands	(4.1)	153	161	153	..	..
Business and professional	Thousands	(4.2)	3	2	2	..	..
Other	Thousands	(4.3)	46	48	49	..	..
Overnight stays and length of stay							
Overnight stays in H&S	Thousand nights	(5.1)	..	..	..	..	..
Overnight stays in CE	Thousand nights	(5.2)	..	..	..	..	..
ALS of non resident tourists	Nights	(5.5)	..	..	..	..	..
Tourism expenditure in the country of reference	US$ Million	(8.1)	258	269	256	290	290
DOMESTIC TOURISM							
Overnight stays							
Overnight stays in H&S	Thousand nights	(5.3)	..	..	..	..	..
Overnight stays in CE	Thousand nights	(5.4)	..	..	..	..	..
OUTBOUND TOURISM							
Departures	Thousands	(6.1)	369	..	..	..	..
Tourism expenditure in other countries	US$ Million	(8.2)	26	..	..	..	..
TOURISM ACTIVITIES							
Hotels and similar establishments							
Number of rooms	H&S	(7.1)	3,185	3,185	3,185	3,185	..
Number of bed-places	H&S	(7.2)	..	..	..	..	..
Occupancy rate	Percent	(7.3)	81.40	..	..	..	..
Average length of stay	Nights	(5.6)	..	..	..	..	..
ECONOMIC AGGREGATES							
Gross National Product (GNP)	US$ Million	(9.1)	519	547	547	568	625
Exports (F.O.B.)	US$ Million	(9.2)	38	38	36	38	..
Imports (C.I.F.)	US$ Million	(9.3)	365	370	385	414	..

Abbreviations used in tables and notes:
H&S: Hotels and similar establishments; **CE:** All types of tourism accommodation establishments; **ALS:** Average length of stay; **THS:** Non-resident tourists staying in H&S; **TCE:** Non-resident tourists staying in CE; **TF:** Arrivals of international (or non-resident) tourists; **VF:** Arrivals of international (or non-resident) visitors; **NHS:** Overnight stays at H&S; **NCE:** Overnight stays at CE.

..	data not available
incl	including
excl	excluding
nra	nationals residing abroad

Notes:
(1.2) Air and sea arrivals, excl nra; (1.4) Incl cruise ships, windjammer cruises and yacht arrivals; (4.1-4.3) Air arrivals; (6.1) Trips abroad include departing residents.

ARGENTINA

Basic Indicators	Units	Code	1996	1997	1998	1999	2000
INBOUND TOURISM							
Arrivals							
Visitors	Thousands	(1.1)	..	..	..	..	..
Tourists (overnight visitors)	Thousands	(1.2)	2,614	2,764	3,012	2,898	2,949
Same-day visitors	Thousands	(1.3)	..	..	..	..	..
Cruise passengers	Thousands	(1.4)	..	..	..	..	..
Arrivals by region							
Africa	Thousands	(2.1)	..	..	..	..	..
Americas	Thousands	(2.2)	2,252	2,378	2,595	2,491	2,520
Europe	Thousands	(2.3)	299	320	344	337	354
East Asia and the Pacific	Thousands	(2.4)	..	..	..	..	..
South Asia	Thousands	(2.5)	..	..	..	..	..
Middle East	Thousands	(2.6)	..	..	..	..	..
Arrivals by mode of transport							
Air	Thousands	(3.1)	..	..	..	..	1,208
Rail	Thousands	(3.2)	..	..	..	..	..
Road	Thousands	(3.3)	..	..	..	..	1,347
Sea	Thousands	(3.4)	..	..	..	..	394
Arrivals by purpose of visit							
Leisure, recreation and holidays	Thousands	(4.1)	..	..	..	..	..
Business and professional	Thousands	(4.2)	..	..	..	..	..
Other	Thousands	(4.3)	..	..	..	..	..
Overnight stays and length of stay							
Overnight stays in H&S	Thousand nights	(5.1)	..	..	..	..	..
Overnight stays in CE	Thousand nights	(5.2)	..	..	..	..	..
ALS of non resident tourists	Nights	(5.5)	..	..	..	..	..
Tourism expenditure in the country of reference	US$ Million	(8.1)	2,542	2,693	2,936	2,812	2,874
DOMESTIC TOURISM							
Overnight stays							
Overnight stays in H&S	Thousand nights	(5.3)	..	..	..	..	..
Overnight stays in CE	Thousand nights	(5.4)	..	..	..	..	..
OUTBOUND TOURISM							
Departures	Thousands	(6.1)	4,296	4,517	4,592	4,786	4,953
Tourism expenditure in other countries	US$ Million	(8.2)	3,497	3,874	3,993	4,107	4,338
TOURISM ACTIVITIES							
Hotels and similar establishments							
Number of rooms	H&S	(7.1)	85,170	155,435	162,462	162,234	166,087
Number of bed-places	H&S	(7.2)	317,535	390,072	364,713	368,929	378,246
Occupancy rate	Percent	(7.3)	..	..	..	..	..
Average length of stay	Nights	(5.6)	..	..	..	..	..
ECONOMIC AGGREGATES							
Gross National Product (GNP)	US$ Million	(9.1)	273,303	290,980	290,042	276,199	275,547
Exports (F.O.B.)	US$ Million	(9.2)	23,811	26,370	26,441	23,333	26,409
Imports (C.I.F.)	US$ Million	(9.3)	23,762	30,450	31,404	25,508	25,243

Abbreviations used in tables and notes:
H&S: Hotels and similar establishments; **CE:** All types of tourism accommodation establishments; **ALS:** Average length of stay; **THS:** Non-resident tourists staying in H&S; **TCE:** Non-resident tourists staying in CE; **TF:** Arrivals of international (or non-resident) tourists; **VF:** Arrivals of international (or non-resident) visitors; **NHS:** Overnight stays at H&S; **NCE:** Overnight stays at CE.

..   data not available
incl   including
excl   excluding
nra   nationals residing abroad

Notes:
(1.2) Excl nra; (7.1/96) Figures refer to one to five-star and non-classified hotels.
Note: Arrivals and economic receipts from inbound international tourism correspond to a new series from 1990 to 1999. Source: data published by the Sub-Secretary of Macroeconomic Programming, Ministry of Economy and Civil Works and Services.

ARMENIA

Basic Indicators	Units	Code	1996	1997	1998	1999	2000
INBOUND TOURISM							
Arrivals							
Visitors	Thousands	(1.1)	..	..	..	..	45
Tourists (overnight visitors)	Thousands	(1.2)	13	23	32	41	45
Same-day visitors	Thousands	(1.3)	..	..	..	..	..
Cruise passengers	Thousands	(1.4)	..	..	..	..	..
Arrivals by region							
Africa	Thousands	(2.1)	..	..	..	..	..
Americas	Thousands	(2.2)	1	3	5	6	8
Europe	Thousands	(2.3)	11	16	23	27	25
East Asia and the Pacific	Thousands	(2.4)	..	1	1	1	1
South Asia	Thousands	(2.5)	1	2	1	5	9
Middle East	Thousands	(2.6)	..	1	1	2	2
Arrivals by mode of transport							
Air	Thousands	(3.1)	12	20	29	..	..
Rail	Thousands	(3.2)	..	1	1	..	..
Road	Thousands	(3.3)	1	2	2	..	..
Sea	Thousands	(3.4)	..	..	..	..	..
Arrivals by purpose of visit							
Leisure, recreation and holidays	Thousands	(4.1)	9	18	25	..	..
Business and professional	Thousands	(4.2)	2	3	5	..	..
Other	Thousands	(4.3)	2	2	2	..	..
Overnight stays and length of stay							
Overnight stays in H&S	Thousand nights	(5.1)	..	..	..	..	..
Overnight stays in CE	Thousand nights	(5.2)	89	116	161	204	..
ALS of non resident tourists	Nights	(5.5)	6.50	6.50	6.50	..	..
Tourism expenditure							
in the country of reference	US$ Million	(8.1)	5	7	10	27	45
DOMESTIC TOURISM							
Overnight stays							
Overnight stays in H&S	Thousand nights	(5.3)	..	..	..	..	..
Overnight stays in CE	Thousand nights	(5.4)	..	..	..	..	..
OUTBOUND TOURISM							
Departures	Thousands	(6.1)	..	..	..	..	..
Tourism expenditure in other countries	US$ Million	(8.2)	22	41	45	34	37
TOURISM ACTIVITIES							
Hotels and similar establishments							
Number of rooms	H&S	(7.1)	..	3,450	3,600	..	..
Number of bed-places	H&S	(7.2)	..	10,300	10,800	..	..
Occupancy rate	Percent	(7.3)	..	16.00	17.00	19.30	..
Average length of stay	Nights	(5.6)	6.50	6.50	6.50	..	..
ECONOMIC AGGREGATES							
Gross National Product (GNP)	US$ Million	(9.1)	2,323	1,973	1,792	1,850	1,990
Exports (F.O.B.)	US$ Million	(9.2)	290	233	221	232	294
Imports (C.I.F.)	US$ Million	(9.3)	856	892	902	800	882

Abbreviations used in tables and notes:
H&S: Hotels and similar establishments; **CE:** All types of tourism accommodation establishments; **ALS:** Average length of stay; **THS:** Non-resident tourists staying in H&S; **TCE:** Non-resident tourists staying in CE; **TF:** Arrivals of international (or non-resident) tourists; **VF:** Arrivals of international (or non-resident) visitors; **NHS:** Overnight stays at H&S; **NCE:** Overnight stays at CE.

..   data not available
incl   including
excl   excluding
nra   nationals residing abroad

Notes:
(1.2,2.2-2.6) TCE.

Basic Indicators	Units	Code	1996	1997	1998	1999	2000
INBOUND TOURISM							
Arrivals							
Visitors	Thousands	(1.1)	957	947	906	972	1,211
Tourists (overnight visitors)	Thousands	(1.2)	641	650	647	683	721
Same-day visitors	Thousands	(1.3)	..	..	..	..	..
Cruise passengers	Thousands	(1.4)	316	297	259	289	490
Arrivals by region							
Africa	Thousands	(2.1)	..	..	..	..	..
Americas	Thousands	(2.2)	582	588	595	629	670
Europe	Thousands	(2.3)	55	57	49	49	47
East Asia and the Pacific	Thousands	(2.4)	..	..	..	..	..
South Asia	Thousands	(2.5)	..	..	..	..	..
Middle East	Thousands	(2.6)	..	..	..	..	..
Arrivals by mode of transport							
Air	Thousands	(3.1)	637	641	644	683	721
Rail	Thousands	(3.2)	..	..	..	..	..
Road	Thousands	(3.3)	..	..	..	..	..
Sea	Thousands	(3.4)	4	5	3	..	..
Arrivals by purpose of visit							
Leisure, recreation and holidays	Thousands	(4.1)	619	606	598	631	660
Business and professional	Thousands	(4.2)	17	36	38	40	40
Other	Thousands	(4.3)	4	4	11	12	21
Overnight stays and length of stay							
Overnight stays in H&S	Thousand nights	(5.1)	3,824	3,879	3,959	3,998	4,250
Overnight stays in CE	Thousand nights	(5.2)	4,714	4,843	4,890	5,142	5,248
ALS of non resident tourists	Nights	(5.5)	7.36	7.50	8.50	9.30	8.60
Tourism expenditure							
in the country of reference	US$ Million	(8.1)	613	668	732	778	638
DOMESTIC TOURISM							
Overnight stays							
Overnight stays in H&S	Thousand nights	(5.3)	..	..	..	..	..
Overnight stays in CE	Thousand nights	(5.4)	..	..	..	..	..
OUTBOUND TOURISM							
Departures	Thousands	(6.1)	..	..	..	..	..
Tourism expenditure in other countries	US$ Million	(8.2)	96	131	111	122	..
TOURISM ACTIVITIES							
Hotels and similar establishments							
Number of rooms	H&S	(7.1)	6,781	7,233	7,233	7,783	7,783
Number of bed-places	H&S	(7.2)	13,562	14,466	14,466	15,566	15,566
Occupancy rate	Percent	(7.3)	71.50	73.50	78.46	78.60	74.04
Average length of stay	Nights	(5.6)	..	..	..	..	..
ECONOMIC AGGREGATES							
Gross National Product (GNP)	US$ Million	(9.1)	1,556	1,647	1,728	1,821	..
Exports (F.O.B.)	US$ Million	(9.2)	12	24	29	29	..
Imports (C.I.F.)	US$ Million	(9.3)	578	614	815	782	..

Abbreviations used in tables and notes:
H&S: Hotels and similar establishments; **CE:** All types of tourism accommodation establishments; **ALS:** Average length of stay; **THS:** Non-resident tourists staying in H&S; **TCE:** Non-resident tourists staying in CE; **TF:** Arrivals of international (or non-resident) tourists; **VF:** Arrivals of international (or non-resident) visitors; **NHS:** Overnight stays at H&S; **NCE:** Overnight stays at CE.

..   data not available
incl   including
excl   excluding
nra   nationals residing abroad

Notes:
(1.2,2.2-4.3) TF; (5.5) THS; (7.3) Rooms; (9.1) GDP.

AUSTRALIA

Basic Indicators	Units	Code	1996	1997	1998	1999	2000
INBOUND TOURISM							
Arrivals							
Visitors	Thousands	(1.1)	4,165	4,318	4,167	4,459	4,946
Tourists (overnight visitors)	Thousands	(1.2)	..	..	..	..	..
Same-day visitors	Thousands	(1.3)	..	..	..	..	..
Cruise passengers	Thousands	(1.4)	..	..	..	..	..
Arrivals by region							
Africa	Thousands	(2.1)	53	56	71	71	..
Americas	Thousands	(2.2)	401	420	474	534	..
Europe	Thousands	(2.3)	811	885	964	1,084	..
East Asia and the Pacific	Thousands	(2.4)	2,843	2,893	2,584	2,683	..
South Asia	Thousands	(2.5)	33	38	43	50	..
Middle East	Thousands	(2.6)	20	21	28	34	..
Arrivals by mode of transport							
Air	Thousands	(3.1)	4,149	4,305	4,146	4,427	..
Rail	Thousands	(3.2)	..	..	..	..	..
Road	Thousands	(3.3)	..	..	..	..	..
Sea	Thousands	(3.4)	15	13	21	32	..
Arrivals by purpose of visit							
Leisure, recreation and holidays	Thousands	(4.1)	2,518	2,535	2,219	2,503	..
Business and professional	Thousands	(4.2)	659	692	667	745	..
Other	Thousands	(4.3)	986	1,091	1,281	1,211	..
Overnight stays and length of stay							
Overnight stays in H&S	Thousand nights	(5.1)	19,139	18,112	17,731	19,128	..
Overnight stays in CE	Thousand nights	(5.2)	34,653	32,808	34,512	39,029	..
ALS of non resident tourists	Nights	(5.5)	24.00	23.00	25.00	26.00	..
Tourism expenditure in the country of reference	US$ Million	(8.1)	9,113	9,057	7,335	7,525	8,006
DOMESTIC TOURISM							
Overnight stays							
Overnight stays in H&S	Thousand nights	(5.3)	52,784	50,661	66,687	69,005	67,284
Overnight stays in CE	Thousand nights	(5.4)	86,743	84,862	104,833	111,059	134,831
OUTBOUND TOURISM							
Departures	Thousands	(6.1)	2,732	2,933	3,161	3,210	..
Tourism expenditure in other countries	US$ Million	(8.2)	5,445	6,150	5,388	5,792	5,740
TOURISM ACTIVITIES							
Hotels and similar establishments							
Number of rooms	H&S	(7.1)	173,876	172,334	182,061	190,097	194,926
Number of bed-places	H&S	(7.2)	504,123	507,807	536,754	559,665	567,546
Occupancy rate	Percent	(7.3)	58.40	57.40	57.70	58.70	58.10
Average length of stay	Nights	(5.6)	2.10	2.00	2.20	2.20	2.30
ECONOMIC AGGREGATES							
Gross National Product (GNP)	US$ Million	(9.1)	392,825	412,779	402,328	397,222	394,068
Exports (F.O.B.)	US$ Million	(9.2)	60,300	62,910	55,893	56,080	64,898
Imports (C.I.F.)	US$ Million	(9.3)	65,428	65,892	64,630	69,158	71,537

Abbreviations used in tables and notes:
H&S: Hotels and similar establishments; **CE:** All types of tourism accommodation establishments; **ALS:** Average length of stay; **THS:** Non-resident tourists staying in H&S; **TCE:** Non-resident tourists staying in CE; **TF:** Arrivals of international (or non-resident) tourists; **VF:** Arrivals of international (or non-resident) visitors; **NHS:** Overnight stays at H&S; **NCE:** Overnight stays at CE.

..   data not available
incl   including
excl   excluding
nra   nationals residing abroad

Notes:
(1.1) Excl nra and crew members; (5.5) Commercial; (5.6) Inbound tourism in commercial accommodation; (7.1-7.3) Hotels, motels and guests houses with 15 rooms or more; (7.3) Rooms.

Basic Indicators	Units	Code	1996	1997	1998	1999	2000
INBOUND TOURISM							
Arrivals							
Visitors	Thousands	(1.1)	..	..	..	..	..
Tourists (overnight visitors)	Thousands	(1.2)	17,090	16,647	17,352	17,467	17,982
Same-day visitors	Thousands	(1.3)	..	..	..	..	..
Cruise passengers	Thousands	(1.4)	..	..	..	..	..
Arrivals by region							
Africa	Thousands	(2.1)	22	23	33	33	36
Americas	Thousands	(2.2)	708	719	828	767	934
Europe	Thousands	(2.3)	15,570	15,063	15,680	15,843	16,084
East Asia and the Pacific	Thousands	(2.4)	515	530	500	535	624
South Asia	Thousands	(2.5)	28	24	22	31	35
Middle East	Thousands	(2.6)	21	26	26	25	29
Arrivals by mode of transport							
Air	Thousands	(3.1)	..	..	..	..	..
Rail	Thousands	(3.2)	..	..	..	..	..
Road	Thousands	(3.3)	..	..	..	..	..
Sea	Thousands	(3.4)	..	..	..	..	..
Arrivals by purpose of visit							
Leisure, recreation and holidays	Thousands	(4.1)	..	..	..	..	..
Business and professional	Thousands	(4.2)	..	..	..	..	..
Other	Thousands	(4.3)	..	..	..	..	..
Overnight stays and length of stay							
Overnight stays in H&S	Thousand nights	(5.1)	55,126	53,393	56,371	57,072	58,029
Overnight stays in CE	Thousand nights	(5.2)	62,411	60,115	63,195	63,831	64,468
ALS of non resident tourists	Nights	(5.5)	..	..	..	..	..
Tourism expenditure							
in the country of reference	US$ Million	(8.1)	13,930	12,248	12,628	12,533	10,031
DOMESTIC TOURISM							
Overnight stays							
Overnight stays in H&S	Thousand nights	(5.3)	15,892	16,085	17,102	18,034	18,897
Overnight stays in CE	Thousand nights	(5.4)	23,417	23,453	24,421	25,466	26,242
OUTBOUND TOURISM							
Departures	Thousands	(6.1)	3,713	..	3,784	3,954	4,660
Tourism expenditure in other countries	US$ Million	(8.2)	11,782	10,712	10,324	9,803	9,291
TOURISM ACTIVITIES							
Hotels and similar establishments							
Number of rooms	H&S	(7.1)	307,187	301,479	302,364	309,402	304,928
Number of bed-places	H&S	(7.2)	640,199	633,601	632,409	648,757	642,623
Occupancy rate	Percent	(7.3)	32.50	32.30	34.20	34.50	34.50
Average length of stay	Nights	(5.6)	4.70	4.60	4.50	4.40	4.00
ECONOMIC AGGREGATES							
Gross National Product (GNP)	US$ Million	(9.1)	232,282	227,858	214,524	205,719	204,250
Exports (F.O.B.)	US$ Million	(9.2)	57,822	58,599	62,747	64,126	64,167
Imports (C.I.F.)	US$ Million	(9.3)	67,336	64,786	68,187	69,557	68,986

Abbreviations used in tables and notes:
H&S: Hotels and similar establishments; **CE:** All types of tourism accommodation establishments; **ALS:** Average length of stay; **THS:** Non-resident tourists staying in H&S; **TCE:** Non-resident tourists staying in CE; **TF:** Arrivals of international (or non-resident) tourists; **VF:** Arrivals of international (or non-resident) visitors; **NHS:** Overnight stays at H&S; **NCE:** Overnight stays at CE.

Notes:
(1.2-2.6) TCE; (5.1,5.3/96/97) Hotels only; (5.1,5.3/98/99) Incl holiday villages; (5.2,5.4) Excl private accommodation; (8.1,8.2) Incl international transport.

..	data not available
incl	including
excl	excluding
nra	nationals residing abroad

AZERBAIJAN

Basic Indicators	Units	Code	1996	1997	1998	1999	2000
INBOUND TOURISM							
Arrivals							
Visitors	Thousands	(1.1)	..	..	..	..	..
Tourists (overnight visitors)	Thousands	(1.2)	210	306	483	602	681
Same-day visitors	Thousands	(1.3)	..	..	..	..	..
Cruise passengers	Thousands	(1.4)	..	..	..	..	..
Arrivals by region							
Africa	Thousands	(2.1)	..	..	..	..	..
Americas	Thousands	(2.2)	..	5	3	2	..
Europe	Thousands	(2.3)	..	183	331	443	359
East Asia and the Pacific	Thousands	(2.4)	..	..	..	..	..
South Asia	Thousands	(2.5)	..	106	140	122	242
Middle East	Thousands	(2.6)	..	..	..	..	..
Arrivals by mode of transport							
Air	Thousands	(3.1)	195	286	466	564	658
Rail	Thousands	(3.2)	..	..	2	..	3
Road	Thousands	(3.3)	14	17	14	37	20
Sea	Thousands	(3.4)	1	3	1	1	..
Arrivals by purpose of visit							
Leisure, recreation and holidays	Thousands	(4.1)	15	22	17	11	6
Business and professional	Thousands	(4.2)	167	210	438	538	606
Other	Thousands	(4.3)	28	74	28	53	69
Overnight stays and length of stay							
Overnight stays in H&S	Thousand nights	(5.1)	..	67	143	34	..
Overnight stays in CE	Thousand nights	(5.2)	..	..	..	..	..
ALS of non resident tourists	Nights	(5.5)	..	..	..	..	..
Tourism expenditure							
in the country of reference	US$ Million	(8.1)	46	162	125	81	63
DOMESTIC TOURISM							
Overnight stays							
Overnight stays in H&S	Thousand nights	(5.3)	..	..	..	..	..
Overnight stays in CE	Thousand nights	(5.4)	..	..	..	..	..
OUTBOUND TOURISM							
Departures	Thousands	(6.1)	432	654	1,146	1,204	..
Tourism expenditure in other countries	US$ Million	(8.2)	100	186	170	139	132
TOURISM ACTIVITIES							
Hotels and similar establishments							
Number of rooms	H&S	(7.1)	5,600	6,000	6,400	..	..
Number of bed-places	H&S	(7.2)	..	..	..	..	..
Occupancy rate	Percent	(7.3)	..	49.80	37.00	31.50	..
Average length of stay	Nights	(5.6)	..	..	..	..	..
ECONOMIC AGGREGATES							
Gross National Product (GNP)	US$ Million	(9.1)	3,060	3,469	3,961	4,431	4,881
Exports (F.O.B.)	US$ Million	(9.2)	631	781	606	929	..
Imports (C.I.F.)	US$ Million	(9.3)	961	794	1,077	1,036	..

Abbreviations used in tables and notes:
H&S: Hotels and similar establishments; **CE:** All types of tourism accommodation establishments; **ALS:** Average length of stay; **THS:** Non-resident tourists staying in H&S; **TCE:** Non-resident tourists staying in CE; **TF:** Arrivals of international (or non-resident) tourists; **VF:** Arrivals of international (or non-resident) visitors; **NHS:** Overnight stays at H&S; **NCE:** Overnight stays at CE.

..	data not available
incl	including
excl	excluding
nra	nationals residing abroad

Notes:
(8.1,8.2) International Monetary Fund.

Basic Indicators	Units	Code	1996	1997	1998	1999	2000
INBOUND TOURISM							
Arrivals							
Visitors	Thousands	(1.1)	3,416	3,446	3,348	3,648	4,204
Tourists (overnight visitors)	Thousands	(1.2)	1,633	1,618	1,528	1,577	1,596
Same-day visitors	Thousands	(1.3)	99	77	90	90	95
Cruise passengers	Thousands	(1.4)	1,686	1,751	1,730	1,981	2,513
Arrivals by region							
Africa	Thousands	(2.1)	..	..	..	..	..
Americas	Thousands	(2.2)	1,445	..	..	..	..
Europe	Thousands	(2.3)	128	130	118	125	128
East Asia and the Pacific	Thousands	(2.4)	26	..	..	..	..
South Asia	Thousands	(2.5)	..	..	..	..	..
Middle East	Thousands	(2.6)	..	..	..	..	..
Arrivals by mode of transport							
Air	Thousands	(3.1)	1,368	1,368	1,305	1,439	1,482
Rail	Thousands	(3.2)	..	..	..	..	..
Road	Thousands	(3.3)	..	..	..	..	..
Sea	Thousands	(3.4)	2,048	2,078	2,043	2,209	2,722
Arrivals by purpose of visit							
Leisure, recreation and holidays	Thousands	(4.1)	1,421	1,375	..	1,246	..
Business and professional	Thousands	(4.2)	147	178	..	158	..
Other	Thousands	(4.3)	65	65	..	173	..
Overnight stays and length of stay							
Overnight stays in H&S	Thousand nights	(5.1)	..	..	..	..	..
Overnight stays in CE	Thousand nights	(5.2)	9,466	..	..	..	..
ALS of non resident tourists	Nights	(5.5)	5.80	6.00	5.40	5.40	..
Tourism expenditure							
in the country of reference	US$ Million	(8.1)	1,398	1,416	1,354	1,583	1,814
DOMESTIC TOURISM							
Overnight stays							
Overnight stays in H&S	Thousand nights	(5.3)	..	..	..	..	..
Overnight stays in CE	Thousand nights	(5.4)	..	..	..	..	..
OUTBOUND TOURISM							
Departures	Thousands	(6.1)	..	..	..	..	..
Tourism expenditure in other countries	US$ Million	(8.2)	235	250	256	309	293
TOURISM ACTIVITIES							
Hotels and similar establishments							
Number of rooms	H&S	(7.1)	13,288	13,288	14,243	14,153	14,701
Number of bed-places	H&S	(7.2)	26,576	26,576	28,486	28,306	29,402
Occupancy rate	Percent	(7.3)	66.40	68.00	68.70	68.60	67.20
Average length of stay	Nights	(5.6)	..	..	..	..	6.50
ECONOMIC AGGREGATES							
Gross National Product (GNP)	US$ Million	(9.1)	3,594	3,735	3,803	4,201	4,533
Exports (F.O.B.)	US$ Million	(9.2)	180	181	300	450	400
Imports (C.I.F.)	US$ Million	(9.3)	1,366	1,666	1,873	1,911	1,421

Abbreviations used in tables and notes:
H&S: Hotels and similar establishments; **CE:** All types of tourism accommodation establishments; **ALS:** Average length of stay; **THS:** Non-resident tourists staying in H&S; **TCE:** Non-resident tourists staying in CE; **TF:** Arrivals of international (or non-resident) tourists; **VF:** Arrivals of international (or non-resident) visitors; **NHS:** Overnight stays at H&S; **NCE:** Overnight stays at CE.

..   data not available
incl   including
excl   excluding
nra   nationals residing abroad

Notes:
(1.2,2.2-2.4,4.1-4.3) TF; (5.2) Nights in all forms of commercial accommodation; (7.1,7.2) Hotels, apartments, cottages and villas- Licensed properties only; (7.3) Rooms; (8.2) International Monetary Fund.

BAHRAIN

Basic Indicators	Units	Code	1996	1997	1998	1999	2000
INBOUND TOURISM							
Arrivals							
Visitors	Thousands	(1.1)	1,988	2,600	2,898	3,280	3,869
Tourists (overnight visitors)	Thousands	(1.2)	1,201	1,611	1,640	2,019	2,420
Same-day visitors	Thousands	(1.3)	787	989	1,258	1,261	1,449
Cruise passengers	Thousands	(1.4)	..	..	..	..	..
Arrivals by region							
Africa	Thousands	(2.1)	12	18	22	26	32
Americas	Thousands	(2.2)	77	86	97	102	103
Europe	Thousands	(2.3)	148	173	179	191	216
East Asia and the Pacific	Thousands	(2.4)	84	83	97	101	107
South Asia	Thousands	(2.5)	193	222	261	299	332
Middle East	Thousands	(2.6)	1,474	2,018	2,242	2,561	3,060
Arrivals by mode of transport							
Air	Thousands	(3.1)	505	552	606	656	720
Rail	Thousands	(3.2)	..	..	..	..	..
Road	Thousands	(3.3)	1,481	2,044	2,286	2,619	3,143
Sea	Thousands	(3.4)	2	4	5	5	6
Arrivals by purpose of visit							
Leisure, recreation and holidays	Thousands	(4.1)	1,461	2,089	2,136	2,637	3,115
Business and professional	Thousands	(4.2)	175	157	153	190	277
Other	Thousands	(4.3)	352	354	608	453	477
Overnight stays and length of stay							
Overnight stays in H&S	Thousand nights	(5.1)	1,123	1,563	1,287	1,263	1,764
Overnight stays in CE	Thousand nights	(5.2)	..	..	..	..	..
ALS of non resident tourists	Nights	(5.5)	..	..	..	..	2.33
Tourism expenditure in the country of reference	US$ Million	(8.1)	263	311	366	408	469
DOMESTIC TOURISM							
Overnight stays							
Overnight stays in H&S	Thousand nights	(5.3)	..	..	..	..	..
Overnight stays in CE	Thousand nights	(5.4)	..	..	..	..	..
OUTBOUND TOURISM							
Departures	Thousands	(6.1)	..	..	..	..	..
Tourism expenditure in other countries	US$ Million	(8.2)	109	122	142	159	169
TOURISM ACTIVITIES							
Hotels and similar establishments							
Number of rooms	H&S	(7.1)	4,946	5,148	6,100	6,202	6,766
Number of bed-places	H&S	(7.2)	6,601	6,511	8,068	8,393	9,002
Occupancy rate	Percent	(7.3)	..	..	..	47.96	55.40
Average length of stay	Nights	(5.6)	..	..	..	..	..
ECONOMIC AGGREGATES							
Gross National Product (GNP)	US$ Million	(9.1)	5,177	5,135	4,909	..	..
Exports (F.O.B.)	US$ Million	(9.2)	4,702	4,384	3,270	4,140	5,701
Imports (C.I.F.)	US$ Million	(9.3)	4,273	4,026	3,566	3,698	4,612

Abbreviations used in tables and notes:
H&S: Hotels and similar establishments; **CE:** All types of tourism accommodation establishments; **ALS:** Average length of stay; **THS:** Non-resident tourists staying in H&S; **TCE:** Non-resident tourists staying in CE; **TF:** Arrivals of international (or non-resident) tourists; **VF:** Arrivals of international (or non-resident) visitors; **NHS:** Overnight stays at H&S; **NCE:** Overnight stays at CE.

..	data not available
incl	including
excl	excluding
nra	nationals residing abroad

Notes:
(1.1,2.1-4.3) VF, Excl nra; (3.3) Arrivals through King Fahad Causeway; (5.1,7.1,7.2) Classified hotels only; (8.1,8.2) International Monetary Fund.

Basic Indicators	Units	Code	1996	1997	1998	1999	2000
INBOUND TOURISM							
Arrivals							
Visitors	Thousands	(1.1)	..	..	..	..	..
Tourists (overnight visitors)	Thousands	(1.2)	166	182	172	173	199
Same-day visitors	Thousands	(1.3)	..	..	..	..	..
Cruise passengers	Thousands	(1.4)	..	..	..	..	..
Arrivals by region							
Africa	Thousands	(2.1)	1	1	2	2	2
Americas	Thousands	(2.2)	14	15	16	12	15
Europe	Thousands	(2.3)	51	48	37	40	46
East Asia and the Pacific	Thousands	(2.4)	30	34	36	35	38
South Asia	Thousands	(2.5)	66	82	77	79	94
Middle East	Thousands	(2.6)	3	2	4	5	4
Arrivals by mode of transport							
Air	Thousands	(3.1)	136	148	139	134	151
Rail	Thousands	(3.2)	..	..	..	..	..
Road	Thousands	(3.3)	30	34	33	39	48
Sea	Thousands	(3.4)	..	..	..	..	..
Arrivals by purpose of visit							
Leisure, recreation and holidays	Thousands	(4.1)	63	57	51	49	41
Business and professional	Thousands	(4.2)	43	58	55	36	40
Other	Thousands	(4.3)	59	67	66	88	118
Overnight stays and length of stay							
Overnight stays in H&S	Thousand nights	(5.1)	..	..	..	..	..
Overnight stays in CE	Thousand nights	(5.2)	..	..	..	..	..
ALS of non resident tourists	Nights	(5.5)	9.50	9.00	8.50	7.00	6.50
Tourism expenditure in the country of reference	US$ Million	(8.1)	32	59	51	50	50
DOMESTIC TOURISM							
Overnight stays							
Overnight stays in H&S	Thousand nights	(5.3)	..	..	..	..	..
Overnight stays in CE	Thousand nights	(5.4)	..	..	..	..	..
OUTBOUND TOURISM							
Departures	Thousands	(6.1)	911	866	992	1,103	1,128
Tourism expenditure in other countries	US$ Million	(8.2)	200	170	198	212	301
TOURISM ACTIVITIES							
Hotels and similar establishments							
Number of rooms	H&S	(7.1)	4,166	4,249	4,461	4,506	4,550
Number of bed-places	H&S	(7.2)	8,386	8,552	9,407	9,502	9,789
Occupancy rate	Percent	(7.3)	39.52	45.00	41.97	42.00	49.10
Average length of stay	Nights	(5.6)	..	..	..	..	..
ECONOMIC AGGREGATES							
Gross National Product (GNP)	US$ Million	(9.1)	41,605	44,150	45,107	47,071	49,930
Exports (F.O.B.)	US$ Million	(9.2)	3,297	3,778	3,831	3,919	4,692
Imports (C.I.F.)	US$ Million	(9.3)	6,621	6,896	6,978	7,685	8,358

Abbreviations used in tables and notes:
H&S: Hotels and similar establishments; **CE:** All types of tourism accommodation establishments; **ALS:** Average length of stay; **THS:** Non-resident tourists staying in H&S; **TCE:** Non-resident tourists staying in CE; **TF:** Arrivals of international (or non-resident) tourists; **VF:** Arrivals of international (or non-resident) visitors; **NHS:** Overnight stays at H&S; **NCE:** Overnight stays at CE.

..   data not available
incl   including
excl   excluding
nra   nationals residing abroad

BARBADOS

Basic Indicators	Units	Code	1996	1997	1998	1999	2000
INBOUND TOURISM							
Arrivals							
Visitors	Thousands	(1.1)	957	990	1,019	947	1,078
Tourists (overnight visitors)	Thousands	(1.2)	447	472	512	515	545
Same-day visitors	Thousands	(1.3)	..	..	..	..	..
Cruise passengers	Thousands	(1.4)	510	518	507	433	533
Arrivals by region							
Africa	Thousands	(2.1)	..	..	..	1	1
Americas	Thousands	(2.2)	239	245	255	264	278
Europe	Thousands	(2.3)	201	221	252	245	263
East Asia and the Pacific	Thousands	(2.4)	2	1	2	4	2
South Asia	Thousands	(2.5)	..	..	..	..	..
Middle East	Thousands	(2.6)	..	..	..	..	..
Arrivals by mode of transport							
Air	Thousands	(3.1)	438	461	499	507	538
Rail	Thousands	(3.2)	..	..	..	..	..
Road	Thousands	(3.3)	..	..	..	..	..
Sea	Thousands	(3.4)	9	11	13	8	7
Arrivals by purpose of visit							
Leisure, recreation and holidays	Thousands	(4.1)	416	422	444	435	462
Business and professional	Thousands	(4.2)	24	37	41	55	56
Other	Thousands	(4.3)	7	13	27	25	27
Overnight stays and length of stay							
Overnight stays in H&S	Thousand nights	(5.1)	..	..	..	..	..
Overnight stays in CE	Thousand nights	(5.2)	2,603	2,434	2,303	..	2,695
ALS of non resident tourists	Nights	(5.5)	10.70	10.50	11.10	10.10	10.10
Tourism expenditure							
in the country of reference	US$ Million	(8.1)	644	657	703	677	711
DOMESTIC TOURISM							
Overnight stays							
Overnight stays in H&S	Thousand nights	(5.3)	..	..	..	..	..
Overnight stays in CE	Thousand nights	(5.4)	..	..	..	..	..
OUTBOUND TOURISM							
Departures	Thousands	(6.1)	..	..	..	..	..
Tourism expenditure in other countries	US$ Million	(8.2)	74	79	82	87	..
TOURISM ACTIVITIES							
Hotels and similar establishments							
Number of rooms	H&S	(7.1)	6,315	5,349	5,752	5,761	6,456
Number of bed-places	H&S	(7.2)	11,432	10,283	11,661	12,274	12,240
Occupancy rate	Percent	(7.3)	60.60	57.20	58.60	55.90	56.90
Average length of stay	Nights	(5.6)	7.20	6.60	6.60	7.60	7.30
ECONOMIC AGGREGATES							
Gross National Product (GNP)	US$ Million	(9.1)	1,894	2,076	2,185	2,302	2,487
Exports (F.O.B.)	US$ Million	(9.2)	281	283	252	264	272
Imports (C.I.F.)	US$ Million	(9.3)	834	996	1,010	1,108	1,156

Abbreviations used in tables and notes:
H&S: Hotels and similar establishments; **CE:** All types of tourism accommodation establishments; **ALS:** Average length of stay; **THS:** Non-resident tourists staying in H&S; **TCE:** Non-resident tourists staying in CE; **TF:** Arrivals of international (or non-resident) tourists; **VF:** Arrivals of international (or non-resident) visitors; **NHS:** Overnight stays at H&S; **NCE:** Overnight stays at CE.

..   data not available
incl   including
excl   excluding
nra   nationals residing abroad

Notes:
(1.2,2.2-4.3) TF; (7.1,7.2) Hotels, apartment hotels, apartments and cottages, guest houses; (7.3) Rooms; (8.2) International Monetary Fund.

Basic Indicators	Units	Code	1996	1997	1998	1999	2000
INBOUND TOURISM							
Arrivals							
Visitors	Thousands	(1.1)	..	..	..	..	..
Tourists (overnight visitors)	Thousands	(1.2)	234	254	355	..	..
Same-day visitors	Thousands	(1.3)	..	..	..	..	..
Cruise passengers	Thousands	(1.4)	..	..	..	..	..
Arrivals by region							
Africa	Thousands	(2.1)	..	..	1	..	..
Americas	Thousands	(2.2)	8	9	10	..	..
Europe	Thousands	(2.3)	222	241	339	..	..
East Asia and the Pacific	Thousands	(2.4)	3	2	4	..	..
South Asia	Thousands	(2.5)	..	..	..	..	..
Middle East	Thousands	(2.6)	1	1	1	..	..
Arrivals by mode of transport							
Air	Thousands	(3.1)	..	..	..	..	..
Rail	Thousands	(3.2)	..	..	..	..	..
Road	Thousands	(3.3)	..	..	..	..	..
Sea	Thousands	(3.4)	..	..	..	..	..
Arrivals by purpose of visit							
Leisure, recreation and holidays	Thousands	(4.1)	..	..	..	..	..
Business and professional	Thousands	(4.2)	..	..	..	..	..
Other	Thousands	(4.3)	..	..	..	..	..
Overnight stays and length of stay							
Overnight stays in H&S	Thousand nights	(5.1)	..	..	..	..	..
Overnight stays in CE	Thousand nights	(5.2)	..	..	..	..	..
ALS of non resident tourists	Nights	(5.5)	..	..	..	..	..
Tourism expenditure **in the country of reference**	US$ Million	(8.1)	55	25	22	12	19
DOMESTIC TOURISM							
Overnight stays							
Overnight stays in H&S	Thousand nights	(5.3)	..	..	..	..	..
Overnight stays in CE	Thousand nights	(5.4)	..	..	..	..	..
OUTBOUND TOURISM							
Departures	Thousands	(6.1)	703	969	..	..	..
Tourism expenditure in other countries	US$ Million	(8.2)	119	114	124	116	133
TOURISM ACTIVITIES							
Hotels and similar establishments							
Number of rooms	H&S	(7.1)	877	800	..	..	..
Number of bed-places	H&S	(7.2)	1,438	1,326	..	..	..
Occupancy rate	Percent	(7.3)	..	..	..	..	..
Average length of stay	Nights	(5.6)	..	..	..	..	..
ECONOMIC AGGREGATES							
Gross National Product (GNP)	US$ Million	(9.1)	20,689	23,090	24,314	25,617	29,959
Exports (F.O.B.)	US$ Million	(9.2)	5,652	7,301	7,070	5,909	7,331
Imports (C.I.F.)	US$ Million	(9.3)	6,939	8,689	8,549	6,674	8,492

Abbreviations used in tables and notes:
H&S: Hotels and similar establishments; **CE:** All types of tourism accommodation establishments; **ALS:** Average length of stay; **THS:** Non-resident tourists staying in H&S; **TCE:** Non-resident tourists staying in CE; **TF:** Arrivals of international (or non-resident) tourists; **VF:** Arrivals of international (or non-resident) visitors; **NHS:** Overnight stays at H&S; **NCE:** Overnight stays at CE.

..	data not available
incl	including
excl	excluding
nra	nationals residing abroad

Notes:
(8.1,8.2) International Monetary Fund.

BELGIUM

Basic Indicators	Units	Code	1996	1997	1998	1999	2000
INBOUND TOURISM							
Arrivals							
Visitors	Thousands	(1.1)	..	..	..	..	..
Tourists (overnight visitors)	Thousands	(1.2)	5,829	6,037	6,179	6,369	6,457
Same-day visitors	Thousands	(1.3)	..	..	..	..	..
Cruise passengers	Thousands	(1.4)	..	..	..	..	..
Arrivals by region							
Africa	Thousands	(2.1)	63	63	61	57	64
Americas	Thousands	(2.2)	389	411	420	434	449
Europe	Thousands	(2.3)	5,046	5,197	5,364	5,522	5,550
East Asia and the Pacific	Thousands	(2.4)	266	286	267	287	297
South Asia	Thousands	(2.5)	30	28	17	19	23
Middle East	Thousands	(2.6)	16	18	19	18	20
Arrivals by mode of transport							
Air	Thousands	(3.1)	6,657	7,865	9,174	9,973	10,771
Rail	Thousands	(3.2)	..	..	..	..	..
Road	Thousands	(3.3)	..	..	..	..	..
Sea	Thousands	(3.4)	..	..	..	..	..
Arrivals by purpose of visit							
Leisure, recreation and holidays	Thousands	(4.1)	3,313	3,425	3,611	3,770	3,811
Business and professional	Thousands	(4.2)	2,176	2,287	2,278	2,346	2,483
Other	Thousands	(4.3)	340	325	290	252	163
Overnight stays and length of stay							
Overnight stays in H&S	Thousand nights	(5.1)	8,695	9,267	9,483	9,749	10,184
Overnight stays in CE	Thousand nights	(5.2)	14,441	14,762	14,838	15,366	15,526
ALS of non resident tourists	Nights	(5.5)	..	..	..	..	..
Tourism expenditure							
in the country of reference	US$ Million	(8.1)	4,893	5,267	5,443	7,331	7,422
DOMESTIC TOURISM							
Overnight stays							
Overnight stays in H&S	Thousand nights	(5.3)	3,140	3,366	3,498	3,652	4,045
Overnight stays in CE	Thousand nights	(5.4)	14,288	13,760	13,185	13,111	13,689
OUTBOUND TOURISM							
Departures	Thousands	(6.1)	5,645	7,548	7,773	7,665	9,444
Tourism expenditure in other countries	US$ Million	(8.2)	8,562	8,281	8,794	10,426	10,151
TOURISM ACTIVITIES							
Hotels and similar establishments							
Number of rooms	H&S	(7.1)	60,948	61,052	60,368	60,419	61,890
Number of bed-places	H&S	(7.2)	157,265	158,982	155,878	155,274	158,599
Occupancy rate	Percent	(7.3)	..	..	..	..	..
Average length of stay	Nights	(5.6)	..	..	..	..	..
ECONOMIC AGGREGATES							
Gross National Product (GNP)	US$ Million	(9.1)	274,008	273,524	258,249	252,057	252,461
Exports (F.O.B.)	US$ Million	(9.2)	175,367	171,906	177,666	178,965	186,265
Imports (C.I.F.)	US$ Million	(9.3)	163,615	157,283	162,212	164,620	173,444

Abbreviations used in tables and notes:
H&S: Hotels and similar establishments; **CE:** All types of tourism accommodation establishments; **ALS:** Average length of stay; **THS:** Non-resident tourists staying in H&S; **TCE:** Non-resident tourists staying in CE; **TF:** Arrivals of international (or non-resident) tourists; **VF:** Arrivals of international (or non-resident) visitors; **NHS:** Overnight stays at H&S; **NCE:** Overnight stays at CE.

..   data not available
incl   including
excl   excluding
nra   nationals residing abroad

Notes:
(1.2,2.1-2.4,4.1-4.3) TCE; (6.1/96) Holiday trips of 4 nights and more; (6.1/97) Holiday and business trips; (8.1,8.2) International Monetary Fund; Belgium and Luxembourg.

BELIZE

Basic Indicators	Units	Code	1996	1997	1998	1999	2000
INBOUND TOURISM							
Arrivals							
Visitors	Thousands	(1.1)	349	305	300	340	374
Tourists (overnight visitors)	Thousands	(1.2)	133	146	177	181	196
Same-day visitors	Thousands	(1.3)	215	156	109	125	120
Cruise passengers	Thousands	(1.4)	1	3	14	34	58
Arrivals by region							
Africa	Thousands	(2.1)	..	..	..	..	..
Americas	Thousands	(2.2)	323	276	248	288	320
Europe	Thousands	(2.3)	39	47	45	44	48
East Asia and the Pacific	Thousands	(2.4)	5	4	4	4	3
South Asia	Thousands	(2.5)	..	..	..	..	..
Middle East	Thousands	(2.6)	..	..	..	..	..
Arrivals by mode of transport							
Air	Thousands	(3.1)	94	98	114	120	129
Rail	Thousands	(3.2)	..	..	..	..	..
Road	Thousands	(3.3)	244	192	159	174	177
Sea	Thousands	(3.4)	12	14	26	46	67
Arrivals by purpose of visit							
Leisure, recreation and holidays	Thousands	(4.1)	124	137	181	206	245
Business and professional	Thousands	(4.2)	9	12	9	9	9
Other	Thousands	(4.3)	216	157	109	125	120
Overnight stays and length of stay							
Overnight stays in H&S	Thousand nights	(5.1)	416	455	432	489	516
Overnight stays in CE	Thousand nights	(5.2)	..	..	..	..	..
ALS of non resident tourists	Nights	(5.5)	7.00	7.00	7.10	7.10	7.60
Tourism expenditure							
in the country of reference	US$ Million	(8.1)	89	88	108	112	121
DOMESTIC TOURISM							
Overnight stays							
Overnight stays in H&S	Thousand nights	(5.3)	..	..	..	..	..
Overnight stays in CE	Thousand nights	(5.4)	55	58	53	59	61
OUTBOUND TOURISM							
Departures	Thousands	(6.1)	..	..	..	..	..
Tourism expenditure in other countries	US$ Million	(8.2)	26	34	24	24	24
TOURISM ACTIVITIES							
Hotels and similar establishments							
Number of rooms	H&S	(7.1)	3,690	3,905	3,921	3,963	4,106
Number of bed-places	H&S	(7.2)	6,111	6,425	6,617	6,810	7,045
Occupancy rate	Percent	(7.3)	26.90	27.10	29.90	31.40	41.70
Average length of stay	Nights	(5.6)	..	..	..	..	..
ECONOMIC AGGREGATES							
Gross National Product (GNP)	US$ Million	(9.1)	601	626	637	675	751
Exports (F.O.B.)	US$ Million	(9.2)	168	176	191	169	210
Imports (C.I.F.)	US$ Million	(9.3)	255	286	325	375	480

Abbreviations used in tables and notes:
H&S: Hotels and similar establishments; **CE:** All types of tourism accommodation establishments; **ALS:** Average length of stay; **THS:** Non-resident tourists staying in H&S; **TCE:** Non-resident tourists staying in CE; **TF:** Arrivals of international (or non-resident) tourists; **VF:** Arrivals of international (or non-resident) visitors; **NHS:** Overnight stays at H&S; **NCE:** Overnight stays at CE.

..   data not available
incl   including
excl   excluding
nra   nationals residing abroad

Notes:
(1.1,2.2-4.3) VF; (1.3,4.3) In transit and border permits; (2.2) Incl border permits and returning residents; (2.4) China.

BENIN

Basic Indicators	Units	Code	1996	1997	1998	1999	2000
INBOUND TOURISM							
Arrivals							
Visitors	Thousands	(1.1)	516	541	575	..	..
Tourists (overnight visitors)	Thousands	(1.2)	143	148	152	..	..
Same-day visitors	Thousands	(1.3)	..	..	..	..	..
Cruise passengers	Thousands	(1.4)	..	..	..	..	..
Arrivals by region							
Africa	Thousands	(2.1)	..	..	..	..	..
Americas	Thousands	(2.2)	..	..	..	..	..
Europe	Thousands	(2.3)	..	..	..	..	..
East Asia and the Pacific	Thousands	(2.4)	..	..	..	..	..
South Asia	Thousands	(2.5)	..	..	..	..	..
Middle East	Thousands	(2.6)	..	..	..	..	..
Arrivals by mode of transport							
Air	Thousands	(3.1)	..	..	..	..	..
Rail	Thousands	(3.2)	..	..	..	..	..
Road	Thousands	(3.3)	..	..	..	..	..
Sea	Thousands	(3.4)	..	..	..	..	..
Arrivals by purpose of visit							
Leisure, recreation and holidays	Thousands	(4.1)	..	..	..	..	..
Business and professional	Thousands	(4.2)	..	..	..	..	..
Other	Thousands	(4.3)	..	..	..	..	..
Overnight stays and length of stay							
Overnight stays in H&S	Thousand nights	(5.1)	..	..	..	..	..
Overnight stays in CE	Thousand nights	(5.2)	362	445	525	..	..
ALS of non resident tourists	Nights	(5.5)	..	..	..	..	..
Tourism expenditure in the country of reference	US$ Million	(8.1)	29	31	33	..	..
DOMESTIC TOURISM							
Overnight stays							
Overnight stays in H&S	Thousand nights	(5.3)	..	..	..	..	..
Overnight stays in CE	Thousand nights	(5.4)	..	..	..	..	..
OUTBOUND TOURISM							
Departures	Thousands	(6.1)	..	..	..	..	..
Tourism expenditure in other countries	US$ Million	(8.2)	6	7	7	..	..
TOURISM ACTIVITIES							
Hotels and similar establishments							
Number of rooms	H&S	(7.1)	..	..	..	..	..
Number of bed-places	H&S	(7.2)	..	..	..	..	..
Occupancy rate	Percent	(7.3)	34.00	36.00	33.00	..	..
Average length of stay	Nights	(5.6)	..	..	..	..	..
ECONOMIC AGGREGATES							
Gross National Product (GNP)	US$ Million	(9.1)	1,990	2,227	2,266	2,320	2,398
Exports (F.O.B.)	US$ Million	(9.2)	653	681	414	422	184
Imports (C.I.F.)	US$ Million	(9.3)	654	681	674	824	699

Abbreviations used in tables and notes:
H&S: Hotels and similar establishments; **CE:** All types of tourism accommodation establishments; **ALS:** Average length of stay; **THS:** Non-resident tourists staying in H&S; **TCE:** Non-resident tourists staying in CE; **TF:** Arrivals of international (or non-resident) tourists; **VF:** Arrivals of international (or non-resident) visitors; **NHS:** Overnight stays at H&S; **NCE:** Overnight stays at CE.

..   data not available
incl   including
excl   excluding
nra   nationals residing abroad

Notes:
(1.2) THS. 1998: Estimates.

BERMUDA

Basic Indicators	Units	Code	1996	1997	1998	1999	2000
INBOUND TOURISM							
Arrivals							
Visitors	Thousands	(1.1)	570	562	558	547	538
Tourists (overnight visitors)	Thousands	(1.2)	390	380	369	354	328
Same-day visitors	Thousands	(1.3)	..	..	..	..	..
Cruise passengers	Thousands	(1.4)	180	182	189	193	210
Arrivals by region							
Africa	Thousands	(2.1)	..	..	..	..	..
Americas	Thousands	(2.2)	351	339	324	311	284
Europe	Thousands	(2.3)	30	32	37	36	35
East Asia and the Pacific	Thousands	(2.4)	1	1	1	1	1
South Asia	Thousands	(2.5)	..	..	..	..	..
Middle East	Thousands	(2.6)	..	..	..	..	..
Arrivals by mode of transport							
Air	Thousands	(3.1)	390	380	369	354	328
Rail	Thousands	(3.2)	..	..	..	..	..
Road	Thousands	(3.3)	..	..	..	..	..
Sea	Thousands	(3.4)	180	182	189	193	210
Arrivals by purpose of visit							
Leisure, recreation and holidays	Thousands	(4.1)	300	286	..	..	..
Business and professional	Thousands	(4.2)	57	61	..	..	..
Other	Thousands	(4.3)	33	33	..	..	..
Overnight stays and length of stay							
Overnight stays in H&S	Thousand nights	(5.1)	..	..	..	..	..
Overnight stays in CE	Thousand nights	(5.2)	2,365	2,283	2,274	2,144	1,966
ALS of non resident tourists	Nights	(5.5)	6.10	6.10	6.20	..	..
Tourism expenditure in the country of reference	US$ Million	(8.1)	472	478	484	480	431
DOMESTIC TOURISM							
Overnight stays							
Overnight stays in H&S	Thousand nights	(5.3)	..	..	..	..	..
Overnight stays in CE	Thousand nights	(5.4)	..	..	..	..	..
OUTBOUND TOURISM							
Departures	Thousands	(6.1)	..	..	..	..	..
Tourism expenditure in other countries	US$ Million	(8.2)	..	..	..	..	..
TOURISM ACTIVITIES							
Hotels and similar establishments							
Number of rooms	H&S	(7.1)	4,152	4,135	3,857	3,276	3,339
Number of bed-places	H&S	(7.2)	..	..	..	..	..
Occupancy rate	Percent	(7.3)	57.00	58.40	60.00	..	..
Average length of stay	Nights	(5.6)	..	5.17	5.26	..	..
ECONOMIC AGGREGATES							
Gross National Product (GNP)	US$ Million	(9.1)	1,870	1,872	2,019	2,087	..
Exports (F.O.B.)	US$ Million	(9.2)	68	57	45	..	..
Imports (C.I.F.)	US$ Million	(9.3)	569	619	629	..	..

Abbreviations used in tables and notes:
H&S: Hotels and similar establishments; **CE:** All types of tourism accommodation establishments; **ALS:** Average length of stay; **THS:** Non-resident tourists staying in H&S; **TCE:** Non-resident tourists staying in CE; **TF:** Arrivals of international (or non-resident) tourists; **VF:** Arrivals of international (or non-resident) visitors; **NHS:** Overnight stays at H&S; **NCE:** Overnight stays at CE.

.. data not available
incl including
excl excluding
nra nationals residing abroad

Notes:
(1.1) Excl nra; (1.2,2.2,2.3,4.1-4.3) Air arrivals; (5.2) Incl overnight stays at private houses; (7.3) Rooms; (9.1) GDP.

BHUTAN

Basic Indicators	Units	Code	1996	1997	1998	1999	2000
INBOUND TOURISM							
Arrivals							
Visitors	Thousands	(1.1)	..	..	..	..	..
Tourists (overnight visitors)	Thousands	(1.2)	5.2	5.4	6.2	7.2	7.6
Same-day visitors	Thousands	(1.3)	..	..	..	..	..
Cruise passengers	Thousands	(1.4)	..	..	..	..	..
Arrivals by region							
Africa	Thousands	(2.1)	..	..	..	..	..
Americas	Thousands	(2.2)	1.1	1.0	1.6	2.3	3.0
Europe	Thousands	(2.3)	2.4	2.6	3.2	3.1	3.0
East Asia and the Pacific	Thousands	(2.4)	1.6	1.7	1.4	1.6	1.4
South Asia	Thousands	(2.5)	..	..	..	..	..
Middle East	Thousands	(2.6)	..	..	..	..	..
Arrivals by mode of transport							
Air	Thousands	(3.1)	5.2	5.4	6.2	7.2	7.6
Rail	Thousands	(3.2)	..	..	..	..	..
Road	Thousands	(3.3)	..	..	..	..	..
Sea	Thousands	(3.4)	..	..	..	..	..
Arrivals by purpose of visit							
Leisure, recreation and holidays	Thousands	(4.1)	5.2	5.4	6.2	7.2	7.6
Business and professional	Thousands	(4.2)	..	..	..	..	..
Other	Thousands	(4.3)	..	..	..	..	..
Overnight stays and length of stay							
Overnight stays in H&S	Thousand nights	(5.1)	..	..	46	53	61
Overnight stays in CE	Thousand nights	(5.2)	..	..	..	..	..
ALS of non resident tourists	Nights	(5.5)	..	..	..	..	7.00
Tourism expenditure							
in the country of reference	US$ Million	(8.1)	6	6	8	9	10
DOMESTIC TOURISM							
Overnight stays							
Overnight stays in H&S	Thousand nights	(5.3)	..	..	..	..	..
Overnight stays in CE	Thousand nights	(5.4)	..	..	..	..	..
OUTBOUND TOURISM							
Departures	Thousands	(6.1)	..	..	..	..	..
Tourism expenditure in other countries	US$ Million	(8.2)	..	..	..	..	..
TOURISM ACTIVITIES							
Hotels and similar establishments							
Number of rooms	H&S	(7.1)	..	..	..	..	1,215
Number of bed-places	H&S	(7.2)	..	..	..	..	2,153
Occupancy rate	Percent	(7.3)	..	..	..	..	50.34
Average length of stay	Nights	(5.6)	..	..	..	..	7.00
ECONOMIC AGGREGATES							
Gross National Product (GNP)	US$ Million	(9.1)	295	342	368	407	441
Exports (F.O.B.)	US$ Million	(9.2)	..	..	..	..	..
Imports (C.I.F.)	US$ Million	(9.3)	..	..	..	..	..

Abbreviations used in tables and notes:
H&S: Hotels and similar establishments; **CE:** All types of tourism accommodation establishments; **ALS:** Average length of stay; **THS:** Non-resident tourists staying in H&S; **TCE:** Non-resident tourists staying in CE; **TF:** Arrivals of international (or non-resident) tourists; **VF:** Arrivals of international (or non-resident) visitors; **NHS:** Overnight stays at H&S; **NCE:** Overnight stays at CE.

..	data not available
incl	including
excl	excluding
nra	nationals residing abroad

Basic Indicators	Units	Code	1996	1997	1998	1999	2000
INBOUND TOURISM							
Arrivals							
Visitors	Thousands	(1.1)	..	..	..	..	..
Tourists (overnight visitors)	Thousands	(1.2)	313	355	388	342	306
Same-day visitors	Thousands	(1.3)	..	..	..	..	..
Cruise passengers	Thousands	(1.4)	..	..	..	..	..
Arrivals by region							
Africa	Thousands	(2.1)	1	1	1	1	1
Americas	Thousands	(2.2)	187	230	262	203	177
Europe	Thousands	(2.3)	112	111	106	115	107
East Asia and the Pacific	Thousands	(2.4)	13	13	19	23	21
South Asia	Thousands	(2.5)	..	..	..	..	..
Middle East	Thousands	(2.6)	..	..	..	..	..
Arrivals by mode of transport							
Air	Thousands	(3.1)	194	245	279	236	231
Rail	Thousands	(3.2)	34	21	11	10	7
Road	Thousands	(3.3)	80	84	92	91	64
Sea	Thousands	(3.4)	5	5	5	5	4
Arrivals by purpose of visit							
Leisure, recreation and holidays	Thousands	(4.1)	221	250	274	241	191
Business and professional	Thousands	(4.2)	46	53	57	51	43
Other	Thousands	(4.3)	46	52	57	50	71
Overnight stays and length of stay							
Overnight stays in H&S	Thousand nights	(5.1)	1,041	1,109	1,142	1,095	991
Overnight stays in CE	Thousand nights	(5.2)	..	..	..	..	..
ALS of non resident tourists	Nights	(5.5)	11.00	10.00	10.00	10.00	10.00
Tourism expenditure							
in the country of reference	US$ Million	(8.1)	159	166	174	179	160
DOMESTIC TOURISM							
Overnight stays							
Overnight stays in H&S	Thousand nights	(5.3)	1,380	1,420	1,443	1,365	1,293
Overnight stays in CE	Thousand nights	(5.4)	..	..	..	..	..
OUTBOUND TOURISM							
Departures	Thousands	(6.1)	269	285	299	253	196
Tourism expenditure in other countries	US$ Million	(8.2)	138	145	153	131	102
TOURISM ACTIVITIES							
Hotels and similar establishments							
Number of rooms	H&S	(7.1)	14,342	14,260	15,126	15,497	15,795
Number of bed-places	H&S	(7.2)	24,383	23,649	25,449	26,176	26,852
Occupancy rate	Percent	(7.3)	29.10	29.70	28.30	26.10	23.60
Average length of stay	Nights	(5.6)	2.30	2.30	2.30	2.20	2.20
ECONOMIC AGGREGATES							
Gross National Product (GNP)	US$ Million	(9.1)	7,004	7,537	8,017	8,080	8,305
Exports (F.O.B.)	US$ Million	(9.2)	1,137	1,167	1,104	1,051	1,230
Imports (C.I.F.)	US$ Million	(9.3)	1,635	1,851	1,983	1,755	1,830

Abbreviations used in tables and notes:
H&S: Hotels and similar establishments; **CE:** All types of tourism accommodation establishments; **ALS:** Average length of stay; **THS:** Non-resident tourists staying in H&S; **TCE:** Non-resident tourists staying in CE; **TF:** Arrivals of international (or non-resident) tourists; **VF:** Arrivals of international (or non-resident) visitors; **NHS:** Overnight stays at H&S; **NCE:** Overnight stays at CE.

Notes:
(1.2-4.3) Data based on surveys. As from 2000 a new survey was applied; (1.2-4.3,8.1,8.2/99/2000) Provisional data; (3.4) Arrivals by lake; (5.1,5.3,7.1,7.2) Department capitals only; (5.6) Days, H&S, inbound tourism; (7.3) Bed-places (hotels).

..   data not available
incl   including
excl   excluding
nra   nationals residing abroad

BONAIRE

Basic Indicators	Units	Code	1996	1997	1998	1999	2000
INBOUND TOURISM							
Arrivals							
Visitors	Thousands	(1.1)	80	83	82	81	94
Tourists (overnight visitors)	Thousands	(1.2)	65	63	62	61	51
Same-day visitors	Thousands	(1.3)	..	..		..	43
Cruise passengers	Thousands	(1.4)	15	20	20	20	43
Arrivals by region							
Africa	Thousands	(2.1)					
Americas	Thousands	(2.2)	42	40	40	41	33
Europe	Thousands	(2.3)	23	22	22	20	18
East Asia and the Pacific	Thousands	(2.4)	..	..	..	..	..
South Asia	Thousands	(2.5)			..		
Middle East	Thousands	(2.6)	..	..	..	..	..
Arrivals by mode of transport							
Air	Thousands	(3.1)	65	63	62	61	51
Rail	Thousands	(3.2)	..	..	..	..	..
Road	Thousands	(3.3)			..		..
Sea	Thousands	(3.4)	..	..	..	..	..
Arrivals by purpose of visit							
Leisure, recreation and holidays	Thousands	(4.1)	..	..		..	
Business and professional	Thousands	(4.2)	..	..	..	..	..
Other	Thousands	(4.3)			..	..	
Overnight stays and length of stay							
Overnight stays in H&S	Thousand nights	(5.1)	..	..	406	423	378
Overnight stays in CE	Thousand nights	(5.2)	523	518	520	523	481
ALS of non resident tourists	Nights	(5.5)	8.00	8.30	8.30	8.20	9.30
Tourism expenditure **in the country of reference**	US$ Million	(8.1)	42	44	43	44	87
DOMESTIC TOURISM							
Overnight stays							
Overnight stays in H&S	Thousand nights	(5.3)	..	..	..	..	..
Overnight stays in CE	Thousand nights	(5.4)	..	..	..	..	..
OUTBOUND TOURISM							
Departures	Thousands	(6.1)	..	..	..	..	..
Tourism expenditure in other countries	US$ Million	(8.2)	..	..	10	8	5
TOURISM ACTIVITIES							
Hotels and similar establishments							
Number of rooms	H&S	(7.1)	1,128	1,069	1,086	989	1,050
Number of bed-places	H&S	(7.2)	2,875	3,013	3,007	..	2,963
Occupancy rate	Percent	(7.3)	63.00	47.00	59.50	67.00	57.00
Average length of stay	Nights	(5.6)	8.00	8.30	8.30	8.60	9.30
ECONOMIC AGGREGATES							
Gross National Product (GNP)	US$ Million	(9.1)	..	..	..	..	..
Exports (F.O.B.)	US$ Million	(9.2)	8	5	5	4	..
Imports (C.I.F.)	US$ Million	(9.3)	..	..	..	..	..

Abbreviations used in tables and notes:
H&S: Hotels and similar establishments; **CE:** All types of tourism accommodation establishments; **ALS:** Average length of stay; **THS:** Non-resident tourists staying in H&S; **TCE:** Non-resident tourists staying in CE; **TF:** Arrivals of international (or non-resident) tourists; **VF:** Arrivals of international (or non-resident) visitors; **NHS:** Overnight stays at H&S; **NCE:** Overnight stays at CE.

..   data not available
incl   including
excl   excluding
nra   nationals residing abroad

Notes:
(8.1/2000) The total expenditure is derived from a newly estimated expenditure rate per day in 2001. The figure is also widely used by the Economic Department.

Basic Indicators	Units	Code	1996	1997	1998	1999	2000
INBOUND TOURISM							
Arrivals							
Visitors	Thousands	(1.1)	..	..	..	..	..
Tourists (overnight visitors)	Thousands	(1.2)	99	..	90	89	..
Same-day visitors	Thousands	(1.3)	..	..	..	..	..
Cruise passengers	Thousands	(1.4)	..	..	..	..	..
Arrivals by region							
Africa	Thousands	(2.1)	..	..	..	..	..
Americas	Thousands	(2.2)	9	..	..	..	..
Europe	Thousands	(2.3)	87	..	..	..	..
East Asia and the Pacific	Thousands	(2.4)	..	..	..	..	..
South Asia	Thousands	(2.5)	..	..	..	..	..
Middle East	Thousands	(2.6)	..	..	..	..	..
Arrivals by mode of transport							
Air	Thousands	(3.1)	..	..	..	..	..
Rail	Thousands	(3.2)	..	..	..	..	..
Road	Thousands	(3.3)	..	..	..	..	..
Sea	Thousands	(3.4)	..	..	..	..	..
Arrivals by purpose of visit							
Leisure, recreation and holidays	Thousands	(4.1)	..	..	..	..	..
Business and professional	Thousands	(4.2)	..	..	..	..	..
Other	Thousands	(4.3)	..	..	..	..	..
Overnight stays and length of stay							
Overnight stays in H&S	Thousand nights	(5.1)	..	..	229	206	..
Overnight stays in CE	Thousand nights	(5.2)	..	..	231	214	..
ALS of non resident tourists	Nights	(5.5)	..	..	..	..	..
Tourism expenditure							
in the country of reference	US$ Million	(8.1)	16	..	21	21	..
DOMESTIC TOURISM							
Overnight stays							
Overnight stays in H&S	Thousand nights	(5.3)	..	..	..	..	..
Overnight stays in CE	Thousand nights	(5.4)	..	..	..	..	..
OUTBOUND TOURISM							
Departures	Thousands	(6.1)	..	..	..	..	..
Tourism expenditure in other countries	US$ Million	(8.2)	..	..	..	..	..
TOURISM ACTIVITIES							
Hotels and similar establishments							
Number of rooms	H&S	(7.1)	1,275	..	..	..	..
Number of bed-places	H&S	(7.2)	2,650	..	..	..	..
Occupancy rate	Percent	(7.3)	..	..	..	..	..
Average length of stay	Nights	(5.6)	..	..	..	..	..
ECONOMIC AGGREGATES							
Gross National Product (GNP)	US$ Million	(9.1)	..	3,724	4,384	4,709	4,930
Exports (F.O.B.)	US$ Million	(9.2)	58	..	..	..	..
Imports (C.I.F.)	US$ Million	(9.3)	1,171	..	..	..	..

Abbreviations used in tables and notes:
H&S: Hotels and similar establishments; **CE:** All types of tourism accommodation establishments; **ALS:** Average length of stay; **THS:** Non-resident tourists staying in H&S; **TCE:** Non-resident tourists staying in CE; **TF:** Arrivals of international (or non-resident) tourists; **VF:** Arrivals of international (or non-resident) visitors; **NHS:** Overnight stays at H&S; **NCE:** Overnight stays at CE.

..   data not available
incl   including
excl   excluding
nra   nationals residing abroad

Notes:
(8.1/96) Tourism payments: May-December 1996.

BOTSWANA

Basic Indicators	Units	Code	1996	1997	1998	1999	2000
INBOUND TOURISM							
Arrivals							
Visitors	Thousands	(1.1)	656	765	940	1,051	..
Tourists (overnight visitors)	Thousands	(1.2)	512	607	750	843	995
Same-day visitors	Thousands	(1.3)	144	158	190	208	..
Cruise passengers	Thousands	(1.4)	..	..	..	..	..
Arrivals by region							
Africa	Thousands	(2.1)	439	516	629	720	..
Americas	Thousands	(2.2)	8	9	11	12	..
Europe	Thousands	(2.3)	31	38	39	44	..
East Asia and the Pacific	Thousands	(2.4)	8	9	9	10	..
South Asia	Thousands	(2.5)	1	1	1	1	..
Middle East	Thousands	(2.6)	..	..	..	..	..
Arrivals by mode of transport							
Air	Thousands	(3.1)	30	34	37	41	..
Rail	Thousands	(3.2)	19	23	29	6	..
Road	Thousands	(3.3)	463	547	681	792	..
Sea	Thousands	(3.4)	..	..	..	..	..
Arrivals by purpose of visit							
Leisure, recreation and holidays	Thousands	(4.1)	130	152	170	183	..
Business and professional	Thousands	(4.2)	49	60	79	81	..
Other	Thousands	(4.3)	332	395	501	579	..
Overnight stays and length of stay							
Overnight stays in H&S	Thousand nights	(5.1)	..	..	..	..	..
Overnight stays in CE	Thousand nights	(5.2)	..	..	..	..	..
ALS of non resident tourists	Nights	(5.5)	..	..	..	..	..
Tourism expenditure in the country of reference	US$ Million	(8.1)	93	136	175	234	313
DOMESTIC TOURISM							
Overnight stays							
Overnight stays in H&S	Thousand nights	(5.3)	..	..	..	..	..
Overnight stays in CE	Thousand nights	(5.4)	..	..	..	..	..
OUTBOUND TOURISM							
Departures	Thousands	(6.1)	..	..	..	..	..
Tourism expenditure in other countries	US$ Million	(8.2)	78	92	126	143	..
TOURISM ACTIVITIES							
Hotels and similar establishments							
Number of rooms	H&S	(7.1)	1,760	1,960	1,800	2,100	..
Number of bed-places	H&S	(7.2)	3,340	3,560	3,260	3,720	..
Occupancy rate	Percent	(7.3)	51.50	57.90	48.00	53.30	..
Average length of stay	Nights	(5.6)	..	..	9.40	9.80	..
ECONOMIC AGGREGATES							
Gross National Product (GNP)	US$ Million	(9.1)	5,149	4,981	5,072	4,824	5,280
Exports (F.O.B.)	US$ Million	(9.2)	..	..	..	..	..
Imports (C.I.F.)	US$ Million	(9.3)	..	..	..	..	..

Abbreviations used in tables and notes:
H&S: Hotels and similar establishments; **CE:** All types of tourism accommodation establishments; **ALS:** Average length of stay; **THS:** Non-resident tourists staying in H&S; **TCE:** Non-resident tourists staying in CE; **TF:** Arrivals of international (or non-resident) tourists; **VF:** Arrivals of international (or non-resident) visitors; **NHS:** Overnight stays at H&S; **NCE:** Overnight stays at CE.

..   data not available
incl   including
excl   excluding
nra   nationals residing abroad

Notes:
(8.1,8.2/96-99) International Monetary Fund.

Basic Indicators	Units	Code	1996	1997	1998	1999	2000
INBOUND TOURISM							
Arrivals							
Visitors	Thousands	(1.1)	..	..	..	..	..
Tourists (overnight visitors)	Thousands	(1.2)	2,666	2,850	4,818	5,107	5,313
Same-day visitors	Thousands	(1.3)	..	..	..	..	..
Cruise passengers	Thousands	(1.4)	..	..	..	..	..
Arrivals by region							
Africa	Thousands	(2.1)	23	24	41	41	35
Americas	Thousands	(2.2)	1,830	1,999	3,449	3,643	3,803
Europe	Thousands	(2.3)	681	713	1,161	1,246	1,320
East Asia and the Pacific	Thousands	(2.4)	110	95	122	130	122
South Asia	Thousands	(2.5)	..	..	..	..	..
Middle East	Thousands	(2.6)	7	8	14	15	11
Arrivals by mode of transport							
Air	Thousands	(3.1)	1,894	2,005	2,421	2,534	2,723
Rail	Thousands	(3.2)	..	..	..	..	..
Road	Thousands	(3.3)	718	775	2,274	2,446	2,429
Sea	Thousands	(3.4)	53	70	123	127	161
Arrivals by purpose of visit							
Leisure, recreation and holidays	Thousands	(4.1)	1,791	1,861	3,459	3,963	3,768
Business and professional	Thousands	(4.2)	765	929	1,286	1,084	1,480
Other	Thousands	(4.3)	110	60	73	60	65
Overnight stays and length of stay							
Overnight stays in H&S	Thousand nights	(5.1)	29,816	31,211	50,108	52,553	46,676
Overnight stays in CE	Thousand nights	(5.2)	..	..	..	..	..
ALS of non resident tourists	Nights	(5.5)	13.16	12.90	13.00	14.00	12.06
Tourism expenditure							
in the country of reference	US$ Million	(8.1)	2,469	2,595	3,678	3,994	4,228
DOMESTIC TOURISM							
Overnight stays							
Overnight stays in H&S	Thousand nights	(5.3)	95,752	124,844	200,432	210,211	215,528
Overnight stays in CE	Thousand nights	(5.4)	..	..	..	..	..
OUTBOUND TOURISM							
Departures	Thousands	(6.1)	3,797	4,014	4,171	2,863	2,888
Tourism expenditure in other countries	US$ Million	(8.2)	5,825	5,446	5,731	3,085	3,893
TOURISM ACTIVITIES							
Hotels and similar establishments							
Number of rooms	H&S	(7.1)	139,454	212,580	..	..	..
Number of bed-places	H&S	(7.2)	278,908	425,160	..	..	..
Occupancy rate	Percent	(7.3)	..	62.40	61.70	59.30	60.80
Average length of stay	Nights	(5.6)	..	..	..	..	..
ECONOMIC AGGREGATES							
Gross National Product (GNP)	US$ Million	(9.1)	697,952	776,481	764,341	651,045	606,775
Exports (F.O.B.)	US$ Million	(9.2)	47,747	52,994	51,140	48,011	55,086
Imports (C.I.F.)	US$ Million	(9.3)	56,947	64,996	60,631	51,675	58,532

Abbreviations used in tables and notes:
H&S: Hotels and similar establishments; **CE:** All types of tourism accommodation establishments; **ALS:** Average length of stay; **THS:** Non-resident tourists staying in H&S; **TCE:** Non-resident tourists staying in CE; **TF:** Arrivals of international (or non-resident) tourists; **VF:** Arrivals of international (or non-resident) visitors; **NHS:** Overnight stays at H&S; **NCE:** Overnight stays at CE.

..   data not available
incl   including
excl   excluding
nra   nationals residing abroad

Notes:
(3.4) Incl arrivals by river; (5.5) Days; (7.1,7.2/96) Hotels, residential hotels, resort hotels and national inns ("pousadas") classified by EMBRATUR; (7.1,7.2/97) Classified and unclassified hotels; (8.1) Data based on the sample survey conducted by EMBRATUR.
NOTE 1998: Change in methodology.

BRITISH VIRGIN ISLANDS

Basic Indicators	Units	Code	1996	1997	1998	1999	2000
INBOUND TOURISM							
Arrivals							
Visitors	Thousands	(1.1)	412	378	392	484	469
Tourists (overnight visitors)	Thousands	(1.2)	244	244	279	286	281
Same-day visitors	Thousands	(1.3)	8	29	8	17	..
Cruise passengers	Thousands	(1.4)	160	105	105	181	188
Arrivals by region							
Africa	Thousands	(2.1)	..	..	..	..	..
Americas	Thousands	(2.2)	213	214	224	236	..
Europe	Thousands	(2.3)	23	22	31	33	39
East Asia and the Pacific	Thousands	(2.4)	..	..	..	..	..
South Asia	Thousands	(2.5)	..	..	..	..	..
Middle East	Thousands	(2.6)	..	..	..	..	..
Arrivals by mode of transport							
Air	Thousands	(3.1)	108	120	121	..	..
Rail	Thousands	(3.2)	..	..	..	..	..
Road	Thousands	(3.3)	..	..	..	..	..
Sea	Thousands	(3.4)	304	258	271	..	..
Arrivals by purpose of visit							
Leisure, recreation and holidays	Thousands	(4.1)	239	240	246	277	..
Business and professional	Thousands	(4.2)	2	2	5	3	..
Other	Thousands	(4.3)	3	2	28	6	..
Overnight stays and length of stay							
Overnight stays in H&S	Thousand nights	(5.1)	..	..	..	..	..
Overnight stays in CE	Thousand nights	(5.2)	..	..	..	..	..
ALS of non resident tourists	Nights	(5.5)	7.40	8.00	8.40	9.40	..
Tourism expenditure in the country of reference	US$ Million	(8.1)	228	220	255	300	315
DOMESTIC TOURISM							
Overnight stays							
Overnight stays in H&S	Thousand nights	(5.3)	..	..	..	..	..
Overnight stays in CE	Thousand nights	(5.4)	..	..	..	..	..
OUTBOUND TOURISM							
Departures	Thousands	(6.1)					
Tourism expenditure in other countries	US$ Million	(8.2)	..	..	..	..	..
TOURISM ACTIVITIES							
Hotels and similar establishments							
Number of rooms	H&S	(7.1)	1,555	1,594	1,594	1,626	1,637
Number of bed-places	H&S	(7.2)	..	..	..	..	..
Occupancy rate	Percent	(7.3)	56.50	52.40	59.30	58.80	..
Average length of stay	Nights	(5.6)	7.10	7.00	7.10	..	..
ECONOMIC AGGREGATES							
Gross National Product (GNP)	US$ Million	(9.1)	504	573	617	..	..
Exports (F.O.B.)	US$ Million	(9.2)	21	22	23	26	..
Imports (C.I.F.)	US$ Million	(9.3)	158	166	165	..	..

Abbreviations used in tables and notes:
H&S: Hotels and similar establishments; **CE:** All types of tourism accommodation establishments; **ALS:** Average length of stay; **THS:** Non-resident tourists staying in H&S; **TCE:** Non-resident tourists staying in CE; **TF:** Arrivals of international (or non-resident) tourists; **VF:** Arrivals of international (or non-resident) visitors; **NHS:** Overnight stays at H&S; **NCE:** Overnight stays at CE.

..   data not available
incl   including
excl   excluding
nra   nationals residing abroad

Notes:
(7.1) Hotels and guest houses; (7.3) Rooms; (9.1) GDP.

Basic Indicators	Units	Code	1996	1997	1998	1999	2000
INBOUND TOURISM							
Arrivals							
Visitors	Thousands	(1.1)	837	643	964	967	984
Tourists (overnight visitors)	Thousands	(1.2)	..	..	..	..	..
Same-day visitors	Thousands	(1.3)	..	..	..	..	..
Cruise passengers	Thousands	(1.4)	..	..	10	..	..
Arrivals by region							
Africa	Thousands	(2.1)	..	..	..	..	..
Americas	Thousands	(2.2)	..	..	10	9	9
Europe	Thousands	(2.3)	..	..	48	45	42
East Asia and the Pacific	Thousands	(2.4)	..	..	893	897	913
South Asia	Thousands	(2.5)	..	..	13	13	16
Middle East	Thousands	(2.6)	..	..	..	1	1
Arrivals by mode of transport							
Air	Thousands	(3.1)	..	..	..	..	..
Rail	Thousands	(3.2)	..	..	..	..	..
Road	Thousands	(3.3)	..	..	..	..	..
Sea	Thousands	(3.4)	..	..	..	..	..
Arrivals by purpose of visit							
Leisure, recreation and holidays	Thousands	(4.1)	55	..	33	38	41
Business and professional	Thousands	(4.2)	48	..	38	30	27
Other	Thousands	(4.3)	734	..	893	898	916
Overnight stays and length of stay							
Overnight stays in H&S	Thousand nights	(5.1)	..	..	..	..	..
Overnight stays in CE	Thousand nights	(5.2)	..	..	..	..	..
ALS of non resident tourists	Nights	(5.5)	..	..	..	..	..
Tourism expenditure							
in the country of reference	US$ Million	(8.1)	..	..	..	..	..
DOMESTIC TOURISM							
Overnight stays							
Overnight stays in H&S	Thousand nights	(5.3)	..	..	..	..	..
Overnight stays in CE	Thousand nights	(5.4)	..	..	..	..	..
OUTBOUND TOURISM							
Departures	Thousands	(6.1)	..	..	..	..	..
Tourism expenditure in other countries	US$ Million	(8.2)	..	..	..	..	..
TOURISM ACTIVITIES							
Hotels and similar establishments							
Number of rooms	H&S	(7.1)	1,170	1,098	1,186	1,726	2,412
Number of bed-places	H&S	(7.2)	..	..	..	..	..
Occupancy rate	Percent	(7.3)	66.90	61.20	54.45	49.07	62.84
Average length of stay	Nights	(5.6)	2.60	2.14	1.84	2.93	1.88
ECONOMIC AGGREGATES							
Gross National Product (GNP)	US$ Million	(9.1)	7,847	8,401	7,754	..	..
Exports (F.O.B.)	US$ Million	(9.2)	2,481	2,467	2,058	..	..
Imports (C.I.F.)	US$ Million	(9.3)	2,494	2,203	1,552	..	..

Abbreviations used in tables and notes:
H&S: Hotels and similar establishments; **CE:** All types of tourism accommodation establishments; **ALS:** Average length of stay; **THS:** Non-resident tourists staying in H&S; **TCE:** Non-resident tourists staying in CE; **TF:** Arrivals of international (or non-resident) tourists; **VF:** Arrivals of international (or non-resident) visitors; **NHS:** Overnight stays at H&S; **NCE:** Overnight stays at CE.

..	data not available
incl	including
excl	excluding
nra	nationals residing abroad

BULGARIA

Basic Indicators	Units	Code	1996	1997	1998	1999	2000
INBOUND TOURISM							
Arrivals							
Visitors	Thousands	(1.1)	6,811	7,543	5,240	5,056	4,922
Tourists (overnight visitors)	Thousands	(1.2)	2,795	2,980	2,667	2,472	2,785
Same-day visitors	Thousands	(1.3)	..	..	..	..	..
Cruise passengers	Thousands	(1.4)	..	..	..	..	..
Arrivals by region							
Africa	Thousands	(2.1)	3	7	6	4	3
Americas	Thousands	(2.2)	19	22	40	39	42
Europe	Thousands	(2.3)	6,407	7,248	4,822	4,912	4,780
East Asia and the Pacific	Thousands	(2.4)	14	19	21	21	24
South Asia	Thousands	(2.5)	10	16	15	14	16
Middle East	Thousands	(2.6)	18	21	20	18	17
Arrivals by mode of transport							
Air	Thousands	(3.1)	947	981	933	651	776
Rail	Thousands	(3.2)	376	1,469	884	79	172
Road	Thousands	(3.3)	5,425	5,002	3,346	4,234	3,874
Sea	Thousands	(3.4)	62	91	77	92	100
Arrivals by purpose of visit							
Leisure, recreation and holidays	Thousands	(4.1)	2,192	2,336	1,973	2,085	2,354
Business and professional	Thousands	(4.2)	154	188	132	170	178
Other	Thousands	(4.3)	4,465	5,019	3,134	2,801	2,390
Overnight stays and length of stay							
Overnight stays in H&S	Thousand nights	(5.1)	5,764	5,287	5,037	4,323	5,100
Overnight stays in CE	Thousand nights	(5.2)	5,922	5,477	5,197	4,382	5,170
ALS of non resident tourists	Nights	(5.5)	7.60	8.05	8.30	8.30	8.35
Tourism expenditure							
in the country of reference	US$ Million	(8.1)	450	496	966	932	1,074
DOMESTIC TOURISM							
Overnight stays							
Overnight stays in H&S	Thousand nights	(5.3)	3,200	2,509	2,897	2,648	3,024
Overnight stays in CE	Thousand nights	(5.4)	3,884	3,025	3,437	3,118	3,384
OUTBOUND TOURISM							
Departures	Thousands	(6.1)	3,006	3,059	2,592	2,376	2,337
Tourism expenditure in other countries	US$ Million	(8.2)	199	222	519	526	538
TOURISM ACTIVITIES							
Hotels and similar establishments							
Number of rooms	H&S	(7.1)	..	..	..	..	..
Number of bed-places	H&S	(7.2)	103,619	97,974	110,235	99,538	120,150
Occupancy rate	Percent	(7.3)	35.50	33.60	32.90	29.90	28.30
Average length of stay	Nights	(5.6)	3.90	4.10	3.80	3.80	3.90
ECONOMIC AGGREGATES							
Gross National Product (GNP)	US$ Million	(9.1)	10,024	9,739	10,123	11,387	12,355
Exports (F.O.B.)	US$ Million	(9.2)	6,602	5,322	4,302	3,964	4,810
Imports (C.I.F.)	US$ Million	(9.3)	6,861	5,223	5,021	5,454	6,492

Abbreviations used in tables and notes:
H&S: Hotels and similar establishments; **CE:** All types of tourism accommodation establishments; **ALS:** Average length of stay; **THS:** Non-resident tourists staying in H&S; **TCE:** Non-resident tourists staying in CE; **TF:** Arrivals of international (or non-resident) tourists; **VF:** Arrivals of international (or non-resident) visitors; **NHS:** Overnight stays at H&S; **NCE:** Overnight stays at CE.

..   data not available
incl   including
excl   excluding
nra   nationals residing abroad

Notes:
(1.1,1.2/98-2000) Excluding children without own passports; (3.4) Sea and inland waterways; (5.1-5.6,7.2,7.3) Covers mainly former Stateowned and Public Sector in accommodation. Considerable part of the private sector (more than 70% in 1998) is not included in the data; (7.2) Hotels only; (7.3) Bed-places in hotels; (8.1,8.2/98-2000) New methodology of the Bulgarian Central Bank & Ministry of Economy.

BURKINA FASO

Basic Indicators	Units	Code	1996	1997	1998	1999	2000
INBOUND TOURISM							
Arrivals							
Visitors	Thousands	(1.1)	..	..	..	..	..
Tourists (overnight visitors)	Thousands	(1.2)	131	138	160	..	..
Same-day visitors	Thousands	(1.3)	..	..	..	..	..
Cruise passengers	Thousands	(1.4)	..	..	..	..	..
Arrivals by region							
Africa	Thousands	(2.1)	54	57	63	..	..
Americas	Thousands	(2.2)	8	8	10	..	..
Europe	Thousands	(2.3)	55	58	78	..	..
East Asia and the Pacific	Thousands	(2.4)	2	2	3	..	..
South Asia	Thousands	(2.5)	..	..	..	..	..
Middle East	Thousands	(2.6)	..	..	..	..	..
Arrivals by mode of transport							
Air	Thousands	(3.1)	..	..	..	..	..
Rail	Thousands	(3.2)	..	..	..	..	..
Road	Thousands	(3.3)	..	..	..	..	..
Sea	Thousands	(3.4)	..	..	..	..	..
Arrivals by purpose of visit							
Leisure, recreation and holidays	Thousands	(4.1)	44	44	38	..	..
Business and professional	Thousands	(4.2)	105	112	123	..	..
Other	Thousands	(4.3)	34	37	49	..	..
Overnight stays and length of stay							
Overnight stays in H&S	Thousand nights	(5.1)	304	320	613	..	..
Overnight stays in CE	Thousand nights	(5.2)	..	..	..	..	..
ALS of non resident tourists	Nights	(5.5)	2.32	2.30	3.55	..	..
Tourism expenditure							
in the country of reference	US$ Million	(8.1)	31	39	42	..	..
DOMESTIC TOURISM							
Overnight stays							
Overnight stays in H&S	Thousand nights	(5.3)	120	126	138	..	..
Overnight stays in CE	Thousand nights	(5.4)	..	..	..	..	..
OUTBOUND TOURISM							
Departures	Thousands	(6.1)	..	..	..	..	..
Tourism expenditure in other countries	US$ Million	(8.2)	..	..	..	..	..
TOURISM ACTIVITIES							
Hotels and similar establishments							
Number of rooms	H&S	(7.1)	..	..	..	..	..
Number of bed-places	H&S	(7.2)	..	..	..	..	..
Occupancy rate	Percent	(7.3)	54.20	59.88	58.45	..	..
Average length of stay	Nights	(5.6)	..	..	..	..	..
ECONOMIC AGGREGATES							
Gross National Product (GNP)	US$ Million	(9.1)	2,412	2,556	2,574	2,602	2,640
Exports (F.O.B.)	US$ Million	(9.2)	234	232	319	255	213
Imports (C.I.F.)	US$ Million	(9.3)	647	588	732	579	550

Abbreviations used in tables and notes:
H&S: Hotels and similar establishments; **CE:** All types of tourism accommodation establishments; **ALS:** Average length of stay; **THS:** Non-resident tourists staying in H&S; **TCE:** Non-resident tourists staying in CE; **TF:** Arrivals of international (or non-resident) tourists; **VF:** Arrivals of international (or non-resident) visitors; **NHS:** Overnight stays at H&S; **NCE:** Overnight stays at CE.

..   data not available
incl including
excl excluding
nra nationals residing abroad

Notes:
(1.2,2.1-2.4) THS; (4.1-4.3) Incl domestic tourism; (7.3) Rooms.

BURUNDI

Basic Indicators	Units	Code	1996	1997	1998	1999	2000
INBOUND TOURISM							
Arrivals							
Visitors	Thousands	(1.1)	..	..	..	..	..
Tourists (overnight visitors)	Thousands	(1.2)	27	11	15	26	..
Same-day visitors	Thousands	(1.3)	..	..	..	..	..
Cruise passengers	Thousands	(1.4)	..	..	..	..	..
Arrivals by region							
Africa	Thousands	(2.1)	13	5	7	..	..
Americas	Thousands	(2.2)	2	1	1	..	..
Europe	Thousands	(2.3)	10	1	6	..	..
East Asia and the Pacific	Thousands	(2.4)	2	4	1	..	..
South Asia	Thousands	(2.5)	..	..	..	..	..
Middle East	Thousands	(2.6)	..	..	..	..	..
Arrivals by mode of transport							
Air	Thousands	(3.1)	11	3	6	..	..
Rail	Thousands	(3.2)	..	..	..	..	..
Road	Thousands	(3.3)	15	5	8	..	..
Sea	Thousands	(3.4)	1	1	1	..	..
Arrivals by purpose of visit							
Leisure, recreation and holidays	Thousands	(4.1)	7	2	4	..	..
Business and professional	Thousands	(4.2)	9	3	5	..	..
Other	Thousands	(4.3)	11	3	5	..	..
Overnight stays and length of stay							
Overnight stays in H&S	Thousand nights	(5.1)	52	47	82	83	..
Overnight stays in CE	Thousand nights	(5.2)	..	..	..	..	..
ALS of non resident tourists	Nights	(5.5)	..	..	..	..	..
Tourism expenditure in the country of reference	US$ Million	(8.1)	1.2	0.6	0.4	0.7	0.8
DOMESTIC TOURISM							
Overnight stays							
Overnight stays in H&S	Thousand nights	(5.3)	..	..	..	..	..
Overnight stays in CE	Thousand nights	(5.4)	..	..	..	..	..
OUTBOUND TOURISM							
Departures	Thousands	(6.1)	35	8	16	..	..
Tourism expenditure in other countries	US$ Million	(8.2)	12	12	11	8	14
TOURISM ACTIVITIES							
Hotels and similar establishments							
Number of rooms	H&S	(7.1)	551	551	551	..	..
Number of bed-places	H&S	(7.2)	888	888	888	..	..
Occupancy rate	Percent	(7.3)	32.14	15.40	18.20	..	..
Average length of stay	Nights	(5.6)	1.24	1.12	1.96	..	..
ECONOMIC AGGREGATES							
Gross National Product (GNP)	US$ Million	(9.1)	880	924	913	818	732
Exports (F.O.B.)	US$ Million	(9.2)	40	87	65	54	50
Imports (C.I.F.)	US$ Million	(9.3)	127	121	158	118	148

Abbreviations used in tables and notes:
H&S: Hotels and similar establishments; **CE:** All types of tourism accommodation establishments; **ALS:** Average length of stay; **THS:** Non-resident tourists staying in H&S; **TCE:** Non-resident tourists staying in CE; **TF:** Arrivals of international (or non-resident) tourists; **VF:** Arrivals of international (or non-resident) visitors; **NHS:** Overnight stays at H&S; **NCE:** Overnight stays at CE.

..   data not available
incl   including
excl   excluding
nra   nationals residing abroad

Notes:
(1.2,2.1-2.4,3.1-4.3) TF, incl nra; (3.4) Arrivals by lake; (5.6) Days; (7.1,7.2) Hotels; (8.1,8.2) International Monetary Fund.

Basic Indicators	Units	Code	1996	1997	1998	1999	2000
INBOUND TOURISM							
Arrivals							
Visitors	Thousands	(1.1)	..	..	575	644	..
Tourists (overnight visitors)	Thousands	(1.2)	260	219	286	368	466
Same-day visitors	Thousands	(1.3)	..	..	289	276	..
Cruise passengers	Thousands	(1.4)	..	..	..	..	..
Arrivals by region							
Africa	Thousands	(2.1)	..	..	..	5	..
Americas	Thousands	(2.2)	28	25	22	36	42
Europe	Thousands	(2.3)	54	43	46	60	66
East Asia and the Pacific	Thousands	(2.4)	174	147	105	136	152
South Asia	Thousands	(2.5)	4	3	2	2	3
Middle East	Thousands	(2.6)	..	..	..	24	..
Arrivals by mode of transport							
Air	Thousands	(3.1)	260	219	186	263	351
Rail	Thousands	(3.2)	..	..	..	..	..
Road	Thousands	(3.3)	..	..	100	105	115
Sea	Thousands	(3.4)	..	..	..	..	..
Arrivals by purpose of visit							
Leisure, recreation and holidays	Thousands	(4.1)	194	163	142	200	296
Business and professional	Thousands	(4.2)	58	49	37	55	47
Other	Thousands	(4.3)	8	7	7	8	8
Overnight stays and length of stay							
Overnight stays in H&S	Thousand nights	(5.1)	..	..	..	..	..
Overnight stays in CE	Thousand nights	(5.2)	..	..	..	..	..
ALS of non resident tourists	Nights	(5.5)	7.50	6.40	5.20	5.50	5.50
Tourism expenditure							
in the country of reference	US$ Million	(8.1)	118	103	166	190	228
DOMESTIC TOURISM							
Overnight stays							
Overnight stays in H&S	Thousand nights	(5.3)	..	..	..	..	..
Overnight stays in CE	Thousand nights	(5.4)	..	..	..	..	..
OUTBOUND TOURISM							
Departures	Thousands	(6.1)	38	45	41	49	..
Tourism expenditure in other countries	US$ Million	(8.2)	15	13	7	18	19
TOURISM ACTIVITIES							
Hotels and similar establishments							
Number of rooms	H&S	(7.1)	6,397	6,385	8,385	9,105	..
Number of bed-places	H&S	(7.2)	10,367	10,845	13,081	14,805	..
Occupancy rate	Percent	(7.3)	40.00	30.00	40.00	44.00	45.00
Average length of stay	Nights	(5.6)	..	..	..	..	..
ECONOMIC AGGREGATES							
Gross National Product (GNP)	US$ Million	(9.1)	3,080	3,128	2,973	3,037	3,144
Exports (F.O.B.)	US$ Million	(9.2)	809	696	..	..	..
Imports (C.I.F.)	US$ Million	(9.3)	1,362	1,039	..	..	..

Abbreviations used in tables and notes:
H&S: Hotels and similar establishments; **CE:** All types of tourism accommodation establishments; **ALS:** Average length of stay; **THS:** Non-resident tourists staying in H&S; **TCE:** Non-resident tourists staying in CE; **TF:** Arrivals of international (or non-resident) tourists; **VF:** Arrivals of international (or non-resident) visitors; **NHS:** Overnight stays at H&S; **NCE:** Overnight stays at CE.

..   data not available
incl   including
excl   excluding
nra   nationals residing abroad

Notes:
(1.2/96/97) Arrivals by air; (1.2/98-2000) International tourist arrivals by all means of transport; (1.3) Preah Vihear Temple; (2.2-2.6,4.1-4.3) Arrivals by air; (3.3) Arrivals by land and boat; (4.1/98,2000) Incl arrivals at Siem Reap Airport by direct-flights; 1998: 10,423; 2000: 87,012; (5.5) Days; (8.2) International Monetary Fund.

CAMEROON

Basic Indicators	Units	Code	1996	1997	1998	1999	2000
INBOUND TOURISM							
Arrivals							
Visitors	Thousands	(1.1)	..	..	..	..	..
Tourists (overnight visitors)	Thousands	(1.2)	101	133	..	..	..
Same-day visitors	Thousands	(1.3)	..	..	..	..	..
Cruise passengers	Thousands	(1.4)	..	..	..	..	..
Arrivals by region							
Africa	Thousands	(2.1)	27	48	..	..	..
Americas	Thousands	(2.2)	8	14	..	..	..
Europe	Thousands	(2.3)	62	66	..	..	..
East Asia and the Pacific	Thousands	(2.4)	2	3	..	..	..
South Asia	Thousands	(2.5)	..	..	..	..	..
Middle East	Thousands	(2.6)	1	1	..	..	..
Arrivals by mode of transport							
Air	Thousands	(3.1)	..	..	..	..	..
Rail	Thousands	(3.2)	..	..	..	..	..
Road	Thousands	(3.3)	..	..	..	..	..
Sea	Thousands	(3.4)	..	..	..	..	..
Arrivals by purpose of visit							
Leisure, recreation and holidays	Thousands	(4.1)	..	..	..	..	..
Business and professional	Thousands	(4.2)	..	..	..	..	..
Other	Thousands	(4.3)	..	..	..	..	..
Overnight stays and length of stay							
Overnight stays in H&S	Thousand nights	(5.1)	227	239	..	..	..
Overnight stays in CE	Thousand nights	(5.2)	..	..	..	..	..
ALS of non resident tourists	Nights	(5.5)	..	..	..	..	..
Tourism expenditure in the country of reference	US$ Million	(8.1)	..	..	..	..	..
DOMESTIC TOURISM							
Overnight stays							
Overnight stays in H&S	Thousand nights	(5.3)	350	468	..	..	..
Overnight stays in CE	Thousand nights	(5.4)	..	..	..	..	..
OUTBOUND TOURISM							
Departures	Thousands	(6.1)	..	..	..	..	..
Tourism expenditure in other countries	US$ Million	(8.2)	..	..	..	..	..
TOURISM ACTIVITIES							
Hotels and similar establishments							
Number of rooms	H&S	(7.1)	..	..	..	..	..
Number of bed-places	H&S	(7.2)	..	..	..	..	..
Occupancy rate	Percent	(7.3)	16.88	16.07	..	..	..
Average length of stay	Nights	(5.6)	..	..	..	..	..
ECONOMIC AGGREGATES							
Gross National Product (GNP)	US$ Million	(9.1)	8,360	8,627	8,734	8,779	8,564
Exports (F.O.B.)	US$ Million	(9.2)	1,768	1,860	1,675	1,595	..
Imports (C.I.F.)	US$ Million	(9.3)	1,226	1,359	1,503	1,314	..

Abbreviations used in tables and notes:
H&S: Hotels and similar establishments; **CE:** All types of tourism accommodation establishments; **ALS:** Average length of stay; **THS:** Non-resident tourists staying in H&S; **TCE:** Non-resident tourists staying in CE; **TF:** Arrivals of international (or non-resident) tourists; **VF:** Arrivals of international (or non-resident) visitors; **NHS:** Overnight stays at H&S; **NCE:** Overnight stays at CE.

..   data not available
incl   including
excl   excluding
nra   nationals residing abroad

Notes:
(1.2,2.1-2.6) THS.

Basic Indicators	Units	Code	1996	1997	1998	1999	2000
INBOUND TOURISM							
Arrivals							
Visitors	Thousands	(1.1)	43,256	45,076	48,064	49,055	48,637
Tourists (overnight visitors)	Thousands	(1.2)	17,329	17,669	18,870	19,411	19,650
Same-day visitors	Thousands	(1.3)	25,927	27,407	29,194	29,644	28,987
Cruise passengers	Thousands	(1.4)	..	..	..	..	..
Arrivals by region							
Africa	Thousands	(2.1)	55	59	59	66	73
Americas	Thousands	(2.2)	13,240	13,742	15,256	15,564	15,628
Europe	Thousands	(2.3)	2,371	2,330	2,274	2,382	2,497
East Asia and the Pacific	Thousands	(2.4)	1,509	1,393	1,145	1,251	1,342
South Asia	Thousands	(2.5)	73	78	56	63	74
Middle East	Thousands	(2.6)	35	35	38	41	36
Arrivals by mode of transport							
Air	Thousands	(3.1)	6,319	6,622	6,941	7,351	7,657
Rail	Thousands	(3.2)	72	86	88	100	108
Road	Thousands	(3.3)	10,658	10,606	11,460	11,601	11,403
Sea	Thousands	(3.4)	280	355	380	359	482
Arrivals by purpose of visit							
Leisure, recreation and holidays	Thousands	(4.1)	9,753	9,693	10,556	10,785	10,692
Business and professional	Thousands	(4.2)	2,641	2,868	3,045	3,087	3,145
Other	Thousands	(4.3)	4,892	5,074	5,227	5,495	5,781
Overnight stays and length of stay							
Overnight stays in H&S	Thousand nights	(5.1)	..	..	..	..	..
Overnight stays in CE	Thousand nights	(5.2)	96,685	96,648	98,283	105,720	107,816
ALS of non resident tourists	Nights	(5.5)	5.59	5.50	5.22	..	..
Tourism expenditure							
in the country of reference	US$ Million	(8.1)	8,616	8,828	9,396	10,171	10,704
DOMESTIC TOURISM							
Overnight stays							
Overnight stays in H&S	Thousand nights	(5.3)	39,002	37,597	44,653	43,980	..
Overnight stays in CE	Thousand nights	(5.4)	227,879	218,484	241,515	240,212	..
OUTBOUND TOURISM							
Departures	Thousands	(6.1)	18,973	19,111	17,640	18,368	19,163
Tourism expenditure in other countries	US$ Million	(8.2)	11,253	11,464	10,765	11,345	12,140
TOURISM ACTIVITIES							
Hotels and similar establishments							
Number of rooms	H&S	(7.1)	331,584	327,383	330,003	..	..
Number of bed-places	H&S	(7.2)	..	..	..	..	..
Occupancy rate	Percent	(7.3)	62.40	63.70	64.00	63.40	..
Average length of stay	Nights	(5.6)	5.59	5.50	5.22	..	..
ECONOMIC AGGREGATES							
Gross National Product (GNP)	US$ Million	(9.1)	587,555	608,437	597,490	614,071	647,126
Exports (F.O.B.)	US$ Million	(9.2)	201,636	214,428	214,335	238,422	276,645
Imports (C.I.F.)	US$ Million	(9.3)	170,694	195,980	201,061	214,791	238,812

Abbreviations used in tables and notes:
H&S: Hotels and similar establishments; **CE:** All types of tourism accommodation establishments; **ALS:** Average length of stay; **THS:** Non-resident tourists staying in H&S; **TCE:** Non-resident tourists staying in CE; **TF:** Arrivals of international (or non-resident) tourists; **VF:** Arrivals of international (or non-resident) visitors; **NHS:** Overnight stays at H&S; **NCE:** Overnight stays at CE.

..   data not available
incl   including
excl   excluding
nra   nationals residing abroad

Notes:
(1.1,1.3) Data based on customs counts and adjusted using questionnaire surveys; (1.2,2.1-4.3) TF; (4.2) Incl convention; (5.6) Inbound tourism; (6.1) Person-trips (one or more nights); (8.1,8.2) Incl. medical, education and crew spending. Excl. international fares.
Note: Statistics Canada's Tourism Program uses two methods for collecting statistics on international travellers: the frontier counts and the mail-back questionnaires (characteristics). However, due to methodological differences, both sources yield slightly different estimates of the number of same-day overseas visitors entering Canada by commercial plane or boat.

CAPE VERDE

Basic Indicators	Units	Code	1996	1997	1998	1999	2000
INBOUND TOURISM							
Arrivals							
Visitors	Thousands	(1.1)	..	..	..	..	
Tourists (overnight visitors)	Thousands	(1.2)	37	45	52	67	83
Same-day visitors	Thousands	(1.3)	..	..	..	..	..
Cruise passengers	Thousands	(1.4)	..	..	..	..	..
Arrivals by region							
Africa	Thousands	(2.1)	..	..	..	..	
Americas	Thousands	(2.2)	..	..	..	..	3
Europe	Thousands	(2.3)	31	38	44	..	71
East Asia and the Pacific	Thousands	(2.4)	..	..	..	..	..
South Asia	Thousands	(2.5)	..	..	..	..	..
Middle East	Thousands	(2.6)	..	..	..	..	..
Arrivals by mode of transport							
Air	Thousands	(3.1)	37	45	52	67	83
Rail	Thousands	(3.2)	..	..	..	..	..
Road	Thousands	(3.3)	..	..	..	..	
Sea	Thousands	(3.4)	..	..	..	..	..
Arrivals by purpose of visit							
Leisure, recreation and holidays	Thousands	(4.1)	..	..	..	..	..
Business and professional	Thousands	(4.2)	..	..	..	..	..
Other	Thousands	(4.3)	..	..	..	..	..
Overnight stays and length of stay							
Overnight stays in H&S	Thousand nights	(5.1)	..	..	..	..	..
Overnight stays in CE	Thousand nights	(5.2)	..	..	..	..	
ALS of non resident tourists	Nights	(5.5)	..	7.00	7.00	..	..
Tourism expenditure **in the country of reference**	US$ Million	(8.1)	11	15	20	23	..
DOMESTIC TOURISM							
Overnight stays							
Overnight stays in H&S	Thousand nights	(5.3)	..	..	..	..	..
Overnight stays in CE	Thousand nights	(5.4)	..	..	..	..	..
OUTBOUND TOURISM							
Departures	Thousands	(6.1)	..	..	..	..	..
Tourism expenditure in other countries	US$ Million	(8.2)	18	17	24	..	..
TOURISM ACTIVITIES							
Hotels and similar establishments							
Number of rooms	H&S	(7.1)	..	1,461	1,800	1,825	2,391
Number of bed-places	H&S	(7.2)	..	2,687	3,240	3,165	4,475
Occupancy rate	Percent	(7.3)	70.00	70.00	80.00	41.00	52.00
Average length of stay	Nights	(5.6)	..	..	..	3.80	4.20
ECONOMIC AGGREGATES							
Gross National Product (GNP)	US$ Million	(9.1)	499	521	535	569	587
Exports (F.O.B.)	US$ Million	(9.2)	..	..	..	..	..
Imports (C.I.F.)	US$ Million	(9.3)	..	..	..	..	..

Abbreviations used in tables and notes:
H&S: Hotels and similar establishments; **CE:** All types of tourism accommodation establishments; **ALS:** Average length of stay; **THS:** Non-resident tourists staying in H&S; **TCE:** Non-resident tourists staying in CE; **TF:** Arrivals of international (or non-resident) tourists; **VF:** Arrivals of international (or non-resident) visitors; **NHS:** Overnight stays at H&S; **NCE:** Overnight stays at CE.

.. data not available
incl including
excl excluding
nra nationals residing abroad

Notes:
(1.2) Arrivals by air; (5.5) Days; (8.2) International Monetary Fund.

Basic Indicators	Units	Code	1996	1997	1998	1999	2000
INBOUND TOURISM							
Arrivals							
Visitors	Thousands	(1.1)	1,173	1,248	1,275	1,430	1,385
Tourists (overnight visitors)	Thousands	(1.2)	373	381	404	395	354
Same-day visitors	Thousands	(1.3)	..	..	..	..	..
Cruise passengers	Thousands	(1.4)	800	867	871	1,035	1,031
Arrivals by region							
Africa	Thousands	(2.1)	..	..	..	1	..
Americas	Thousands	(2.2)	336	344	365	356	..
Europe	Thousands	(2.3)	33	33	35	35	..
East Asia and the Pacific	Thousands	(2.4)	2	3	3	3	..
South Asia	Thousands	(2.5)	..	..	..	..	..
Middle East	Thousands	(2.6)	..	..	..	..	..
Arrivals by mode of transport							
Air	Thousands	(3.1)	373	381	404	395	354
Rail	Thousands	(3.2)	..	..	..	..	..
Road	Thousands	(3.3)	..	..	..	..	..
Sea	Thousands	(3.4)	800	867	871	1,035	1,031
Arrivals by purpose of visit							
Leisure, recreation and holidays	Thousands	(4.1)	354	364	385	373	..
Business and professional	Thousands	(4.2)	15	15	16	18	..
Other	Thousands	(4.3)	4	2	3	4	..
Overnight stays and length of stay							
Overnight stays in H&S	Thousand nights	(5.1)	..	..	..	..	..
Overnight stays in CE	Thousand nights	(5.2)	..	..	..	..	..
ALS of non resident tourists	Nights	(5.5)	6.90	7.39	6.92	6.52	..
Tourism expenditure							
in the country of reference	US$ Million	(8.1)	368	436	450	439	..
DOMESTIC TOURISM							
Overnight stays							
Overnight stays in H&S	Thousand nights	(5.3)	..	..	..	..	..
Overnight stays in CE	Thousand nights	(5.4)	..	..	..	..	..
OUTBOUND TOURISM							
Departures	Thousands	(6.1)	..	..	..	..	..
Tourism expenditure in other countries	US$ Million	(8.2)	..	..	..	..	..
TOURISM ACTIVITIES							
Hotels and similar establishments							
Number of rooms	H&S	(7.1)	4,477	4,501	4,216	4,318	..
Number of bed-places	H&S	(7.2)	13,222	13,262	12,193	11,811	..
Occupancy rate	Percent	(7.3)	..	62.90	68.81	64.68	..
Average length of stay	Nights	(5.6)	4.50	4.85	5.30	5.05	..
ECONOMIC AGGREGATES							
Gross National Product (GNP)	US$ Million	(9.1)	674	711	745	..	..
Exports (F.O.B.)	US$ Million	(9.2)	3	2	1	2	..
Imports (C.I.F.)	US$ Million	(9.3)	378	..	..	..	..

Abbreviations used in tables and notes:
H&S: Hotels and similar establishments; **CE:** All types of tourism accommodation establishments; **ALS:** Average length of stay; **THS:** Non-resident tourists staying in H&S; **TCE:** Non-resident tourists staying in CE; **TF:** Arrivals of international (or non-resident) tourists; **VF:** Arrivals of international (or non-resident) visitors; **NHS:** Overnight stays at H&S; **NCE:** Overnight stays at CE.

.. data not available
incl including
excl excluding
nra nationals residing abroad

Notes:
(1.2,2.2-2.4,4.1-4.3) Arrivals by air; (5.5,5.6) Days; (7.1,7.2) Hotels and apartments; (7.3) Hotels (rooms); (8.1) Incl expenditure by cruise passengers; (9.1) GDP.

CENTRAL AFRICAN REPUBLIC

Basic Indicators	Units	Code	1996	1997	1998	1999	2000
INBOUND TOURISM							
Arrivals							
Visitors	Thousands	(1.1)	..	..	..	..	..
Tourists (overnight visitors)	Thousands	(1.2)	21	17	7	10	..
Same-day visitors	Thousands	(1.3)	..	..	..	..	..
Cruise passengers	Thousands	(1.4)	..	..	..	..	..
Arrivals by region							
Africa	Thousands	(2.1)	..	..	3	..	..
Americas	Thousands	(2.2)	..	..	..	..	..
Europe	Thousands	(2.3)	..	..	3	..	..
East Asia and the Pacific	Thousands	(2.4)	..	..	..	..	..
South Asia	Thousands	(2.5)	..	..	..	..	..
Middle East	Thousands	(2.6)	..	..	..	..	..
Arrivals by mode of transport							
Air	Thousands	(3.1)	21	17	7	10	..
Rail	Thousands	(3.2)	..	..	..	..	..
Road	Thousands	(3.3)	..	..	..	..	..
Sea	Thousands	(3.4)	..	..	..	..	..
Arrivals by purpose of visit							
Leisure, recreation and holidays	Thousands	(4.1)	..	..	1	..	..
Business and professional	Thousands	(4.2)	..	..	3	..	..
Other	Thousands	(4.3)	..	..	3	..	..
Overnight stays and length of stay							
Overnight stays in H&S	Thousand nights	(5.1)	31	29	30	..	..
Overnight stays in CE	Thousand nights	(5.2)	..	..	..	..	..
ALS of non resident tourists	Nights	(5.5)	..	..	..	..	..
Tourism expenditure in the country of reference	US$ Million	(8.1)	..	..	..	..	..
DOMESTIC TOURISM							
Overnight stays							
Overnight stays in H&S	Thousand nights	(5.3)	..	..	5	..	..
Overnight stays in CE	Thousand nights	(5.4)	..	..	..	..	..
OUTBOUND TOURISM							
Departures	Thousands	(6.1)	..	..	..	..	..
Tourism expenditure in other countries	US$ Million	(8.2)	..	..	..	..	..
TOURISM ACTIVITIES							
Hotels and similar establishments							
Number of rooms	H&S	(7.1)	227	227	..	..	..
Number of bed-places	H&S	(7.2)	347	347	..	..	..
Occupancy rate	Percent	(7.3)	51.72	55.42	49.10	..	..
Average length of stay	Nights	(5.6)	..	..	..	..	..
ECONOMIC AGGREGATES							
Gross National Product (GNP)	US$ Million	(9.1)	1,014	1,075	1,047	1,036	1,053
Exports (F.O.B.)	US$ Million	(9.2)	147	154	..	..	..
Imports (C.I.F.)	US$ Million	(9.3)	141	145	..	..	..

Abbreviations used in tables and notes:
H&S: Hotels and similar establishments; **CE:** All types of tourism accommodation establishments; **ALS:** Average length of stay; **THS:** Non-resident tourists staying in H&S; **TCE:** Non-resident tourists staying in CE; **TF:** Arrivals of international (or non-resident) tourists; **VF:** Arrivals of international (or non-resident) visitors; **NHS:** Overnight stays at H&S; **NCE:** Overnight stays at CE.

..	data not available
incl	including
excl	excluding
nra	nationals residing abroad

Notes:
(1.2) Arrivals by air.

CHAD

Basic Indicators	Units	Code	1996	1997	1998	1999	2000
INBOUND TOURISM							
Arrivals							
Visitors	Thousands	(1.1)	67	77	89	98	..
Tourists (overnight visitors)	Thousands	(1.2)	20	27	41	47	54
Same-day visitors	Thousands	(1.3)	..	..	..	..	..
Cruise passengers	Thousands	(1.4)	..	..	..	..	..
Arrivals by region							
Africa	Thousands	(2.1)	2	4	12	14	13
Americas	Thousands	(2.2)	1	1	4	5	8
Europe	Thousands	(2.3)	5	5	21	24	21
East Asia and the Pacific	Thousands	(2.4)	..	..	..	..	..
South Asia	Thousands	(2.5)	..	..	..	..	..
Middle East	Thousands	(2.6)	..	..	..	1	1
Arrivals by mode of transport							
Air	Thousands	(3.1)	..	..	27	31	38
Rail	Thousands	(3.2)	..	..	..	..	..
Road	Thousands	(3.3)	..	..	14	15	16
Sea	Thousands	(3.4)	..	..	..	..	..
Arrivals by purpose of visit							
Leisure, recreation and holidays	Thousands	(4.1)	..	..	..	..	..
Business and professional	Thousands	(4.2)	..	..	..	..	..
Other	Thousands	(4.3)	..	..	..	..	..
Overnight stays and length of stay							
Overnight stays in H&S	Thousand nights	(5.1)	42	46	116	121	107
Overnight stays in CE	Thousand nights	(5.2)	..	..	..	..	..
ALS of non resident tourists	Nights	(5.5)	..	..	..	..	..
Tourism expenditure							
in the country of reference	US$ Million	(8.1)	..	..	..	..	..
DOMESTIC TOURISM							
Overnight stays							
Overnight stays in H&S	Thousand nights	(5.3)	1	2	3	3	10
Overnight stays in CE	Thousand nights	(5.4)	..	..	..	..	..
OUTBOUND TOURISM							
Departures	Thousands	(6.1)	..	..	..	..	..
Tourism expenditure in other countries	US$ Million	(8.2)	..	..	..	..	..
TOURISM ACTIVITIES							
Hotels and similar establishments							
Number of rooms	H&S	(7.1)	374	374	389	586	677
Number of bed-places	H&S	(7.2)	688	688	693	983	1,250
Occupancy rate	Percent	(7.3)	18.50	23.29	79.66	83.12	..
Average length of stay	Nights	(5.6)	2.00	2.00	3.00	3.00	3.62
ECONOMIC AGGREGATES							
Gross National Product (GNP)	US$ Million	(9.1)	1,455	1,570	1,638	1,549	1,504
Exports (F.O.B.)	US$ Million	(9.2)	238	238	262	202	184
Imports (C.I.F.)	US$ Million	(9.3)	332	335	356	317	291

Abbreviations used in tables and notes:
H&S: Hotels and similar establishments; **CE:** All types of tourism accommodation establishments; **ALS:** Average length of stay; **THS:** Non-resident tourists staying in H&S; **TCE:** Non-resident tourists staying in CE; **TF:** Arrivals of international (or non-resident) tourists; **VF:** Arrivals of international (or non-resident) visitors; **NHS:** Overnight stays at H&S; **NCE:** Overnight stays at CE.

.. data not available
incl including
excl excluding
nra nationals residing abroad

Notes:
(1.2,3.1,3.3/96-99) THS; (1.2,3.1,3.3/2000) TF; (2.1-2.6) THS; (7.3) Rooms.

CHILE

Basic Indicators	Units	Code	1996	1997	1998	1999	2000
INBOUND TOURISM							
Arrivals							
Visitors	Thousands	(1.1)	..	..	..	..	..
Tourists (overnight visitors)	Thousands	(1.2)	1,450	1,644	1,759	1,622	1,742
Same-day visitors	Thousands	(1.3)	..	..	..	..	..
Cruise passengers	Thousands	(1.4)	..	..	..	..	..
Arrivals by region							
Africa	Thousands	(2.1)	..	2	2	2	2
Americas	Thousands	(2.2)	1,243	1,403	1,493	1,356	1,457
Europe	Thousands	(2.3)	168	203	227	224	240
East Asia and the Pacific	Thousands	(2.4)	28	32	34	35	37
South Asia	Thousands	(2.5)	..	2	2	2	3
Middle East	Thousands	(2.6)	..	1	..	1	1
Arrivals by mode of transport							
Air	Thousands	(3.1)	571	655	683	638	662
Rail	Thousands	(3.2)	6	7	8	8	44
Road	Thousands	(3.3)	866	968	1,049	957	1,009
Sea	Thousands	(3.4)	6	13	17	19	27
Arrivals by purpose of visit							
Leisure, recreation and holidays	Thousands	(4.1)	902	1,062	1,256	1,161	1,224
Business and professional	Thousands	(4.2)	223	173	144	165	248
Other	Thousands	(4.3)	325	409	357	296	270
Overnight stays and length of stay							
Overnight stays in H&S	Thousand nights	(5.1)	2,650	2,953	2,657	2,108	2,181
Overnight stays in CE	Thousand nights	(5.2)	..	..	..	..	..
ALS of non resident tourists	Nights	(5.5)	11.30	11.00	11.60	10.00	10.10
Tourism expenditure **in the country of reference**	US$ Million	(8.1)	905	1,020	1,062	898	827
DOMESTIC TOURISM							
Overnight stays							
Overnight stays in H&S	Thousand nights	(5.3)	4,051	4,321	5,116	4,079	4,224
Overnight stays in CE	Thousand nights	(5.4)	..	..	..	..	..
OUTBOUND TOURISM							
Departures	Thousands	(6.1)	1,092	1,263	1,351	1,567	1,830
Tourism expenditure in other countries	US$ Million	(8.2)	806	945	906	806	752
TOURISM ACTIVITIES							
Hotels and similar establishments							
Number of rooms	H&S	(7.1)	40,412	40,829	44,720	46,097	47,204
Number of bed-places	H&S	(7.2)	91,339	91,854	102,439	108,068	110,137
Occupancy rate	Percent	(7.3)	34.70	36.10	35.00	30.20	30.80
Average length of stay	Nights	(5.6)	2.20	2.30	2.20	2.00	2.10
ECONOMIC AGGREGATES							
Gross National Product (GNP)	US$ Million	(9.1)	65,706	72,719	72,396	69,042	69,936
Exports (F.O.B.)	US$ Million	(9.2)	15,405	16,663	14,830	15,616	18,158
Imports (C.I.F.)	US$ Million	(9.3)	17,823	19,662	18,779	15,137	18,107

Abbreviations used in tables and notes:

H&S: Hotels and similar establishments; **CE:** All types of tourism accommodation establishments; **ALS:** Average length of stay; **THS:** Non-resident tourists staying in H&S; **TCE:** Non-resident tourists staying in CE; **TF:** Arrivals of international (or non-resident) tourists; **VF:** Arrivals of international (or non-resident) visitors; **NHS:** Overnight stays at H&S; **NCE:** Overnight stays at CE.

..   data not available
incl   including
excl   excluding
nra   nationals residing abroad

Basic Indicators	Units	Code	1996	1997	1998	1999	2000
INBOUND TOURISM							
Arrivals							
Visitors	Thousands	(1.1)	51,128	57,588	63,478	72,796	83,444
Tourists (overnight visitors)	Thousands	(1.2)	22,765	23,770	25,073	27,047	31,229
Same-day visitors	Thousands	(1.3)	..	..	..	..	..
Cruise passengers	Thousands	(1.4)	..	..	..	..	..
Arrivals by region							
Africa	Thousands	(2.1)	39	38	39	43	54
Americas	Thousands	(2.2)	809	867	948	1,026	1,217
Europe	Thousands	(2.3)	1,770	2,039	1,896	2,149	2,537
East Asia and the Pacific	Thousands	(2.4)	3,972	4,313	4,058	5,023	6,104
South Asia	Thousands	(2.5)	120	131	133	161	210
Middle East	Thousands	(2.6)	18	22	21	26	35
Arrivals by mode of transport							
Air	Thousands	(3.1)	5,325	5,856	5,559	6,627	7,745
Rail	Thousands	(3.2)	1,014	898	820	1,016	1,119
Road	Thousands	(3.3)	40,624	46,256	53,345	61,339	70,719
Sea	Thousands	(3.4)	4,164	4,578	3,754	3,814	3,860
Arrivals by purpose of visit							
Leisure, recreation and holidays	Thousands	(4.1)	..	..	..	..	..
Business and professional	Thousands	(4.2)	..	..	..	..	..
Other	Thousands	(4.3)	..	..	..	..	..
Overnight stays and length of stay							
Overnight stays in H&S	Thousand nights	(5.1)	47,340	53,200	57,925	63,104	78,310
Overnight stays in CE	Thousand nights	(5.2)	..	..	..	..	..
ALS of non resident tourists	Nights	(5.5)	..	..	..	..	..
Tourism expenditure in the country of reference	US$ Million	(8.1)	10,200	12,074	12,602	14,099	16,224
DOMESTIC TOURISM							
Overnight stays							
Overnight stays in H&S	Thousand nights	(5.3)	160,975	185,250	207,078	313,904	354,031
Overnight stays in CE	Thousand nights	(5.4)	..	..	..	..	..
OUTBOUND TOURISM							
Departures	Thousands	(6.1)	5,061	5,324	8,426	9,232	10,473
Tourism expenditure in other countries	US$ Million	(8.2)	4,474	8,130	9,205	10,864	13,114
TOURISM ACTIVITIES							
Hotels and similar establishments							
Number of rooms	H&S	(7.1)	593,696	701,736	764,797	889,430	948,185
Number of bed-places	H&S	(7.2)	1,199,714	1,411,708	1,524,224	1,769,825	1,855,965
Occupancy rate	Percent	(7.3)	55.27	53.78	51.67	53.41	55.85
Average length of stay	Nights	(5.6)	2.43	2.44	2.64	2.53	2.52
ECONOMIC AGGREGATES							
Gross National Product (GNP)	US$ Million	(9.1)	755,266	866,702	922,088	977,462	1,064,537
Exports (F.O.B.)	US$ Million	(9.2)	151,197	182,877	183,589	195,150	249,297
Imports (C.I.F.)	US$ Million	(9.3)	138,944	142,189	140,305	165,788	206,132

Abbreviations used in tables and notes:
H&S: Hotels and similar establishments; **CE:** All types of tourism accommodation establishments; **ALS:** Average length of stay; **THS:** Non-resident tourists staying in H&S; **TCE:** Non-resident tourists staying in CE; **TF:** Arrivals of international (or non-resident) tourists; **VF:** Arrivals of international (or non-resident) visitors; **NHS:** Overnight stays at H&S; **NCE:** Overnight stays at CE.

.. data not available
incl including
excl excluding
nra nationals residing abroad

Notes:
(1.1,3.1-3.4) Incl ethnic Chinese arriving from HK, Macau, Taiwan and overseas Chinese (1996= 44,383,182; 1997= 50,159,917; 1998= 56,370,654; 1999= 64,363,298; 2000= 73,283,449) of which most same-day visitors are from HK and Macau; (2.1-2.6) Excl ethnic Chinese arriving from HK, Macau, Taiwan and overseas Chinese; (5.6) Inbound tourism only; (6.1/98-2000) Incl air crew members and other servicemen; (7.3) Rooms.

COLOMBIA

Basic Indicators	Units	Code	1996	1997	1998	1999	2000
INBOUND TOURISM							
Arrivals							
Visitors	Thousands	(1.1)	846	793	844	725	749
Tourists (overnight visitors)	Thousands	(1.2)	757	639	674	546	557
Same-day visitors	Thousands	(1.3)	..	..	..	..	..
Cruise passengers	Thousands	(1.4)	89	154	170	179	192
Arrivals by region							
Africa	Thousands	(2.1)	..	..	..	..	..
Americas	Thousands	(2.2)	500	513	561	475	486
Europe	Thousands	(2.3)	61	70	70	71	70
East Asia and the Pacific	Thousands	(2.4)	..	..	..	..	..
South Asia	Thousands	(2.5)	..	..	..	..	..
Middle East	Thousands	(2.6)	..	..	..	..	..
Arrivals by mode of transport							
Air	Thousands	(3.1)	620	524	553	447	456
Rail	Thousands	(3.2)	..	..	..	..	..
Road	Thousands	(3.3)	67	57	60	49	50
Sea	Thousands	(3.4)	69	58	61	50	51
Arrivals by purpose of visit							
Leisure, recreation and holidays	Thousands	(4.1)	..	..	..	126	131
Business and professional	Thousands	(4.2)	..	..	..	420	426
Other	Thousands	(4.3)	..	..	..	..	..
Overnight stays and length of stay							
Overnight stays in H&S	Thousand nights	(5.1)	..	..	..	..	..
Overnight stays in CE	Thousand nights	(5.2)	..	..	..	..	..
ALS of non resident tourists	Nights	(5.5)	3.00	2.64	..	..	..
Tourism expenditure **in the country of reference**	US$ Million	(8.1)	1,120	1,044	929	928	1,028
DOMESTIC TOURISM							
Overnight stays							
Overnight stays in H&S	Thousand nights	(5.3)	..	..	..	..	..
Overnight stays in CE	Thousand nights	(5.4)	..	..	..	..	..
OUTBOUND TOURISM							
Departures	Thousands	(6.1)	929	1,071	1,093	1,098	1,235
Tourism expenditure in other countries	US$ Million	(8.2)	1,116	1,209	1,120	1,078	1,057
TOURISM ACTIVITIES							
Hotels and similar establishments							
Number of rooms	H&S	(7.1)	51,598	52,588	53,346	53,195	53,970
Number of bed-places	H&S	(7.2)	98,036	99,917	101,357	103,060	104,132
Occupancy rate	Percent	(7.3)	48.29	49.00	40.00	39.10	41.76
Average length of stay	Nights	(5.6)	2.65	2.64	..	..	..
ECONOMIC AGGREGATES							
Gross National Product (GNP)	US$ Million	(9.1)	92,139	100,270	98,583	90,014	88,047
Exports (F.O.B.)	US$ Million	(9.2)	10,587	11,522	10,852	11,576	13,040
Imports (C.I.F.)	US$ Million	(9.3)	13,684	15,378	14,635	10,659	11,539

Abbreviations used in tables and notes:
H&S: Hotels and similar establishments; **CE:** All types of tourism accommodation establishments; **ALS:** Average length of stay; **THS:** Non-resident tourists staying in H&S; **TCE:** Non-resident tourists staying in CE; **TF:** Arrivals of international (or non-resident) tourists; **VF:** Arrivals of international (or non-resident) visitors; **NHS:** Overnight stays at H&S; **NCE:** Overnight stays at CE.

..   data not available
incl   including
excl   excluding
nra   nationals residing abroad

Notes:
(7.3) Rooms.
Source: "Departamento Administrativo de Seguridad (DAS), Banco de la República, COTELCO".

COMOROS

Basic Indicators	Units	Code	1996	1997	1998	1999	2000
INBOUND TOURISM							
Arrivals							
Visitors	Thousands	(1.1)	..	..	..	..	..
Tourists (overnight visitors)	Thousands	(1.2)	24	26	27	24	24
Same-day visitors	Thousands	(1.3)	..	..	..	..	..
Cruise passengers	Thousands	(1.4)	..	..	..	..	..
Arrivals by region							
Africa	Thousands	(2.1)	11	14	11	14	16
Americas	Thousands	(2.2)	..	..	..	..	..
Europe	Thousands	(2.3)	11	11	13	9	7
East Asia and the Pacific	Thousands	(2.4)	..	1	..	..	..
South Asia	Thousands	(2.5)	..	..	..	..	..
Middle East	Thousands	(2.6)	..	..	..	..	..
Arrivals by mode of transport							
Air	Thousands	(3.1)	24	26	27	24	24
Rail	Thousands	(3.2)	..	..	..	..	..
Road	Thousands	(3.3)	..	..	..	..	..
Sea	Thousands	(3.4)	..	..	..	..	..
Arrivals by purpose of visit							
Leisure, recreation and holidays	Thousands	(4.1)	14	16	15	12	13
Business and professional	Thousands	(4.2)	3	3	4	2	2
Other	Thousands	(4.3)	7	7	8	10	9
Overnight stays and length of stay							
Overnight stays in H&S	Thousand nights	(5.1)	..	..	..	..	..
Overnight stays in CE	Thousand nights	(5.2)	178	209	206	184	138
ALS of non resident tourists	Nights	(5.5)	..	..	..	..	..
Tourism expenditure							
in the country of reference	US$ Million	(8.1)	23	26	16	19	15
DOMESTIC TOURISM							
Overnight stays							
Overnight stays in H&S	Thousand nights	(5.3)	..	..	..	..	..
Overnight stays in CE	Thousand nights	(5.4)	..	..	..	..	..
OUTBOUND TOURISM							
Departures	Thousands	(6.1)	..	..	..	..	..
Tourism expenditure in other countries	US$ Million	(8.2)	..	..	3	..	..
TOURISM ACTIVITIES							
Hotels and similar establishments							
Number of rooms	H&S	(7.1)	392	392	386	389	389
Number of bed-places	H&S	(7.2)	784	742	772	778	778
Occupancy rate	Percent	(7.3)	..	..	45.00	30.00	27.00
Average length of stay	Nights	(5.6)	..	..	..	..	..
ECONOMIC AGGREGATES							
Gross National Product (GNP)	US$ Million	(9.1)	208	210	204	211	213
Exports (F.O.B.)	US$ Million	(9.2)	..	..	..	..	..
Imports (C.I.F.)	US$ Million	(9.3)	..	..	..	..	..

Abbreviations used in tables and notes:
H&S: Hotels and similar establishments; **CE:** All types of tourism accommodation establishments; **ALS:** Average length of stay; **THS:** Non-resident tourists staying in H&S; **TCE:** Non-resident tourists staying in CE; **TF:** Arrivals of international (or non-resident) tourists; **VF:** Arrivals of international (or non-resident) visitors; **NHS:** Overnight stays at H&S; **NCE:** Overnight stays at CE.

.. data not available
incl including
excl excluding
nra nationals residing abroad

Notes:
(1.2,2.1-2.4,4.1-4.3) Air arrivals.

CONGO

Basic Indicators	Units	Code	1996	1997	1998	1999	2000
INBOUND TOURISM							
Arrivals							
Visitors	Thousands	(1.1)	..	..	..	..	..
Tourists (overnight visitors)	Thousands	(1.2)	39	27	20	14	19
Same-day visitors	Thousands	(1.3)	..	..	..	..	..
Cruise passengers	Thousands	(1.4)	..	..	..	..	..
Arrivals by region							
Africa	Thousands	(2.1)	14	10	7	6	9
Americas	Thousands	(2.2)	3	2	1	1	1
Europe	Thousands	(2.3)	21	14	11	7	8
East Asia and the Pacific	Thousands	(2.4)	..	..	..	..	..
South Asia	Thousands	(2.5)	..	..	..	..	..
Middle East	Thousands	(2.6)	..	..	..	..	..
Arrivals by mode of transport							
Air	Thousands	(3.1)	..	..	..	..	..
Rail	Thousands	(3.2)	..	..	..	..	..
Road	Thousands	(3.3)	..	..	..	..	..
Sea	Thousands	(3.4)	..	..	..	..	..
Arrivals by purpose of visit							
Leisure, recreation and holidays	Thousands	(4.1)	..	..	..	..	..
Business and professional	Thousands	(4.2)	..	..	..	..	..
Other	Thousands	(4.3)	..	..	..	..	..
Overnight stays and length of stay							
Overnight stays in H&S	Thousand nights	(5.1)	119	93	55	63	76
Overnight stays in CE	Thousand nights	(5.2)	..	..	..	..	..
ALS of non resident tourists	Nights	(5.5)	..	..	..	..	..
Tourism expenditure **in the country of reference**	US$ Million	(8.1)	10	10	9	12	..
DOMESTIC TOURISM							
Overnight stays							
Overnight stays in H&S	Thousand nights	(5.3)	66	78	40	27	..
Overnight stays in CE	Thousand nights	(5.4)	..	..	..	..	..
OUTBOUND TOURISM							
Departures	Thousands	(6.1)	..	..	..	..	..
Tourism expenditure in other countries	US$ Million	(8.2)	77	64	57	60	..
TOURISM ACTIVITIES							
Hotels and similar establishments							
Number of rooms	H&S	(7.1)	3,313	3,774	1,929	2,032	2,522
Number of bed-places	H&S	(7.2)	..	..	..	..	..
Occupancy rate	Percent	(7.3)	48.70	68.50	55.70	39.80	40.70
Average length of stay	Nights	(5.6)	3.00	3.70	2.70	4.10	3.70
ECONOMIC AGGREGATES							
Gross National Product (GNP)	US$ Million	(9.1)	1,212	1,357	1,795	1,495	1,847
Exports (F.O.B.)	US$ Million	(9.2)	1,552	1,666	1,373	1,555	..
Imports (C.I.F.)	US$ Million	(9.3)	1,399	925	682	820	..

Abbreviations used in tables and notes:
H&S: Hotels and similar establishments; **CE:** All types of tourism accommodation establishments; **ALS:** Average length of stay; **THS:** Non-resident tourists staying in H&S; **TCE:** Non-resident tourists staying in CE; **TF:** Arrivals of international (or non-resident) tourists; **VF:** Arrivals of international (or non-resident) visitors; **NHS:** Overnight stays at H&S; **NCE:** Overnight stays at CE.

..   data not available
incl   including
excl   excluding
nra   nationals residing abroad

Notes:
(1.2-2.3) THS; (7.3) Rooms.

Basic Indicators	Units	Code	1996	1997	1998	1999	2000
INBOUND TOURISM							
Arrivals							
Visitors	Thousands	(1.1)	..	..	..	..	..
Tourists (overnight visitors)	Thousands	(1.2)	48	50	49	56	73
Same-day visitors	Thousands	(1.3)	..	..	..	..	..
Cruise passengers	Thousands	(1.4)	..	..	..	..	..
Arrivals by region							
Africa	Thousands	(2.1)	..	..	..	..	..
Americas	Thousands	(2.2)	9	9	9	11	13
Europe	Thousands	(2.3)	18	20	19	18	24
East Asia and the Pacific	Thousands	(2.4)	21	20	20	26	36
South Asia	Thousands	(2.5)	..	..	..	..	..
Middle East	Thousands	(2.6)	..	..	..	..	..
Arrivals by mode of transport							
Air	Thousands	(3.1)	..	..	..	..	..
Rail	Thousands	(3.2)	..	..	..	..	..
Road	Thousands	(3.3)	..	..	..	..	..
Sea	Thousands	(3.4)	..	..	..	..	..
Arrivals by purpose of visit							
Leisure, recreation and holidays	Thousands	(4.1)	45	46	43	46	64
Business and professional	Thousands	(4.2)	2	2	2	2	3
Other	Thousands	(4.3)	2	2	3	7	7
Overnight stays and length of stay							
Overnight stays in H&S	Thousand nights	(5.1)	156	157	161	175	219
Overnight stays in CE	Thousand nights	(5.2)	..	..	..	..	..
ALS of non resident tourists	Nights	(5.5)	9.00	9.00	10.00	10.00	11.00
Tourism expenditure							
in the country of reference	US$ Million	(8.1)	50	35	34	39	36
DOMESTIC TOURISM							
Overnight stays							
Overnight stays in H&S	Thousand nights	(5.3)	..	..	..	..	..
Overnight stays in CE	Thousand nights	(5.4)	..	..	..	..	..
OUTBOUND TOURISM							
Departures	Thousands	(6.1)	7	8	8	8	9
Tourism expenditure in other countries	US$ Million	(8.2)	..	..	..	..	..
TOURISM ACTIVITIES							
Hotels and similar establishments							
Number of rooms	H&S	(7.1)	750	733	724	777	783
Number of bed-places	H&S	(7.2)	1,935	1,974	1,880	2,130	2,180
Occupancy rate	Percent	(7.3)	57.50	61.20	58.40	61.60	76.30
Average length of stay	Nights	(5.6)	..	..	..	..	..
ECONOMIC AGGREGATES							
Gross National Product (GNP)	US$ Million	(9.1)	..	..	..	..	..
Exports (F.O.B.)	US$ Million	(9.2)	3	3	3	4	..
Imports (C.I.F.)	US$ Million	(9.3)	43	48	38	41	..

Abbreviations used in tables and notes:
H&S: Hotels and similar establishments; **CE:** All types of tourism accommodation establishments; **ALS:** Average length of stay; **THS:** Non-resident tourists staying in H&S; **TCE:** Non-resident tourists staying in CE; **TF:** Arrivals of international (or non-resident) tourists; **VF:** Arrivals of international (or non-resident) visitors; **NHS:** Overnight stays at H&S; **NCE:** Overnight stays at CE.

..   data not available
incl   including
excl   excluding
nra   nationals residing abroad

Notes:
(1.2,2.2-2.4,4.1-4.3) Air and sea arrivals; (7.3) Rooms.

COSTA RICA

Basic Indicators	Units	Code	1996	1997	1998	1999	2000
INBOUND TOURISM							
Arrivals							
Visitors	Thousands	(1.1)	940	1,013	1,167	1,267	1,278
Tourists (overnight visitors)	Thousands	(1.2)	781	811	943	1,032	1,088
Same-day visitors	Thousands	(1.3)	..	..	..	..	..
Cruise passengers	Thousands	(1.4)	159	201	224	235	190
Arrivals by region							
Africa	Thousands	(2.1)	1	1	1	1	1
Americas	Thousands	(2.2)	630	662	791	863	907
Europe	Thousands	(2.3)	132	131	132	146	157
East Asia and the Pacific	Thousands	(2.4)	15	14	14	16	16
South Asia	Thousands	(2.5)	..	..	..	..	..
Middle East	Thousands	(2.6)	..	..	..	..	..
Arrivals by mode of transport							
Air	Thousands	(3.1)	560	582	669	734	801
Rail	Thousands	(3.2)	..	..	..	..	..
Road	Thousands	(3.3)	215	223	266	287	264
Sea	Thousands	(3.4)	6	7	7	10	23
Arrivals by purpose of visit							
Leisure, recreation and holidays	Thousands	(4.1)	586	640	659	682	740
Business and professional	Thousands	(4.2)	122	114	214	260	259
Other	Thousands	(4.3)	73	57	70	90	89
Overnight stays and length of stay							
Overnight stays in H&S	Thousand nights	(5.1)	..	..	..	..	..
Overnight stays in CE	Thousand nights	(5.2)	..	..	..	..	..
ALS of non resident tourists	Nights	(5.5)	10.35	9.73	9.52	11.10	11.30
Tourism expenditure							
in the country of reference	US$ Million	(8.1)	689	719	884	1,036	1,229
DOMESTIC TOURISM							
Overnight stays							
Overnight stays in H&S	Thousand nights	(5.3)	..	..	..	..	..
Overnight stays in CE	Thousand nights	(5.4)	..	..	..	..	..
OUTBOUND TOURISM							
Departures	Thousands	(6.1)	283	288	330	353	381
Tourism expenditure in other countries	US$ Million	(8.2)	335	358	408	446	482
TOURISM ACTIVITIES							
Hotels and similar establishments							
Number of rooms	H&S	(7.1)	27,103	27,860	28,084	28,826	29,497
Number of bed-places	H&S	(7.2)	..	..	..	..	..
Occupancy rate	Percent	(7.3)	48.10	46.70	51.00	53.00	59.60
Average length of stay	Nights	(5.6)	..	..	..	..	..
ECONOMIC AGGREGATES							
Gross National Product (GNP)	US$ Million	(9.1)	11,760	12,472	13,112	13,272	14,448
Exports (F.O.B.)	US$ Million	(9.2)	3,730	4,268	5,511	6,577	5,865
Imports (C.I.F.)	US$ Million	(9.3)	4,300	4,924	6,230	6,320	6,372

Abbreviations used in tables and notes:
H&S: Hotels and similar establishments; **CE:** All types of tourism accommodation establishments; **ALS:** Average length of stay; **THS:** Non-resident tourists staying in H&S; **TCE:** Non-resident tourists staying in CE; **TF:** Arrivals of international (or non-resident) tourists; **VF:** Arrivals of international (or non-resident) visitors; **NHS:** Overnight stays at H&S; **NCE:** Overnight stays at CE.

..   data not available
incl   including
excl   excluding
nra   nationals residing abroad

Notes:
(4.1) Pleasure trips and visits to relatives; (5.5) In the central area of the country; (7.3) "Five category" establishments in San José Metropolitan Area (survey).

COTE D´IVOIRE

Basic Indicators	Units	Code	1996	1997	1998	1999	2000
INBOUND TOURISM							
Arrivals							
Visitors	Thousands	(1.1)	..	..	..	..	..
Tourists (overnight visitors)	Thousands	(1.2)	237	274	301	..	..
Same-day visitors	Thousands	(1.3)	..	..	..	..	..
Cruise passengers	Thousands	(1.4)	..	..	..	..	..
Arrivals by region							
Africa	Thousands	(2.1)	113	138	159	..	..
Americas	Thousands	(2.2)	19	21	23	..	..
Europe	Thousands	(2.3)	97	107	109	..	..
East Asia and the Pacific	Thousands	(2.4)	5	6	6	..	..
South Asia	Thousands	(2.5)	1	..	1	..	..
Middle East	Thousands	(2.6)	1	2	3	..	..
Arrivals by mode of transport							
Air	Thousands	(3.1)	237	260	..	..	..
Rail	Thousands	(3.2)	..	..	..	..	..
Road	Thousands	(3.3)	..	14	..	..	..
Sea	Thousands	(3.4)	..	..	..	..	..
Arrivals by purpose of visit							
Leisure, recreation and holidays	Thousands	(4.1)	97	94	..	..	..
Business and professional	Thousands	(4.2)	107	135	..	..	..
Other	Thousands	(4.3)	33	31	..	..	..
Overnight stays and length of stay							
Overnight stays in H&S	Thousand nights	(5.1)	1,314	1,479	..	..	..
Overnight stays in CE	Thousand nights	(5.2)	..	..	..	..	..
ALS of non resident tourists	Nights	(5.5)	..	3.60	..	..	..
Tourism expenditure **in the country of reference**	US$ Million	(8.1)	93	90	98	100	57
DOMESTIC TOURISM							
Overnight stays							
Overnight stays in H&S	Thousand nights	(5.3)	..	413	..	..	..
Overnight stays in CE	Thousand nights	(5.4)	..	..	..	..	..
OUTBOUND TOURISM							
Departures	Thousands	(6.1)	..	..			
Tourism expenditure in other countries	US$ Million	(8.2)	221	200	213	222	226
TOURISM ACTIVITIES							
Hotels and similar establishments							
Number of rooms	H&S	(7.1)	7,786	7,786	..	..	..
Number of bed-places	H&S	(7.2)	11,374	11,374	..	..	..
Occupancy rate	Percent	(7.3)	52.00	70.00	..	..	..
Average length of stay	Nights	(5.6)	..	3.40	..	..	..
ECONOMIC AGGREGATES							
Gross National Product (GNP)	US$ Million	(9.1)	9,434	10,363	10,385	10,398	10,527
Exports (F.O.B.)	US$ Million	(9.2)	4,444	4,460	4,610	4,739	3,990
Imports (C.I.F.)	US$ Million	(9.3)	2,900	2,782	3,002	3,262	3,003

Abbreviations used in tables and notes:
H&S: Hotels and similar establishments; **CE:** All types of tourism accommodation establishments; **ALS:** Average length of stay; **THS:** Non-resident tourists staying in H&S; **TCE:** Non-resident tourists staying in CE; **TF:** Arrivals of international (or non-resident) tourists; **VF:** Arrivals of international (or non-resident) visitors; **NHS:** Overnight stays at H&S; **NCE:** Overnight stays at CE.

..   data not available
incl   including
excl   excluding
nra   nationals residing abroad

Notes:
(1.2,2.1-3.1,4.1-4.3) Air arrivals at the international FHB airport at Port Bouet. Arrivals at land frontiers, Bouaké airport and Air Ivoire airport at Abidjan are not taken into consideration; (1.2/97/98) Air arrivals at the international FHB airport at Port Bouet and arrivals at land frontiers; (5.1,5.3) Hotels; (7.3) Rooms; (8.1,8.2) International Monetary Fund; 1998: Preliminary.

49

CROATIA

Basic Indicators	Units	Code	1996	1997	1998	1999	2000
INBOUND TOURISM							
Arrivals							
Visitors	Thousands	(1.1)	19,085	23,660	25,499	29,215	37,226
Tourists (overnight visitors)	Thousands	(1.2)	2,914	4,178	4,499	3,805	5,831
Same-day visitors	Thousands	(1.3)	..	..	..	..	..
Cruise passengers	Thousands	(1.4)	..	..	..	..	..
Arrivals by region							
Africa	Thousands	(2.1)	..	..	..	..	..
Americas	Thousands	(2.2)	65	60	53	47	67
Europe	Thousands	(2.3)	2,815	4,072	4,412	3,730	5,720
East Asia and the Pacific	Thousands	(2.4)	8	11	16	15	23
South Asia	Thousands	(2.5)			..	..	
Middle East	Thousands	(2.6)	..	..	..	..	
Arrivals by mode of transport							
Air	Thousands	(3.1)	522	577	631	580	740
Rail	Thousands	(3.2)	377	294	311	302	342
Road	Thousands	(3.3)	18,077	22,625	24,379	28,211	35,961
Sea	Thousands	(3.4)	109	164	178	122	183
Arrivals by purpose of visit							
Leisure, recreation and holidays	Thousands	(4.1)	..	..	..	..	..
Business and professional	Thousands	(4.2)	..	..	..	..	..
Other	Thousands	(4.3)	..	..	..	..	..
Overnight stays and length of stay							
Overnight stays in H&S	Thousand nights	(5.1)	8,482	11,931	12,164	9,792	15,125
Overnight stays in CE	Thousand nights	(5.2)	16,919	25,114	26,545	21,885	34,045
ALS of non resident tourists	Nights	(5.5)	..	..	..	..	..
Tourism expenditure **in the country of reference**	US$ Million	(8.1)	2,014	2,523	2,733	2,493	2,758
DOMESTIC TOURISM							
Overnight stays							
Overnight stays in H&S	Thousand nights	(5.3)	3,341	3,379	3,147	3,243	2,949
Overnight stays in CE	Thousand nights	(5.4)	4,941	5,661	5,307	5,241	5,138
OUTBOUND TOURISM							
Departures	Thousands	(6.1)	..	..	..	..	..
Tourism expenditure in other countries	US$ Million	(8.2)	510	530	600	751	568
TOURISM ACTIVITIES							
Hotels and similar establishments							
Number of rooms	H&S	(7.1)	83,445	82,668	83,199	80,009	81,272
Number of bed-places	H&S	(7.2)	200,968	199,127	199,571	193,716	199,474
Occupancy rate	Percent	(7.3)	16.07	22.81	22.92	18.44	24.80
Average length of stay	Nights	(5.6)	5.22	5.51	5.44	5.29	5.49
ECONOMIC AGGREGATES							
Gross National Product (GNP)	US$ Million	(9.1)	16,865	19,951	20,592	20,137	20,124
Exports (F.O.B.)	US$ Million	(9.2)	4,512	4,171	4,541	4,303	4,432
Imports (C.I.F.)	US$ Million	(9.3)	7,788	9,104	8,383	7,799	7,887

Abbreviations used in tables and notes:
H&S: Hotels and similar establishments; **CE:** All types of tourism accommodation establishments; **ALS:** Average length of stay; **THS:** Non-resident tourists staying in H&S; **TCE:** Non-resident tourists staying in CE; **TF:** Arrivals of international (or non-resident) tourists; **VF:** Arrivals of international (or non-resident) visitors; **NHS:** Overnight stays at H&S; **NCE:** Overnight stays at CE.

..   data not available
incl   including
excl   excluding
nra   nationals residing abroad

Notes:
(1.2,2.2-2.6) TCE, incl arrivals in ports of nautical tourism; (3.1-3.4) VF; (5.2,5.4) Incl nights in ports of nautical tourism; (5.6) Internal tourism (domestic and inbound) in all accommodation facilities (incl Ports of nautical tourism).

CUBA

Basic Indicators	Units	Code	1996	1997	1998	1999	2000
INBOUND TOURISM							
Arrivals							
Visitors	Thousands	(1.1)	1,004	1,170	1,416	1,603	1,774
Tourists (overnight visitors)	Thousands	(1.2)	999	1,153	1,390	1,561	1,741
Same-day visitors	Thousands	(1.3)	5	17	26	42	33
Cruise passengers	Thousands	(1.4)	2	2	8	4	10
Arrivals by region							
Africa	Thousands	(2.1)	3	5	6	6	7
Americas	Thousands	(2.2)	419	497	595	697	784
Europe	Thousands	(2.3)	563	648	793	875	949
East Asia and the Pacific	Thousands	(2.4)	15	14	17	20	27
South Asia	Thousands	(2.5)	3	4	4	3	5
Middle East	Thousands	(2.6)	1	2	1	2	2
Arrivals by mode of transport							
Air	Thousands	(3.1)	999	1,153	1,390	1,561	1,741
Rail	Thousands	(3.2)	..	..	..	..	..
Road	Thousands	(3.3)	..	..	..	..	..
Sea	Thousands	(3.4)	..	..	..	..	..
Arrivals by purpose of visit							
Leisure, recreation and holidays	Thousands	(4.1)	921	1,073	1,307	1,467	1,641
Business and professional	Thousands	(4.2)	10	11	11	12	12
Other	Thousands	(4.3)	68	69	72	82	88
Overnight stays and length of stay							
Overnight stays in H&S	Thousand nights	(5.1)	6,631	7,400	9,164	9,824	10,323
Overnight stays in CE	Thousand nights	(5.2)	7,431	8,214	10,095	10,976	11,557
ALS of non resident tourists	Nights	(5.5)	11.70	11.30	11.30	10.00	10.50
Tourism expenditure							
in the country of reference	US$ Million	(8.1)	1,185	1,326	1,571	1,714	1,756
DOMESTIC TOURISM							
Overnight stays							
Overnight stays in H&S	Thousand nights	(5.3)	3,308	3,500	3,285	3,154	3,261
Overnight stays in CE	Thousand nights	(5.4)	7,045	7,020	6,948	6,800	7,281
OUTBOUND TOURISM							
Departures	Thousands	(6.1)	55	54	55	56	58
Tourism expenditure in other countries	US$ Million	(8.2)	..	..	..	..	..
TOURISM ACTIVITIES							
Hotels and similar establishments							
Number of rooms	H&S	(7.1)	29,663	31,757	35,708	37,114	38,072
Number of bed-places	H&S	(7.2)	60,719	64,087	71,841	76,496	77,625
Occupancy rate	Percent	(7.3)	64.90	75.40	76.10	71.70	74.20
Average length of stay	Nights	(5.6)	3.10	3.10	3.30	3.00	..
ECONOMIC AGGREGATES							
Gross National Product (GNP)	US$ Million	(9.1)	..	..	..	..	..
Exports (F.O.B.)	US$ Million	(9.2)	2,015	..	..	..	..
Imports (C.I.F.)	US$ Million	(9.3)	3,205	..	..	..	..

Abbreviations used in tables and notes:
H&S: Hotels and similar establishments; **CE:** All types of tourism accommodation establishments; **ALS:** Average length of stay; **THS:** Non-resident tourists staying in H&S; **TCE:** Non-resident tourists staying in CE; **TF:** Arrivals of international (or non-resident) tourists; **VF:** Arrivals of international (or non-resident) visitors; **NHS:** Overnight stays at H&S; **NCE:** Overnight stays at CE.

.. data not available
incl including
excl excluding
nra nationals residing abroad

Notes:
(1.1,2.1-2.4) VF; (1.2,4.1-4.3) Air arrivals; (1.3) Incl cruise passengers; (5.1,5.3,7.1,7.2) Hotels, motels & apart-hotels; (5.2,5.4) Hotels, motels, apart-hotels, camping/caravaning and other; (6.1) Incl only tours authorized by the "Instituto de Turismo"; (7.3) Rooms.

CURAÇAO

Basic Indicators	Units	Code	1996	1997	1998	1999	2000
INBOUND TOURISM							
Arrivals							
Visitors	Thousands	(1.1)	387	420	430	419	500
Tourists (overnight visitors)	Thousands	(1.2)	214	205	199	198	191
Same-day visitors	Thousands	(1.3)	..	..	..	..	
Cruise passengers	Thousands	(1.4)	173	215	231	221	309
Arrivals by region							
Africa	Thousands	(2.1)	..	..	..	..	
Americas	Thousands	(2.2)	127	125	125	120	..
Europe	Thousands	(2.3)	84	77	70	71	61
East Asia and the Pacific	Thousands	(2.4)	..	..	..	..	
South Asia	Thousands	(2.5)	..	..	..	..	
Middle East	Thousands	(2.6)	..	..	..	..	..
Arrivals by mode of transport							
Air	Thousands	(3.1)	214	205	199	198	191
Rail	Thousands	(3.2)	..	..	..	..	
Road	Thousands	(3.3)	..	..	..	..	
Sea	Thousands	(3.4)	173	215	231	221	309
Arrivals by purpose of visit							
Leisure, recreation and holidays	Thousands	(4.1)	166	..	..	172	
Business and professional	Thousands	(4.2)	24	..	..	12	..
Other	Thousands	(4.3)	24	..	..	14	
Overnight stays and length of stay							
Overnight stays in H&S	Thousand nights	(5.1)	732	633	..	..	
Overnight stays in CE	Thousand nights	(5.2)	1,855	1,733	..	..	
ALS of non resident tourists	Nights	(5.5)	8.20	8.10	7.20	8.50	
Tourism expenditure in the country of reference	US$ Million	(8.1)	186	201	261	267	227
DOMESTIC TOURISM							
Overnight stays							
Overnight stays in H&S	Thousand nights	(5.3)	..	..	..	..	..
Overnight stays in CE	Thousand nights	(5.4)	..	..	..	..	..
OUTBOUND TOURISM							
Departures	Thousands	(6.1)	..	..	..	..	
Tourism expenditure in other countries	US$ Million	(8.2)	174	178	..	..	..
TOURISM ACTIVITIES							
Hotels and similar establishments							
Number of rooms	H&S	(7.1)	2,343	2,696	2,528	2,768	..
Number of bed-places	H&S	(7.2)	..	..	..	..	..
Occupancy rate	Percent	(7.3)	74.20	67.30	59.70	71.00	..
Average length of stay	Nights	(5.6)	6.28	5.89	..	..	..
ECONOMIC AGGREGATES							
Gross National Product (GNP)	US$ Million	(9.1)	..	..	..	..	..
Exports (F.O.B.)	US$ Million	(9.2)	..	..	273	216	..
Imports (C.I.F.)	US$ Million	(9.3)	..	..	..	..	..

Abbreviations used in tables and notes:
H&S: Hotels and similar establishments; **CE:** All types of tourism accommodation establishments; **ALS:** Average length of stay; **THS:** Non-resident tourists staying in H&S; **TCE:** Non-resident tourists staying in CE; **TF:** Arrivals of international (or non-resident) tourists; **VF:** Arrivals of international (or non-resident) visitors; **NHS:** Overnight stays at H&S; **NCE:** Overnight stays at CE.

..   data not available
incl   including
excl   excluding
nra   nationals residing abroad

Notes:
(1.2,2.2,2.3,3.1,4.1-4.3) Arrivals by air; Incl nra; (3.4) Cruise ship arrivals; (7.1) Hotels, guest houses, appartments; (7.3) Rooms.

CYPRUS

Basic Indicators	Units	Code	1996	1997	1998	1999	2000
INBOUND TOURISM							
Arrivals							
Visitors	Thousands	(1.1)	2,089	2,194	2,357	2,578	2,912
Tourists (overnight visitors)	Thousands	(1.2)	1,950	2,088	2,223	2,434	2,686
Same-day visitors	Thousands	(1.3)	138	106	134	143	226
Cruise passengers	Thousands	(1.4)	41	55	75	77	87
Arrivals by region							
Africa	Thousands	(2.1)	..	..	6	9	10
Americas	Thousands	(2.2)	..	..	26	31	38
Europe	Thousands	(2.3)	1,773	1,979	2,112	2,312	2,554
East Asia and the Pacific	Thousands	(2.4)	..	..	10	11	14
South Asia	Thousands	(2.5)	..	..	11	13	16
Middle East	Thousands	(2.6)	105	53	51	56	51
Arrivals by mode of transport							
Air	Thousands	(3.1)	1,744	1,836	1,989	2,166	2,446
Rail	Thousands	(3.2)	..	..	..	..	..
Road	Thousands	(3.3)	..	..	..	..	..
Sea	Thousands	(3.4)	344	358	368	412	466
Arrivals by purpose of visit							
Leisure, recreation and holidays	Thousands	(4.1)	..	..	2,102	2,308	2,541
Business and professional	Thousands	(4.2)	..	..	121	126	145
Other	Thousands	(4.3)	..	..	..	..	..
Overnight stays and length of stay							
Overnight stays in H&S	Thousand nights	(5.1)	12,702	13,193	14,442	..	..
Overnight stays in CE	Thousand nights	(5.2)	12,718	13,206	14,456	..	..
ALS of non resident tourists	Nights	(5.5)	10.92	11.50	11.27	11.00	11.00
Tourism expenditure in the country of reference	US$ Million	(8.1)	1,669	1,639	1,696	1,878	1,894
DOMESTIC TOURISM							
Overnight stays							
Overnight stays in H&S	Thousand nights	(5.3)	486	529	575	..	..
Overnight stays in CE	Thousand nights	(5.4)	511	554	594	..	..
OUTBOUND TOURISM							
Departures	Thousands	(6.1)	365	422	417	470	503
Tourism expenditure in other countries	US$ Million	(8.2)	263	278	276	289	285
TOURISM ACTIVITIES							
Hotels and similar establishments							
Number of rooms	H&S	(7.1)	40,370	40,173	40,886	42,783	43,363
Number of bed-places	H&S	(7.2)	83,537	83,288	85,161	84,173	84,479
Occupancy rate	Percent	(7.3)	52.74	52.23	55.65	..	..
Average length of stay	Nights	(5.6)	10.41	10.87	10.62	11.00	11.00
ECONOMIC AGGREGATES							
Gross National Product (GNP)	US$ Million	(9.1)	8,959	9,068	8,975	9,086	..
Exports (F.O.B.)	US$ Million	(9.2)	1,391	1,250	1,062	997	954
Imports (C.I.F.)	US$ Million	(9.3)	3,983	3,655	3,687	3,618	3,846

Abbreviations used in tables and notes:
H&S: Hotels and similar establishments; **CE:** All types of tourism accommodation establishments; **ALS:** Average length of stay; **THS:** Non-resident tourists staying in H&S; **TCE:** Non-resident tourists staying in CE; **TF:** Arrivals of international (or non-resident) tourists; **VF:** Arrivals of international (or non-resident) visitors; **NHS:** Overnight stays at H&S; **NCE:** Overnight stays at CE.

.. data not available
incl including
excl excluding
nra nationals residing abroad

Notes:
(1.2,2.1-2.6) TF; (1.3) Incl transit & cruise passengers; (3.4) Incl transit passengers; (7.3) Bed-places.

53

CZECH REPUBLIC

Basic Indicators	Units	Code	1996	1997	1998	1999	2000
INBOUND TOURISM							
Arrivals							
Visitors	Thousands	(1.1)	109,405	107,884	102,843	100,832	104,247
Tourists (overnight visitors)	Thousands	(1.2)	4,558	4,976	5,482	5,610	4,666
Same-day visitors	Thousands	(1.3)	..	..	..	..	..
Cruise passengers	Thousands	(1.4)	..	..	..	..	..
Arrivals by region							
Africa	Thousands	(2.1)	15	16	22	26	14
Americas	Thousands	(2.2)	234	257	318	313	285
Europe	Thousands	(2.3)	4,150	4,507	4,926	5,037	4,168
East Asia and the Pacific	Thousands	(2.4)	159	195	217	233	200
South Asia	Thousands	(2.5)	..	..	..	..	..
Middle East	Thousands	(2.6)	..	..	..	..	..
Arrivals by mode of transport							
Air	Thousands	(3.1)	1,514	1,492	1,480	1,438	1,918
Rail	Thousands	(3.2)	4,578	4,532	4,870	4,079	4,011
Road	Thousands	(3.3)	103,313	101,860	96,493	95,315	98,317
Sea	Thousands	(3.4)	..	..	..	..	..
Arrivals by purpose of visit							
Leisure, recreation and holidays	Thousands	(4.1)	..	..	..	..	..
Business and professional	Thousands	(4.2)	..	..	..	..	..
Other	Thousands	(4.3)	..	..	..	..	..
Overnight stays and length of stay							
Overnight stays in H&S	Thousand nights	(5.1)	10,858	11,726	11,547	11,921	12,811
Overnight stays in CE	Thousand nights	(5.2)	14,186	15,670	16,933	16,857	16,471
ALS of non resident tourists	Nights	(5.5)	3.10	3.10	3.10	3.00	3.50
Tourism expenditure in the country of reference	US$ Million	(8.1)	4,075	3,647	3,719	3,035	2,869
DOMESTIC TOURISM							
Overnight stays							
Overnight stays in H&S	Thousand nights	(5.3)	9,908	10,737	9,919	10,608	12,358
Overnight stays in CE	Thousand nights	(5.4)	23,100	27,326	28,561	27,145	30,598
OUTBOUND TOURISM							
Departures	Thousands	(6.1)	48,614	46,070	43,608	39,977	38,177
Tourism expenditure in other countries	US$ Million	(8.2)	2,953	2,380	1,869	1,474	1,257
TOURISM ACTIVITIES							
Hotels and similar establishments							
Number of rooms	H&S	(7.1)	74,161	90,201	91,720	92,138	96,399
Number of bed-places	H&S	(7.2)	186,210	218,780	228,474	228,906	236,476
Occupancy rate	Percent	(7.3)	35.60	34.70	34.60	33.60	46.00
Average length of stay	Nights	(5.6)	2.90	2.90	2.80	2.90	3.30
ECONOMIC AGGREGATES							
Gross National Product (GNP)	US$ Million	(9.1)	53,349	54,313	52,310	51,406	50,593
Exports (F.O.B.)	US$ Million	(9.2)	21,917	22,751	26,417	26,245	29,057
Imports (C.I.F.)	US$ Million	(9.3)	27,716	27,188	28,814	28,784	32,241

Abbreviations used in tables and notes:
H&S: Hotels and similar establishments; **CE:** All types of tourism accommodation establishments; **ALS:** Average length of stay; **THS:** Non-resident tourists staying in H&S; **TCE:** Non-resident tourists staying in CE; **TF:** Arrivals of international (or non-resident) tourists; **VF:** Arrivals of international (or non-resident) visitors; **NHS:** Overnight stays at H&S; **NCE:** Overnight stays at CE.

..   data not available
incl   including
excl   excluding
nra   nationals residing abroad

Notes:
(1.1,3.1-3.3) VF; (1.2,2.1-2.4) TCE; (1.2,2.1-2.4,5.1-5.4/2000) Preliminary data; (6.1) Visitor trips abroad (tourists and same-day visitors).

DEMOCRATIC REPUBLIC OF THE CONGO

Basic Indicators	Units	Code	1996	1997	1998	1999	2000
INBOUND TOURISM							
Arrivals							
Visitors	Thousands	(1.1)	..	..	..	..	..
Tourists (overnight visitors)	Thousands	(1.2)	37	30	53	80	103
Same-day visitors	Thousands	(1.3)	..	..	..	..	..
Cruise passengers	Thousands	(1.4)	..	..	..	..	..
Arrivals by region							
Africa	Thousands	(2.1)	..	..	22	73	96
Americas	Thousands	(2.2)	..	..	1	1	..
Europe	Thousands	(2.3)	..	..	8	4	6
East Asia and the Pacific	Thousands	(2.4)	..	..	1	1	..
South Asia	Thousands	(2.5)					
Middle East	Thousands	(2.6)	..	..	..	..	..
Arrivals by mode of transport							
Air	Thousands	(3.1)	..	..	..	..	..
Rail	Thousands	(3.2)	..	..	..	..	..
Road	Thousands	(3.3)	..	..	..	..	..
Sea	Thousands	(3.4)	..	..	..	..	..
Arrivals by purpose of visit							
Leisure, recreation and holidays	Thousands	(4.1)	..	..	5	9	40
Business and professional	Thousands	(4.2)	..	..	9	15	10
Other	Thousands	(4.3)	..	..	39	56	53
Overnight stays and length of stay							
Overnight stays in H&S	Thousand nights	(5.1)	..	..	..	..	..
Overnight stays in CE	Thousand nights	(5.2)	..	..	103	114	..
ALS of non resident tourists	Nights	(5.5)	..	..	..	..	..
Tourism expenditure **in the country of reference**	US$ Million	(8.1)	..	..		..	..
DOMESTIC TOURISM							
Overnight stays							
Overnight stays in H&S	Thousand nights	(5.3)	..	..	..	..	..
Overnight stays in CE	Thousand nights	(5.4)	..	..	61	26	..
OUTBOUND TOURISM							
Departures	Thousands	(6.1)	..	..	50	50	..
Tourism expenditure in other countries	US$ Million	(8.2)	..	..	..	..	..
TOURISM ACTIVITIES							
Hotels and similar establishments							
Number of rooms	H&S	(7.1)	..	..	..	6,000	..
Number of bed-places	H&S	(7.2)	..	..	..	9,000	..
Occupancy rate	Percent	(7.3)	..	..	..	40.00	..
Average length of stay	Nights	(5.6)	..	..	..	7.00	..
ECONOMIC AGGREGATES							
Gross National Product (GNP)	US$ Million	(9.1)	5,203	4,858	5,024	..	..
Exports (F.O.B.)	US$ Million	(9.2)	592	..	..	..	..
Imports (C.I.F.)	US$ Million	(9.3)	424	..	..	..	..

Abbreviations used in tables and notes:
H&S: Hotels and similar establishments; **CE:** All types of tourism accommodation establishments; **ALS:** Average length of stay; **THS:** Non-resident tourists staying in H&S; **TCE:** Non-resident tourists staying in CE; **TF:** Arrivals of international (or non-resident) tourists; **VF:** Arrivals of international (or non-resident) visitors; **NHS:** Overnight stays at H&S; **NCE:** Overnight stays at CE.

.. data not available
incl including
excl excluding
nra nationals residing abroad

Notes:
(1.2/96/97) Excl nra; (1.2,4.1-4.3/98) Incl nra; (1.2-4.3/98) Arrivals through "Ndjili" and "Beach" posts; (2.1-2.4) Excl nra; (7.1) Registered hotels.

DENMARK

Basic Indicators	Units	Code	1996	1997	1998	1999	2000
INBOUND TOURISM							
Arrivals							
Visitors	Thousands	(1.1)	..	..	..	..	..
Tourists (overnight visitors)	Thousands	(1.2)	2,125	2,158	2,073	2,023	2,088
Same-day visitors	Thousands	(1.3)	..	..	..	..	..
Cruise passengers	Thousands	(1.4)	..	..	..	..	..
Arrivals by region							
Africa	Thousands	(2.1)	..	..	..	..	..
Americas	Thousands	(2.2)	94	95	101	101	113
Europe	Thousands	(2.3)	1,824	1,851	1,793	1,748	1,795
East Asia and the Pacific	Thousands	(2.4)	56	51	56	61	62
South Asia	Thousands	(2.5)	..	..	..	..	..
Middle East	Thousands	(2.6)	..	..	..	..	..
Arrivals by mode of transport							
Air	Thousands	(3.1)	..	..	..	..	..
Rail	Thousands	(3.2)	..	..	..	..	..
Road	Thousands	(3.3)	..	..	..	..	..
Sea	Thousands	(3.4)	..	..	..	..	..
Arrivals by purpose of visit							
Leisure, recreation and holidays	Thousands	(4.1)	..	..	..	..	..
Business and professional	Thousands	(4.2)	..	..	..	..	..
Other	Thousands	(4.3)	..	..	..	..	..
Overnight stays and length of stay							
Overnight stays in H&S	Thousand nights	(5.1)	4,473	4,505	4,462	4,350	4,611
Overnight stays in CE	Thousand nights	(5.2)	10,810	10,919	10,288	9,966	10,008
ALS of non resident tourists	Nights	(5.5)	..	..	..	..	..
Tourism expenditure **in the country of reference**	US$ Million	(8.1)	3,425	3,185	3,211	3,460	4,025
DOMESTIC TOURISM							
Overnight stays							
Overnight stays in H&S	Thousand nights	(5.3)	4,200	4,171	4,339	4,417	4,599
Overnight stays in CE	Thousand nights	(5.4)	14,878	15,108	14,883	15,246	15,166
OUTBOUND TOURISM							
Departures	Thousands	(6.1)	5,035	4,685	4,807	4,841	5,125
Tourism expenditure in other countries	US$ Million	(8.2)	4,142	4,137	4,462	4,884	5,139
TOURISM ACTIVITIES							
Hotels and similar establishments							
Number of rooms	H&S	(7.1)	38,656	38,182	38,386	38,769	39,459
Number of bed-places	H&S	(7.2)	99,762	98,440	99,795	100,815	102,110
Occupancy rate	Percent	(7.3)	37.40	37.80	37.80	36.70	37.40
Average length of stay	Nights	(5.6)	..	..	..	..	..
ECONOMIC AGGREGATES							
Gross National Product (GNP)	US$ Million	(9.1)	178,759	180,842	173,156	170,687	170,995
Exports (F.O.B.)	US$ Million	(9.2)	50,099	47,720	47,481	48,698	53,840
Imports (C.I.F.)	US$ Million	(9.3)	44,434	44,044	45,427	44,067	43,711

Abbreviations used in tables and notes:
H&S: Hotels and similar establishments; **CE:** All types of tourism accommodation establishments; **ALS:** Average length of stay; **THS:** Non-resident tourists staying in H&S; **TCE:** Non-resident tourists staying in CE; **TF:** Arrivals of international (or non-resident) tourists; **VF:** Arrivals of international (or non-resident) visitors; **NHS:** Overnight stays at H&S; **NCE:** Overnight stays at CE.

.. data not available
incl including
excl excluding
nra nationals residing abroad

Notes:
(1.2,2.2-2.4) TCE; (7.1,7.2) Incl holiday dwellings; (7.3) Bed-places; (8.2) Incl international fare expenditure.

Basic Indicators	Units	Code	1996	1997	1998	1999	2000
INBOUND TOURISM							
Arrivals							
Visitors	Thousands	(1.1)	..	..	..	..	..
Tourists (overnight visitors)	Thousands	(1.2)	20	20	21	..	..
Same-day visitors	Thousands	(1.3)	..	..	..	..	..
Cruise passengers	Thousands	(1.4)	..	..	..	..	..
Arrivals by region							
Africa	Thousands	(2.1)	..	..	..	..	..
Americas	Thousands	(2.2)	..	..	..	..	..
Europe	Thousands	(2.3)	..	..	..	..	..
East Asia and the Pacific	Thousands	(2.4)	..	..	..	..	..
South Asia	Thousands	(2.5)	..	..	..	..	..
Middle East	Thousands	(2.6)	..	..	..	..	..
Arrivals by mode of transport							
Air	Thousands	(3.1)	..	..	..	..	..
Rail	Thousands	(3.2)	..	..	..	..	..
Road	Thousands	(3.3)	..	..	..	..	..
Sea	Thousands	(3.4)	..	..	..	..	..
Arrivals by purpose of visit							
Leisure, recreation and holidays	Thousands	(4.1)	..	..	..	..	..
Business and professional	Thousands	(4.2)	..	..	..	..	..
Other	Thousands	(4.3)	..	..	..	..	..
Overnight stays and length of stay							
Overnight stays in H&S	Thousand nights	(5.1)	..	38	27	..	..
Overnight stays in CE	Thousand nights	(5.2)	..	..	..	..	..
ALS of non resident tourists	Nights	(5.5)	..	..	..	..	..
Tourism expenditure							
in the country of reference	US$ Million	(8.1)	..	..	..	..	..
DOMESTIC TOURISM							
Overnight stays							
Overnight stays in H&S	Thousand nights	(5.3)	..	..	..	..	..
Overnight stays in CE	Thousand nights	(5.4)	..	..	..	..	..
OUTBOUND TOURISM							
Departures	Thousands	(6.1)	..	..	..	..	..
Tourism expenditure in other countries	US$ Million	(8.2)	..	..	..	..	..
TOURISM ACTIVITIES							
Hotels and similar establishments							
Number of rooms	H&S	(7.1)	330	330	360	..	..
Number of bed-places	H&S	(7.2)	545	575	..	..	..
Occupancy rate	Percent	(7.3)	..	..	..	..	..
Average length of stay	Nights	(5.6)	..	..	..	..	..
ECONOMIC AGGREGATES							
Gross National Product (GNP)	US$ Million	(9.1)	..	509	503	522	556
Exports (F.O.B.)	US$ Million	(9.2)	14	11	12	12	..
Imports (C.I.F.)	US$ Million	(9.3)	179	148	158	153	..

Abbreviations used in tables and notes:
H&S: Hotels and similar establishments; **CE:** All types of tourism accommodation establishments; **ALS:** Average length of stay; **THS:** Non-resident tourists staying in H&S; **TCE:** Non-resident tourists staying in CE; **TF:** Arrivals of international (or non-resident) tourists; **VF:** Arrivals of international (or non-resident) visitors; **NHS:** Overnight stays at H&S; **NCE:** Overnight stays at CE.

..   data not available
incl   including
excl   excluding
nra   nationals residing abroad

DOMINICA

Basic Indicators	Units	Code	1996	1997	1998	1999	2000
INBOUND TOURISM							
Arrivals							
Visitors	Thousands	(1.1)	261	299	312	276	309
Tourists (overnight visitors)	Thousands	(1.2)	63	65	66	74	69
Same-day visitors	Thousands	(1.3)	5	3	1	..	..
Cruise passengers	Thousands	(1.4)	193	231	245	202	240
Arrivals by region							
Africa	Thousands	(2.1)	..	..	..	..	..
Americas	Thousands	(2.2)	51	52	53	60	..
Europe	Thousands	(2.3)	12	12	12	12	..
East Asia and the Pacific	Thousands	(2.4)	..	1	..	..	..
South Asia	Thousands	(2.5)	..	..	..	..	..
Middle East	Thousands	(2.6)	..	..	..	..	..
Arrivals by mode of transport							
Air	Thousands	(3.1)	47	48	47	..	..
Rail	Thousands	(3.2)	..	..	..	..	..
Road	Thousands	(3.3)	..	..	..	..	..
Sea	Thousands	(3.4)	22	20	20	..	..
Arrivals by purpose of visit							
Leisure, recreation and holidays	Thousands	(4.1)	51	53	54	..	..
Business and professional	Thousands	(4.2)	11	12	11	..	..
Other	Thousands	(4.3)	..	..	..	..	..
Overnight stays and length of stay							
Overnight stays in H&S	Thousand nights	(5.1)	..	..	..	..	..
Overnight stays in CE	Thousand nights	(5.2)	..	..	..	..	..
ALS of non resident tourists	Nights	(5.5)	..	..	..	..	..
Tourism expenditure in the country of reference	US$ Million	(8.1)	37	40	38	49	47
DOMESTIC TOURISM							
Overnight stays							
Overnight stays in H&S	Thousand nights	(5.3)	..	..	..	..	..
Overnight stays in CE	Thousand nights	(5.4)	..	..	..	..	..
OUTBOUND TOURISM							
Departures	Thousands	(6.1)	..	..	..	..	..
Tourism expenditure in other countries	US$ Million	(8.2)	7	7	8	..	..
TOURISM ACTIVITIES							
Hotels and similar establishments							
Number of rooms	H&S	(7.1)	764	824	824	857	890
Number of bed-places	H&S	(7.2)	..	..	..	..	..
Occupancy rate	Percent	(7.3)	..	..	..	..	..
Average length of stay	Nights	(5.6)	..	..	..	..	..
ECONOMIC AGGREGATES							
Gross National Product (GNP)	US$ Million	(9.1)	219	224	231	230	238
Exports (F.O.B.)	US$ Million	(9.2)	51	53	63	54	53
Imports (C.I.F.)	US$ Million	(9.3)	130	125	136	141	147

Abbreviations used in tables and notes:
H&S: Hotels and similar establishments; **CE:** All types of tourism accommodation establishments; **ALS:** Average length of stay; **THS:** Non-resident tourists staying in H&S; **TCE:** Non-resident tourists staying in CE; **TF:** Arrivals of international (or non-resident) tourists; **VF:** Arrivals of international (or non-resident) visitors; **NHS:** Overnight stays at H&S; **NCE:** Overnight stays at CE.

..	data not available
incl	including
excl	excluding
nra	nationals residing abroad

Notes:
(1.2,2.2-2.3,4.1-4.3) TF; (3.1-3.4) VF, excl cruise ships; (7.1) Hotels, guest houses, apartments and cottages.

Basic Indicators	Units	Code	1996	1997	1998	1999	2000
INBOUND TOURISM							
Arrivals							
Visitors	Thousands	(1.1)	2,037	2,482	2,702	2,932	3,154
Tourists (overnight visitors)	Thousands	(1.2)	1,926	2,211	2,309	2,649	2,972
Same-day visitors	Thousands	(1.3)	..	..	..	..	..
Cruise passengers	Thousands	(1.4)	111	271	393	283	182
Arrivals by region							
Africa	Thousands	(2.1)	..	..	..	..	..
Americas	Thousands	(2.2)	702	733	805	925	1,131
Europe	Thousands	(2.3)	863	1,014	1,064	1,206	1,302
East Asia and the Pacific	Thousands	(2.4)	3	3	2	2	3
South Asia	Thousands	(2.5)	..	..	..	..	..
Middle East	Thousands	(2.6)	..	..	..	..	..
Arrivals by mode of transport							
Air	Thousands	(3.1)	1,926	2,211	2,309	2,649	2,972
Rail	Thousands	(3.2)	..	..	..	..	..
Road	Thousands	(3.3)	..	..	..	..	..
Sea	Thousands	(3.4)	111	271	393	283	182
Arrivals by purpose of visit							
Leisure, recreation and holidays	Thousands	(4.1)	1,505	1,886	2,098	2,412	2,735
Business and professional	Thousands	(4.2)	122	99	70	90	96
Other	Thousands	(4.3)	321	199	166	147	141
Overnight stays and length of stay							
Overnight stays in H&S	Thousand nights	(5.1)	16,812	18,884	18,942	29,390	32,849
Overnight stays in CE	Thousand nights	(5.2)	..	..	..	..	..
ALS of non resident tourists	Nights	(5.5)	10.60	10.42	10.02	11.09	11.05
Tourism expenditure							
in the country of reference	US$ Million	(8.1)	1,763	2,099	2,142	2,483	2,860
DOMESTIC TOURISM							
Overnight stays							
Overnight stays in H&S	Thousand nights	(5.3)	..	..	..	..	..
Overnight stays in CE	Thousand nights	(5.4)	..	..	..	..	..
OUTBOUND TOURISM							
Departures	Thousands	(6.1)	358	355	354	363	360
Tourism expenditure in other countries	US$ Million	(8.2)	198	221	254	264	309
TOURISM ACTIVITIES							
Hotels and similar establishments							
Number of rooms	H&S	(7.1)	35,451	38,505	43,027	49,410	52,192
Number of bed-places	H&S	(7.2)	88,628	96,263	107,568	123,525	130,480
Occupancy rate	Percent	(7.3)	72.80	76.30	59.70	66.90	70.20
Average length of stay	Nights	(5.6)	..	..	..	..	..
ECONOMIC AGGREGATES							
Gross National Product (GNP)	US$ Million	(9.1)	12,318	13,814	14,645	16,130	17,959
Exports (F.O.B.)	US$ Million	(9.2)	945	1,017	880	805	966
Imports (C.I.F.)	US$ Million	(9.3)	3,581	4,192	4,897	5,207	6,416

Abbreviations used in tables and notes:
H&S: Hotels and similar establishments; **CE:** All types of tourism accommodation establishments; **ALS:** Average length of stay; **THS:** Non-resident tourists staying in H&S; **TCE:** Non-resident tourists staying in CE; **TF:** Arrivals of international (or non-resident) tourists; **VF:** Arrivals of international (or non-resident) visitors; **NHS:** Overnight stays at H&S; **NCE:** Overnight stays at CE.

.. data not available
incl including
excl excluding
nra nationals residing abroad

Notes:
(1.2) Arrivals by air only, incl nra; (1.4) All arrivals by sea; (2.2-2.4) Departures by air, excl nra; (2.4) Japan only; (7.1,7.2) Hotels; (7.3) Rooms.

ECUADOR

Basic Indicators	Units	Code	1996	1997	1998	1999	2000
INBOUND TOURISM							
Arrivals							
Visitors	Thousands	(1.1)	494	529	511	518	615
Tourists (overnight visitors)	Thousands	(1.2)	..	..	..	..	..
Same-day visitors	Thousands	(1.3)	..	..	..	..	..
Cruise passengers	Thousands	(1.4)	..	..	..	..	..
Arrivals by region							
Africa	Thousands	(2.1)	1	1	1	1	1
Americas	Thousands	(2.2)	374	406	388	396	471
Europe	Thousands	(2.3)	105	108	108	107	127
East Asia and the Pacific	Thousands	(2.4)	14	14	14	14	16
South Asia	Thousands	(2.5)	..	..	..	..	..
Middle East	Thousands	(2.6)	..	..	..	..	..
Arrivals by mode of transport							
Air	Thousands	(3.1)	307	348	340	343	366
Rail	Thousands	(3.2)	..	..	..	..	..
Road	Thousands	(3.3)	176	173	160	168	240
Sea	Thousands	(3.4)	11	9	11	6	9
Arrivals by purpose of visit							
Leisure, recreation and holidays	Thousands	(4.1)	..	..	..	..	..
Business and professional	Thousands	(4.2)	..	..	..	..	..
Other	Thousands	(4.3)	..	..	..	..	..
Overnight stays and length of stay							
Overnight stays in H&S	Thousand nights	(5.1)	..	..	..	..	..
Overnight stays in CE	Thousand nights	(5.2)	..	..	..	..	..
ALS of non resident tourists	Nights	(5.5)	..	..	..	..	..
Tourism expenditure **in the country of reference**	US$ Million	(8.1)	281	290	291	343	402
DOMESTIC TOURISM							
Overnight stays							
Overnight stays in H&S	Thousand nights	(5.3)	..	..	..	..	..
Overnight stays in CE	Thousand nights	(5.4)	..	..	..	..	..
OUTBOUND TOURISM							
Departures	Thousands	(6.1)	275	321	330	386	504
Tourism expenditure in other countries	US$ Million	(8.2)	219	227	241	271	299
TOURISM ACTIVITIES							
Hotels and similar establishments							
Number of rooms	H&S	(7.1)	31,961	32,443	33,299	34,023	36,726
Number of bed-places	H&S	(7.2)	64,482	67,583	69,371	70,844	78,349
Occupancy rate	Percent	(7.3)	..	..	..	..	..
Average length of stay	Nights	(5.6)	..	..	..	..	..
ECONOMIC AGGREGATES							
Gross National Product (GNP)	US$ Million	(9.1)	17,589	18,745	18,555	17,144	15,261
Exports (F.O.B.)	US$ Million	(9.2)	4,900	5,264	4,203	4,451	4,927
Imports (C.I.F.)	US$ Million	(9.3)	3,935	4,955	5,576	3,017	3,721

Abbreviations used in tables and notes:
H&S: Hotels and similar establishments; **CE:** All types of tourism accommodation establishments; **ALS:** Average length of stay; **THS:** Non-resident tourists staying in H&S; **TCE:** Non-resident tourists staying in CE; **TF:** Arrivals of international (or non-resident) tourists; **VF:** Arrivals of international (or non-resident) visitors; **NHS:** Overnight stays at H&S; **NCE:** Overnight stays at CE.

..   data not available
incl   including
excl   excluding
nra   nationals residing abroad

Notes:
(1.1) Excl nra.

EGYPT

Basic Indicators	Units	Code	1996	1997	1998	1999	2000
INBOUND TOURISM							
Arrivals							
Visitors	Thousands	(1.1)	3,896	3,961	3,454	4,797	5,506
Tourists (overnight visitors)	Thousands	(1.2)	3,528	3,656	3,213	4,490	5,116
Same-day visitors	Thousands	(1.3)	368	305	241	307	390
Cruise passengers	Thousands	(1.4)	..	..	..	..	..
Arrivals by region							
Africa	Thousands	(2.1)	116	120	131	151	147
Americas	Thousands	(2.2)	259	257	217	277	341
Europe	Thousands	(2.3)	2,343	2,394	1,957	3,224	3,805
East Asia and the Pacific	Thousands	(2.4)	252	231	131	211	281
South Asia	Thousands	(2.5)	37	30	30	35	39
Middle East	Thousands	(2.6)	829	893	986	897	890
Arrivals by mode of transport							
Air	Thousands	(3.1)	2,579	2,747	2,281	3,542	4,190
Rail	Thousands	(3.2)	..	..	..	..	..
Road	Thousands	(3.3)	801	738	788	800	733
Sea	Thousands	(3.4)	516	476	385	455	583
Arrivals by purpose of visit							
Leisure, recreation and holidays	Thousands	(4.1)	..	3,493	3,055	4,301	4,914
Business and professional	Thousands	(4.2)	..	92	84	159	117
Other	Thousands	(4.3)	..	71	74	30	85
Overnight stays and length of stay							
Overnight stays in H&S	Thousand nights	(5.1)	23,765	26,579	20,151	31,002	32,788
Overnight stays in CE	Thousand nights	(5.2)	..	..	..	..	..
ALS of non resident tourists	Nights	(5.5)	6.10	6.70	5.80	6.50	6.00
Tourism expenditure in the country of reference	US$ Million	(8.1)	3,204	3,727	2,565	3,903	4,345
DOMESTIC TOURISM							
Overnight stays							
Overnight stays in H&S	Thousand nights	(5.3)	..	3,592	3,425	3,768	..
Overnight stays in CE	Thousand nights	(5.4)	..	..	..	..	..
OUTBOUND TOURISM							
Departures	Thousands	(6.1)	2,812	2,722	2,854	2,886	2,964
Tourism expenditure in other countries	US$ Million	(8.2)	1,317	1,347	1,148	1,078	1,073
TOURISM ACTIVITIES							
Hotels and similar establishments							
Number of rooms	H&S	(7.1)	70,471	75,679	82,925	93,822	113,611
Number of bed-places	H&S	(7.2)	140,741	150,986	166,817	187,284	227,222
Occupancy rate	Percent	(7.3)	63.00	62.00	46.00	67.00	73.00
Average length of stay	Nights	(5.6)	..	..	..	4.00	6.00
ECONOMIC AGGREGATES							
Gross National Product (GNP)	US$ Million	(9.1)	64,990	72,701	78,718	86,547	95,244
Exports (F.O.B.)	US$ Million	(9.2)	3,539	3,921	3,130	3,559	4,691
Imports (C.I.F.)	US$ Million	(9.3)	13,038	13,211	16,166	16,022	14,010

Abbreviations used in tables and notes:
H&S: Hotels and similar establishments; **CE:** All types of tourism accommodation establishments; **ALS:** Average length of stay; **THS:** Non-resident tourists staying in H&S; **TCE:** Non-resident tourists staying in CE; **TF:** Arrivals of international (or non-resident) tourists; **VF:** Arrivals of international (or non-resident) visitors; **NHS:** Overnight stays at H&S; **NCE:** Overnight stays at CE.

.. data not available
incl including
excl excluding
nra nationals residing abroad

Notes:
(1.1,2.1-3.4) VF; (4.1-4.3) TF; (5.3) Hotels only. Main regions only, namely: Cairo, Giza, South Sinai, Red Sea, Luxor, Aswan, Alexandria; (6.1) Travel for tourism and non-tourism purposes (more than 50% for work purpose); (7.3) Rooms.

EL SALVADOR

Basic Indicators	Units	Code	1996	1997	1998	1999	2000
INBOUND TOURISM							
Arrivals							
Visitors	Thousands	(1.1)	..	..	..	..	..
Tourists (overnight visitors)	Thousands	(1.2)	283	387	542	658	795
Same-day visitors	Thousands	(1.3)	..	..	..	..	..
Cruise passengers	Thousands	(1.4)	..	..	..	..	..
Arrivals by region							
Africa	Thousands	(2.1)	..	..	..	..	..
Americas	Thousands	(2.2)	245	343	498	596	720
Europe	Thousands	(2.3)	33	27	27	26	27
East Asia and the Pacific	Thousands	(2.4)	5	4	4	3	3
South Asia	Thousands	(2.5)	..	..	..	..	..
Middle East	Thousands	(2.6)	..	..	..	..	..
Arrivals by mode of transport							
Air	Thousands	(3.1)	164	206	189	230	234
Rail	Thousands	(3.2)	..	..	..	..	..
Road	Thousands	(3.3)	119	181	352	423	556
Sea	Thousands	(3.4)	..	..	..	5	5
Arrivals by purpose of visit							
Leisure, recreation and holidays	Thousands	(4.1)	264	136	100	193	232
Business and professional	Thousands	(4.2)	11	174	341	252	304
Other	Thousands	(4.3)	8	77	100	213	258
Overnight stays and length of stay							
Overnight stays in H&S	Thousand nights	(5.1)	608	937	1,584	2,590	3,133
Overnight stays in CE	Thousand nights	(5.2)	..	..	..	..	..
ALS of non resident tourists	Nights	(5.5)	2.30	2.50	3.00	4.00	4.00
Tourism expenditure							
in the country of reference	US$ Million	(8.1)	44	75	125	211	254
DOMESTIC TOURISM							
Overnight stays							
Overnight stays in H&S	Thousand nights	(5.3)	38	47	..	..	..
Overnight stays in CE	Thousand nights	(5.4)	..	..	..	..	..
OUTBOUND TOURISM							
Departures	Thousands	(6.1)	492	627	868	787	923
Tourism expenditure in other countries	US$ Million	(8.2)	73	153	179	169	171
TOURISM ACTIVITIES							
Hotels and similar establishments							
Number of rooms	H&S	(7.1)	3,500	3,750	4,000	4,535	4,899
Number of bed-places	H&S	(7.2)	7,000	7,500	8,000	9,070	9,798
Occupancy rate	Percent	(7.3)	58.00	65.00	68.00	70.00	61.00
Average length of stay	Nights	(5.6)	2.30	2.50	3.00	4.00	4.00
ECONOMIC AGGREGATES							
Gross National Product (GNP)	US$ Million	(9.1)	9,746	10,658	11,158	11,769	12,507
Exports (F.O.B.)	US$ Million	(9.2)	1,024	1,359	1,263	1,164	1,342
Imports (C.I.F.)	US$ Million	(9.3)	2,671	2,973	3,112	3,130	3,796

Abbreviations used in tables and notes:
H&S: Hotels and similar establishments; **CE:** All types of tourism accommodation establishments; **ALS:** Average length of stay; **THS:** Non-resident tourists staying in H&S; **TCE:** Non-resident tourists staying in CE; **TF:** Arrivals of international (or non-resident) tourists; **VF:** Arrivals of international (or non-resident) visitors; **NHS:** Overnight stays at H&S; **NCE:** Overnight stays at CE.

..	data not available
incl	including
excl	excluding
nra	nationals residing abroad

Notes:
(1.2) Excl nra; (7.3) Bed-places; (8.2) International Monetary Fund.

ERITREA

Basic Indicators	Units	Code	1996	1997	1998	1999	2000
INBOUND TOURISM							
Arrivals							
Visitors	Thousands	(1.1)	417	410	188	57	70
Tourists (overnight visitors)	Thousands	(1.2)	..	..	..	..	..
Same-day visitors	Thousands	(1.3)	..	..	..	..	..
Cruise passengers	Thousands	(1.4)	..	..	..	..	..
Arrivals by region							
Africa	Thousands	(2.1)	255	280	119	4	4
Americas	Thousands	(2.2)	3	3	2	1	2
Europe	Thousands	(2.3)	11	12	8	4	6
East Asia and the Pacific	Thousands	(2.4)	2	2	1	2	3
South Asia	Thousands	(2.5)	..	..	..	..	..
Middle East	Thousands	(2.6)	1	1	2	2	2
Arrivals by mode of transport							
Air	Thousands	(3.1)	58	62	35	26	34
Rail	Thousands	(3.2)	..	..	..	..	..
Road	Thousands	(3.3)	356	343	151	28	33
Sea	Thousands	(3.4)	3	5	2	3	3
Arrivals by purpose of visit							
Leisure, recreation and holidays	Thousands	(4.1)	40	67	33	3	4
Business and professional	Thousands	(4.2)	178	175	96	15	21
Other	Thousands	(4.3)	199	168	59	39	45
Overnight stays and length of stay							
Overnight stays in H&S	Thousand nights	(5.1)	..	..	..	..	..
Overnight stays in CE	Thousand nights	(5.2)	..	..	..	..	..
ALS of non resident tourists	Nights	(5.5)	14.00	19.00	22.00	24.00	17.00
Tourism expenditure in the country of reference	US$ Million	(8.1)	69	90	34	28	36
DOMESTIC TOURISM							
Overnight stays							
Overnight stays in H&S	Thousand nights	(5.3)	..	..	..	..	..
Overnight stays in CE	Thousand nights	(5.4)	..	..	..	..	..
OUTBOUND TOURISM							
Departures	Thousands	(6.1)	..	..	..	..	..
Tourism expenditure in other countries	US$ Million	(8.2)	..	..	..	..	..
TOURISM ACTIVITIES							
Hotels and similar establishments							
Number of rooms	H&S	(7.1)	3,402	3,846	4,111	4,309	4,497
Number of bed-places	H&S	(7.2)	7,114	7,546	8,845	8,845	9,287
Occupancy rate	Percent	(7.3)	55.00	57.00	44.00	37.00	45.00
Average length of stay	Nights	(5.6)	..	..	..	..	..
ECONOMIC AGGREGATES							
Gross National Product (GNP)	US$ Million	(9.1)	748	852	799	792	699
Exports (F.O.B.)	US$ Million	(9.2)	86	53	..	..	..
Imports (C.I.F.)	US$ Million	(9.3)	488	489	..	..	..

Abbreviations used in tables and notes:
H&S: Hotels and similar establishments; **CE:** All types of tourism accommodation establishments; **ALS:** Average length of stay; **THS:** Non-resident tourists staying in H&S; **TCE:** Non-resident tourists staying in CE; **TF:** Arrivals of international (or non-resident) tourists; **VF:** Arrivals of international (or non-resident) visitors; **NHS:** Overnight stays at H&S; **NCE:** Overnight stays at CE.

..	data not available
incl	including
excl	excluding
nra	nationals residing abroad

Notes:
(1.1) Incl nra; (2.1-2.6) Excl nra.

ESTONIA

Basic Indicators	Units	Code	1996	1997	1998	1999	2000
INBOUND TOURISM							
Arrivals							
Visitors	Thousands	(1.1)	2,444	2,619	2,909	3,181	3,310
Tourists (overnight visitors)	Thousands	(1.2)	665	730	825	950	1,240
Same-day visitors	Thousands	(1.3)	1,735	1,839	1,992	2,125	1,961
Cruise passengers	Thousands	(1.4)	44	50	92	106	109
Arrivals by region							
Africa	Thousands	(2.1)	..	..	..	..	..
Americas	Thousands	(2.2)	56	45	79	65	100
Europe	Thousands	(2.3)	2,365	2,548	2,784	3,091	3,186
East Asia and the Pacific	Thousands	(2.4)	16	24	28	14	14
South Asia	Thousands	(2.5)	..	..	..	..	..
Middle East	Thousands	(2.6)	..	..	..	..	..
Arrivals by mode of transport							
Air	Thousands	(3.1)	130	135	150	..	149
Rail	Thousands	(3.2)	66	84	70	..	34
Road	Thousands	(3.3)	513	629	789	..	907
Sea	Thousands	(3.4)	1,735	1,770	1,900	..	2,220
Arrivals by purpose of visit							
Leisure, recreation and holidays	Thousands	(4.1)	1,490	1,280	1,338	1,558	1,622
Business and professional	Thousands	(4.2)	460	590	640	723	761
Other	Thousands	(4.3)	494	749	931	900	927
Overnight stays and length of stay							
Overnight stays in H&S	Thousand nights	(5.1)	693	835	926	1,045	1,253
Overnight stays in CE	Thousand nights	(5.2)	890	1,048	1,185	1,230	1,598
ALS of non resident tourists	Nights	(5.5)	5.30	5.60	5.90	6.00	5.40
Tourism expenditure in the country of reference	US$ Million	(8.1)	470	465	534	560	506
DOMESTIC TOURISM							
Overnight stays							
Overnight stays in H&S	Thousand nights	(5.3)	292	333	413	439	459
Overnight stays in CE	Thousand nights	(5.4)	..	..	..	..	613
OUTBOUND TOURISM							
Departures	Thousands	(6.1)	1,547	1,616	1,659	1,780	1,800
Tourism expenditure in other countries	US$ Million	(8.2)	98	118	133	217	204
TOURISM ACTIVITIES							
Hotels and similar establishments							
Number of rooms	H&S	(7.1)	4,678	4,822	5,749	7,323	7,599
Number of bed-places	H&S	(7.2)	9,118	9,679	11,912	13,830	16,292
Occupancy rate	Percent	(7.3)	40.00	46.00	46.00	44.00	48.00
Average length of stay	Nights	(5.6)	1.74	1.60	1.60	1.53	1.53
ECONOMIC AGGREGATES							
Gross National Product (GNP)	US$ Million	(9.1)	4,665	4,848	4,855	4,837	4,894
Exports (F.O.B.)	US$ Million	(9.2)	2,087	2,924	3,130	2,937	3,132
Imports (C.I.F.)	US$ Million	(9.3)	3,245	4,429	4,611	4,094	4,242

Abbreviations used in tables and notes:
H&S: Hotels and similar establishments; **CE:** All types of tourism accommodation establishments; **ALS:** Average length of stay; **THS:** Non-resident tourists staying in H&S; **TCE:** Non-resident tourists staying in CE; **TF:** Arrivals of international (or non-resident) tourists; **VF:** Arrivals of international (or non-resident) visitors; **NHS:** Overnight stays at H&S; **NCE:** Overnight stays at CE.

.. data not available
incl including
excl excluding
nra nationals residing abroad

Notes:
(1.1,2.2-4.3) VF; (4.3) Shopping, transit, visiting friends.

Basic Indicators	Units	Code	1996	1997	1998	1999	2000
INBOUND TOURISM							
Arrivals							
Visitors	Thousands	(1.1)	..	..	..	..	..
Tourists (overnight visitors)	Thousands	(1.2)	109	115	91	92	136
Same-day visitors	Thousands	(1.3)	..	..	..	..	..
Cruise passengers	Thousands	(1.4)	..	..	..	..	..
Arrivals by region							
Africa	Thousands	(2.1)	28	29	25	28	49
Americas	Thousands	(2.2)	15	16	15	16	14
Europe	Thousands	(2.3)	39	41	30	26	35
East Asia and the Pacific	Thousands	(2.4)	4	5	4	4	7
South Asia	Thousands	(2.5)	2	2	2	2	3
Middle East	Thousands	(2.6)	13	14	15	15	9
Arrivals by mode of transport							
Air	Thousands	(3.1)	109	115	91	92	112
Rail	Thousands	(3.2)	..	..	..	..	11
Road	Thousands	(3.3)	..	..	..	..	13
Sea	Thousands	(3.4)	..	..	..	..	..
Arrivals by purpose of visit							
Leisure, recreation and holidays	Thousands	(4.1)	21	24	29	..	46
Business and professional	Thousands	(4.2)	40	44	30	..	33
Other	Thousands	(4.3)	47	47	32	..	57
Overnight stays and length of stay							
Overnight stays in H&S	Thousand nights	(5.1)	103	143	73	74	210
Overnight stays in CE	Thousand nights	(5.2)	..	..	..	..	..
ALS of non resident tourists	Nights	(5.5)	..	..	..	..	..
Tourism expenditure in the country of reference	US$ Million	(8.1)	28	36	16	16	68
DOMESTIC TOURISM							
Overnight stays							
Overnight stays in H&S	Thousand nights	(5.3)	..	..	..	..	..
Overnight stays in CE	Thousand nights	(5.4)	..	..	..	..	..
OUTBOUND TOURISM							
Departures	Thousands	(6.1)	133	..	..	..	..
Tourism expenditure in other countries	US$ Million	(8.2)	25	40	50	51	74
TOURISM ACTIVITIES							
Hotels and similar establishments							
Number of rooms	H&S	(7.1)	2,445	6,053	2,357	..	6,499
Number of bed-places	H&S	(7.2)	4,273	8,279	4,042	..	9,406
Occupancy rate	Percent	(7.3)	60.50	..	..	..	40.00
Average length of stay	Nights	(5.6)	5.30	2.36	4.55	..	2.06
ECONOMIC AGGREGATES							
Gross National Product (GNP)	US$ Million	(9.1)	6,194	6,436	6,165	6,522	6,660
Exports (F.O.B.)	US$ Million	(9.2)	417	587	560	..	..
Imports (C.I.F.)	US$ Million	(9.3)	1,401	..	1,034	1,317	..

Abbreviations used in tables and notes:
H&S: Hotels and similar establishments; **CE:** All types of tourism accommodation establishments; **ALS:** Average length of stay; **THS:** Non-resident tourists staying in H&S; **TCE:** Non-resident tourists staying in CE; **TF:** Arrivals of international (or non-resident) tourists; **VF:** Arrivals of international (or non-resident) visitors; **NHS:** Overnight stays at H&S; **NCE:** Overnight stays at CE.

..   data not available
incl   including
excl   excluding
nra   nationals residing abroad

Notes:
(1.2,2.1-2.6,3.1,4.1-4.3/96-99) Arrivals to Bole airport only; (1.2,2.1-2.6,3.1-3.3,4.1-4.3/2000) Arrivals through all ports of entry; (1.2) Incl nra; (5.6) Ethiopian Fiscal Year; (7.1,7.2/97,2000) Incl all government and private hotels; (7.3) Bed-places; (8.1/96-99) Incl revenues from hotel services, tour operators and travel agency services, duty free, gift articles and souvenir sales; excl: National Bank of Ethiopia foreign currency earning report & Revenue from private sector; (8.1/2000) Incorporates all revenues obtained from the sector based on estimation; (8.2) International Monetary Fund.

FIJI

Basic Indicators	Units	Code	1996	1997	1998	1999	2000
INBOUND TOURISM							
Arrivals							
Visitors	Thousands	(1.1)	357	372	389	424	304
Tourists (overnight visitors)	Thousands	(1.2)	340	359	371	410	294
Same-day visitors	Thousands	(1.3)	..	..	..	..	..
Cruise passengers	Thousands	(1.4)	17	13	18	14	10
Arrivals by region							
Africa	Thousands	(2.1)	..	..	..	..	..
Americas	Thousands	(2.2)	50	58	61	76	63
Europe	Thousands	(2.3)	61	68	69	69	52
East Asia and the Pacific	Thousands	(2.4)	227	232	240	264	178
South Asia	Thousands	(2.5)	..	..	..	..	..
Middle East	Thousands	(2.6)	..	..	..	..	..
Arrivals by mode of transport							
Air	Thousands	(3.1)	334	355	..	..	..
Rail	Thousands	(3.2)	..	..	..	..	..
Road	Thousands	(3.3)	..	..	..	..	..
Sea	Thousands	(3.4)	23	17	..	..	..
Arrivals by purpose of visit							
Leisure, recreation and holidays	Thousands	(4.1)	275	291	..	..	..
Business and professional	Thousands	(4.2)	26	28	..	..	..
Other	Thousands	(4.3)	39	40	..	..	..
Overnight stays and length of stay							
Overnight stays in H&S	Thousand nights	(5.1)	1,716	1,806	1,991	2,143	1,519
Overnight stays in CE	Thousand nights	(5.2)	..	..	..	..	..
ALS of non resident tourists	Nights	(5.5)	..	..	..	..	..
Tourism expenditure in the country of reference	US$ Million	(8.1)	299	297	244	284	195
DOMESTIC TOURISM							
Overnight stays							
Overnight stays in H&S	Thousand nights	(5.3)	299	301	320	344	330
Overnight stays in CE	Thousand nights	(5.4)	..	..	..	..	..
OUTBOUND TOURISM							
Departures	Thousands	(6.1)	72	74	78	89	83
Tourism expenditure in other countries	US$ Million	(8.2)	70	69	52	66	..
TOURISM ACTIVITIES							
Hotels and similar establishments							
Number of rooms	H&S	(7.1)	5,286	5,437	5,745	5,777	5,283
Number of bed-places	H&S	(7.2)	13,327	13,592	14,717	14,214	13,463
Occupancy rate	Percent	(7.3)	53.50	54.40	50.80	51.10	..
Average length of stay	Nights	(5.6)	8.30	8.20	8.50	8.40	8.50
ECONOMIC AGGREGATES							
Gross National Product (GNP)	US$ Million	(9.1)	2,021	2,009	1,764	1,755	1,480
Exports (F.O.B.)	US$ Million	(9.2)	749	619	510	..	585
Imports (C.I.F.)	US$ Million	(9.3)	987	965	721	..	830

Abbreviations used in tables and notes:
H&S: Hotels and similar establishments; **CE:** All types of tourism accommodation establishments; **ALS:** Average length of stay; **THS:** Non-resident tourists staying in H&S; **TCE:** Non-resident tourists staying in CE; **TF:** Arrivals of international (or non-resident) tourists; **VF:** Arrivals of international (or non-resident) visitors; **NHS:** Overnight stays at H&S; **NCE:** Overnight stays at CE.

..   data not available
incl   including
excl   excluding
nra   nationals residing abroad

Notes:
(1.2,2.2-2.4,4.1-4.3) TF, excl nra; (3.4) Incl cruise passengers; (5.6) Days; (7.3) Rooms; (8.2) International Monetary Fund.

Basic Indicators	Units	Code	1996	1997	1998	1999	2000
INBOUND TOURISM							
Arrivals							
Visitors	Thousands	(1.1)	..	..	3,432	3,363	3,789
Tourists (overnight visitors)	Thousands	(1.2)	1,724	1,832	2,644	2,454	2,714
Same-day visitors	Thousands	(1.3)	..	..	788	909	1,075
Cruise passengers	Thousands	(1.4)	..	..	..	..	..
Arrivals by region							
Africa	Thousands	(2.1)	..	..	9	10	10
Americas	Thousands	(2.2)	..	..	164	161	154
Europe	Thousands	(2.3)	..	..	3,095	3,059	3,469
East Asia and the Pacific	Thousands	(2.4)	..	..	135	126	130
South Asia	Thousands	(2.5)	..	..	6	5	20
Middle East	Thousands	(2.6)	..	..	3	2	2
Arrivals by mode of transport							
Air	Thousands	(3.1)	..	..	1,222	1,208	1,427
Rail	Thousands	(3.2)	..	..	..	49	64
Road	Thousands	(3.3)	..	..	963	1,002	1,080
Sea	Thousands	(3.4)	..	..	1,247	1,104	1,218
Arrivals by purpose of visit							
Leisure, recreation and holidays	Thousands	(4.1)	..	..	1,291	1,255	1,450
Business and professional	Thousands	(4.2)	..	..	1,165	1,139	1,262
Other	Thousands	(4.3)	..	..	976	969	1,077
Overnight stays and length of stay							
Overnight stays in H&S	Thousand nights	(5.1)	2,907	3,171	3,226	3,271	3,562
Overnight stays in CE	Thousand nights	(5.2)	3,285	3,646	3,700	3,774	4,066
ALS of non resident tourists	Nights	(5.5)	..	..	5.50	4.40	5.86
Tourism expenditure in the country of reference	US$ Million	(8.1)	1,637	1,644	1,631	1,517	1,397
DOMESTIC TOURISM							
Overnight stays							
Overnight stays in H&S	Thousand nights	(5.3)	8,755	9,115	9,494	9,600	9,786
Overnight stays in CE	Thousand nights	(5.4)	10,729	11,280	11,627	11,804	11,976
OUTBOUND TOURISM							
Departures	Thousands	(6.1)	4,918	5,233	4,743	5,314	5,914
Tourism expenditure in other countries	US$ Million	(8.2)	2,287	2,082	2,063	2,021	1,836
TOURISM ACTIVITIES							
Hotels and similar establishments							
Number of rooms	H&S	(7.1)	51,453	51,889	53,033	54,063	54,855
Number of bed-places	H&S	(7.2)	108,418	109,391	112,289	114,892	117,322
Occupancy rate	Percent	(7.3)	45.70	48.00	49.00	49.40	49.30
Average length of stay	Nights	(5.6)	1.86	1.88	2.00	1.90	1.90
ECONOMIC AGGREGATES							
Gross National Product (GNP)	US$ Million	(9.1)	122,873	131,666	127,711	127,662	128,999
Exports (F.O.B.)	US$ Million	(9.2)	38,435	39,318	42,963	40,666	44,533
Imports (C.I.F.)	US$ Million	(9.3)	29,265	29,786	32,301	30,727	32,610

Abbreviations used in tables and notes:
H&S: Hotels and similar establishments; **CE:** All types of tourism accommodation establishments; **ALS:** Average length of stay; **THS:** Non-resident tourists staying in H&S; **TCE:** Non-resident tourists staying in CE; **TF:** Arrivals of international (or non-resident) tourists; **VF:** Arrivals of international (or non-resident) visitors; **NHS:** Overnight stays at H&S; **NCE:** Overnight stays at CE.

..   data not available
incl   including
excl   excluding
nra   nationals residing abroad

Notes:
(1.1,3.1-3.4,4.1-4.3) VF, Border Survey; (1.2/96/97) TCE; (1.2/98-2000) TF, new series; (2.1-2.6) VF; (5.1,5.3,7.1,7.2) Hotels and similar establishments; (5.2,5.4) Collective tourism establishments; (6.1) Overnight trips abroad; (7.3) Rooms (hotels only); (8.1,8.2) Data collected by travel surveys.

FRANCE

Basic Indicators	Units	Code	1996	1997	1998	1999	2000
INBOUND TOURISM							
Arrivals							
Visitors	Thousands	(1.1)	148,263	159,252	..	..	..
Tourists (overnight visitors)	Thousands	(1.2)	62,406	67,310	70,040	73,042	75,595
Same-day visitors	Thousands	(1.3)	85,857	91,942	..	..	..
Cruise passengers	Thousands	(1.4)	..	..	..	..	..
Arrivals by region							
Africa	Thousands	(2.1)	996	1,086	1,118	987	1,051
Americas	Thousands	(2.2)	4,191	4,433	4,704	4,609	5,053
Europe	Thousands	(2.3)	54,788	59,180	61,556	64,785	66,606
East Asia and the Pacific	Thousands	(2.4)	1,986	2,133	2,229	2,236	2,423
South Asia	Thousands	(2.5)	..	..	..	..	..
Middle East	Thousands	(2.6)	262	288	246	234	259
Arrivals by mode of transport							
Air	Thousands	(3.1)	9,136	9,774	..	..	..
Rail	Thousands	(3.2)	4,082	4,722	..	..	..
Road	Thousands	(3.3)	44,660	47,770	..	..	..
Sea	Thousands	(3.4)	4,527	5,044	..	..	..
Arrivals by purpose of visit							
Leisure, recreation and holidays	Thousands	(4.1)	45,144	48,652	..	..	..
Business and professional	Thousands	(4.2)	7,984	8,756	..	..	..
Other	Thousands	(4.3)	9,278	9,901	..	..	..
Overnight stays and length of stay							
Overnight stays in H&S	Thousand nights	(5.1)	54,994	60,786	66,330	71,768	74,979
Overnight stays in CE	Thousand nights	(5.2)	459,524	497,480	512,001	538,680	559,196
ALS of non resident tourists	Nights	(5.5)	7.36	7.39	7.31	7.37	7.48
Tourism expenditure in the country of reference	US$ Million	(8.1)	28,357	28,009	29,931	31,507	29,900
DOMESTIC TOURISM							
Overnight stays							
Overnight stays in H&S	Thousand nights	(5.3)	90,761	94,060	96,696	108,774	110,343
Overnight stays in CE	Thousand nights	(5.4)	1,074,841	1,050,058	1,054,916	991,561	991,903
OUTBOUND TOURISM							
Departures	Thousands	(6.1)	18,151	17,115	18,077	16,709	17,369
Tourism expenditure in other countries	US$ Million	(8.2)	17,746	16,576	17,791	18,631	17,166
TOURISM ACTIVITIES							
Hotels and similar establishments							
Number of rooms	H&S	(7.1)	608,353	600,883	586,944	583,578	589,174
Number of bed-places	H&S	(7.2)	1,216,706	1,201,766	1,173,888	1,167,156	1,178,348
Occupancy rate	Percent	(7.3)	50.30	53.50	55.60	57.50	59.60
Average length of stay	Nights	(5.6)	..	..	..	..	..
ECONOMIC AGGREGATES							
Gross National Product (GNP)	US$ Million	(9.1)	1,549,956	1,543,147	1,481,349	1,453,211	1,429,390
Exports (F.O.B.)	US$ Million	(9.2)	287,643	290,972	305,991	300,763	298,899
Imports (C.I.F.)	US$ Million	(9.3)	281,776	372,721	290,273	289,799	301,085

Abbreviations used in tables and notes:
H&S: Hotels and similar establishments; **CE:** All types of tourism accommodation establishments; **ALS:** Average length of stay; **THS:** Non-resident tourists staying in H&S; **TCE:** Non-resident tourists staying in CE; **TF:** Arrivals of international (or non-resident) tourists; **VF:** Arrivals of international (or non-resident) visitors; **NHS:** Overnight stays at H&S; **NCE:** Overnight stays at CE.

..	data not available
incl	including
excl	excluding
nra	nationals residing abroad

Notes:
(1.1-4.3/96/97) Frontier surveys; (1.1-4.3/98-2000) Estimates; (2.4) Inc. South Asia; (5.1,5.3,7.1-7.3) Hotels only; (5.2,5.4) All types of accommodation; (5.4) Revised and back-extrapolated series; (5.5) Inbound ALS; (7.3) Net room occupancy rate; (8.1,8.2) New series since 1999 excluding frontier workers paid in foreign currency (voir: 5th edition of the International Monetary Fund Manual).

Basic Indicators	Units	Code	1996	1997	1998	1999	2000
INBOUND TOURISM							
Arrivals							
Visitors	Thousands	(1.1)	..	..	..	..	..
Tourists (overnight visitors)	Thousands	(1.2)	..	..	68	70	..
Same-day visitors	Thousands	(1.3)	..	..	..	..	..
Cruise passengers	Thousands	(1.4)	..	..	..	..	..
Arrivals by region							
Africa	Thousands	(2.1)	..	..	..	..	..
Americas	Thousands	(2.2)	..	..	..	..	..
Europe	Thousands	(2.3)	..	..	..	..	..
East Asia and the Pacific	Thousands	(2.4)	..	..	..	..	..
South Asia	Thousands	(2.5)	..	..	..	..	..
Middle East	Thousands	(2.6)	..	..	..	..	..
Arrivals by mode of transport							
Air	Thousands	(3.1)	..	..	..	..	..
Rail	Thousands	(3.2)	..	..	..	..	..
Road	Thousands	(3.3)	..	..	..	..	..
Sea	Thousands	(3.4)	..	..	..	..	..
Arrivals by purpose of visit							
Leisure, recreation and holidays	Thousands	(4.1)	..	..	..	..	..
Business and professional	Thousands	(4.2)	..	..	..	..	..
Other	Thousands	(4.3)	..	..	..	..	..
Overnight stays and length of stay							
Overnight stays in H&S	Thousand nights	(5.1)	..	..	..	..	..
Overnight stays in CE	Thousand nights	(5.2)	..	..	..	..	..
ALS of non resident tourists	Nights	(5.5)	..	..	..	..	..
Tourism expenditure in the country of reference	US$ Million	(8.1)	..	..	51	50	..
DOMESTIC TOURISM							
Overnight stays							
Overnight stays in H&S	Thousand nights	(5.3)	..	..	..	..	..
Overnight stays in CE	Thousand nights	(5.4)	..	..	..	..	..
OUTBOUND TOURISM							
Departures	Thousands	(6.1)	..	..	..	..	..
Tourism expenditure in other countries	US$ Million	(8.2)	..	..	..	..	..
TOURISM ACTIVITIES							
Hotels and similar establishments							
Number of rooms	H&S	(7.1)	..	..	1,302	..	..
Number of bed-places	H&S	(7.2)	..	..	..	..	..
Occupancy rate	Percent	(7.3)	..	..	50.00	50.00	..
Average length of stay	Nights	(5.6)	..	..	..	..	..
ECONOMIC AGGREGATES							
Gross National Product (GNP)	US$ Million	(9.1)	..	..	..	..	..
Exports (F.O.B.)	US$ Million	(9.2)	..	..	..	..	..
Imports (C.I.F.)	US$ Million	(9.3)	..	..	..	..	..

Abbreviations used in tables and notes:
H&S: Hotels and similar establishments; **CE:** All types of tourism accommodation establishments; **ALS:** Average length of stay; **THS:** Non-resident tourists staying in H&S; **TCE:** Non-resident tourists staying in CE; **TF:** Arrivals of international (or non-resident) tourists; **VF:** Arrivals of international (or non-resident) visitors; **NHS:** Overnight stays at H&S; **NCE:** Overnight stays at CE.

..   data not available
incl   including
excl   excluding
nra   nationals residing abroad

FRENCH POLYNESIA

Basic Indicators	Units	Code	1996	1997	1998	1999	2000
INBOUND TOURISM							
Arrivals							
Visitors	Thousands	(1.1)	184	201	211	236	..
Tourists (overnight visitors)	Thousands	(1.2)	164	180	189	211	252
Same-day visitors	Thousands	(1.3)	12	12	15	14	..
Cruise passengers	Thousands	(1.4)	9	9	7	11	..
Arrivals by region							
Africa	Thousands	(2.1)	..	..	..	..	..
Americas	Thousands	(2.2)	55	54	62	80	..
Europe	Thousands	(2.3)	74	84	87	92	..
East Asia and the Pacific	Thousands	(2.4)	34	42	38	38	..
South Asia	Thousands	(2.5)	..	..	..		..
Middle East	Thousands	(2.6)	..	..	..	..	..
Arrivals by mode of transport							
Air	Thousands	(3.1)	164	180	189	211	252
Rail	Thousands	(3.2)	..	..	..	..	..
Road	Thousands	(3.3)	..	..	..	..	..
Sea	Thousands	(3.4)	..	..	..	..	..
Arrivals by purpose of visit							
Leisure, recreation and holidays	Thousands	(4.1)	149	161	171	..	..
Business and professional	Thousands	(4.2)	7	12	10	..	..
Other	Thousands	(4.3)	8	7	9	..	..
Overnight stays and length of stay							
Overnight stays in H&S	Thousand nights	(5.1)	1,250	1,431	1,467	1,645	..
Overnight stays in CE	Thousand nights	(5.2)	1,902	2,160	2,217	2,493	..
ALS of non resident tourists	Nights	(5.5)	11.61	11.97	11.73	11.82	12.14
Tourism expenditure **in the country of reference**	US$ Million	(8.1)	322	345	354	394	..
DOMESTIC TOURISM							
Overnight stays							
Overnight stays in H&S	Thousand nights	(5.3)	..	..	..	..	..
Overnight stays in CE	Thousand nights	(5.4)	..	..	..	..	..
OUTBOUND TOURISM							
Departures	Thousands	(6.1)	65	..	..	..	..
Tourism expenditure in other countries	US$ Million	(8.2)	..	..	..	..	..
TOURISM ACTIVITIES							
Hotels and similar establishments							
Number of rooms	H&S	(7.1)	3,075	3,012	3,021	3,396	3,357
Number of bed-places	H&S	(7.2)	6,150	6,024	6,042	6,772	6,714
Occupancy rate	Percent	(7.3)	53.28	54.07	59.20	57.51	60.27
Average length of stay	Nights	(5.6)	9.07	9.45	9.20	9.20	10.56
ECONOMIC AGGREGATES							
Gross National Product (GNP)	US$ Million	(9.1)	3,952	3,912	3,950	3,908	4,064
Exports (F.O.B.)	US$ Million	(9.2)	251	222	..	..	..
Imports (C.I.F.)	US$ Million	(9.3)	1,016	936	..	..	..

Abbreviations used in tables and notes:
H&S: Hotels and similar establishments; **CE:** All types of tourism accommodation establishments; **ALS:** Average length of stay; **THS:** Non-resident tourists staying in H&S; **TCE:** Non-resident tourists staying in CE; **TF:** Arrivals of international (or non-resident) tourists; **VF:** Arrivals of international (or non-resident) visitors; **NHS:** Overnight stays at H&S; **NCE:** Overnight stays at CE.

..   data not available
incl   including
excl   excluding
nra   nationals residing abroad

Notes:
(1.2,2.2-4.3) TF, excl nra; (1.2/2000) The figure of 252,200 has been estimated by the "Institut de la Statistique (ISPF)"; (5.5,5.6) Days; (7.1,7.2) Hotels only; at 31st December of each year; (7.3) Rooms in hotels.

Basic Indicators	Units	Code	1996	1997	1998	1999	2000
INBOUND TOURISM							
Arrivals							
Visitors	Thousands	(1.1)	217	247	274	262	230
Tourists (overnight visitors)	Thousands	(1.2)	145	167	195	178	155
Same-day visitors	Thousands	(1.3)	70	75	72	76	70
Cruise passengers	Thousands	(1.4)	2	5	7	8	5
Arrivals by region							
Africa	Thousands	(2.1)	28	33	48	38	38
Americas	Thousands	(2.2)	21	24	27	6	2
Europe	Thousands	(2.3)	82	94	103	104	112
East Asia and the Pacific	Thousands	(2.4)	1	1	1	5	1
South Asia	Thousands	(2.5)	..	..	..	..	..
Middle East	Thousands	(2.6)	3	3	4	5	2
Arrivals by mode of transport							
Air	Thousands	(3.1)	145	167	195	178	155
Rail	Thousands	(3.2)	..	..	..	..	..
Road	Thousands	(3.3)	..	..	..	..	..
Sea	Thousands	(3.4)	..	..	..	..	..
Arrivals by purpose of visit							
Leisure, recreation and holidays	Thousands	(4.1)	69	66	88	82	..
Business and professional	Thousands	(4.2)	23	33	44	41	..
Other	Thousands	(4.3)	53	68	63	55	..
Overnight stays and length of stay							
Overnight stays in H&S	Thousand nights	(5.1)	..	..	203	252	250
Overnight stays in CE	Thousand nights	(5.2)	..	..	..	..	..
ALS of non resident tourists	Nights	(5.5)	..	..	..	..	..
Tourism expenditure in the country of reference	US$ Million	(8.1)	7	7	8	11	7
DOMESTIC TOURISM							
Overnight stays							
Overnight stays in H&S	Thousand nights	(5.3)	..	..	..	..	..
Overnight stays in CE	Thousand nights	(5.4)	..	..	..	..	..
OUTBOUND TOURISM							
Departures	Thousands	(6.1)	..	..	..	..	..
Tourism expenditure in other countries	US$ Million	(8.2)	176	178	180	183	174
TOURISM ACTIVITIES							
Hotels and similar establishments							
Number of rooms	H&S	(7.1)	2,450	2,450	2,450	2,450	2,450
Number of bed-places	H&S	(7.2)	..	..	..	..	..
Occupancy rate	Percent	(7.3)	60.00	60.00	60.00	70.00	70.00
Average length of stay	Nights	(5.6)	..	..	..	..	..
ECONOMIC AGGREGATES							
Gross National Product (GNP)	US$ Million	(9.1)	4,572	5,006	4,645	3,960	3,928
Exports (F.O.B.)	US$ Million	(9.2)	3,183	3,021	..	..	..
Imports (C.I.F.)	US$ Million	(9.3)	956	1,103	..	..	..

Abbreviations used in tables and notes:
H&S: Hotels and similar establishments; **CE:** All types of tourism accommodation establishments; **ALS:** Average length of stay; **THS:** Non-resident tourists staying in H&S; **TCE:** Non-resident tourists staying in CE; **TF:** Arrivals of international (or non-resident) tourists; **VF:** Arrivals of international (or non-resident) visitors; **NHS:** Overnight stays at H&S; **NCE:** Overnight stays at CE.

.. data not available
incl including
excl excluding
nra nationals residing abroad

Notes:
(1.2,2.1-2.6,3.1,4.1-4.3) TF, arrivals at Libreville airport.
Note: 1996-1998: Estimates.

GAMBIA

Basic Indicators	Units	Code	1996	1997	1998	1999	2000
INBOUND TOURISM							
Arrivals							
Visitors	Thousands	(1.1)	..	..	..	..	..
Tourists (overnight visitors)	Thousands	(1.2)	77	85	91	96	..
Same-day visitors	Thousands	(1.3)	..	..	..	..	..
Cruise passengers	Thousands	(1.4)	..	..	..	..	..
Arrivals by region							
Africa	Thousands	(2.1)	1	1	1	1	..
Americas	Thousands	(2.2)	1	1	1	1	..
Europe	Thousands	(2.3)	72	81	86	90	..
East Asia and the Pacific	Thousands	(2.4)	..	..	..	..	..
South Asia	Thousands	(2.5)	..	..	..	..	..
Middle East	Thousands	(2.6)	..	..	..	..	..
Arrivals by mode of transport							
Air	Thousands	(3.1)	77	85	91	96	..
Rail	Thousands	(3.2)	..	..	..	..	..
Road	Thousands	(3.3)	..	..	..	..	..
Sea	Thousands	(3.4)	..	..	..	..	..
Arrivals by purpose of visit							
Leisure, recreation and holidays	Thousands	(4.1)	77	85	91	96	..
Business and professional	Thousands	(4.2)	..	..	..	..	..
Other	Thousands	(4.3)	..	..	..	..	..
Overnight stays and length of stay							
Overnight stays in H&S	Thousand nights	(5.1)	..	..	..	..	..
Overnight stays in CE	Thousand nights	(5.2)	..	..	..	..	..
ALS of non resident tourists	Nights	(5.5)	12.27	13.42	..	..	..
Tourism expenditure in the country of reference	US$ Million	(8.1)	31	32	49	..	..
DOMESTIC TOURISM							
Overnight stays							
Overnight stays in H&S	Thousand nights	(5.3)	..	..	..	..	..
Overnight stays in CE	Thousand nights	(5.4)	..	..	..	..	..
OUTBOUND TOURISM							
Departures	Thousands	(6.1)	..	..	..	..	..
Tourism expenditure in other countries	US$ Million	(8.2)	15	16	..	..	..
TOURISM ACTIVITIES							
Hotels and similar establishments							
Number of rooms	H&S	(7.1)	..	..	..	..	..
Number of bed-places	H&S	(7.2)	5,734	5,914	..	..	..
Occupancy rate	Percent	(7.3)	37.60	59.30	..	..	..
Average length of stay	Nights	(5.6)	..	..	..	..	..
ECONOMIC AGGREGATES							
Gross National Product (GNP)	US$ Million	(9.1)	392	406	410	415	422
Exports (F.O.B.)	US$ Million	(9.2)	21	15	27	7	..
Imports (C.I.F.)	US$ Million	(9.3)	258	174	245	192	..

Abbreviations used in tables and notes:
H&S: Hotels and similar establishments; **CE:** All types of tourism accommodation establishments; **ALS:** Average length of stay; **THS:** Non-resident tourists staying in H&S; **TCE:** Non-resident tourists staying in CE; **TF:** Arrivals of international (or non-resident) tourists; **VF:** Arrivals of international (or non-resident) visitors; **NHS:** Overnight stays at H&S; **NCE:** Overnight stays at CE.

..   data not available
incl   including
excl   excluding
nra   nationals residing abroad

Notes:
(1.2,2.1-2.3,3.1) Charter tourists only.

Basic Indicators	Units	Code	1996	1997	1998	1999	2000
INBOUND TOURISM							
Arrivals							
Visitors	Thousands	(1.1)	..	..	..	..	..
Tourists (overnight visitors)	Thousands	(1.2)	117	313	317	384	387
Same-day visitors	Thousands	(1.3)	..	..	..	..	..
Cruise passengers	Thousands	(1.4)	..	..	..	..	..
Arrivals by region							
Africa	Thousands	(2.1)	..	1	..	..	..
Americas	Thousands	(2.2)	3	4	5	9	11
Europe	Thousands	(2.3)	106	304	304	363	358
East Asia and the Pacific	Thousands	(2.4)	..	1	2	5	7
South Asia	Thousands	(2.5)	2	2	5	5	6
Middle East	Thousands	(2.6)	..	1	1	2	2
Arrivals by mode of transport							
Air	Thousands	(3.1)	27	200	72	200	72
Rail	Thousands	(3.2)	..	..	..	..	67
Road	Thousands	(3.3)	90	113	245	184	196
Sea	Thousands	(3.4)	..	..	..	..	52
Arrivals by purpose of visit							
Leisure, recreation and holidays	Thousands	(4.1)	60	140	144	160	161
Business and professional	Thousands	(4.2)	50	160	160	190	192
Other	Thousands	(4.3)	7	13	13	34	34
Overnight stays and length of stay							
Overnight stays in H&S	Thousand nights	(5.1)	100	280	295	512	516
Overnight stays in CE	Thousand nights	(5.2)	702	1,515	1,585	2,667	2,730
ALS of non resident tourists	Nights	(5.5)	..	..	..	..	7.10
Tourism expenditure in the country of reference	US$ Million	(8.1)	170	416	423	400	413
DOMESTIC TOURISM							
Overnight stays							
Overnight stays in H&S	Thousand nights	(5.3)	85	102	101	103	115
Overnight stays in CE	Thousand nights	(5.4)	..	..	..	..	..
OUTBOUND TOURISM							
Departures	Thousands	(6.1)	219	355	433	373	315
Tourism expenditure in other countries	US$ Million	(8.2)	..	156	226	130	110
TOURISM ACTIVITIES							
Hotels and similar establishments							
Number of rooms	H&S	(7.1)	..	..	..	..	..
Number of bed-places	H&S	(7.2)	2,333	2,333	2,350	2,400	3,182
Occupancy rate	Percent	(7.3)	30.00	33.70	34.00	36.00	34.00
Average length of stay	Nights	(5.6)	..	..	..	..	..
ECONOMIC AGGREGATES							
Gross National Product (GNP)	US$ Million	(9.1)	..	3,107	3,554	3,363	3,243
Exports (F.O.B.)	US$ Million	(9.2)	199	240	192	..	..
Imports (C.I.F.)	US$ Million	(9.3)	687	944	878	..	..

Abbreviations used in tables and notes:
H&S: Hotels and similar establishments; **CE:** All types of tourism accommodation establishments; **ALS:** Average length of stay; **THS:** Non-resident tourists staying in H&S; **TCE:** Non-resident tourists staying in CE; **TF:** Arrivals of international (or non-resident) tourists; **VF:** Arrivals of international (or non-resident) visitors; **NHS:** Overnight stays at H&S; **NCE:** Overnight stays at CE.

..   data not available
incl   including
excl   excluding
nra   nationals residing abroad

Notes:
(8.2) International Monetary Fund.

GERMANY

Basic Indicators	Units	Code	1996	1997	1998	1999	2000
INBOUND TOURISM							
Arrivals							
Visitors	Thousands	(1.1)	..	..	..	..	..
Tourists (overnight visitors)	Thousands	(1.2)	15,205	15,837	16,511	17,116	18,983
Same-day visitors	Thousands	(1.3)	..	..	..	..	..
Cruise passengers	Thousands	(1.4)	..	..	..	..	..
Arrivals by region							
Africa	Thousands	(2.1)	124	134	137	142	160
Americas	Thousands	(2.2)	1,942	2,127	2,351	2,400	2,865
Europe	Thousands	(2.3)	11,112	11,491	11,979	12,497	13,516
East Asia and the Pacific	Thousands	(2.4)	1,573	1,590	1,515	1,567	1,799
South Asia	Thousands	(2.5)	..	..	..	..	..
Middle East	Thousands	(2.6)	76	84	97	93	106
Arrivals by mode of transport							
Air	Thousands	(3.1)	38,412	41,046	42,576	45,957	49,258
Rail	Thousands	(3.2)	..	..	..	..	..
Road	Thousands	(3.3)	..	..	..	..	..
Sea	Thousands	(3.4)	..	..	..	..	..
Arrivals by purpose of visit							
Leisure, recreation and holidays	Thousands	(4.1)	..	..	..	..	..
Business and professional	Thousands	(4.2)	..	..	..	..	..
Other	Thousands	(4.3)	..	..	..	..	..
Overnight stays and length of stay							
Overnight stays in H&S	Thousand nights	(5.1)	29,016	30,178	31,245	32,466	36,354
Overnight stays in CE	Thousand nights	(5.2)	35,461	36,355	37,260	38,655	42,629
ALS of non resident tourists	Nights	(5.5)	..	..	..	..	..
Tourism expenditure							
in the country of reference	US$ Million	(8.1)	17,706	16,696	16,766	16,730	17,879
DOMESTIC TOURISM							
Overnight stays							
Overnight stays in H&S	Thousand nights	(5.3)	149,396	149,640	152,686	159,890	170,947
Overnight stays in CE	Thousand nights	(5.4)	285,806	271,967	277,212	290,706	304,751
OUTBOUND TOURISM							
Departures	Thousands	(6.1)	..	55,800	69,200	73,400	74,400
Tourism expenditure in other countries	US$ Million	(8.2)	52,938	47,920	48,911	48,495	47,785
TOURISM ACTIVITIES							
Hotels and similar establishments							
Number of rooms	H&S	(7.1)	798,894	822,547	833,375	868,728	877,070
Number of bed-places	H&S	(7.2)	1,527,426	1,565,850	1,590,861	1,633,681	1,649,218
Occupancy rate	Percent	(7.3)	32.70	32.20	32.30	33.40	35.00
Average length of stay	Nights	(5.6)	2.17	2.15	2.12	2.13	2.13
ECONOMIC AGGREGATES							
Gross National Product (GNP)	US$ Million	(9.1)	2,394,474	2,346,503	2,189,533	2,103,848	2,057,633
Exports (F.O.B.)	US$ Million	(9.2)	524,226	512,503	543,431	542,883	549,686
Imports (C.I.F.)	US$ Million	(9.3)	458,808	445,683	471,448	473,551	497,902

Abbreviations used in tables and notes:
H&S: Hotels and similar establishments; **CE:** All types of tourism accommodation establishments; **ALS:** Average length of stay; **THS:** Non-resident tourists staying in H&S; **TCE:** Non-resident tourists staying in CE; **TF:** Arrivals of international (or non-resident) tourists; **VF:** Arrivals of international (or non-resident) visitors; **NHS:** Overnight stays at H&S; **NCE:** Overnight stays at CE.

..   data not available
incl   including
excl   excluding
nra   nationals residing abroad

Notes:
(1.2,2.1-2.6) TCE; (5.6) Inbound tourism in H&S; ALS for internal tourism are as follows (Nights): 96=3.36; 97=3.15; 98=3.09; 99=3.07; 2000=3.05; (7.3) Bed-places in H&S; (8.1,8.2) Including border merchandise transactions and including purchases of inward-bound and outward-bound commuters.

GHANA

Basic Indicators	Units	Code	1996	1997	1998	1999	2000
INBOUND TOURISM							
Arrivals							
Visitors	Thousands	(1.1)	..	..	..	..	..
Tourists (overnight visitors)	Thousands	(1.2)	305	325	348	373	
Same-day visitors	Thousands	(1.3)			..	..	..
Cruise passengers	Thousands	(1.4)	..	..	..	..	..
Arrivals by region							
Africa	Thousands	(2.1)	104	111	118	127	..
Americas	Thousands	(2.2)	26	27	29	31	..
Europe	Thousands	(2.3)	76	81	86	92	..
East Asia and the Pacific	Thousands	(2.4)	15	16	17	18	..
South Asia	Thousands	(2.5)	..	..	..	..	..
Middle East	Thousands	(2.6)	2	2	3	3	..
Arrivals by mode of transport							
Air	Thousands	(3.1)	..	..	..	..	..
Rail	Thousands	(3.2)	..	..	..	..	..
Road	Thousands	(3.3)	..	..	..	..	..
Sea	Thousands	(3.4)	..	..	..	..	..
Arrivals by purpose of visit							
Leisure, recreation and holidays	Thousands	(4.1)	..	..	..	..	..
Business and professional	Thousands	(4.2)	..	..	..	..	..
Other	Thousands	(4.3)	..	..	..	..	..
Overnight stays and length of stay							
Overnight stays in H&S	Thousand nights	(5.1)	..	..	..	..	..
Overnight stays in CE	Thousand nights	(5.2)	3,172	3,393	3,601	..	..
ALS of non resident tourists	Nights	(5.5)	10.40	10.44	10.35	..	..
Tourism expenditure							
in the country of reference	US$ Million	(8.1)	249	266	284	304	335
DOMESTIC TOURISM							
Overnight stays							
Overnight stays in H&S	Thousand nights	(5.3)	..	..	..	..	..
Overnight stays in CE	Thousand nights	(5.4)	..	..	..	..	..
OUTBOUND TOURISM							
Departures	Thousands	(6.1)	..	..	..	..	..
Tourism expenditure in other countries	US$ Million	(8.2)	22	23	85	91	100
TOURISM ACTIVITIES							
Hotels and similar establishments							
Number of rooms	H&S	(7.1)	10,263	10,921	10,879	..	..
Number of bed-places	H&S	(7.2)	13,791	14,164	14,289	..	..
Occupancy rate	Percent	(7.3)	69.00	71.00	..	..	..
Average length of stay	Nights	(5.6)	..	..	..	..	..
ECONOMIC AGGREGATES							
Gross National Product (GNP)	US$ Million	(9.1)	6,588	6,977	7,130	7,432	6,785
Exports (F.O.B.)	US$ Million	(9.2)	1,670	1,636	1,792	..	..
Imports (C.I.F.)	US$ Million	(9.3)	2,101	2,310	2,561	3,533	3,055

Abbreviations used in tables and notes:
H&S: Hotels and similar establishments; **CE:** All types of tourism accommodation establishments; **ALS:** Average length of stay; **THS:** Non-resident tourists staying in H&S; **TCE:** Non-resident tourists staying in CE; **TF:** Arrivals of international (or non-resident) tourists; **VF:** Arrivals of international (or non-resident) visitors; **NHS:** Overnight stays at H&S; **NCE:** Overnight stays at CE.

..   data not available
incl   including
excl   excluding
nra   nationals residing abroad

Notes:
(1.2) Incl nra; (2.1-2.6) Excl nra; (8.1,8.2) International Monetary Fund.

GREECE

Basic Indicators	Units	Code	1996	1997	1998	1999	2000
INBOUND TOURISM							
Arrivals							
Visitors	Thousands	(1.1)	9,782	10,588	11,364	12,606	..
Tourists (overnight visitors)	Thousands	(1.2)	9,233	10,070	10,916	12,164	..
Same-day visitors	Thousands	(1.3)	..	..	..	..	..
Cruise passengers	Thousands	(1.4)	549	518	448	442	..
Arrivals by region							
Africa	Thousands	(2.1)	24	23	21	24	..
Americas	Thousands	(2.2)	298	314	292	305	..
Europe	Thousands	(2.3)	8,541	9,405	10,334	11,556	..
East Asia and the Pacific	Thousands	(2.4)	314	281	224	225	..
South Asia	Thousands	(2.5)	5	4	4	4	..
Middle East	Thousands	(2.6)	51	44	42	50	..
Arrivals by mode of transport							
Air	Thousands	(3.1)	7,684	8,148	8,646	9,962	..
Rail	Thousands	(3.2)	28	37	32	39	..
Road	Thousands	(3.3)	943	1,320	1,404	1,366	..
Sea	Thousands	(3.4)	1,127	1,084	1,282	1,239	..
Arrivals by purpose of visit							
Leisure, recreation and holidays	Thousands	(4.1)	..	..	..	..	..
Business and professional	Thousands	(4.2)	..	..	..	..	..
Other	Thousands	(4.3)	..	..	..	..	..
Overnight stays and length of stay							
Overnight stays in H&S	Thousand nights	(5.1)	35,498	39,992	42,565	45,803	..
Overnight stays in CE	Thousand nights	(5.2)	..	..	..	..	..
ALS of non resident tourists	Nights	(5.5)	..	..	..	..	..
Tourism expenditure in the country of reference	US$ Million	(8.1)	3,723	5,151	6,188	8,783	9,219
DOMESTIC TOURISM							
Overnight stays							
Overnight stays in H&S	Thousand nights	(5.3)	12,448	13,373	13,984	14,454	..
Overnight stays in CE	Thousand nights	(5.4)	..	..	..	..	..
OUTBOUND TOURISM							
Departures	Thousands	(6.1)	..	..	..	..	..
Tourism expenditure in other countries	US$ Million	(8.2)	1,210	1,327	1,756	3,989	4,558
TOURISM ACTIVITIES							
Hotels and similar establishments							
Number of rooms	H&S	(7.1)	289,446	296,096	304,232	308,452	311,841
Number of bed-places	H&S	(7.2)	548,785	561,068	576,876	584,973	591,652
Occupancy rate	Percent	(7.3)	54.37	58.37	61.55	64.00	..
Average length of stay	Nights	(5.6)	..	..	..	..	..
ECONOMIC AGGREGATES							
Gross National Product (GNP)	US$ Million	(9.1)	123,542	129,711	127,880	127,651	126,245
Exports (F.O.B.)	US$ Million	(9.2)	11,948	11,128	10,732	9,815	..
Imports (C.I.F.)	US$ Million	(9.3)	24,136	23,644	23,247	25,433	..

Abbreviations used in tables and notes:
H&S: Hotels and similar establishments; **CE:** All types of tourism accommodation establishments; **ALS:** Average length of stay; **THS:** Non-resident tourists staying in H&S; **TCE:** Non-resident tourists staying in CE; **TF:** Arrivals of international (or non-resident) tourists; **VF:** Arrivals of international (or non-resident) visitors; **NHS:** Overnight stays at H&S; **NCE:** Overnight stays at CE.

.. data not available
incl including
excl excluding
nra nationals residing abroad

Notes:
(1.1,3.1-4.3) VF; (1.2,2.1-2.6) Data based on surveys; (3.4) Incl cruise passengers; (8.1,8.2/98/99) Including registrations through new methodology; (8.1,8.2/2000) International Monetary Fund.

Basic Indicators	Units	Code	1996	1997	1998	1999	2000
INBOUND TOURISM							
Arrivals							
Visitors	Thousands	(1.1)	386	368	392	379	316
Tourists (overnight visitors)	Thousands	(1.2)	108	111	116	125	129
Same-day visitors	Thousands	(1.3)	11	10	10	8	7
Cruise passengers	Thousands	(1.4)	267	247	266	246	180
Arrivals by region							
Africa	Thousands	(2.1)	..	..	..	..	..
Americas	Thousands	(2.2)	50	52	55	64	62
Europe	Thousands	(2.3)	38	38	38	41	46
East Asia and the Pacific	Thousands	(2.4)	1	1	1	2	1
South Asia	Thousands	(2.5)	..	..	..	..	..
Middle East	Thousands	(2.6)	..	..	..	..	..
Arrivals by mode of transport							
Air	Thousands	(3.1)	94	98	104	..	118
Rail	Thousands	(3.2)	..	..	..	..	..
Road	Thousands	(3.3)	..	..	..	..	..
Sea	Thousands	(3.4)	14	13	12	..	10
Arrivals by purpose of visit							
Leisure, recreation and holidays	Thousands	(4.1)	..	63	57	..	..
Business and professional	Thousands	(4.2)	..	12	13	..	..
Other	Thousands	(4.3)	..	35	34	..	..
Overnight stays and length of stay							
Overnight stays in H&S	Thousand nights	(5.1)	..	..	..	..	329
Overnight stays in CE	Thousand nights	(5.2)	..	..	..	..	626
ALS of non resident tourists	Nights	(5.5)	..	..	..	..	7.20
Tourism expenditure in the country of reference	US$ Million	(8.1)	55	55	59	63	67
DOMESTIC TOURISM							
Overnight stays							
Overnight stays in H&S	Thousand nights	(5.3)	..	..	..	..	..
Overnight stays in CE	Thousand nights	(5.4)	..	..	..	..	..
OUTBOUND TOURISM							
Departures	Thousands	(6.1)	..	..	..	..	..
Tourism expenditure in other countries	US$ Million	(8.2)	5	5	5	..	..
TOURISM ACTIVITIES							
Hotels and similar establishments							
Number of rooms	H&S	(7.1)	1,669	1,775	1,802	1,928	1,822
Number of bed-places	H&S	(7.2)	2,964	3,118	2,995	3,274	3,091
Occupancy rate	Percent	(7.3)	59.33	62.10	62.31	64.77	71.00
Average length of stay	Nights	(5.6)	7.54	7.40	7.36	7.32	7.20
ECONOMIC AGGREGATES							
Gross National Product (GNP)	US$ Million	(9.1)	280	294	301	320	345
Exports (F.O.B.)	US$ Million	(9.2)	20	23	27	..	..
Imports (C.I.F.)	US$ Million	(9.3)	152	173	200	..	..

Abbreviations used in tables and notes:
H&S: Hotels and similar establishments; **CE:** All types of tourism accommodation establishments; **ALS:** Average length of stay; **THS:** Non-resident tourists staying in H&S; **TCE:** Non-resident tourists staying in CE; **TF:** Arrivals of international (or non-resident) tourists; **VF:** Arrivals of international (or non-resident) visitors; **NHS:** Overnight stays at H&S; **NCE:** Overnight stays at CE.

..   data not available
incl   including
excl   excluding
nra   nationals residing abroad

Notes:
(1.2,2.2-4.3) TF; (7.1,7.2) Hotels, cottages/apartments and guest houses; (7.3) Rooms.

GUADELOUPE

Basic Indicators	Units	Code	1996	1997	1998	1999	2000
INBOUND TOURISM							
Arrivals							
Visitors	Thousands	(1.1)	1,236	1,204	1,111	940	1,015
Tourists (overnight visitors)	Thousands	(1.2)	625	660	693	561	623
Same-day visitors	Thousands	(1.3)	..	..	..	..	..
Cruise passengers	Thousands	(1.4)	611	544	418	379	392
Arrivals by region							
Africa	Thousands	(2.1)	..	..	..	..	..
Americas	Thousands	(2.2)	11	17	7	8	126
Europe	Thousands	(2.3)	135	129	125	137	495
East Asia and the Pacific	Thousands	(2.4)	..	..	..	..	..
South Asia	Thousands	(2.5)	..	..	..	..	..
Middle East	Thousands	(2.6)	..	..	..	..	..
Arrivals by mode of transport							
Air	Thousands	(3.1)	625	660	693	561	623
Rail	Thousands	(3.2)	..	..	..	..	..
Road	Thousands	(3.3)	..	..	..	..	..
Sea	Thousands	(3.4)	611	544	418	379	392
Arrivals by purpose of visit							
Leisure, recreation and holidays	Thousands	(4.1)	..	..	..	..	..
Business and professional	Thousands	(4.2)	..	..	..	..	..
Other	Thousands	(4.3)	..	..	..	..	..
Overnight stays and length of stay							
Overnight stays in H&S	Thousand nights	(5.1)	876	849	850	847	3,233
Overnight stays in CE	Thousand nights	(5.2)	3,750	3,960	4,158	..	..
ALS of non resident tourists	Nights	(5.5)	..	..	..	..	..
Tourism expenditure in the country of reference	US$ Million	(8.1)	496	372	466	375	418
DOMESTIC TOURISM							
Overnight stays							
Overnight stays in H&S	Thousand nights	(5.3)	..	..	..	..	..
Overnight stays in CE	Thousand nights	(5.4)	..	..	..	..	..
OUTBOUND TOURISM							
Departures	Thousands	(6.1)	..	..	..	..	..
Tourism expenditure in other countries	US$ Million	(8.2)	..	..	..	..	..
TOURISM ACTIVITIES							
Hotels and similar establishments							
Number of rooms	H&S	(7.1)	8,294	8,530	8,371	8,260	8,136
Number of bed-places	H&S	(7.2)	..	..	..	..	..
Occupancy rate	Percent	(7.3)	68.91	69.75	65.25	66.25	56.90
Average length of stay	Nights	(5.6)	5.96	5.74	6.06	5.80	5.20
ECONOMIC AGGREGATES							
Gross National Product (GNP)	US$ Million	(9.1)	..	..	..	..	..
Exports (F.O.B.)	US$ Million	(9.2)	93	137	125	147	..
Imports (C.I.F.)	US$ Million	(9.3)	1,669	1,707	..	..	..

Abbreviations used in tables and notes:
H&S: Hotels and similar establishments; **CE:** All types of tourism accommodation establishments; **ALS:** Average length of stay; **THS:** Non-resident tourists staying in H&S; **TCE:** Non-resident tourists staying in CE; **TF:** Arrivals of international (or non-resident) tourists; **VF:** Arrivals of international (or non-resident) visitors; **NHS:** Overnight stays at H&S; **NCE:** Overnight stays at CE.

.. data not available
incl including
excl excluding
nra nationals residing abroad

Notes:
(1.2) THS; (2.2,2.3,5.1/96-99) HS, arrivals and nights at 21 traditional hotel establishments; (2.2,2.3,5.1/2000) HS, arrivals and nights at 83 traditional hotel establishments; (7.1) Hotels; (7.3) Rooms.

Basic Indicators	Units	Code	1996	1997	1998	1999	2000
INBOUND TOURISM							
Arrivals							
Visitors	Thousands	(1.1)	..	..	..	..	..
Tourists (overnight visitors)	Thousands	(1.2)	1,363	1,382	1,137	1,162	1,288
Same-day visitors	Thousands	(1.3)	..	..	..	..	..
Cruise passengers	Thousands	(1.4)	10	8	8	6	9
Arrivals by region							
Africa	Thousands	(2.1)	..	..	..	..	..
Americas	Thousands	(2.2)	36	44	42	42	42
Europe	Thousands	(2.3)	1	2	2	2	2
East Asia and the Pacific	Thousands	(2.4)	1,308	1,324	1,079	1,105	1,231
South Asia	Thousands	(2.5)	..	..	..	..	..
Middle East	Thousands	(2.6)	..	..	..	..	..
Arrivals by mode of transport							
Air	Thousands	(3.1)	1,352	1,373	1,129	1,156	1,279
Rail	Thousands	(3.2)	..	..	..	..	..
Road	Thousands	(3.3)	..	..	..	..	..
Sea	Thousands	(3.4)	10	8	8	6	9
Arrivals by purpose of visit							
Leisure, recreation and holidays	Thousands	(4.1)	..	..	..	..	..
Business and professional	Thousands	(4.2)	..	..	..	..	..
Other	Thousands	(4.3)	..	..	..	..	..
Overnight stays and length of stay							
Overnight stays in H&S	Thousand nights	(5.1)	..	..	..	..	..
Overnight stays in CE	Thousand nights	(5.2)	..	..	..	..	..
ALS of non resident tourists	Nights	(5.5)	..	..	..	..	..
Tourism expenditure							
in the country of reference	US$ Million	(8.1)	..	2,818	2,361	1,908	..
DOMESTIC TOURISM							
Overnight stays							
Overnight stays in H&S	Thousand nights	(5.3)	..	..	..	..	..
Overnight stays in CE	Thousand nights	(5.4)	..	..	..	..	..
OUTBOUND TOURISM							
Departures	Thousands	(6.1)	..	..	..	..	..
Tourism expenditure in other countries	US$ Million	(6.2)	..	..	..	..	..
TOURISM ACTIVITIES							
Hotels and similar establishments							
Number of rooms	H&S	(7.1)	7,928	8,119	8,705	10,084	10,110
Number of bed-places	H&S	(7.2)	..	..	..	..	..
Occupancy rate	Percent	(7.3)	85.00	82.00	67.00	61.00	63.00
Average length of stay	Nights	(5.6)	..	..	..	..	..
ECONOMIC AGGREGATES							
Gross National Product (GNP)	US$ Million	(9 1)	2,993	3,000	3,303	..	..
Exports (F.O.B.)	US$ Million	(9 2)	..	..	..	..	..
Imports (C.I.F.)	US$ Million	(9 3)	..	..	..	..	..

Abbreviations used in tables and notes:
H&S: Hotels and similar establishments; **CE:** All types of tourism accommodation establishments; **ALS:** Average length of stay; **THS:** Non-resident tourists staying in H&S; **TCE:** Non-resident tourists staying in CE; **TF:** Arrivals of international (or non-resident) tourists; **VF:** Arrivals of international (or non-resident) visitors; **NHS:** Overnight stays at H&S; **NCE:** Overnight stays at CE.

..   data not available
incl   including
excl   excluding
nra   nationals residing abroad

Notes:
(1.2) Air and sea arrivals; (2.2) Incl Hawaii; (7.3) Reporting for fiscal year ending 30 September (weighted); (9.1) GDP.

GUATEMALA

Basic Indicators	Units	Code	1996	1997	1998	1999	2000
INBOUND TOURISM							
Arrivals							
Visitors	Thousands	(1.1)	..	..	..	..	..
Tourists (overnight visitors)	Thousands	(1.2)	520	576	636	823	826
Same-day visitors	Thousands	(1.3)	..	..	..	..	..
Cruise passengers	Thousands	(1.4)	..	..	..	..	..
Arrivals by region							
Africa	Thousands	(2.1)	..	..	..	..	..
Americas	Thousands	(2.2)	409	457	505	693	..
Europe	Thousands	(2.3)	97	104	115	114	..
East Asia and the Pacific	Thousands	(2.4)	12	14	15	15	..
South Asia	Thousands	(2.5)	..	..	..	..	..
Middle East	Thousands	(2.6)	..	..	..	..	..
Arrivals by mode of transport							
Air	Thousands	(3.1)	269	303	331	..	..
Rail	Thousands	(3.2)	..	..	..	..	..
Road	Thousands	(3.3)	232	232	256	..	..
Sea	Thousands	(3.4)	19	42	47	..	..
Arrivals by purpose of visit							
Leisure, recreation and holidays	Thousands	(4.1)	229	259	..	..	..
Business and professional	Thousands	(4.2)	161	179	..	..	..
Other	Thousands	(4.3)	130	138	..	..	..
Overnight stays and length of stay							
Overnight stays in H&S	Thousand nights	(5.1)	..	..	..	..	..
Overnight stays in CE	Thousand nights	(5.2)	3,691	4,380	..	..	..
ALS of non resident tourists	Nights	(5.5)	7.30	7.50	..	..	..
Tourism expenditure **in the country of reference**	US$ Million	(8.1)	284	325	394	570	518
DOMESTIC TOURISM							
Overnight stays							
Overnight stays in H&S	Thousand nights	(5.3)	..	..	..	..	..
Overnight stays in CE	Thousand nights	(5.4)	..	..	..	..	..
OUTBOUND TOURISM							
Departures	Thousands	(6.1)	333	331	391	..	..
Tourism expenditure in other countries	US$ Million	(8.2)	135	119	157	183	182
TOURISM ACTIVITIES							
Hotels and similar establishments							
Number of rooms	H&S	(7.1)	13,113	13,854	14,744	..	..
Number of bed-places	H&S	(7.2)	33,120	35,707	37,863	..	..
Occupancy rate	Percent	(7.3)	61.20	63.40	57.50	56.80	..
Average length of stay	Nights	(5.6)	..	..	..	..	..
ECONOMIC AGGREGATES							
Gross National Product (GNP)	US$ Million	(9.1)	15,199	16,546	17,807	18,625	19,224
Exports (F.O.B.)	US$ Million	(9.2)	2,031	2,344	2,582	2,398	2,696
Imports (C.I.F.)	US$ Million	(9.3)	3,146	3,852	4,651	4,382	4,791

Abbreviations used in tables and notes:
H&S: Hotels and similar establishments; **CE:** All types of tourism accommodation establishments; **ALS:** Average length of stay; **THS:** Non-resident tourists staying in H&S; **TCE:** Non-resident tourists staying in CE; **TF:** Arrivals of international (or non-resident) tourists; **VF:** Arrivals of international (or non-resident) visitors; **NHS:** Overnight stays at H&S; **NCE:** Overnight stays at CE.

..   data not available
incl   including
excl   excluding
nra   nationals residing abroad

Notes:
(5.5) Days; (8.2) International Monetary Fund.

Basic Indicators	Units	Code	1996	1997	1998	1999	2000
INBOUND TOURISM							
Arrivals							
Visitors	Thousands	(1.1)	..		..	..	..
Tourists (overnight visitors)	Thousands	(1.2)	12	17	23	27	33
Same-day visitors	Thousands	(1.3)	..	..	..	..	..
Cruise passengers	Thousands	(1.4)	..	..	..	..	..
Arrivals by region							
Africa	Thousands	(2.1)	..	3	4	9	12
Americas	Thousands	(2.2)	..	2	2	4	4
Europe	Thousands	(2.3)	..	9	12	11	14
East Asia and the Pacific	Thousands	(2.4)	..	1	1	2	1
South Asia	Thousands	(2.5)	..	..	..	..	..
Middle East	Thousands	(2.6)	..	2	4	..	..
Arrivals by mode of transport							
Air	Thousands	(3.1)	12	17	23	27	33
Rail	Thousands	(3.2)	..	..	..	..	..
Road	Thousands	(3.3)	..	..	..	..	..
Sea	Thousands	(3.4)	..	..	..	..	..
Arrivals by purpose of visit							
Leisure, recreation and holidays	Thousands	(4.1)	..	..	3	6	7
Business and professional	Thousands	(4.2)	..	..	19	14	16
Other	Thousands	(4.3)	..	..	1	7	9
Overnight stays and length of stay							
Overnight stays in H&S	Thousand nights	(5.1)	..	..	..	70	..
Overnight stays in CE	Thousand nights	(5.2)	..	..	..	..	..
ALS of non resident tourists	Nights	(5.5)	..	..	..	..	4.40
Tourism expenditure in the country of reference	US$ Million	(8.1)	6	..	1	7	..
DOMESTIC TOURISM							
Overnight stays							
Overnight stays in H&S	Thousand nights	(5.3)	..	..	..	..	..
Overnight stays in CE	Thousand nights	(5.4)	..	..	..	..	..
OUTBOUND TOURISM							
Departures	Thousands	(3.1)	..	..	..	..	..
Tourism expenditure in other countries	US$ Million	(3.2)	27	23	27	31	36
TOURISM ACTIVITIES							
Hotels and similar establishments							
Number of rooms	H&S	(7.1)	..	2,287	2,409	3,115	3,594
Number of bed-places	H&S	(7.2)	..	..	..	..	..
Occupancy rate	Percent	(7.3)	..	..	..	..	..
Average length of stay	Nights	(5.6)	..	..	..	..	..
ECONOMIC AGGREGATES							
Gross National Product (GNP)	US$ Million	(9.1)	3,856	3,867	3,695	3,587	3,345
Exports (F.O.B.)	US$ Million	(9.2)	613	660	679	..	..
Imports (C.I.F.)	US$ Million	(9.3)	612	624	604	..	..

Abbreviations used in tables and notes:
H&S: Hotels and similar establishments; **CE:** All types of tourism accommodation establishments; **ALS:** Average length of stay; **THS:** Non-resident tourists staying in H&S; **TCE:** Non-resident tourists staying in CE; **TF:** Arrivals of international (or non-resident) tourists; **VF:** Arrivals of international (or non-resident) visitors; **NHS:** Overnight stays at H&S; **NCE:** Overnight stays at CE.

..   data not available
incl including
excl excluding
nra nationals residing abroad

Notes:
(1.2,2.1-2.6,4.1-4.3) Arrivals by air at Conakry airport.

GUYANA

Basic Indicators	Units	Code	1996	1997	1998	1999	2000
INBOUND TOURISM							
Arrivals							
Visitors	Thousands	(1.1)	..	..	..	..	..
Tourists (overnight visitors)	Thousands	(1.2)	92	76	68	75	105
Same-day visitors	Thousands	(1.3)	..	..	..	..	
Cruise passengers	Thousands	(1.4)	..	..	..	..	..
Arrivals by region							
Africa	Thousands	(2.1)	..	..	..	..	..
Americas	Thousands	(2.2)	85	69	63	..	..
Europe	Thousands	(2.3)	6	5	5	..	..
East Asia and the Pacific	Thousands	(2.4)	..	..	..	..	..
South Asia	Thousands	(2.5)	..	..	..	..	..
Middle East	Thousands	(2.6)	..	..	..	..	..
Arrivals by mode of transport							
Air	Thousands	(3.1)	81	68	62	..	..
Rail	Thousands	(3.2)	..	..	..	..	..
Road	Thousands	(3.3)	..	..	..	..	..
Sea	Thousands	(3.4)	11	7	6	..	..
Arrivals by purpose of visit							
Leisure, recreation and holidays	Thousands	(4.1)	29	54	51	..	..
Business and professional	Thousands	(4.2)	2	2	1	..	..
Other	Thousands	(4.3)	61	20	16	..	..
Overnight stays and length of stay							
Overnight stays in H&S	Thousand nights	(5.1)	..	..	..	..	..
Overnight stays in CE	Thousand nights	(5.2)	..	..	..	..	..
ALS of non resident tourists	Nights	(5.5)	..	19.00	19.00	..	..
Tourism expenditure in the country of reference	US$ Million	(8.1)	70	60	54	59	..
DOMESTIC TOURISM							
Overnight stays							
Overnight stays in H&S	Thousand nights	(5.3)	..	..	..	..	..
Overnight stays in CE	Thousand nights	(5.4)	..	..	..	..	..
OUTBOUND TOURISM							
Departures	Thousands	(6.1)	..	..	..	..	..
Tourism expenditure in other countries	US$ Million	(8.2)	..	..	..	..	..
TOURISM ACTIVITIES							
Hotels and similar establishments							
Number of rooms	H&S	(7.1)	639	730	730	730	730
Number of bed-places	H&S	(7.2)	..	..	..	..	..
Occupancy rate	Percent	(7.3)	..	..	..	..	..
Average length of stay	Nights	(5.6)	..	..	..	..	..
ECONOMIC AGGREGATES							
Gross National Product (GNP)	US$ Million	(9.1)	631	671	660	651	667
Exports (F.O.B.)	US$ Million	(9.2)	517	643	485	523	498
Imports (C.I.F.)	US$ Million	(9.3)	598	629	..	..	..

Abbreviations used in tables and notes:
H&S: Hotels and similar establishments; **CE:** All types of tourism accommodation establishments; **ALS:** Average length of stay; **THS:** Non-resident tourists staying in H&S; **TCE:** Non-resident tourists staying in CE; **TF:** Arrivals of international (or non-resident) tourists; **VF:** Arrivals of international (or non-resident) visitors; **NHS:** Overnight stays at H&S; **NCE:** Overnight stays at CE.

..   data not available
incl   including
excl   excluding
nra   nationals residing abroad

Notes:
(7.1) Hotels only.

82

Basic Indicators	Units	Code	1996	1997	1998	1999	2000
INBOUND TOURISM							
Arrivals							
Visitors	Thousands	(1.1)	400	387	393	386	445
Tourists (overnight visitors)	Thousands	(1.2)	150	149	147	143	140
Same-day visitors	Thousands	(1.3)	..	..	..	..	..
Cruise passengers	Thousands	(1.4)	250	238	246	243	305
Arrivals by region							
Africa	Thousands	(2.1)	..	..	..	..	..
Americas	Thousands	(2.2)	133	133	131	130	128
Europe	Thousands	(2.3)	15	14	14	12	11
East Asia and the Pacific	Thousands	(2.4)	..	..	..	..	..
South Asia	Thousands	(2.5)	..	..	..	..	..
Middle East	Thousands	(2.6)	..	..	..	..	..
Arrivals by mode of transport							
Air	Thousands	(3.1)	150	149	147	143	140
Rail	Thousands	(3.2)	..	..	..	..	..
Road	Thousands	(3.3)	..	..	..	..	..
Sea	Thousands	(3.4)	..	..	..	..	..
Arrivals by purpose of visit							
Leisure, recreation and holidays	Thousands	(4.1)	..	48	45	44	..
Business and professional	Thousands	(4.2)	..	27	27	26	..
Other	Thousands	(4.3)	..	74	75	73	..
Overnight stays and length of stay							
Overnight stays in H&S	Thousand nights	(5.1)	..	..	..	..	..
Overnight stays in CE	Thousand nights	(5.2)	..	..	..	..	..
ALS of non resident tourists	Nights	(5.5)	..	..	..	..	..
Tourism expenditure							
in the country of reference	US$ Million	(8.1)	58	57	56	55	54
DOMESTIC TOURISM							
Overnight stays							
Overnight stays in H&S	Thousand nights	(5.3)	..	..	..	..	..
Overnight stays in CE	Thousand nights	(5.4)	..	..	..	..	..
OUTBOUND TOURISM							
Departures	Thousands	(6.1)	..	..	..	..	..
Tourism expenditure in other countries	US$ Million	(6.2)	37	35	37	..	..
TOURISM ACTIVITIES							
Hotels and similar establishments							
Number of rooms	H&S	(7.1)	1,758	1,758	1,758	1,758	..
Number of bed-places	H&S	(7.2)	..	..	..	..	..
Occupancy rate	Percent	(7.3)	..	..	..	..	..
Average length of stay	Nights	(5.6)	..	..	..	..	..
ECONOMIC AGGREGATES							
Gross National Product (GNP)	US$ Million	(9.1)	2,620	2,871	3,182	3,572	4,034
Exports (F.O.B.)	US$ Million	(9.2)	90	119	175	199	165
Imports (C.I.F.)	US$ Million	(9.3)	666	648	800	1,035	1,041

Abbreviations used in tables and notes:
H&S: Hotels and similar establishments; CE: All types of tourism accommodation establishments; ALS: Average length of stay; THS: Non-resident tourists staying in H&S; TCE: Non-resident tourists staying in CE; TF: Arrivals of international (or non-resident) tourists; VF: Arrivals of international (or non-resident) visitors; NHS: Overnight stays at H&S; NCE: Overnight stays at CE.

..	data not available
incl	including
excl	excluding
nra	nationals residing abroad

Notes:
(7.1) Hotels, beach hotels and guest houses.

HAWAII (USA)

Basic Indicators	Units	Code	1996	1997	1998	1999	2000
INBOUND TOURISM							
Arrivals							
Visitors	Thousands	(1.1)	..	..	..	..	..
Tourists (overnight visitors)	Thousands	(1.2)	6,829	6,876	6,738	..	..
Same-day visitors	Thousands	(1.3)	..	..	..	..	..
Cruise passengers	Thousands	(1.4)	..	..	..	..	..
Arrivals by region							
Africa	Thousands	(2.1)	..	..	..	..	..
Americas	Thousands	(2.2)	3,986	3,923	4,190	..	..
Europe	Thousands	(2.3)	260	255	238	..	..
East Asia and the Pacific	Thousands	(2.4)	2,548	2,652	2,273	..	..
South Asia	Thousands	(2.5)	..	..	..	..	..
Middle East	Thousands	(2.6)	..	..	..	..	..
Arrivals by mode of transport							
Air	Thousands	(3.1)	6,829	6,876	6,738	..	..
Rail	Thousands	(3.2)	..	..	..	..	..
Road	Thousands	(3.3)	..	..	..	..	..
Sea	Thousands	(3.4)	..	..	..	..	..
Arrivals by purpose of visit							
Leisure, recreation and holidays	Thousands	(4.1)	5,783	5,703	5,513	..	..
Business and professional	Thousands	(4.2)	694	760	757	..	..
Other	Thousands	(4.3)	377	413	468	..	..
Overnight stays and length of stay							
Overnight stays in H&S	Thousand nights	(5.1)	..	..	..	..	..
Overnight stays in CE	Thousand nights	(5.2)	59,149	57,604	58,342	..	..
ALS of non resident tourists	Nights	(5.5)	8.66	8.38	8.66	..	..
Tourism expenditure in the country of reference	US$ Million	(8.1)	10,685	10,770	11,133	..	..
DOMESTIC TOURISM							
Overnight stays							
Overnight stays in H&S	Thousand nights	(5.3)	..	..	..	..	..
Overnight stays in CE	Thousand nights	(5.4)	..	..	..	..	..
OUTBOUND TOURISM							
Departures	Thousands	(6.1)	..	..	..	..	..
Tourism expenditure in other countries	US$ Million	(8.2)	..	..	..	..	..
TOURISM ACTIVITIES							
Hotels and similar establishments							
Number of rooms	H&S	(7.1)	70,288	71,025	71,480	..	..
Number of bed-places	H&S	(7.2)	..	..	..	..	..
Occupancy rate	Percent	(7.3)	76.00	74.00	71.80	..	..
Average length of stay	Nights	(5.6)	..	..	..	..	..
ECONOMIC AGGREGATES							
Gross National Product (GNP)	US$ Million	(9.1)	..	..	..	..	..
Exports (F.O.B.)	US$ Million	(9.2)	..	..	..	..	..
Imports (C.I.F.)	US$ Million	(9.3)	..	..	..	..	..

Abbreviations used in tables and notes:
H&S: Hotels and similar establishments; **CE:** All types of tourism accommodation establishments; **ALS:** Average length of stay; **THS:** Non-resident tourists staying in H&S; **TCE:** Non-resident tourists staying in CE; **TF:** Arrivals of international (or non-resident) tourists; **VF:** Arrivals of international (or non-resident) visitors; **NHS:** Overnight stays at H&S; **NCE:** Overnight stays at CE.

..   data not available
incl   including
excl   excluding
nra   nationals residing abroad

Notes:
(4.1) Pleasure traveler; (4.2) Convention, corp. meeting, incentive, other business, government, school; (4.3) Incl visitors to friends and relative; (5.2,5.5) Days.

Basic Indicators	Units	Code	1996	1997	1998	1999	2000
INBOUND TOURISM							
Arrivals							
Visitors	Thousands	(1.1)	271	310	324	428	689
Tourists (overnight visitors)	Thousands	(1.2)	263	307	321	371	471
Same-day visitors	Thousands	(1.3)	..	..	..	..	..
Cruise passengers	Thousands	(1.4)	8	3	3	57	218
Arrivals by region							
Africa	Thousands	(2.1)	..	..	..	..	..
Americas	Thousands	(2.2)	225	266	280	331	420
Europe	Thousands	(2.3)	32	33	33	34	43
East Asia and the Pacific	Thousands	(2.4)	6	8	8	6	7
South Asia	Thousands	(2.5)	..	..	..	..	..
Middle East	Thousands	(2.6)	..	..	..	..	..
Arrivals by mode of transport							
Air	Thousands	(3.1)	201	189	206	227	237
Rail	Thousands	(3.2)	..	..	..	..	..
Road	Thousands	(3.3)	59	110	110	139	221
Sea	Thousands	(3.4)	3	7	5	5	13
Arrivals by purpose of visit							
Leisure, recreation and holidays	Thousands	(4.1)	165	237	186	206	247
Business and professional	Thousands	(4.2)	59	46	56	65	69
Other	Thousands	(4.3)	39	23	79	100	155
Overnight stays and length of stay							
Overnight stays in H&S	Thousand nights	(5.1)	..	..	..	..	..
Overnight stays in CE	Thousand nights	(5.2)	..	..	..	..	..
ALS of non resident tourists	Nights	(5.5)	7.40	7.60	7.80	9.27	10.40
Tourism expenditure in the country of reference	US$ Million	(6.1)	115	146	168	195	262
DOMESTIC TOURISM							
Overnight stays							
Overnight stays in H&S	Thousand nights	(6.3)	..	..	..	..	..
Overnight stays in CE	Thousand nights	(6.4)	..	..	..	..	..
OUTBOUND TOURISM							
Departures	Thousands	(8.1)	162	183	202	235	277
Tourism expenditure in other countries	US$ Million	(8.2)	60	62	81	94	99
TOURISM ACTIVITIES							
Hotels and similar establishments							
Number of rooms	H&S	(7.1)	10,772	11,428	12,205	12,891	13,943
Number of bed-places	H&S	(7.2)	18,264	19,542	20,910	20,086	22,309
Occupancy rate	Percent	(7.3)	..	..	..	47.30	..
Average length of stay	Nights	(5.6)	..	..	..	..	..
ECONOMIC AGGREGATES							
Gross National Product (GNP)	US$ Million	(9.1)	3,828	4,272	4,534	4,865	5,517
Exports (F.O.B.)	US$ Million	(9.2)	1,316	1,446	1,575	1,249	1,322
Imports (C.I.F.)	US$ Million	(9.3)	1,840	2,149	2,500	2,728	2,885

Abbreviations used in tables and notes:
H&S: Hotels and similar establishments; **CE:** All types of tourism accommodation establishments; **ALS:** Average length of stay; **THS:** Non-resident tourists staying in H&S; **TCE:** Non-resident tourists staying in CE; **TF:** Arrivals of international (or non-resident) tourists; **VF:** Arrivals of international (or non-resident) visitors; **NHS:** Overnight stays at H&S; **NCE:** Overnight stays at CE.

..   data not available
incl   including
excl   excluding
nra   nationals residing abroad

Notes:
(1.1,2.2-4.3) VF; (5.5) Days; (8.2) International Monetary Fund.

HONG KONG, CHINA

Basic Indicators	Units	Code	1996	1997	1998	1999	2000
INBOUND TOURISM							
Arrivals							
Visitors	Thousands	(1.1)	12,974	11,273	10,160	11,328	13,059
Tourists (overnight visitors)	Thousands	(1.2)	..	..	..	..	..
Same-day visitors	Thousands	(1.3)	..	..	..	..	..
Cruise passengers	Thousands	(1.4)	7	8	11	8	9
Arrivals by region							
Africa	Thousands	(2.1)	65	74	64	65	73
Americas	Thousands	(2.2)	1,083	1,125	1,105	1,155	1,296
Europe	Thousands	(2.3)	1,374	1,195	1,042	1,059	1,117
East Asia and the Pacific	Thousands	(2.4)	10,256	8,695	7,762	8,853	10,336
South Asia	Thousands	(2.5)	180	168	168	172	206
Middle East	Thousands	(2.6)	16	16	19	24	32
Arrivals by mode of transport							
Air	Thousands	(3.1)	7,532	6,343	5,571	6,062	6,709
Rail	Thousands	(3.2)	..	..	..	..	..
Road	Thousands	(3.3)	2,560	2,568	2,632	3,266	4,254
Sea	Thousands	(3.4)	2,882	2,363	1,957	1,999	2,096
Arrivals by purpose of visit							
Leisure, recreation and holidays	Thousands	(4.1)	7,596	6,903	4,985	5,568	7,166
Business and professional	Thousands	(4.2)	3,733	2,923	3,287	3,449	3,872
Other	Thousands	(4.3)	1,644	1,447	1,888	2,311	2,022
Overnight stays and length of stay							
Overnight stays in H&S	Thousand nights	(5.1)	..	..	..	..	..
Overnight stays in CE	Thousand nights	(5.2)	..	..	..	..	..
ALS of non resident tourists	Nights	(5.5)	3.70	3.59	3.38	3.36	3.00
Tourism expenditure **in the country of reference**	US$ Million	(8.1)	11,994	9,979	7,496	7,210	7,886
DOMESTIC TOURISM							
Overnight stays							
Overnight stays in H&S	Thousand nights	(5.3)	..	..	..	..	..
Overnight stays in CE	Thousand nights	(5.4)	..	..	..	..	..
OUTBOUND TOURISM							
Departures	Thousands	(6.1)	3,445	3,758	4,197	4,175	4,611
Tourism expenditure in other countries	US$ Million	(8.2)	..	..	..	..	..
TOURISM ACTIVITIES							
Hotels and similar establishments							
Number of rooms	H&S	(7.1)	33,536	33,425	33,981	35,420	36,438
Number of bed-places	H&S	(7.2)	..	..	..	..	..
Occupancy rate	Percent	(7.3)	88.00	76.00	76.00	79.00	83.00
Average length of stay	Nights	(5.6)	..	..	..	..	..
ECONOMIC AGGREGATES							
Gross National Product (GNP)	US$ Million	(9.1)	151,955	164,464	159,508	166,064	176,438
Exports (F.O.B.)	US$ Million	(9.2)	180,750	188,059	174,002	173,885	201,860
Imports (C.I.F.)	US$ Million	(9.3)	198,550	208,614	184,518	179,520	212,805

Abbreviations used in tables and notes:
H&S: Hotels and similar establishments; **CE:** All types of tourism accommodation establishments; **ALS:** Average length of stay; **THS:** Non-resident tourists staying in H&S; **TCE:** Non-resident tourists staying in CE; **TF:** Arrivals of international (or non-resident) tourists; **VF:** Arrivals of international (or non-resident) visitors; **NHS:** Overnight stays at H&S; **NCE:** Overnight stays at CE.

.. data not available
incl including
excl excluding
nra nationals residing abroad

Notes:
(1.4) Cruise passengers (incl in VF); (6.1) Excl HK residents to Macau and Mainland China; (7.1) Hotels (high/medium tariffs) and hostels/ guest houses; (7.3) Rooms; (8.1) Incl receipts from servicemen, air crew members and transit passengers.
Note: From 1996 and onwards, figures include arrivals of non-Macau residents via "Macau, China".

HUNGARY

Basic Indicators	Units	Code	1996	1997	1998	1999	2000
INBOUND TOURISM							
Arrivals							
Visitors	Thousands	(1.1)	39,833	37,315	33,624	28,803	31,141
Tourists (overnight visitors)	Thousands	(1.2)	20,674	17,248	..	..	..
Same-day visitors	Thousands	(1.3)	19,159	20,067	..	..	..
Cruise passengers	Thousands	(1.4)	..	..	..	..	..
Arrivals by region							
Africa	Thousands	(2.1)	17	12	12	14	16
Americas	Thousands	(2.2)	366	404	452	405	448
Europe	Thousands	(2.3)	39,212	36,652	32,968	28,148	30,408
East Asia and the Pacific	Thousands	(2.4)	167	172	124	166	198
South Asia	Thousands	(2.5)	11	13	15	18	22
Middle East	Thousands	(2.6)	31	34	31	24	23
Arrivals by mode of transport							
Air	Thousands	(3.1)	1,183	1,349	1,496	1,823	1,735
Rail	Thousands	(3.2)	2,327	2,019	1,862	1,618	1,791
Road	Thousands	(3.3)	36,245	33,863	30,169	25,273	27,478
Sea	Thousands	(3.4)	78	83	97	89	138
Arrivals by purpose of visit							
Leisure, recreation and holidays	Thousands	(4.1)	..	..	..	..	..
Business and professional	Thousands	(4.2)	..	..	..	..	..
Other	Thousands	(4.3)	..	..	..	..	..
Overnight stays and length of stay							
Overnight stays in H&S	Thousand nights	(5.1)	7,449	7,619	7,714	7,539	8,062
Overnight stays in CE	Thousand nights	(5.2)	10,676	10,272	10,138	9,943	10,514
ALS of non resident tourists	Nights	(5.5)	6.71	7.64	..	..	..
Tourism expenditure							
in the country of reference	US$ Million	(8.1)	3,222	3,440	3,514	3,394	3,429
DOMESTIC TOURISM							
Overnight stays							
Overnight stays in H&S	Thousand nights	(5 3)	4,135	4,334	4,714	5,196	5,479
Overnight stays in CE	Thousand nights	(5 4)	6,466	6,255	6,778	7,384	7,855
OUTBOUND TOURISM							
Departures	Thousands	(6.1)	12,064	12,173	12,317	10,622	11,065
Tourism expenditure in other countries	US$ Million	(8.2)	957	925	1,115	1,193	1,094
TOURISM ACTIVITIES							
Hotels and similar establishments							
Number of rooms	H&S	(7.1)	50,691	52,670	54,653	57,674	57,870
Number of bed-places	H&S	(7.2)	127,650	133,362	136,413	144,600	143,573
Occupancy rate	Percent	(7.3)	47.20	47.70	47.50	45.50	46.70
Average length of stay	Nights	(5.6)	2.82	2.87	2.86	2.87	2.86
ECONOMIC AGGREGATES							
Gross National Product (GNP)	US$ Million	(9.1)	44,343	45,754	45,329	46,757	47,462
Exports (F.O.B.)	US$ Million	(9.2)	12,652	18,628	22,958	24,950	28,013
Imports (C.I.F.)	US$ Million	(9.3)	15,853	20,668	25,600	27,923	31,955

Abbreviations used in tables and notes:
H&S: Hotels and similar establishments; **CE:** All types of tourism accommodation establishments; **ALS:** Average length of stay; **THS:** Non-resident tourists staying in H&S; **TCE:** Non-resident tourists staying in CE; **TF:** Arrivals of international (or non-resident) tourists; **VF:** Arrivals of international (or non-resident) visitors; **NHS:** Overnight stays at H&S; **NCE:** Overnight stays at CE.

Notes:
(1.1,2.1-2.6,3.1-3.4) VF, departures; (1.2,4.1-4.3) TF, departures, excl nra; (3.4) By river; (5.2,5.4/96/97) Incl organized private room service; (7.3) Rooms, July-June; (8.2) International Monetary Fund.

..   data not available
incl   including
excl   excluding
nra   nationals residing abroad

ICELAND

Basic Indicators	Units	Code	1996	1997	1998	1999	2000
INBOUND TOURISM							
Arrivals							
Visitors	Thousands	(1.1)	..	..	..	..	..
Tourists (overnight visitors)	Thousands	(1.2)	201	202	232	263	303
Same-day visitors	Thousands	(1.3)	..	..	..	..	..
Cruise passengers	Thousands	(1.4)	22	21	23	18	26
Arrivals by region							
Africa	Thousands	(2.1)	..	..	..	1	1
Americas	Thousands	(2.2)	34	36	44	48	59
Europe	Thousands	(2.3)	160	159	180	205	232
East Asia and the Pacific	Thousands	(2.4)	6	6	7	8	10
South Asia	Thousands	(2.5)	..	..	..	1	1
Middle East	Thousands	(2.6)	..	..	..	..	..
Arrivals by mode of transport							
Air	Thousands	(3.1)	195	195	225	255	296
Rail	Thousands	(3.2)	..	..	..	..	..
Road	Thousands	(3.3)	..	..	..	..	..
Sea	Thousands	(3.4)	5	7	7	8	7
Arrivals by purpose of visit							
Leisure, recreation and holidays	Thousands	(4.1)	..	..	..	..	..
Business and professional	Thousands	(4.2)	..	..	..	..	..
Other	Thousands	(4.3)	..	..	..	..	..
Overnight stays and length of stay							
Overnight stays in H&S	Thousand nights	(5.1)	636	702	791	862	895
Overnight stays in CE	Thousand nights	(5.2)	866	918	1,017	1,102	1,147
ALS of non resident tourists	Nights	(5.5)	4.30	..	..	..	..
Tourism expenditure in the country of reference	US$ Million	(8.1)	176	173	207	221	227
DOMESTIC TOURISM							
Overnight stays							
Overnight stays in H&S	Thousand nights	(5.3)	260	290	309	321	291
Overnight stays in CE	Thousand nights	(5.4)	483	521	524	583	590
OUTBOUND TOURISM							
Departures	Thousands	(6.1)	190	203	227	257	283
Tourism expenditure in other countries	US$ Million	(8.2)	308	324	396	434	467
TOURISM ACTIVITIES							
Hotels and similar establishments							
Number of rooms	H&S	(7.1)	5,062	5,359	5,957	6,163	6,045
Number of bed-places	H&S	(7.2)	10,209	10,713	12,030	12,507	12,471
Occupancy rate	Percent	(7.3)	45.90	44.50	45.25	46.00	45.97
Average length of stay	Nights	(5.6)	..	..	..	..	2.00
ECONOMIC AGGREGATES							
Gross National Product (GNP)	US$ Million	(9.1)	7,165	7,552	7,736	8,197	8,736
Exports (F.O.B.)	US$ Million	(9.2)	1,638	1,852	2,050	2,005	1,891
Imports (C.I.F.)	US$ Million	(9.3)	2,031	1,992	2,489	2,503	2,591

Abbreviations used in tables and notes:
H&S: Hotels and similar establishments; **CE:** All types of tourism accommodation establishments; **ALS:** Average length of stay; **THS:** Non-resident tourists staying in H&S; **TCE:** Non-resident tourists staying in CE; **TF:** Arrivals of international (or non-resident) tourists; **VF:** Arrivals of international (or non-resident) visitors; **NHS:** Overnight stays at H&S; **NCE:** Overnight stays at CE.

..	data not available
incl	including
excl	excluding
nra	nationals residing abroad

INDIA

Basic Indicators	Units	Code	1996	1997	1998	1999	2000
INBOUND TOURISM							
Arrivals							
Visitors	Thousands	(1.1)	2,303	2,395	2,382	2,508	2,669
Tourists (overnight visitors)	Thousands	(1.2)	2,288	2,374	2,359	2,482	2,641
Same-day visitors	Thousands	(1.3)	..	..	..	..	..
Cruise passengers	Thousands	(1.4)	15	21	23	26	28
Arrivals by region							
Africa	Thousands	(2.1)	86	99	106	130	138
Americas	Thousands	(2.2)	322	340	349	373	448
Europe	Thousands	(2.3)	897	899	925	895	896
East Asia and the Pacific	Thousands	(2.4)	335	358	343	369	389
South Asia	Thousands	(2.5)	544	584	559	625	664
Middle East	Thousands	(2.6)	97	94	77	90	106
Arrivals by mode of transport							
Air	Thousands	(3.1)	1,996	2,048	2,041	2,089	2,214
Rail	Thousands	(3.2)	18	15	17	14	16
Road	Thousands	(3.3)	272	310	300	379	411
Sea	Thousands	(3.4)	2	1	1	..	..
Arrivals by purpose of visit							
Leisure, recreation and holidays	Thousands	(4.1)	1,699	1,753	1,811	1,859	1,973
Business and professional	Thousands	(4.2)	169	154	108	110	110
Other	Thousands	(4.3)	55	67	56	56	70
Overnight stays and length of stay							
Overnight stays in H&S	Thousand nights	(5.1)	..	..	..	..	..
Overnight stays in CE	Thousand nights	(5.2)	..	..	..	..	..
ALS of non resident tourists	Nights	(5.5)	29.80	30.80	31.20	..	..
Tourism expenditure in the country of reference	US$ Million	(8.1)	2,832	2,889	2,948	3,009	3,168
DOMESTIC TOURISM							
Overnight stays							
Overnight stays in H&S	Thousand nights	(5.3)	..	..	..	..	..
Overnight stays in CE	Thousand nights	(5.4)	..	..	..	..	..
OUTBOUND TOURISM							
Departures	Thousands	(6.1)	3,464	3,726	3,811	3,883	3,960
Tourism expenditure in other countries	US$ Million	(8.2)	913	1,341	1,712	2,010	2,567
TOURISM ACTIVITIES							
Hotels and similar establishments							
Number of rooms	H&S	(7.1)	61,974	64,573	66,522	72,114	..
Number of bed-places	H&S	(7.2)	123,948	129,146	133,044	144,228	..
Occupancy rate	Percent	(7.3)	71.10	62.90	59.40	50.40	..
Average length of stay	Nights	(5.6)	..	..	..	..	..
ECONOMIC AGGREGATES							
Gross National Product (GNP)	US$ Million	(9.1)	385,881	401,894	415,546	441,103	471,156
Exports (F.O.B.)	US$ Million	(9.2)	33,107	35,006	33,463	35,666	42,379
Imports (C.I.F.)	US$ Million	(9.3)	37,944	41,430	42,999	46,971	51,507

Abbreviations used in tables and notes:
H&S: Hotels and similar establishments; **CE:** All types of tourism accommodation establishments; **ALS:** Average length of stay; **THS:** Non-resident tourists staying in H&S; **TCE:** Non-resident tourists staying in CE; **TF:** Arrivals of international (or non-resident) tourists; **VF:** Arrivals of international (or non-resident) visitors; **NHS:** Overnight stays at H&S; **NCE:** Overnight stays at CE.

.. data not available
incl including
excl excluding
nra nationals residing abroad

Notes:
(1.2,2.1-4.3) TF, excl nra; (4.1-4.3) Excl arrivals of nationals of Pakistan and Bangladesh; (6.1) Departures of nationals only, irrespective of purpose; (7.1,7.2) In classified hotels; (7.3) Rooms.

89

INDONESIA

Basic Indicators	Units	Code	1996	1997	1998	1999	2000
INBOUND TOURISM							
Arrivals							
Visitors	Thousands	(1.1)	..	..	..	..	..
Tourists (overnight visitors)	Thousands	(1.2)	5,034	5,185	4,606	4,728	5,064
Same-day visitors	Thousands	(1.3)	..	..	..	..	..
Cruise passengers	Thousands	(1.4)	..	..	..	..	..
Arrivals by region							
Africa	Thousands	(2.1)	29	24	52	38	38
Americas	Thousands	(2.2)	244	209	201	187	232
Europe	Thousands	(2.3)	754	820	641	688	800
East Asia and the Pacific	Thousands	(2.4)	3,936	4,062	3,608	3,747	3,909
South Asia	Thousands	(2.5)	46	40	59	35	50
Middle East	Thousands	(2.6)	24	30	44	32	35
Arrivals by mode of transport							
Air	Thousands	(3.1)	3,210	3,138	2,346	2,449	2,760
Rail	Thousands	(3.2)	..	..	..	..	..
Road	Thousands	(3.3)	28	23	38	23	33
Sea	Thousands	(3.4)	1,796	2,024	2,223	2,256	2,271
Arrivals by purpose of visit							
Leisure, recreation and holidays	Thousands	(4.1)	2,759	2,684	2,395	2,763	2,837
Business and professional	Thousands	(4.2)	2,116	2,454	1,599	1,899	2,093
Other	Thousands	(4.3)	159	47	612	65	134
Overnight stays and length of stay							
Overnight stays in H&S	Thousand nights	(5.1)	51,397	54,702	42,287	46,520	..
Overnight stays in CE	Thousand nights	(5.2)	..	..	..	..	
ALS of non resident tourists	Nights	(5.5)	10.50	10.55	9.18	10.51	12.26
Tourism expenditure							
in the country of reference	US$ Million	(8.1)	6,307	5,321	4,331	4,710	5,749
DOMESTIC TOURISM							
Overnight stays							
Overnight stays in H&S	Thousand nights	(5.3)	..	..	..	..	..
Overnight stays in CE	Thousand nights	(5.4)	..	..	..	..	..
OUTBOUND TOURISM							
Departures	Thousands	(6.1)	2,076	..	..	..	..
Tourism expenditure in other countries	US$ Million	(8.2)	2,399	2,411	2,102	2,353	3,197
TOURISM ACTIVITIES							
Hotels and similar establishments							
Number of rooms	H&S	(7.1)	196,983	184,507	231,480	248,498	252,984
Number of bed-places	H&S	(7.2)	369,798	394,678	414,483	415,725	422,317
Occupancy rate	Percent	(7.3)	52.90	48.38	38.13	42.22	43.23
Average length of stay	Nights	(5.6)	2.73	2.80	2.62	2.36	2.25
ECONOMIC AGGREGATES							
Gross National Product (GNP)	US$ Million	(9.1)	218,216	222,547	135,080	120,698	119,871
Exports (F.O.B.)	US$ Million	(9.2)	49,814	53,443	48,847	48,665	62,124
Imports (C.I.F.)	US$ Million	(9.3)	42,929	41,694	27,337	24,004	33,515

Abbreviations used in tables and notes:
H&S: Hotels and similar establishments; **CE:** All types of tourism accommodation establishments; **ALS:** Average length of stay; **THS:** Non-resident tourists staying in H&S; **TCE:** Non-resident tourists staying in CE; **TF:** Arrivals of international (or non-resident) tourists; **VF:** Arrivals of international (or non-resident) visitors; **NHS:** Overnight stays at H&S; **NCE:** Overnight stays at CE.

..   data not available
incl   including
excl   excluding
nra   nationals residing abroad

Notes:
(5.5) Days; (5.6,7.3) Classified hotels only; (7.1,7.2) All forms of commercial accommodation; (7.3) Rooms; (8.2) International Monetary Fund.

Basic Indicators	Units	Code	1996	1997	1998	1999	2000
INBOUND TOURISM							
Arrivals							
Visitors	Thousands	(1.1)	693	860	1,124	..	..
Tourists (overnight visitors)	Thousands	(1.2)	567	740	1,008	1,321	..
Same-day visitors	Thousands	(1.3)	..	..	..	..	..
Cruise passengers	Thousands	(1.4)	..	..	..	..	..
Arrivals by region							
Africa	Thousands	(2.1)	2	3	3	3	..
Americas	Thousands	(2.2)	3	3	3	2	..
Europe	Thousands	(2.3)	261	449	631	735	..
East Asia and the Pacific	Thousands	(2.4)	17	11	18	21	..
South Asia	Thousands	(2.5)	209	194	256	299	..
Middle East	Thousands	(2.6)	75	80	97	113	..
Arrivals by mode of transport							
Air	Thousands	(3.1)	195	290	423	236	..
Rail	Thousands	(3.2)	..	..	..	..	..
Road	Thousands	(3.3)	359	444	578	1,075	..
Sea	Thousands	(3.4)	13	6	6	10	..
Arrivals by purpose of visit							
Leisure, recreation and holidays	Thousands	(4.1)	..	..	..	..	..
Business and professional	Thousands	(4.2)	..	..	..	..	..
Other	Thousands	(4.3)	..	..	..	..	..
Overnight stays and length of stay							
Overnight stays in H&S	Thousand nights	(5.1)	967	798	933	977	..
Overnight stays in CE	Thousand nights	(5.2)	..	..	..	..	..
ALS of non resident tourists	Nights	(5.5)	..	..	5.00	..	..
Tourism expenditure **in the country of reference**	US$ Million	(8.1)	244	327	477	662	..
DOMESTIC TOURISM							
Overnight stays							
Overnight stays in H&S	Thousand nights	(5.3)	8,289	7,065	8,266	..	..
Overnight stays in CE	Thousand nights	(5.4)	..	..	..	..	..
OUTBOUND TOURISM							
Departures	Thousands	(6.1)	1,218	1,354	1,450	..	..
Tourism expenditure in other countries	US$ Million	(8.2)	529	677	788	918	..
TOURISM ACTIVITIES							
Hotels and similar establishments							
Number of rooms	H&S	(7.1)	23,897	24,786	27,034	22,321	..
Number of bed-places	H&S	(7.2)	48,879	50,880	55,382	46,826	..
Occupancy rate	Percent	(7.3)	54.00	53.00	..	..	..
Average length of stay	Nights	(5.6)	2.50	..	3.00	..	..
ECONOMIC AGGREGATES							
Gross National Product (GNP)	US$ Million	(9.1)	90,249	101,485	102,052	100,720	104,572
Exports (F.O.B.)	US$ Million	(9.2)	22,391	..	..	..	..
Imports (C.I.F.)	US$ Million	(9.3)	16,274	..	..	..	..

Abbreviations used in tables and notes:
H&S: Hotels and similar establishments; **CE:** All types of tourism accommodation establishments; **ALS:** Average length of stay; **THS:** Non-resident tourists staying in H&S; **TCE:** Non-resident tourists staying in CE; **TF:** Arrivals of international (or non-resident) tourists; **VF:** Arrivals of international (or non-resident) visitors; **NHS:** Overnight stays at H&S; **NCE:** Overnight stays at CE.

..   data not available
incl   including
excl   excluding
nra   nationals residing abroad

Notes:
(1.2,2.1-3.4) TF; (3.3) Incl rail; (7.1,7.2) Hotels only, 21 March-20 March; (7.3) Est. (Bed-places).

IRAQ

Basic Indicators	Units	Code	1996	1997	1998	1999	2000
INBOUND TOURISM							
Arrivals							
Visitors	Thousands	(1.1)	51	15	45	30	78
Tourists (overnight visitors)	Thousands	(1.2)	..	..	..	..	..
Same-day visitors	Thousands	(1.3)	..	..	..	..	..
Cruise passengers	Thousands	(1.4)	..	..	..	..	..
Arrivals by region							
Africa	Thousands	(2.1)	1	..	..	..	
Americas	Thousands	(2.2)	1	..	..	..	
Europe	Thousands	(2.3)	3	1	1	1	1
East Asia and the Pacific	Thousands	(2.4)	2	..	..	..	..
South Asia	Thousands	(2.5)	9	10	40	28	76
Middle East	Thousands	(2.6)	35	3	3	1	..
Arrivals by mode of transport							
Air	Thousands	(3.1)	..	..	..	..	..
Rail	Thousands	(3.2)	..	..	..	..	..
Road	Thousands	(3.3)	..	..	..	..	..
Sea	Thousands	(3.4)	..	..	..	..	..
Arrivals by purpose of visit							
Leisure, recreation and holidays	Thousands	(4.1)	..	..	..	..	..
Business and professional	Thousands	(4.2)	..	..	..	..	..
Other	Thousands	(4.3)	..	..	..	..	..
Overnight stays and length of stay							
Overnight stays in H&S	Thousand nights	(5.1)	..	..	..	..	..
Overnight stays in CE	Thousand nights	(5.2)	..	..	..	..	..
ALS of non resident tourists	Nights	(5.5)	..	..	..	..	..
Tourism expenditure in the country of reference	US$ Million	(8.1)	..	..	..	..	..
DOMESTIC TOURISM							
Overnight stays							
Overnight stays in H&S	Thousand nights	(5.3)	..	..	..	..	..
Overnight stays in CE	Thousand nights	(5.4)	..	..	..	..	..
OUTBOUND TOURISM							
Departures	Thousands	(6.1)	..	..	..	..	..
Tourism expenditure in other countries	US$ Million	(8.2)	..	..	..	..	..
TOURISM ACTIVITIES							
Hotels and similar establishments							
Number of rooms	H&S	(7.1)	25,882	25,779	25,901	21,604	26,691
Number of bed-places	H&S	(7.2)	55,010	53,987	51,010	42,161	52,946
Occupancy rate	Percent	(7.3)	..	..	..	..	..
Average length of stay	Nights	(5.6)	..	..	..	..	..
ECONOMIC AGGREGATES							
Gross National Product (GNP)	US$ Million	(9.1)	..	..	..	..	..
Exports (F.O.B.)	US$ Million	(9.2)	..	..	..	..	..
Imports (C.I.F.)	US$ Million	(9.3)	..	..	..	..	..

Abbreviations used in tables and notes:
H&S: Hotels and similar establishments; **CE:** All types of tourism accommodation establishments; **ALS:** Average length of stay; **THS:** Non-resident tourists staying in H&S; **TCE:** Non-resident tourists staying in CE; **TF:** Arrivals of international (or non-resident) tourists; **VF:** Arrivals of international (or non-resident) visitors; **NHS:** Overnight stays at H&S; **NCE:** Overnight stays at CE.

..	data not available
incl	including
excl	excluding
nra	nationals residing abroad

Basic Indicators	Units	Code	1996	1997	1998	1999	2000
INBOUND TOURISM							
Arrivals							
Visitors	Thousands	(1.1)	..	..	..	..	..
Tourists (overnight visitors)	Thousands	(1.2)	5,289	5,587	6,064	6,403	6,749
Same-day visitors	Thousands	(1.3)	245	336	364	344	357
Cruise passengers	Thousands	(1.4)	..	..	..	..	..
Arrivals by region							
Africa	Thousands	(2.1)	19	21	23	24	27
Americas	Thousands	(2.2)	738	787	871	961	1,070
Europe	Thousands	(2.3)	4,374	4,598	4,984	5,211	5,428
East Asia and the Pacific	Thousands	(2.4)	157	180	184	205	223
South Asia	Thousands	(2.5)	..	..	..	..	..
Middle East	Thousands	(2.6)	..	..	..	..	..
Arrivals by mode of transport							
Air	Thousands	(3.1)	3,043	3,305	3,708	4,101	4,512
Rail	Thousands	(3.2)	..	..	..	..	..
Road	Thousands	(3.3)	795	780	696	697	671
Sea	Thousands	(3.4)	1,451	1,502	1,660	1,605	1,566
Arrivals by purpose of visit							
Leisure, recreation and holidays	Thousands	(4.1)	2,496	2,582	2,616	2,605	2,999
Business and professional	Thousands	(4.2)	1,213	1,304	1,604	1,740	1,776
Other	Thousands	(4.3)	1,580	1,701	1,844	2,058	1,974
Overnight stays and length of stay							
Overnight stays in H&S	Thousand nights	(5.1)	12,978	13,999	14,464	14,981	17,139
Overnight stays in CE	Thousand nights	(5.2)	16,440	18,022	18,326	18,861	21,720
ALS of non resident tourists	Nights	(5.5)	8.30	8.10	7.70	7.40	7.40
Tourism expenditure							
in the country of reference	US$ Million	(8.1)	3,022	3,189	3,267	3,392	3,387
DOMESTIC TOURISM							
Overnight stays							
Overnight stays in H&S	Thousand nights	(5.3)	5,647	5,583	6,667	6,938	6,786
Overnight stays in CE	Thousand nights	(5.4)	7,979	8,659	8,972	9,036	9,148
OUTBOUND TOURISM							
Departures	Thousands	(6.1)	2,733	3,053	3,330	3,576	3,814
Tourism expenditure in other countries	US$ Million	(8.2)	2,198	2,210	2,374	2,620	2,957
TOURISM ACTIVITIES							
Hotels and similar establishments							
Number of rooms	H&S	(7.1)	46,097	46,811	52,157	55,765	60,000
Number of bed-places	H&S	(7.2)	..	..	..	..	..
Occupancy rate	Percent	(7.3)	62.00	65.00	63.00	64.00	65.00
Average length of stay	Nights	(5.6)	..	..	..	..	..
ECONOMIC AGGREGATES							
Gross National Product (GNP)	US$ Million	(9.1)	65,612	72,607	76,006	80,485	87,108
Exports (F.O.B.)	US$ Million	(9.2)	48,670	53,515	64,574	70,552	76,873
Imports (C.I.F.)	US$ Million	(9.3)	35,895	39,231	44,620	46,535	50,553

Abbreviations used in tables and notes:
H&S: Hotels and similar establishments; **CE:** All types of tourism accommodation establishments; **ALS:** Average length of stay; **THS:** Non-resident tourists staying in H&S; **TCE:** Non-resident tourists staying in CE; **TF:** Arrivals of international (or non-resident) tourists; **VF:** Arrivals of international (or non-resident) visitors; **NHS:** Overnight stays at H&S; **NCE:** Overnight stays at CE.

.. data not available
incl including
excl excluding
nra nationals residing abroad

Notes:
(1.2,2.3,3.3,4.1,4.3,5.5) Incl tourists from North Ireland; (3.3) Incl rail; (5.1-5.4) Excl tourist from North Ireland; (6.1) Incl same-day visitors; (7.3) Rooms, hotels only; (8.2) Excl fare paid to national carriers.

ISRAEL

Basic Indicators	Units	Code	1996	1997	1998	1999	2000
INBOUND TOURISM							
Arrivals							
Visitors	Thousands	(1.1)	2,360	2,295	2,200	2,566	2,672
Tourists (overnight visitors)	Thousands	(1.2)	2,100	2,010	1,942	2,312	2,417
Same-day visitors	Thousands	(1.3)	..	..	..	..	..
Cruise passengers	Thousands	(1.4)	260	285	258	254	255
Arrivals by region							
Africa	Thousands	(2.1)	42	43	37	36	45
Americas	Thousands	(2.2)	559	548	571	645	684
Europe	Thousands	(2.3)	1,246	1,179	1,117	1,341	1,442
East Asia and the Pacific	Thousands	(2.4)	111	107	66	99	111
South Asia	Thousands	(2.5)	13	14	13	17	19
Middle East	Thousands	(2.6)	106	94	101	112	108
Arrivals by mode of transport							
Air	Thousands	(3.1)	1,612	1,561	1,553	1,827	1,955
Rail	Thousands	(3.2)	..	..	..	..	..
Road	Thousands	(3.3)	471	430	373	468	446
Sea	Thousands	(3.4)	17	19	16	18	16
Arrivals by purpose of visit							
Leisure, recreation and holidays	Thousands	(4.1)	798	704	761	948	943
Business and professional	Thousands	(4.2)	420	411	387	370	266
Other	Thousands	(4.3)	881	895	794	994	1,184
Overnight stays and length of stay							
Overnight stays in H&S	Thousand nights	(5.1)	9,180	8,396	8,865	9,047	9,676
Overnight stays in CE	Thousand nights	(5.2)	9,847	9,248	9,385	9,598	10,352
ALS of non resident tourists	Nights	(5.5)	15.60	15.40	16.20	15.00	15.00
Tourism expenditure							
in the country of reference	US$ Million	(8.1)	2,955	2,836	2,657	2,974	3,819
DOMESTIC TOURISM							
Overnight stays							
Overnight stays in H&S	Thousand nights	(5.3)	7,238	7,978	9,742	9,635	9,870
Overnight stays in CE	Thousand nights	(5.4)	7,465	9,536	11,817	11,990	12,104
OUTBOUND TOURISM							
Departures	Thousands	(6.1)	2,505	2,707	2,983	3,203	3,530
Tourism expenditure in other countries	US$ Million	(8.2)	2,278	2,283	2,376	2,566	2,804
TOURISM ACTIVITIES							
Hotels and similar establishments							
Number of rooms	H&S	(7.1)	37,030	38,270	40,268	43,111	45,594
Number of bed-places	H&S	(7.2)	81,173	85,598	89,946	115,655	106,782
Occupancy rate	Percent	(7.3)	58.20	54.30	58.80	61.80	60.00
Average length of stay	Nights	(5.6)	3.20	3.30	3.40	2.65	3.06
ECONOMIC AGGREGATES							
Gross National Product (GNP)	US$ Million	(9.1)	91,992	97,499	98,237	99,574	..
Exports (F.O.B.)	US$ Million	(9.2)	20,610	22,503	22,993	25,794	31,404
Imports (C.I.F.)	US$ Million	(9.3)	29,951	29,084	27,470	31,090	35,750

Abbreviations used in tables and notes:
H&S: Hotels and similar establishments; **CE:** All types of tourism accommodation establishments; **ALS:** Average length of stay; **THS:** Non-resident tourists staying in H&S; **TCE:** Non-resident tourists staying in CE; **TF:** Arrivals of international (or non-resident) tourists; **VF:** Arrivals of international (or non-resident) visitors; **NHS:** Overnight stays at H&S; **NCE:** Overnight stays at CE.

..   data not available
incl   including
excl   excluding
nra   nationals residing abroad

Notes:
(1.1) VF, excl nra; (1.2,2.1-2.6,3.1-3.4,4.1-4.3) TF, excl nra; (3.3) Incl tourists' reentry after a visit of up to 7 days in Sinai; (3.4) Incl US Navy personnel on courtesy visits; (4.3) Incl visit friends and relatives and pilgrimage; (5.1) Tourist hotels and aparthotels; (5.6) Inbound tourism in tourist hotels; (7.3) Bed-occupancy in H&S open.

ITALY

Basic Indicators	Units	Code	1996	1997	1998	1999	2000
INBOUND TOURISM							
Arrivals							
Visitors	Thousands	(1.1)	57,249	57,998	58,499	59,521	62,702
Tourists (overnight visitors)	Thousands	(1.2)	32,943	34,692	34,933	36,516	41,181
Same-day visitors	Thousands	(1.3)	24,306	23,306	23,567	23,005	21,522
Cruise passengers	Thousands	(1.4)	..	..	..	..	..
Arrivals by region							
Africa	Thousands	(2.1)	168	242	181	155	213
Americas	Thousands	(2.2)	2,034	2,646	2,475	2,004	2,292
Europe	Thousands	(2.3)	52,905	52,921	54,049	55,841	58,644
East Asia and the Pacific	Thousands	(2.4)	1,974	2,018	1,627	1,347	1,363
South Asia	Thousands	(2.5)	72	72	73	74	93
Middle East	Thousands	(2.6)	96	100	94	100	98
Arrivals by mode of transport							
Air	Thousands	(3.1)	8,415	8,984	9,200	9,507	10,773
Rail	Thousands	(3.2)	3,080	2,741	2,816	2,854	2,992
Road	Thousands	(3.3)	43,794	43,777	44,146	44,758	45,985
Sea	Thousands	(3.4)	1,961	2,497	2,338	2,403	2,952
Arrivals by purpose of visit							
Leisure, recreation and holidays	Thousands	(4.1)	50,255	49,514	49,577	51,280	52,961
Business and professional	Thousands	(4.2)	6,994	8,484	8,922	8,241	9,741
Other	Thousands	(4.3)	..	..	..	..	..
Overnight stays and length of stay							
Overnight stays in H&S	Thousand nights	(5.1)	87,905	85,377	87,192	90,236	97,221
Overnight stays in CE	Thousand nights	(5.2)	118,024	118,360	121,242	126,668	140,357
ALS of non resident tourists	Nights	(5.5)	..	..	..	..	..
Tourism expenditure in the country of reference	US$ Million	(8.1)	30,017	29,714	29,866	28,359	27,500
DOMESTIC TOURISM							
Overnight stays							
Overnight stays in H&S	Thousand nights	(5.3)	122,918	121,917	126,178	128,238	136,391
Overnight stays in CE	Thousand nights	(5.4)	173,347	173,917	178,266	181,647	198,528
OUTBOUND TOURISM							
Departures	Thousands	(6.1)	18,173	19,078	19,352	18,962	21,993
Tourism expenditure in other countries	US$ Million	(8.2)	15,805	16,631	17,653	16,913	15,693
TOURISM ACTIVITIES							
Hotels and similar establishments							
Number of rooms	H&S	(7.1)	947,429	948,656	949,805	955,757	966,138
Number of bed-places	H&S	(7.2)	1,764,651	1,772,096	1,782,382	1,807,275	1,854,101
Occupancy rate	Percent	(7.3)	..	..	40.40	41.70	42.70
Average length of stay	Nights	(5.6)	..	..	..	..	..
ECONOMIC AGGREGATES							
Gross National Product (GNP)	US$ Million	(9.1)	1,154,753	1,182,446	1,177,351	1,162,891	1,154,271
Exports (F.O.B.)	US$ Million	(9.2)	252,044	240,440	245,715	235,067	238,310
Imports (C.I.F.)	US$ Million	(9.3)	208,097	210,297	218,460	220,327	236,671

Abbreviations used in tables and notes:
H&S: Hotels and similar establishments; **CE:** All types of tourism accommodation establishments; **ALS:** Average length of stay; **THS:** Non-resident tourists staying in H&S; **TCE:** Non-resident tourists staying in CE; **TF:** Arrivals of international (or non-resident) tourists; **VF:** Arrivals of international (or non-resident) visitors; **NHS:** Overnight stays at H&S; **NCE:** Overnight stays at CE.

.. data not available
incl including
excl excluding
nra nationals residing abroad

Notes:
(1.1,2.1-3.4,4.1,4.2) VF, excluding seasonal and border workers; (1.1-4.2,6.1,8.1,8.2) From 1996: new collection system (border survey of the Ufficio Italiano dei Cambi); (1.2) TF, excluding seasonal and border workers; (1.3) Incl cruise passengers; (5.1) Hotels only; (6.1) Number of resident tourists (overnight visitors) abroad; (7.3) Bed-places.

JAMAICA

Basic Indicators	Units	Code	1996	1997	1998	1999	2000
INBOUND TOURISM							
Arrivals							
Visitors	Thousands	(1.1)	1,821	1,904	1,899	2,013	2,230
Tourists (overnight visitors)	Thousands	(1.2)	1,162	1,192	1,225	1,248	1,323
Same-day visitors	Thousands	(1.3)	..	..	..	..	..
Cruise passengers	Thousands	(1.4)	658	712	674	764	907
Arrivals by region							
Africa	Thousands	(2.1)	1	1	1	1	1
Americas	Thousands	(2.2)	926	959	995	1,024	1,109
Europe	Thousands	(2.3)	209	212	214	210	200
East Asia and the Pacific	Thousands	(2.4)	25	20	14	12	11
South Asia	Thousands	(2.5)	..	1	1	1	1
Middle East	Thousands	(2.6)	..	..	..	..	..
Arrivals by mode of transport							
Air	Thousands	(3.1)	1,162	1,192	1,225	1,248	1,323
Rail	Thousands	(3.2)	..	..	..	..	..
Road	Thousands	(3.3)	..	..	..	..	..
Sea	Thousands	(3.4)	..	..	..	..	..
Arrivals by purpose of visit							
Leisure, recreation and holidays	Thousands	(4.1)	930	927	939	969	1,033
Business and professional	Thousands	(4.2)	63	64	68	68	67
Other	Thousands	(4.3)	169	201	218	211	223
Overnight stays and length of stay							
Overnight stays in H&S	Thousand nights	(5.1)	5,698	5,763	5,959	5,903	6,066
Overnight stays in CE	Thousand nights	(5.2)	11,745	11,882	12,232	11,823	12,338
ALS of non resident tourists	Nights	(5.5)	11.10	10.80	10.90	10.30	10.10
Tourism expenditure in the country of reference	US$ Million	(8.1)	1,092	1,131	1,197	1,279	1,333
DOMESTIC TOURISM							
Overnight stays							
Overnight stays in H&S	Thousand nights	(5.3)	..	..	..	..	..
Overnight stays in CE	Thousand nights	(5.4)	..	..	..	..	..
OUTBOUND TOURISM							
Departures	Thousands	(6.1)	..	..	..	..	..
Tourism expenditure in other countries	US$ Million	(8.2)	157	181	198	227	209
TOURISM ACTIVITIES							
Hotels and similar establishments							
Number of rooms	H&S	(7.1)	18,686	19,359	18,947	19,307	19,908
Number of bed-places	H&S	(7.2)	39,060	40,437	39,448	40,080	41,473
Occupancy rate	Percent	(7.3)	57.70	55.70	58.70	57.00	58.50
Average length of stay	Nights	(5.6)	7.10	7.10	7.00	6.90	6.60
ECONOMIC AGGREGATES							
Gross National Product (GNP)	US$ Million	(9.1)	4,367	4,729	5,246	6,228	6,382
Exports (F.O.B.)	US$ Million	(9.2)	1,382	1,382	1,312	1,241	1,296
Imports (C.I.F.)	US$ Million	(9.3)	2,965	3,128	3,033	2,899	3,217

Abbreviations used in tables and notes:
H&S: Hotels and similar establishments; **CE:** All types of tourism accommodation establishments; **ALS:** Average length of stay; **THS:** Non-resident tourists staying in H&S; **TCE:** Non-resident tourists staying in CE; **TF:** Arrivals of international (or non-resident) tourists; **VF:** Arrivals of international (or non-resident) visitors; **NHS:** Overnight stays at H&S; **NCE:** Overnight stays at CE.

..	data not available
incl	including
excl	excluding
nra	nationals residing abroad

Notes:
(1.2,2.1-2.4,3.1,4.1-4.3) TF, air arrivals, incl nra, E/D cards; (5.2) Data obtained by multiplying ALS by number of stopovers of each country of origin; (5.5) Intended length of stay; (5.6) Hotel nights only; (7.3) Rooms; (8.2) International Monetary Fund.

Basic Indicators	Units	Code	1996	1997	1998	1999	2000
INBOUND TOURISM							
Arrivals							
Visitors	Thousands	(1.1)	..	..	..	..	..
Tourists (overnight visitors)	Thousands	(1.2)	3,837	4,218	4,106	4,438	4,757
Same-day visitors	Thousands	(1.3)	..	..	..	..	..
Cruise passengers	Thousands	(1.4)	..	..	..	..	..
Arrivals by region							
Africa	Thousands	(2.1)	11	12	13	13	15
Americas	Thousands	(2.2)	749	781	828	853	899
Europe	Thousands	(2.3)	484	546	577	580	625
East Asia and the Pacific	Thousands	(2.4)	2,540	2,817	2,622	2,925	3,149
South Asia	Thousands	(2.5)	47	56	58	60	64
Middle East	Thousands	(2.6)	3	3	3	3	3
Arrivals by mode of transport							
Air	Thousands	(3.1)	4,143	4,530	4,464	4,717	5,072
Rail	Thousands	(3.2)	..	..	..	..	..
Road	Thousands	(3.3)	..	..	..	..	..
Sea	Thousands	(3.4)	102	140	93	185	200
Arrivals by purpose of visit							
Leisure, recreation and holidays	Thousands	(4.1)	2,114	2,392	2,358	2,560	2,693
Business and professional	Thousands	(4.2)	1,126	1,202	1,105	1,187	1,293
Other	Thousands	(4.3)	597	624	643	690	771
Overnight stays and length of stay							
Overnight stays in H&S	Thousand nights	(5.1)	..	..	..	..	..
Overnight stays in CE	Thousand nights	(5.2)	..	..	..	..	..
ALS of non resident tourists	Nights	(5.5)	8.40	8.60	8.80	8.00	8.00
Tourism expenditure							
in the country of reference	US$ Million	(8.1)	4,078	4,326	3,742	3,428	3,373
DOMESTIC TOURISM							
Overnight stays							
Overnight stays in H&S	Thousand nights	(5.3)	329,000	349,000	345,000	333,000	313,000
Overnight stays in CE	Thousand nights	(5.4)	..	..	..	..	..
OUTBOUND TOURISM							
Departures	Thousands	(6.1)	16,695	16,803	15,806	16,358	17,819
Tourism expenditure in other countries	US$ Million	(8.2)	37,040	33,041	28,815	32,808	31,886
TOURISM ACTIVITIES							
Hotels and similar establishments							
Number of rooms	H&S	(7.1)	1,558,772	1,564,792	1,569,875	1,580,226	..
Number of bed-places	H&S	(7.2)	..	..	..	..	..
Occupancy rate	Percent	(7.3)	70.40	70.30	68.60	68.20	69.20
Average length of stay	Nights	(5.6)	..	..	..	..	..
ECONOMIC AGGREGATES							
Gross National Product (GNP)	US$ Million	(9.1)	5,190,927	4,836,057	4,114,485	4,054,475	4,337,268
Exports (F.O.B.)	US$ Million	(9.2)	410,926	421,050	388,135	417,659	479,227
Imports (C.I.F.)	US$ Million	(9.3)	349,174	338,830	280,631	310,039	379,491

Abbreviations used in tables and notes:
H&S: Hotels and similar establishments; **CE:** All types of tourism accommodation establishments; **ALS:** Average length of stay; **THS:** Non-resident tourists staying in H&S; **TCE:** Non-resident tourists staying in GE; **TF:** Arrivals of international (or non-resident) tourists; **VF:** Arrivals of international (or non-resident) visitors; **NHS:** Overnight stays at H&S; **NCE:** Overnight stays at CE.

..	data not available
incl	including
excl	excluding
nra	nationals residing abroad

Notes:
(1.2,2.1-2.6,4.1-4.3) TF, excl nra; (3.1,3.4) VF, incl foreign residents in Japan; (5.5) Days; (7.1) Government registered and unregistered hotels and "ryokans" (inns); (7.3) Occupancy rate of major government registered hotels (rooms).

JORDAN

Basic Indicators	Units	Code	1996	1997	1998	1999	2000
INBOUND TOURISM							
Arrivals							
Visitors	Thousands	(1.1)	3,164	3,068	3,303	3,315	3,019
Tourists (overnight visitors)	Thousands	(1.2)	1,103	1,127	1,256	1,358	1,427
Same-day visitors	Thousands	(1.3)	..	..	..	..	..
Cruise passengers	Thousands	(1.4)	16	15	12	10	10
Arrivals by region							
Africa	Thousands	(2.1)	55	41	42	44	33
Americas	Thousands	(2.2)	108	108	109	124	126
Europe	Thousands	(2.3)	473	456	430	496	523
East Asia and the Pacific	Thousands	(2.4)	60	61	48	64	71
South Asia	Thousands	(2.5)	48	43	54	50	42
Middle East	Thousands	(2.6)	2,415	2,355	2,614	2,531	2,216
Arrivals by mode of transport							
Air	Thousands	(3.1)	319	316	357	436	492
Rail	Thousands	(3.2)	1	..	..	1	1
Road	Thousands	(3.3)	2,313	2,358	2,644	2,660	2,350
Sea	Thousands	(3.4)	531	394	302	217	176
Arrivals by purpose of visit							
Leisure, recreation and holidays	Thousands	(4.1)	..	..	..	..	..
Business and professional	Thousands	(4.2)	..	..	..	..	..
Other	Thousands	(4.3)	..	..	..	..	..
Overnight stays and length of stay							
Overnight stays in H&S	Thousand nights	(5.1)	2,836	2,720	2,682	3,154	3,291
Overnight stays in CE	Thousand nights	(5.2)	..	..	..	..	..
ALS of non resident tourists	Nights	(5.5)	3.58	3.88	4.14	4.24	4.27
Tourism expenditure in the country of reference	US$ Million	(8.1)	743	774	773	795	722
DOMESTIC TOURISM							
Overnight stays							
Overnight stays in H&S	Thousand nights	(5.3)	519	529	498	577	541
Overnight stays in CE	Thousand nights	(5.4)	..	..	..	..	..
OUTBOUND TOURISM							
Departures	Thousands	(6.1)	1,141	1,233	1,347	1,561	1,625
Tourism expenditure in other countries	US$ Million	(8.2)	381	398	353	355	387
TOURISM ACTIVITIES							
Hotels and similar establishments							
Number of rooms	H&S	(7.1)	11,493	12,109	13,704	16,181	17,485
Number of bed-places	H&S	(7.2)	22,735	23,777	27,050	31,765	34,433
Occupancy rate	Percent	(7.3)	46.80	43.63	37.65	34.90	39.47
Average length of stay	Nights	(5.6)	..	..	..	..	..
ECONOMIC AGGREGATES							
Gross National Product (GNP)	US$ Million	(9.1)	6,991	7,201	7,499	7,720	8,224
Exports (F.O.B.)	US$ Million	(9.2)	1,817	1,836	1,802	1,832	1,897
Imports (C.I.F.)	US$ Million	(9.3)	4,293	4,102	3,828	3,717	4,539

Abbreviations used in tables and notes:
H&S: Hotels and similar establishments; **CE:** All types of tourism accommodation establishments; **ALS:** Average length of stay; **THS:** Non-resident tourists staying in H&S; **TCE:** Non-resident tourists staying in CE; **TF:** Arrivals of international (or non-resident) tourists; **VF:** Arrivals of international (or non-resident) visitors; **NHS:** Overnight stays at H&S; **NCE:** Overnight stays at CE.

.. data not available
incl including
excl excluding
nra nationals residing abroad

Notes:
(1.1,2.1-3.4) VF; (5.5) For organized tours only; (7.3) Rooms; (8.2) Incl education payments; (9.1) For the East Bank only.

KAZAKHSTAN

Basic Indicators	Units	Code	1996	1997	1998	1999	2000
INBOUND TOURISM							
Arrivals							
Visitors	Thousands	(1.1)	202	284	257	394	1,683
Tourists (overnight visitors)	Thousands	(1.2)	..	..	..	..	1,471
Same-day visitors	Thousands	(1.3)	..	..	..	..	212
Cruise passengers	Thousands	(1.4)	..	..	..	..	..
Arrivals by region							
Africa	Thousands	(2.1)	..	..	..	..	..
Americas	Thousands	(2.2)	..	..	..	..	18
Europe	Thousands	(2.3)	..	..	..	..	1,584
East Asia and the Pacific	Thousands	(2.4)	..	..	..	..	69
South Asia	Thousands	(2.5)	..	..	..	..	9
Middle East	Thousands	(2.6)	..	..	..	..	2
Arrivals by mode of transport							
Air	Thousands	(3.1)	..	..	..	..	..
Rail	Thousands	(3.2)	..	..	..	..	..
Road	Thousands	(3.3)	..	..	..	..	..
Sea	Thousands	(3.4)	..	..	..	..	..
Arrivals by purpose of visit							
Leisure, recreation and holidays	Thousands	(4.1)	..	..	..	..	..
Business and professional	Thousands	(4.2)	..	..	..	..	..
Other	Thousands	(4.3)	..	..	..	..	..
Overnight stays and length of stay							
Overnight stays in H&S	Thousand nights	(5.1)	..	..	..	..	281
Overnight stays in CE	Thousand nights	(5.2)	..	..	..	..	..
ALS of non resident tourists	Nights	(5.5)	..	..	..	..	..
Tourism expenditure in the country of reference	US$ Million	(8.1)	199	289	407	363	356
DOMESTIC TOURISM							
Overnight stays							
Overnight stays in H&S	Thousand nights	(5.3)	..	..	..	..	844
Overnight stays in CE	Thousand nights	(5.4)	..	..	..	..	..
OUTBOUND TOURISM							
Departures	Thousands	(6.1)	523	419	502	398	1,247
Tourism expenditure in other countries	US$ Million	(8.2)	319	445	498	394	408
TOURISM ACTIVITIES							
Hotels and similar establishments							
Number of rooms	H&S	(7.1)	2,298	2,298	1,724	2,996	9,124
Number of bed-places	H&S	(7.2)	5,088	5,088	3,896	6,092	..
Occupancy rate	Percent	(7.3)	..	..	..	..	..
Average length of stay	Nights	(5.6)	..	..	..	..	..
ECONOMIC AGGREGATES							
Gross National Product (GNP)	US$ Million	(9.1)	20,169	21,207	20,894	19,322	17,640
Exports (F.O.B.)	US$ Million	(9.2)	5,911	6,497	5,436	5,598	9,140
Imports (C.I.F.)	US$ Million	(9.3)	4,241	4,301	4,350	3,687	5,052

Abbreviations used in tables and notes:
H&S: Hotels and similar establishments; **CE:** All types of tourism accommodation establishments; **ALS:** Average length of stay; **THS:** Non-resident tourists staying in H&S; **TCE:** Non-resident tourists staying in CE; **TF:** Arrivals of international (or non-resident) tourists; **VF:** Arrivals of international (or non-resident) visitors; **NHS:** Overnight stays at H&S; **NCE:** Overnight stays at CE.

..   data not available
incl   including
excl   excluding
nra   nationals residing abroad

Notes:
(2.2-2.6) VF; (8.1,8.2) International Monetary Fund.

KENYA

Basic Indicators	Units	Code	1996	1997	1998	1999	2000
INBOUND TOURISM							
Arrivals							
Visitors	Thousands	(1.1)	1,003	1,001	894	969	1,037
Tourists (overnight visitors)	Thousands	(1.2)	925	907	857	862	899
Same-day visitors	Thousands	(1.3)	56	72	37	107	138
Cruise passengers	Thousands	(1.4)	..	..	..	..	..
Arrivals by region							
Africa	Thousands	(2.1)	216	273	251	264	282
Americas	Thousands	(2.2)	60	85	80	82	88
Europe	Thousands	(2.3)	486	574	504	556	595
East Asia and the Pacific	Thousands	(2.4)	36	44	38	43	46
South Asia	Thousands	(2.5)	12	24	21	23	25
Middle East	Thousands	(2.6)	..	..	..	..	..
Arrivals by mode of transport							
Air	Thousands	(3.1)	..	..	..	..	..
Rail	Thousands	(3.2)	..	..	..	..	..
Road	Thousands	(3.3)	..	..	..	..	..
Sea	Thousands	(3.4)	..	..	..	..	..
Arrivals by purpose of visit							
Leisure, recreation and holidays	Thousands	(4.1)	821	805	687	747	778
Business and professional	Thousands	(4.2)	104	102	87	94	98
Other	Thousands	(4.3)	78	94	120	128	160
Overnight stays and length of stay							
Overnight stays in H&S	Thousand nights	(5.1)	4,279	4,133	2,116	2,241	2,823
Overnight stays in CE	Thousand nights	(5.2)	..	..	..	..	..
ALS of non resident tourists	Nights	(5.5)	..	..	..	..	..
Tourism expenditure							
in the country of reference	US$ Million	(8.1)	448	385	290	304	257
DOMESTIC TOURISM							
Overnight stays							
Overnight stays in H&S	Thousand nights	(5.3)	783	777	697	654	794
Overnight stays in CE	Thousand nights	(5.4)	..	..	..	..	..
OUTBOUND TOURISM							
Departures	Thousands	(6.1)	..	..	..	..	..
Tourism expenditure in other countries	US$ Million	(8.2)	167	194	190	115	132
TOURISM ACTIVITIES							
Hotels and similar establishments							
Number of rooms	H&S	(7.1)	..	..	..	..	..
Number of bed-places	H&S	(7.2)	31,108	26,072	21,850	..	..
Occupancy rate	Percent	(7.3)	44.60	51.60	35.30	33.90	39.30
Average length of stay	Nights	(5.6)	14.20	11.80	9.80	9.40	8.70
ECONOMIC AGGREGATES							
Gross National Product (GNP)	US$ Million	(9.1)	8,790	9,739	10,169	10,695	10,715
Exports (F.O.B.)	US$ Million	(9.2)	2,068	2,054	2,007	1,747	1,734
Imports (C.I.F.)	US$ Million	(9.3)	2,949	3,296	3,195	2,833	3,105

Abbreviations used in tables and notes:
H&S: Hotels and similar establishments; **CE:** All types of tourism accommodation establishments; **ALS:** Average length of stay; **THS:** Non-resident tourists staying in H&S; **TCE:** Non-resident tourists staying in CE; **TF:** Arrivals of international (or non-resident) tourists; **VF:** Arrivals of international (or non-resident) visitors; **NHS:** Overnight stays at H&S; **NCE:** Overnight stays at CE.

..   data not available
incl   including
excl   excluding
nra   nationals residing abroad

Notes:
(1.1-4.3) VF, excl nra, arrivals from all border entry points; (1.1,2.1-2.5) Data are estimates, projected using 1989 market shares; (2.5) India only; (5.6) Days; (7.2) Hotels only (excl unclassified hotels); (7.3) Bed-places; (8.1,8.2) International Monetary Fund.
Source: Economic survey various years.

Basic Indicators	Units	Code	1996	1997	1998	1999	2000
INBOUND TOURISM							
Arrivals							
Visitors	Thousands	(1.1)	4.2	5.1	5.7	4.9	4.0
Tourists (overnight visitors)	Thousands	(1.2)	3.4	5.0	2.0	1.0	..
Same-day visitors	Thousands	(1.3)	..	..	..	..	..
Cruise passengers	Thousands	(1.4)	..	..	..	..	..
Arrivals by region							
Africa	Thousands	(2.1)	..	..	..	..	..
Americas	Thousands	(2.2)	0.3	1.2	..	..	..
Europe	Thousands	(2.3)	0.2	0.3	..	..	..
East Asia and the Pacific	Thousands	(2.4)	2.5	3.3	..	..	..
South Asia	Thousands	(2.5)	..	..	..	..	..
Middle East	Thousands	(2.6)	..	..	..	..	..
Arrivals by mode of transport							
Air	Thousands	(3.1)	3.4	5.0	2.0	1.0	..
Rail	Thousands	(3.2)	..	..	..	..	..
Road	Thousands	(3.3)	..	..	..	..	..
Sea	Thousands	(3.4)	..	..	..	..	..
Arrivals by purpose of visit							
Leisure, recreation and holidays	Thousands	(4.1)	1.3	1.8	..	..	..
Business and professional	Thousands	(4.2)	1.1	1.6	..	..	..
Other	Thousands	(4.3)	1.0	1.6	..	..	..
Overnight stays and length of stay							
Overnight stays in H&S	Thousand nights	(5.1)	..	..	..	..	..
Overnight stays in CE	Thousand nights	(5.2)	..	..	..	..	..
ALS of non resident tourists	Nights	(5.5)	..	..	..	..	..
Tourism expenditure **in the country of reference**	US$ Million	(8.1)	2.0	2.4	2.9	2.5	2.1
DOMESTIC TOURISM							
Overnight stays							
Overnight stays in H&S	Thousand nights	(5.3)	..	..	..	..	..
Overnight stays in CE	Thousand nights	(5.4)	..	..	..	..	..
OUTBOUND TOURISM							
Departures	Thousands	(6.1)	..	..	..		
Tourism expenditure in other countries	US$ Million	(8.2)	4	..	2	2	..
TOURISM ACTIVITIES							
Hotels and similar establishments							
Number of rooms	H&S	(7.1)	404	414	436	..	..
Number of bed-places	H&S	(7.2)	..	..	..	..	..
Occupancy rate	Percent	(7.3)	..	..	..	..	..
Average length of stay	Nights	(5.6)	21.00	21.00	18.00	..	..
ECONOMIC AGGREGATES							
Gross National Product (GNP)	US$ Million	(9.1)	72	94	99	88	86
Exports (F.O.B.)	US$ Million	(9.2)	6	8	7	..	..
Imports (C.I.F.)	US$ Million	(9.3)	38	39	33	..	..

Abbreviations used in tables and notes:
H&S: Hotels and similar establishments; **CE:** All types of tourism accommodation establishments; **ALS:** Average length of stay; **THS:** Non-resident tourists staying in H&S; **TCE:** Non-resident tourists staying in CE; **TF:** Arrivals of international (or non-resident) tourists; **VF:** Arrivals of international (or non-resident) visitors; **NHS:** Overnight stays at H&S; **NCE:** Overnight stays at CE.

..   data not available
incl   including
excl   excluding
nra   nationals residing abroad

Notes:
(1.2) Air arrivals, Tarawa and Christmas Island; (4.1-4.3) TF.

KOREA, REPUBLIC OF

Basic Indicators	Units	Code	1996	1997	1998	1999	2000
INBOUND TOURISM							
Arrivals							
Visitors	Thousands	(1.1)	3,684	3,908	4,250	4,660	5,322
Tourists (overnight visitors)	Thousands	(1.2)	..	..	..	..	..
Same-day visitors	Thousands	(1.3)	..	..	..	..	..
Cruise passengers	Thousands	(1.4)	..	..	..	..	..
Arrivals by region							
Africa	Thousands	(2.1)	9	11	11	14	14
Americas	Thousands	(2.2)	465	494	471	464	535
Europe	Thousands	(2.3)	445	436	401	408	479
East Asia and the Pacific	Thousands	(2.4)	2,382	2,582	2,977	3,381	3,917
South Asia	Thousands	(2.5)	74	71	66	81	96
Middle East	Thousands	(2.6)	7	7	9	11	4
Arrivals by mode of transport							
Air	Thousands	(3.1)	2,656	2,848	3,275	3,646	4,054
Rail	Thousands	(3.2)	..	..	..	..	..
Road	Thousands	(3.3)	..	..	..	..	..
Sea	Thousands	(3.4)	223	239	228	271	314
Arrivals by purpose of visit							
Leisure, recreation and holidays	Thousands	(4.1)	2,373	2,580	3,065	3,454	3,874
Business and professional	Thousands	(4.2)	219	212	182	187	203
Other	Thousands	(4.3)	1,092	1,116	1,003	1,019	1,244
Overnight stays and length of stay							
Overnight stays in H&S	Thousand nights	(5.1)	7,813	..	..	..	..
Overnight stays in CE	Thousand nights	(5.2)	7,951	7,749	..	..	..
ALS of non resident tourists	Nights	(5.5)	5.70	5.50	4.90	4.70	4.90
Tourism expenditure in the country of reference	US$ Million	(8.1)	5,430	5,116	6,865	6,802	6,811
DOMESTIC TOURISM							
Overnight stays							
Overnight stays in H&S	Thousand nights	(5.3)	..	..	..	..	..
Overnight stays in CE	Thousand nights	(5.4)	11,748	..	..	..	..
OUTBOUND TOURISM							
Departures	Thousands	(6.1)	4,649	4,542	3,067	4,342	5,508
Tourism expenditure in other countries	US$ Million	(8.2)	6,963	6,262	2,640	3,975	6,174
TOURISM ACTIVITIES							
Hotels and similar establishments							
Number of rooms	H&S	(7.1)	45,108	46,585	46,998	47,536	51,189
Number of bed-places	H&S	(7.2)	..	..	..	..	..
Occupancy rate	Percent	(7.3)	65.80	62.70	58.10	61.80	65.10
Average length of stay	Nights	(5.6)	..	..	..	..	..
ECONOMIC AGGREGATES							
Gross National Product (GNP)	US$ Million	(9.1)	517,577	523,725	394,540	397,554	421,091
Exports (F.O.B.)	US$ Million	(9.2)	129,715	136,164	132,313	143,686	172,268
Imports (C.I.F.)	US$ Million	(9.3)	150,339	144,616	93,282	119,752	160,481

Abbreviations used in tables and notes:
H&S: Hotels and similar establishments; **CE:** All types of tourism accommodation establishments; **ALS:** Average length of stay; **THS:** Non-resident tourists staying in H&S; **TCE:** Non-resident tourists staying in CE; **TF:** Arrivals of international (or non-resident) tourists; **VF:** Arrivals of international (or non-resident) visitors; **NHS:** Overnight stays at H&S; **NCE:** Overnight stays at CE.

..   data not available
incl   including
excl   excluding
nra   nationals residing abroad

Notes:
(1.1) Incl nra and from June 1988, also crew members; (2.1-2.6) Excl nra; (3.1,3.4) Excl overseas Koreans and crew members; (7.1) Hotels only; (7.3) Rooms; (8.1,8.2) Excl expenses of students studying overseas.

Basic Indicators	Units	Code	1996	1997	1998	1999	2000
INBOUND TOURISM							
Arrivals							
Visitors	Thousands	(1.1)	1,565	1,638	1,763	1,884	1,944
Tourists (overnight visitors)	Thousands	(1.2)	72	76	77	..	79
Same-day visitors	Thousands	(1.3)	..	..	..	..	..
Cruise passengers	Thousands	(1.4)	..	..	..	..	..
Arrivals by region							
Africa	Thousands	(2.1)	11	14	19	18	17
Americas	Thousands	(2.2)	26	32	33	39	39
Europe	Thousands	(2.3)	58	66	66	74	71
East Asia and the Pacific	Thousands	(2.4)	57	55	66	82	95
South Asia	Thousands	(2.5)	459	471	513	537	518
Middle East	Thousands	(2.6)	930	983	1,046	1,118	1,191
Arrivals by mode of transport							
Air	Thousands	(3.1)	859	878	903	961	929
Rail	Thousands	(3.2)	..	..	..	..	..
Road	Thousands	(3.3)	672	731	819	866	953
Sea	Thousands	(3.4)	34	28	41	57	62
Arrivals by purpose of visit							
Leisure, recreation and holidays	Thousands	(4.1)	..	..	..	..	0.4
Business and professional	Thousands	(4.2)	..	..	..	..	36.6
Other	Thousands	(4.3)	..	..	..	..	41.9
Overnight stays and length of stay							
Overnight stays in H&S	Thousand nights	(5.1)	252	266	..	271	246
Overnight stays in CE	Thousand nights	(5.2)	..	..	..	..	..
ALS of non resident tourists	Nights	(5.5)	..	..	..	..	..
Tourism expenditure in the country of reference	US$ Million	(8.1)	184	188	207	92	98
DOMESTIC TOURISM							
Overnight stays							
Overnight stays in H&S	Thousand nights	(5.3)	..	..	..	..	..
Overnight stays in CE	Thousand nights	(5.4)	..	..	..	..	..
OUTBOUND TOURISM							
Departures	Thousands	(6.1)	..	..	..	..	..
Tourism expenditure in other countries	US$ Million	(8.2)	2,492	2,377	2,517	2,270	2,451
TOURISM ACTIVITIES							
Hotels and similar establishments							
Number of rooms	H&S	(7.1)	2,407	2,823	2,224	2,322	1,988
Number of bed-places	H&S	(7.2)	3,482	3,331	3,287	3,222	2,857
Occupancy rate	Percent	(7.3)	..	..	..	..	..
Average length of stay	Nights	(5.6)	..	..	..	..	..
ECONOMIC AGGREGATES							
Gross National Product (GNP)	US$ Million	(9.1)	32,270	..	..	..	..
Exports (F.O.B.)	US$ Million	(9.2)	14,889	14,225	9,553	12,218	18,156
Imports (C.I.F.)	US$ Million	(9.3)	8,373	8,246	8,617	7,617	..

Abbreviations used in tables and notes:
H&S: Hotels and similar establishments; **CE:** All types of tourism accommodation establishments; **ALS:** Average length of stay; **THS:** Non-resident tourists staying in H&S; **TCE:** Non-resident tourists staying in CE; **TF:** Arrivals of international (or non-resident) tourists; **VF:** Arrivals of international (or non-resident) visitors; **NHS:** Overnight stays at H&S; **NCE:** Overnight stays at CE.

.. data not available
incl including
excl excluding
nra nationals residing abroad

Notes:
(1.1,2.1-2.6,3.1-3.4) VF; (1.2,4.1-4.3) THS; (8.1,8.2) International Monetary Fund.

KYRGYZSTAN

Basic Indicators	Units	Code	1996	1997	1998	1999	2000
INBOUND TOURISM							
Arrivals							
Visitors	Thousands	(1.1)	..	..	..	..	..
Tourists (overnight visitors)	Thousands	(1.2)	42	87	59	69	..
Same-day visitors	Thousands	(1.3)	..	..	..	..	..
Cruise passengers	Thousands	(1.4)	..	..	..	..	..
Arrivals by region							
Africa	Thousands	(2.1)	..	..	..	..	..
Americas	Thousands	(2.2)	..	..	1	3	..
Europe	Thousands	(2.3)	..	..	46	50	..
East Asia and the Pacific	Thousands	(2.4)	..	..	7	9	..
South Asia	Thousands	(2.5)	..	..	3	3	..
Middle East	Thousands	(2.6)	..	..	..	..	..
Arrivals by mode of transport							
Air	Thousands	(3.1)	..	..	59	..	..
Rail	Thousands	(3.2)	..	..	..	..	..
Road	Thousands	(3.3)	..	..	..	..	..
Sea	Thousands	(3.4)	..	..	..	..	..
Arrivals by purpose of visit							
Leisure, recreation and holidays	Thousands	(4.1)	..	..	8	..	..
Business and professional	Thousands	(4.2)	..	..	50	..	..
Other	Thousands	(4.3)	..	..	1	..	..
Overnight stays and length of stay							
Overnight stays in H&S	Thousand nights	(5.1)	..	..	..	..	..
Overnight stays in CE	Thousand nights	(5.2)	..	..	..	..	..
ALS of non resident tourists	Nights	(5.5)	..	..	..	..	..
Tourism expenditure in the country of reference	US$ Million	(8.1)	4	7	8	14	15
DOMESTIC TOURISM							
Overnight stays							
Overnight stays in H&S	Thousand nights	(5.3)	..	..	..	..	..
Overnight stays in CE	Thousand nights	(5.4)	..	..	..	..	..
OUTBOUND TOURISM							
Departures	Thousands	(6.1)	..	..	32	..	..
Tourism expenditure in other countries	US$ Million	(8.2)	6	4	3	11	16
TOURISM ACTIVITIES							
Hotels and similar establishments							
Number of rooms	H&S	(7.1)	..	..	..	..	..
Number of bed-places	H&S	(7.2)	..	..	..	..	..
Occupancy rate	Percent	(7.3)	..	..	..	..	..
Average length of stay	Nights	(5.6)	..	..	..	..	..
ECONOMIC AGGREGATES							
Gross National Product (GNP)	US$ Million	(9.1)	2,648	2,205	1,695	1,444	1,330
Exports (F.O.B.)	US$ Million	(9.2)	505	604	514	454	..
Imports (C.I.F.)	US$ Million	(9.3)	838	709	842	600	..

Abbreviations used in tables and notes:
H&S: Hotels and similar establishments; **CE:** All types of tourism accommodation establishments; **ALS:** Average length of stay; **THS:** Non-resident tourists staying in H&S; **TCE:** Non-resident tourists staying in CE; **TF:** Arrivals of international (or non-resident) tourists; **VF:** Arrivals of international (or non-resident) visitors; **NHS:** Overnight stays at H&S; **NCE:** Overnight stays at CE.

..   data not available
incl   including
excl   excluding
nra   nationals residing abroad

Notes:
(8.1, 8.2) International Monetary Fund.

LAO PEOPLE´S DEMOCRATIC REPUBLIC

Basic Indicators	Units	Code	1996	1997	1998	1999	2000
INBOUND TOURISM							
Arrivals							
Visitors	Thousands	(1.1)	403	463	500	614	737
Tourists (overnight visitors)	Thousands	(1.2)	93	193	200	259	191
Same-day visitors	Thousands	(1.3)	310	270	300	355	546
Cruise passengers	Thousands	(1.4)	..	..	..	..	..
Arrivals by region							
Africa	Thousands	(2.1)	..	..	..	..	..
Americas	Thousands	(2.2)	14	18	25	32	42
Europe	Thousands	(2.3)	31	39	53	71	90
East Asia and the Pacific	Thousands	(2.4)	337	397	411	503	600
South Asia	Thousands	(2.5)	20	7	10	7	4
Middle East	Thousands	(2.6)	..	..	..	..	..
Arrivals by mode of transport							
Air	Thousands	(3.1)	47	51	65	66	92
Rail	Thousands	(3.2)	..	..	..	..	..
Road	Thousands	(3.3)	356	412	435	548	645
Sea	Thousands	(3.4)	..	..	..	..	..
Arrivals by purpose of visit							
Leisure, recreation and holidays	Thousands	(4.1)	242	324	350	..	..
Business and professional	Thousands	(4.2)	137	129	140	..	..
Other	Thousands	(4.3)	24	10	10	..	..
Overnight stays and length of stay							
Overnight stays in H&S	Thousand nights	(5.1)	..	..	..	..	..
Overnight stays in CE	Thousand nights	(5.2)	..	..	..	..	..
ALS of non resident tourists	Nights	(5.5)	4.12	5.00	5.00	5.50	5.50
Tourism expenditure in the country of reference	US$ Million	(8.1)	44	73	80	97	114
DOMESTIC TOURISM							
Overnight stays							
Overnight stays in H&S	Thousand nights	(5.3)	..	..	..	..	..
Overnight stays in CE	Thousand nights	(5.4)	..	..	..	..	..
OUTBOUND TOURISM							
Departures	Thousands	(6.1)	..	..	..	..	..
Tourism expenditure in other countries	US$ Million	(8.2)	22	21	23	12	17
TOURISM ACTIVITIES							
Hotels and similar establishments							
Number of rooms	H&S	(7.1)	3,701	4,108	5,019	5,544	7,333
Number of bed-places	H&S	(7.2)	..	7,116	8,659	9,591	12,857
Occupancy rate	Percent	(7.3)	..	62.00	47.00	..	..
Average length of stay	Nights	(5.6)	..	..	..	..	..
ECONOMIC AGGREGATES							
Gross National Product (GNP)	US$ Million	(9.1)	1,893	1,886	1,553	1,473	1,493
Exports (F.O.B.)	US$ Million	(9.2)	323	359	370	311	..
Imports (C.I.F.)	US$ Million	(9.3)	690	706	553	525	..

Abbreviations used in tables and notes:
H&S: Hotels and similar establishments; **CE:** All types of tourism accommodation establishments; **ALS:** Average length of stay; **THS:** Non-resident tourists staying in H&S; **TCE:** Non-resident tourists staying in CE; **TF:** Arrivals of international (or non-resident) tourists; **VF:** Arrivals of international (or non-resident) visitors; **NHS:** Overnight stays at H&S; **NCE:** Overnight stays at CE.

..   data not available
incl   including
excl   excluding
nra   nationals residing abroad

Notes:
(1.2) TF; (2.2-2.5,3.1,3.3,4.1-4.3) VF; (5.5) Days.

LATVIA

Basic Indicators	Units	Code	1996	1997	1998	1999	2000
INBOUND TOURISM							
Arrivals							
Visitors	Thousands	(1.1)	1,750	1,842	1,788	1,738	1,882
Tourists (overnight visitors)	Thousands	(1.2)	560	625	567	490	452
Same-day visitors	Thousands	(1.3)	1,148	1,189	1,225	1,174	1,405
Cruise passengers	Thousands	(1.4)	9	20	36	37	36
Arrivals by region							
Africa	Thousands	(2.1)	..	..	..	..	..
Americas	Thousands	(2.2)	34	40	29	24	16
Europe	Thousands	(2.3)	1,671	1,772	1,763	1,680	1,889
East Asia and the Pacific	Thousands	(2.4)	7	10	7	11	8
South Asia	Thousands	(2.5)	..	1	1	2	1
Middle East	Thousands	(2.6)	..	..	..	..	..
Arrivals by mode of transport							
Air	Thousands	(3.1)	112	127	142	140	140
Rail	Thousands	(3.2)	235	244	173	115	95
Road	Thousands	(3.3)	1,301	1,341	1,326	1,362	1,521
Sea	Thousands	(3.4)	102	130	147	121	126
Arrivals by purpose of visit							
Leisure, recreation and holidays	Thousands	(4.1)	210	189	158	322	265
Business and professional	Thousands	(4.2)	392	398	405	336	430
Other	Thousands	(4.3)	1,111	1,237	1,238	1,060	1,219
Overnight stays and length of stay							
Overnight stays in H&S	Thousand nights	(5.1)	676	744	725	718	691
Overnight stays in CE	Thousand nights	(5.2)	697	763	733	724	697
ALS of non resident tourists	Nights	(5.5)	8.30	6.40	6.00	5.80	6.00
Tourism expenditure **in the country of reference**	US$ Million	(8.1)	215	192	182	118	131
DOMESTIC TOURISM							
Overnight stays							
Overnight stays in H&S	Thousand nights	(5.3)	544	580	551	583	669
Overnight stays in CE	Thousand nights	(5.4)	647	744	708	710	787
OUTBOUND TOURISM							
Departures	Thousands	(6.1)	1,798	1,877	1,961	2,256	2,596
Tourism expenditure in other countries	US$ Million	(8.2)	373	326	305	268	248
TOURISM ACTIVITIES							
Hotels and similar establishments							
Number of rooms	H&S	(7.1)	6,814	7,262	7,172	6,508	6,431
Number of bed-places	H&S	(7.2)	12,388	14,609	13,613	12,453	11,890
Occupancy rate	Percent	(7.3)	..	24.50	25.80	29.60	32.00
Average length of stay	Nights	(5.6)	3.70	3.30	3.10	3.10	2.90
ECONOMIC AGGREGATES							
Gross National Product (GNP)	US$ Million	(9.1)	5,466	5,685	5,841	6,073	6,921
Exports (F.O.B.)	US$ Million	(9.2)	1,443	1,672	1,811	1,723	1,867
Imports (C.I.F.)	US$ Million	(9.3)	2,320	2,721	3,191	2,945	3,187

Abbreviations used in tables and notes:
H&S: Hotels and similar establishments; **CE:** All types of tourism accommodation establishments; **ALS:** Average length of stay; **THS:** Non-resident tourists staying in H&S; **TCE:** Non-resident tourists staying in CE; **TF:** Arrivals of international (or non-resident) tourists; **VF:** Arrivals of international (or non-resident) visitors; **NHS:** Overnight stays at H&S; **NCE:** Overnight stays at CE.

..   data not available
incl   including
excl   excluding
nra   nationals residing abroad

Notes:
(1.1,3.1-3.4) VF, arrivals of non-residents at the border. Data by State Border Guard. (1.2-1.4,2.2-2.5,4.1-4.3,5.5) Non-resident departures. Survey of persons crossing the state border; (1.3) Incl cruise passengers; (7.3) Bed-places.

Basic Indicators	Units	Code	1996	1997	1998	1999	2000
INBOUND TOURISM							
Arrivals							
Visitors	Thousands	(1.1)	..	..	..	..	..
Tourists (overnight visitors)	Thousands	(1.2)	424	558	631	673	742
Same-day visitors	Thousands	(1.3)	..	..	..	..	..
Cruise passengers	Thousands	(1.4)	..	..	..	..	..
Arrivals by region							
Africa	Thousands	(2.1)	14	19	23	28	24
Americas	Thousands	(2.2)	47	59	68	85	90
Europe	Thousands	(2.3)	142	174	196	224	229
East Asia and the Pacific	Thousands	(2.4)	34	41	41	47	56
South Asia	Thousands	(2.5)	20	27	35	36	55
Middle East	Thousands	(2.6)	139	208	236	253	288
Arrivals by mode of transport							
Air	Thousands	(3.1)	..	381	418	448	481
Rail	Thousands	(3.2)	..	..	..	..	..
Road	Thousands	(3.3)	..	174	182	223	260
Sea	Thousands	(3.4)	..	2	3	2	1
Arrivals by purpose of visit							
Leisure, recreation and holidays	Thousands	(4.1)	..	..	..	..	..
Business and professional	Thousands	(4.2)	..	..	..	..	..
Other	Thousands	(4.3)	..	..	..	..	..
Overnight stays and length of stay							
Overnight stays in H&S	Thousand nights	(5.1)	..	..	..	..	..
Overnight stays in CE	Thousand nights	(5.2)	..	..	..	..	..
ALS of non resident tourists	Nights	(5.5)	..	..	..	..	3.00
Tourism expenditure							
in the country of reference	US$ Million	(8.1)	715	1,000	1,221	673	742
DOMESTIC TOURISM							
Overnight stays							
Overnight stays in H&S	Thousand nights	(5.3)	..	..	..	..	..
Overnight stays in CE	Thousand nights	(5.4)	..	..	..	..	..
OUTBOUND TOURISM							
Departures	Thousands	(6.1)	..	..	1,650	..	..
Tourism expenditure in other countries	US$ Million	(8.2)	..	..	..	..	..
TOURISM ACTIVITIES							
Hotels and similar establishments							
Number of rooms	H&S	(7.1)	..	9,681	10,966	14,267	14,500
Number of bed-places	H&S	(7.2)	..	14,858	18,328	25,000	25,450
Occupancy rate	Percent	(7.3)	27.30	32.02	36.74	28.00	28.00
Average length of stay	Nights	(5.6)	..	..	..	..	..
ECONOMIC AGGREGATES							
Gross National Product (GNP)	US$ Million	(9.1)	12,197	13,914	14,852	15,920	16,219
Exports (F.O.B.)	US$ Million	(9.2)	736	643	662	677	714
Imports (C.I.F.)	US$ Million	(9.3)	7,540	7,467	7,070	6,207	6,228

Abbreviations used in tables and notes:
H&S: Hotels and similar establishments; **CE:** All types of tourism accommodation establishments; **ALS:** Average length of stay; **THS:** Non-resident tourists staying in H&S; **TCE:** Non-resident tourists staying in CE; **TF:** Arrivals of international (or non-resident) tourists; **VF:** Arrivals of international (or non-resident) visitors; **NHS:** Overnight stays at H&S; **NCE:** Overnight stays at CE.

.. data not available
incl including
excl excluding
nra nationals residing abroad

Notes:
(1.2) Excl Syrian nationals; (8.1/99-2000) Due to lack of data on international tourism receipts concerning statistics on inbound tourism, the Department of "Internet and Statistics Service of the Ministry of Tourism" considers that a tourist spends an average of US$ 1,000.

LESOTHO

Basic Indicators	Units	Code	1996	1997	1998	1999	2000
INBOUND TOURISM							
Arrivals							
Visitors	Thousands	(1.1)	312	313	290	360	..
Tourists (overnight visitors)	Thousands	(1.2)	134	144	150	186	..
Same-day visitors	Thousands	(1.3)	178	169	140	174	..
Cruise passengers	Thousands	(1.4)	..	..	..	..	..
Arrivals by region							
Africa	Thousands	(2.1)	304	313	286	..	..
Americas	Thousands	(2.2)	1	3	1	..	..
Europe	Thousands	(2.3)	5	5	2	..	..
East Asia and the Pacific	Thousands	(2.4)	1	2	1	..	..
South Asia	Thousands	(2.5)	..	..	..	..	..
Middle East	Thousands	(2.6)	..	..	..	..	..
Arrivals by mode of transport							
Air	Thousands	(3.1)	12	7	9	..	..
Rail	Thousands	(3.2)	..	..	..	..	..
Road	Thousands	(3.3)	300	306	280	..	..
Sea	Thousands	(3.4)	..	..	..	..	..
Arrivals by purpose of visit							
Leisure, recreation and holidays	Thousands	(4.1)	39	39	43	..	..
Business and professional	Thousands	(4.2)	71	53	46	..	..
Other	Thousands	(4.3)	202	220	201	..	..
Overnight stays and length of stay							
Overnight stays in H&S	Thousand nights	(5.1)	150	169	141	165	..
Overnight stays in CE	Thousand nights	(5.2)	315	363	336	417	..
ALS of non resident tourists	Nights	(5.5)	..	..	..	..	..
Tourism expenditure							
in the country of reference	US$ Million	(8.1)	32	32	24	23	24
DOMESTIC TOURISM							
Overnight stays							
Overnight stays in H&S	Thousand nights	(5.3)	..	..	..	..	..
Overnight stays in CE	Thousand nights	(5.4)	45	51	..	..	..
OUTBOUND TOURISM							
Departures	Thousands	(6.1)	..	..	..	..	..
Tourism expenditure in other countries	US$ Million	(8.2)	12	14	13	14	9
TOURISM ACTIVITIES							
Hotels and similar establishments							
Number of rooms	H&S	(7.1)	2,005	1,027	..	..	..
Number of bed-places	H&S	(7.2)	3,922	1,922	..	..	..
Occupancy rate	Percent	(7.3)	20.50	20.80	17.80	22.10	..
Average length of stay	Nights	(5.6)	..	..	..	..	..
ECONOMIC AGGREGATES							
Gross National Product (GNP)	US$ Million	(9.1)	1,399	1,389	1,275	1,209	1,169
Exports (F.O.B.)	US$ Million	(9.2)	..	..	..	..	..
Imports (C.I.F.)	US$ Million	(9.3)	..	..	..	..	..

Abbreviations used in tables and notes:
H&S: Hotels and similar establishments; **CE:** All types of tourism accommodation establishments; **ALS:** Average length of stay; **THS:** Non-resident tourists staying in H&S; **TCE:** Non-resident tourists staying in CE; **TF:** Arrivals of international (or non-resident) tourists; **VF:** Arrivals of international (or non-resident) visitors; **NHS:** Overnight stays at H&S; **NCE:** Overnight stays at CE.

..   data not available
incl   including
excl   excluding
nra   nationals residing abroad

Notes:
(1.1,2.1-4.3) VF; (7.1,7.2) Hotels only; (8.1,8.2) International Monetary Fund.

Basic Indicators	Units	Code	1996	1997	1998	1999	2000
INBOUND TOURISM							
Arrivals							
Visitors	Thousands	(1.1)	1,276	913	850	965	963
Tourists (overnight visitors)	Thousands	(1.2)	88	50	32	178	174
Same-day visitors	Thousands	(1.3)	1,188	863	818	787	789
Cruise passengers	Thousands	(1.4)	..	..	..	..	..
Arrivals by region							
Africa	Thousands	(2.1)	829	572	462	531	533
Americas	Thousands	(2.2)	3	1	..	..	1
Europe	Thousands	(2.3)	55	28	23	33	34
East Asia and the Pacific	Thousands	(2.4)	19	3	3	3	2
South Asia	Thousands	(2.5)	8	2	1	1	1
Middle East	Thousands	(2.6)	362	307	361	396	392
Arrivals by mode of transport							
Air	Thousands	(3.1)	..	..	..	..	..
Rail	Thousands	(3.2)	..	..	..	..	..
Road	Thousands	(3.3)	1,225	..	..	..	..
Sea	Thousands	(3.4)	51	..	..	..	..
Arrivals by purpose of visit							
Leisure, recreation and holidays	Thousands	(4.1)	88	..	..	..	..
Business and professional	Thousands	(4.2)	826	..	..	..	..
Other	Thousands	(4.3)	362	..	..	..	..
Overnight stays and length of stay							
Overnight stays in H&S	Thousand nights	(5.1)	699	397	253	320	..
Overnight stays in CE	Thousand nights	(5.2)	743	422	269	339	..
ALS of non resident tourists	Nights	(5.5)	..	..	..	..	..
Tourism expenditure in the country of reference	US$ Million	(8.1)	6	6	18	28	..
DOMESTIC TOURISM							
Overnight stays							
Overnight stays in H&S	Thousand nights	(5.3)	..	..	..	..	..
Overnight stays in CE	Thousand nights	(5.4)	978	950	960	969	..
OUTBOUND TOURISM							
Departures	Thousands	(6.1)	493	650	..	..	..
Tourism expenditure in other countries	US$ Million	(8.2)	215	154	143	150	..
TOURISM ACTIVITIES							
Hotels and similar establishments							
Number of rooms	H&S	(7.1)	..	7,784	..	..	11,815
Number of bed-places	H&S	(7.2)	..	15,267	..	..	19,969
Occupancy rate	Percent	(7.3)	71.00	57.00	51.00	53.00	..
Average length of stay	Nights	(5.6)	..	..	..	..	..
ECONOMIC AGGREGATES							
Gross National Product (GNP)	US$ Million	(9.1)	..	..	..	..	..
Exports (F.O.B.)	US$ Million	(9.2)	9,805	9,036	6,131	..	..
Imports (C.I.F.)	US$ Million	(9.3)	5,046	5,593	5,692	..	..

Abbreviations used in tables and notes:
H&S: Hotels and similar establishments; **CE:** All types of tourism accommodation establishments; **ALS:** Average length of stay; **THS:** Non-resident tourists staying in H&S; **TCE:** Non-resident tourists staying in CE; **TF:** Arrivals of international (or non-resident) tourists; **VF:** Arrivals of international (or non-resident) visitors; **NHS:** Overnight stays at H&S; **NCE:** Overnight stays at CE.

.. data not available
incl including
excl excluding
nra nationals residing abroad

Notes:
(1.1,2.1-2.6) Incl all travellers (visitors and other travellers not defined as visitors by WTO); (5.1,5.2,5.4,7.3,8.2) Estimates.

LIECHTENSTEIN

Basic Indicators	Units	Code	1996	1997	1998	1999	2000
INBOUND TOURISM							
Arrivals							
Visitors	Thousands	(1.1)	..	..	..	..	..
Tourists (overnight visitors)	Thousands	(1.2)	56	57	59	60	62
Same-day visitors	Thousands	(1.3)	..	..	..	..	..
Cruise passengers	Thousands	(1.4)	..	..	..	..	..
Arrivals by region							
Africa	Thousands	(2.1)	..	..	..	..	..
Americas	Thousands	(2.2)	5	5	5	5	5
Europe	Thousands	(2.3)	49	49	52	53	55
East Asia and the Pacific	Thousands	(2.4)	2	2	2	2	2
South Asia	Thousands	(2.5)	..	..	..	..	..
Middle East	Thousands	(2.6)	..	..	..	..	..
Arrivals by mode of transport							
Air	Thousands	(3.1)	..	..	..	..	..
Rail	Thousands	(3.2)	..	..	..	..	..
Road	Thousands	(3.3)	..	..	..	..	..
Sea	Thousands	(3.4)	..	..	..	..	..
Arrivals by purpose of visit							
Leisure, recreation and holidays	Thousands	(4.1)	..	..	..	..	..
Business and professional	Thousands	(4.2)	..	..	..	..	..
Other	Thousands	(4.3)	..	..	..	..	..
Overnight stays and length of stay							
Overnight stays in H&S	Thousand nights	(5.1)	118	117	120	121	131
Overnight stays in CE	Thousand nights	(5.2)	..	..	..	..	..
ALS of non resident tourists	Nights	(5.5)	2.10	2.06	2.04	..	2.10
Tourism expenditure							
in the country of reference	US$ Million	(8.1)	..	..	..	..	..
DOMESTIC TOURISM							
Overnight stays							
Overnight stays in H&S	Thousand nights	(5.3)	1	3	3	2	3
Overnight stays in CE	Thousand nights	(5.4)	..	..	..	..	..
OUTBOUND TOURISM							
Departures	Thousands	(6.1)	..	..	..	..	..
Tourism expenditure in other countries	US$ Million	(8.2)	..	..	..	..	..
TOURISM ACTIVITIES							
Hotels and similar establishments							
Number of rooms	H&S	(7.1)	..	..	..	..	..
Number of bed-places	H&S	(7.2)	1,180	1,241	1,245	1,194	1,184
Occupancy rate	Percent	(7.3)	27.70	26.50	27.10	..	30.90
Average length of stay	Nights	(5.6)	..	..	..	..	..
ECONOMIC AGGREGATES							
Gross National Product (GNP)	US$ Million	(9.1)	..	..	..	..	..
Exports (F.O.B.)	US$ Million	(9.2)	..	..	..	..	..
Imports (C.I.F.)	US$ Million	(9.3)	..	..	..	..	..

Abbreviations used in tables and notes:
H&S: Hotels and similar establishments; **CE:** All types of tourism accommodation establishments; **ALS:** Average length of stay; **THS:** Non-resident tourists staying in H&S; **TCE:** Non-resident tourists staying in CE; **TF:** Arrivals of international (or non-resident) tourists; **VF:** Arrivals of international (or non-resident) visitors; **NHS:** Overnight stays at H&S; **NCE:** Overnight stays at CE.

..	data not available
incl	including
excl	excluding
nra	nationals residing abroad

Notes:
(1.2,2.2-2.4) THS; (7.3) Bed-places.

Basic Indicators	Units	Code	1996	1997	1998	1999	2000
INBOUND TOURISM							
Arrivals							
Visitors	Thousands	(1.1)	3,497	3,702	4,287	4,454	4,092
Tourists (overnight visitors)	Thousands	(1.2)	832	1,012	1,416	1,422	1,083
Same-day visitors	Thousands	(1.3)	2,665	2,690	2,871	3,032	3,009
Cruise passengers	Thousands	(1.4)	..	..	..	..	..
Arrivals by region							
Africa	Thousands	(2.1)	0.2	0.2	0.2	0.2	0.2
Americas	Thousands	(2.2)	11	12	15	15	15
Europe	Thousands	(2.3)	238	268	284	270	276
East Asia and the Pacific	Thousands	(2.4)	6	8	7	8	9
South Asia	Thousands	(2.5)	..	..	..	..	..
Middle East	Thousands	(2.6)	..	..	..	..	..
Arrivals by mode of transport							
Air	Thousands	(3.1)	111	139	135	145	158
Rail	Thousands	(3.2)	828	863	1,124	1,105	642
Road	Thousands	(3.3)	2,488	2,636	2,954	3,137	3,212
Sea	Thousands	(3.4)	70	64	74	68	80
Arrivals by purpose of visit							
Leisure, recreation and holidays	Thousands	(4.1)	183	169	395	408	237
Business and professional	Thousands	(4.2)	357	348	294	336	337
Other	Thousands	(4.3)	292	495	727	678	509
Overnight stays and length of stay							
Overnight stays in H&S	Thousand nights	(5.1)	505	547	649	619	609
Overnight stays in CE	Thousand nights	(5.2)	901	864	1,034	998	966
ALS of non resident tourists	Nights	(5.5)	9.00	8.30	9.00	9.00	6.00
Tourism expenditure							
in the country of reference	US$ Million	(8.1)	316	360	460	550	391
DOMESTIC TOURISM							
Overnight stays							
Overnight stays in H&S	Thousand nights	(5.3)	319	348	373	365	359
Overnight stays in CE	Thousand nights	(5.4)	2,833	2,609	2,859	2,579	1,987
OUTBOUND TOURISM							
Departures	Thousands	(6.1)	2,864	2,981	3,241	3,482	3,632
Tourism expenditure in other countries	US$ Million	(8.2)	266	277	292	341	253
TOURISM ACTIVITIES							
Hotels and similar establishments							
Number of rooms	H&S	(7.1)	5,555	5,524	6,066	6,505	6,632
Number of bed-places	H&S	(7.2)	11,045	10,976	11,973	12,625	12,897
Occupancy rate	Percent	(7.3)	30.20	32.00	33.20	31.30	28.40
Average length of stay	Nights	(5.6)	5.90	5.10	5.50	5.30	4.70
ECONOMIC AGGREGATES							
Gross National Product (GNP)	US$ Million	(9.1)	7,081	8,242	9,415	9,783	10,741
Exports (F.O.B.)	US$ Million	(9.2)	3,355	3,860	3,711	3,004	3,810
Imports (C.I.F.)	US$ Million	(9.3)	4,559	5,644	5,794	4,835	5,457

Abbreviations used in tables and notes:
H&S: Hotels and similar establishments; **CE:** All types of tourism accommodation establishments; **ALS:** Average length of stay; **THS:** Non-resident tourists staying in H&S; **TCE:** Non-resident tourists staying in CE; **TF:** Arrivals of international (or non-resident) tourists; **VF:** Arrivals of international (or non-resident) visitors; **NHS:** Overnight stays at H&S; **NCE:** Overnight stays at CE.

..   data not available
incl   including
excl   excluding
nra   nationals residing abroad

Notes:
(2.2-2.4) TCE; (2.4) Asia/Pacific; (3.1-3.4) VF; (4.1-4.3) TF; (5.6) CE; (7.3) Rooms, hotels only.

LUXEMBOURG

Basic Indicators	Units	Code	1996	1997	1998	1999	2000
INBOUND TOURISM							
Arrivals							
Visitors	Thousands	(1.1)	..	..	..	..	..
Tourists (overnight visitors)	Thousands	(1.2)	724	778	789	837	807
Same-day visitors	Thousands	(1.3)	..	..	..	..	..
Cruise passengers	Thousands	(1.4)	..	..	..	..	..
Arrivals by region							
Africa	Thousands	(2.1)	..	..	..	..	..
Americas	Thousands	(2.2)	30	36	40	41	39
Europe	Thousands	(2.3)	672	719	722	769	740
East Asia and the Pacific	Thousands	(2.4)	..	..	..	..	..
South Asia	Thousands	(2.5)	..	..	..	..	..
Middle East	Thousands	(2.6)	..	..	..	..	..
Arrivals by mode of transport							
Air	Thousands	(3.1)	640	716	..	..	..
Rail	Thousands	(3.2)	..	..	..	..	..
Road	Thousands	(3.3)	..	..	..	..	..
Sea	Thousands	(3.4)	..	..	..	..	..
Arrivals by purpose of visit							
Leisure, recreation and holidays	Thousands	(4.1)	..	..	..	..	..
Business and professional	Thousands	(4.2)	..	..	..	..	..
Other	Thousands	(4.3)	..	..	..	..	..
Overnight stays and length of stay							
Overnight stays in H&S	Thousand nights	(5.1)	947	1,026	1,089	1,136	1,139
Overnight stays in CE	Thousand nights	(5.2)	2,195	2,334	2,327	2,468	2,340
ALS of non resident tourists	Nights	(5.5)	..	..	..	..	..
Tourism expenditure							
in the country of reference	US$ Million	(8.1)	..	..	..	..	..
DOMESTIC TOURISM							
Overnight stays							
Overnight stays in H&S	Thousand nights	(5.3)	91	83	81	67	68
Overnight stays in CE	Thousand nights	(5.4)	303	281	314	306	272
OUTBOUND TOURISM							
Departures	Thousands	(6.1)	..	..	..	..	..
Tourism expenditure in other countries	US$ Million	(8.2)	..	..	..	..	..
TOURISM ACTIVITIES							
Hotels and similar establishments							
Number of rooms	H&S	(7.1)	7,787	7,683	7,676	7,561	7,708
Number of bed-places	H&S	(7.2)	..	..	..	..	..
Occupancy rate	Percent	(7.3)	38.76	44.70	..	..	..
Average length of stay	Nights	(5.6)	3.27	3.19	3.19	3.15	3.10
ECONOMIC AGGREGATES							
Gross National Product (GNP)	US$ Million	(9.1)	19,337	19,584	17,964	18,554	19,420
Exports (F.O.B.)	US$ Million	(9.2)	7,211	7,000	7,912	7,849	7,825
Imports (C.I.F.)	US$ Million	(9.3)	9,668	9,380	7,409	10,787	10,616

Abbreviations used in tables and notes:
H&S: Hotels and similar establishments; **CE:** All types of tourism accommodation establishments; **ALS:** Average length of stay; **THS:** Non-resident tourists staying in H&S; **TCE:** Non-resident tourists staying in CE; **TF:** Arrivals of international (or non-resident) tourists; **VF:** Arrivals of international (or non-resident) visitors; **NHS:** Overnight stays at H&S; **NCE:** Overnight stays at CE.

..	data not available
incl	including
excl	excluding
nra	nationals residing abroad

Notes:
(1.2,2.1-2.4) TCE; Also incl youth hostels, tourist private accommodation and others; (5.1,5.3) Nights in hotels, inns and guest houses; (5.2,5.4) Also incl tourist private accommodation and others; (7.3) Rooms.

Basic Indicators	Units	Code	1996	1997	1998	1999	2000
INBOUND TOURISM							
Arrivals							
Visitors	Thousands	(1.1)	8,151	7,000	6,949	7,444	9,162
Tourists (overnight visitors)	Thousands	(1.2)	4,690	3,836	4,517	5,050	6,688
Same-day visitors	Thousands	(1.3)	3,461	3,164	2,432	2,394	2,474
Cruise passengers	Thousands	(1.4)	..	..	..	..	..
Arrivals by region							
Africa	Thousands	(2.1)	7	6	5	4	4
Americas	Thousands	(2.2)	149	121	111	106	118
Europe	Thousands	(2.3)	293	239	263	163	148
East Asia and the Pacific	Thousands	(2.4)	7,493	6,434	6,498	7,155	8,872
South Asia	Thousands	(2.5)	18	16	13	14	17
Middle East	Thousands	(2.6)	1	1	1	1	1
Arrivals by mode of transport							
Air	Thousands	(3.1)	409	537	512	673	834
Rail	Thousands	(3.2)	..	..	..	..	..
Road	Thousands	(3.3)	1,701	1,625	1,749	2,335	3,137
Sea	Thousands	(3.4)	6,041	4,838	4,687	4,436	5,191
Arrivals by purpose of visit							
Leisure, recreation and holidays	Thousands	(4.1)	5,738	4,417	4,378	4,690	6,872
Business and professional	Thousands	(4.2)	619	854	764	744	733
Other	Thousands	(4.3)	1,793	1,729	1,807	2,010	1,557
Overnight stays and length of stay							
Overnight stays in H&S	Thousand nights	(5.1)	3,250	2,672	2,753	2,885	3,219
Overnight stays in CE	Thousand nights	(5.2)	..	..	..	..	..
ALS of non resident tourists	Nights	(5.5)	..	..	..	..	..
Tourism expenditure							
in the country of reference	US$ Million	(8.1)	3,085	2,947	2,638	2,466	2,999
DOMESTIC TOURISM							
Overnight stays							
Overnight stays in H&S	Thousand nights	(5.3)	188	172	181	204	227
Overnight stays in CE	Thousand nights	(5.4)	..	..	..	..	..
OUTBOUND TOURISM							
Departures	Thousands	(6.1)	68	83	105	117	144
Tourism expenditure in other countries	US$ Million	(8.2)	..	..	..	..	..
TOURISM ACTIVITIES							
Hotels and similar establishments							
Number of rooms	H&S	(7.1)	8,545	8,786	8,970	9,431	9,201
Number of bed-places	H&S	(7.2)	17,735	20,070	18,909	19,920	19,115
Occupancy rate	Percent	(7.3)	64.11	52.05	53.11	55.42	59.15
Average length of stay	Nights	(5.6)	1.32	1.34	1.43	1.43	1.33
ECONOMIC AGGREGATES							
Gross National Product (GNP)	US$ Million	(9.1)	6,925	6,943	6,404	6,161	..
Exports (F.O.B.)	US$ Million	(9.2)	1,975	2,128	2,122	2,181	2,529
Imports (C.I.F.)	US$ Million	(9.3)	1,979	2,062	1,937	2,024	2,249

Abbreviations used in tables and notes:
H&S: Hotels and similar establishments; **CE:** All types of tourism accommodation establishments; **ALS:** Average length of stay; **THS:** Non-resident tourists staying in H&S; **TCE:** Non-resident tourists staying in CE; **TF:** Arrivals of international (or non-resident) tourists; **VF:** Arrivals of international (or non-resident) visitors; **NHS:** Overnight stays at H&S; **NCE:** Overnight stays at CE.

Notes:
(1.1,2.1-4.3) VF; (1.1-1.3,2.4,3.1-3.4) Incl ethnic Chinese arriving from HK; (1.2,1.3) Estimates; (3.1) Incl entrees by helicopter; (6.1) Package tours; (7.1,7.2) Hotels, guest houses and pousadas (inns); (7.3) Rooms; (8.1) Incl. gambling receipts; (9.1) GDP.

..   data not available
incl   including
excl   excluding
nra   nationals residing abroad

MADAGASCAR

Basic Indicators	Units	Code	1996	1997	1998	1999	2000
INBOUND TOURISM							
Arrivals							
Visitors	Thousands	(1.1)	..	..	..	..	..
Tourists (overnight visitors)	Thousands	(1.2)	83	101	121	138	160
Same-day visitors	Thousands	(1.3)	..	..	..	..	..
Cruise passengers	Thousands	(1.4)	..	..	..	..	..
Arrivals by region							
Africa	Thousands	(2.1)	9	6	15	20	24
Americas	Thousands	(2.2)	6	2	2	7	6
Europe	Thousands	(2.3)	63	64	82	95	110
East Asia and the Pacific	Thousands	(2.4)	4	1	1	2	2
South Asia	Thousands	(2.5)	..	..	..	..	..
Middle East	Thousands	(2.6)	..	..	..	..	..
Arrivals by mode of transport							
Air	Thousands	(3.1)	83	101	121	138	160
Rail	Thousands	(3.2)	..	..	..	..	..
Road	Thousands	(3.3)	..	..	..	..	..
Sea	Thousands	(3.4)	..	..	..	..	..
Arrivals by purpose of visit							
Leisure, recreation and holidays	Thousands	(4.1)	48	58	70	80	101
Business and professional	Thousands	(4.2)	24	29	35	40	29
Other	Thousands	(4.3)	11	13	16	18	30
Overnight stays and length of stay							
Overnight stays in H&S	Thousand nights	(5.1)	1,240	1,511	2,424	2,627	3,041
Overnight stays in CE	Thousand nights	(5.2)	..	..	..	..	..
ALS of non resident tourists	Nights	(5.5)	15.00	15.00	20.00	20.00	20.00
Tourism expenditure							
in the country of reference	US$ Million	(8.1)	65	74	91	100	119
DOMESTIC TOURISM							
Overnight stays							
Overnight stays in H&S	Thousand nights	(5.3)	..	..	..	..	..
Overnight stays in CE	Thousand nights	(5.4)	..	..	..	..	..
OUTBOUND TOURISM							
Departures	Thousands	(6.1)	..	..	..	..	..
Tourism expenditure in other countries	US$ Million	(8.2)	72	80	119	111	114
TOURISM ACTIVITIES							
Hotels and similar establishments							
Number of rooms	H&S	(7.1)	4,987	5,167	5,558	6,128	6,700
Number of bed-places	H&S	(7.2)	9,588	9,911	10,271	11,030	11,945
Occupancy rate	Percent	(7.3)	57.00	57.00	58.00	60.00	63.00
Average length of stay	Nights	(5.6)	4.00	4.00	4.00	4.00	4.00
ECONOMIC AGGREGATES							
Gross National Product (GNP)	US$ Million	(9.1)	3,377	3,587	3,740	3,708	3,959
Exports (F.O.B.)	US$ Million	(9.2)	299	222	243	221	..
Imports (C.I.F.)	US$ Million	(9.3)	507	467	514	377	..

Abbreviations used in tables and notes:
H&S: Hotels and similar establishments; **CE:** All types of tourism accommodation establishments; **ALS:** Average length of stay; **THS:** Non-resident tourists staying in H&S; **TCE:** Non-resident tourists staying in CE; **TF:** Arrivals of international (or non-resident) tourists; **VF:** Arrivals of international (or non-resident) visitors; **NHS:** Overnight stays at H&S; **NCE:** Overnight stays at CE.

.. data not available
incl including
excl excluding
nra nationals residing abroad

Notes:
(1.2,2.1-2.4,3.1,4.1-4.3) TF. Air arrivals; (7.3) Rooms.

Basic Indicators	Units	Code	1996	1997	1998	1999	2000
INBOUND TOURISM							
Arrivals							
Visitors	Thousands	(1.1)	..	..	..	..	..
Tourists (overnight visitors)	Thousands	(1.2)	194	207	220	254	228
Same-day visitors	Thousands	(1.3)	..	..	..	..	..
Cruise passengers	Thousands	(1.4)	..	..	..	..	..
Arrivals by region							
Africa	Thousands	(2.1)	143	153	162	188	179
Americas	Thousands	(2.2)	10	10	11	13	10
Europe	Thousands	(2.3)	31	33	35	40	25
East Asia and the Pacific	Thousands	(2.4)	8	8	9	10	10
South Asia	Thousands	(2.5)	2	2	2	3	3
Middle East	Thousands	(2.6)	..	..	..	..	..
Arrivals by mode of transport							
Air	Thousands	(3.1)	59	70	75	86	100
Rail	Thousands	(3.2)	4	6	7	8	8
Road	Thousands	(3.3)	130	131	138	160	119
Sea	Thousands	(3.4)	..	..	..	..	..
Arrivals by purpose of visit							
Leisure, recreation and holidays	Thousands	(4.1)	49	52	57	66	79
Business and professional	Thousands	(4.2)	84	89	106	122	125
Other	Thousands	(4.3)	61	65	57	66	22
Overnight stays and length of stay							
Overnight stays in H&S	Thousand nights	(5.1)	..	..	..	..	..
Overnight stays in CE	Thousand nights	(5.2)	1,355	1,436	1,235	1,013	1,235
ALS of non resident tourists	Nights	(5.5)	8.00	9.00	8.00	8.00	7.00
Tourism expenditure							
in the country of reference	US$ Million	(8.1)	5	11	15	20	27
DOMESTIC TOURISM							
Overnight stays							
Overnight stays in H&S	Thousand nights	(5.3)	..	..	..	..	..
Overnight stays in CE	Thousand nights	(5.4)	..	..	..	..	..
OUTBOUND TOURISM							
Departures	Thousands	(6.1)	..	..	..	..	..
Tourism expenditure in other countries	US$ Million	(8.2)	..	..	..	..	..
TOURISM ACTIVITIES							
Hotels and similar establishments							
Number of rooms	H&S	(7.1)	1,665	1,715	1,766	3,621	4,150
Number of bed-places	H&S	(7.2)	..	..	..	..	..
Occupancy rate	Percent	(7.3)	38.00	37.00	38.00	40.00	39.00
Average length of stay	Nights	(5.6)	..	..	..	..	..
ECONOMIC AGGREGATES							
Gross National Product (GNP)	US$ Million	(9.1)	1,762	2,108	2,306	2,150	1,884
Exports (F.O.B.)	US$ Million	(9.2)	481	537	517	442	..
Imports (C.I.F.)	US$ Million	(9.3)	623	791	583	697	..

Abbreviations used in tables and notes:
H&S: Hotels and similar establishments; **CE:** All types of tourism accommodation establishments; **ALS:** Average length of stay; **THS:** Non-resident tourists staying in H&S; **TCE:** Non-resident tourists staying in CE; **TF:** Arrivals of international (or non-resident) tourists; **VF:** Arrivals of international (or non-resident) visitors; **NHS:** Overnight stays at H&S; **NCE:** Overnight stays at CE.

..	data not available
incl	including
excl	excluding
nra	nationals residing abroad

Notes:
(1.2-4.3) Departures; (7.1) Incl lodges; (7.3) Bed-places.
Note: All figures for 1999 and 2000 are provisional.

MALAYSIA

Basic Indicators	Units	Code	1996	1997	1998	1999	2000
INBOUND TOURISM							
Arrivals							
Visitors	Thousands	(1.1)	14,084	12,591	10,886	13,910	17,213
Tourists (overnight visitors)	Thousands	(1.2)	7,138	6,211	5,551	7,931	10,222
Same-day visitors	Thousands	(1.3)	6,946	6,380	5,335	5,979	6,991
Cruise passengers	Thousands	(1.4)	..	..	..	..	..
Arrivals by region							
Africa	Thousands	(2.1)	30	24	26	30	74
Americas	Thousands	(2.2)	146	137	122	122	308
Europe	Thousands	(2.3)	411	387	368	309	590
East Asia and the Pacific	Thousands	(2.4)	6,336	5,450	4,697	6,827	8,716
South Asia	Thousands	(2.5)	63	54	56	69	180
Middle East	Thousands	(2.6)	28	16	20	19	45
Arrivals by mode of transport							
Air	Thousands	(3.1)	1,680	1,906	1,559	1,933	3,265
Rail	Thousands	(3.2)	203	118	78	149	197
Road	Thousands	(3.3)	4,668	3,634	3,139	4,612	5,750
Sea	Thousands	(3.4)	224	201	427	762	371
Arrivals by purpose of visit							
Leisure, recreation and holidays	Thousands	(4.1)	3,645	3,088	2,212	3,627	4,775
Business and professional	Thousands	(4.2)	576	505	559	713	1,055
Other	Thousands	(4.3)	2,555	2,266	2,432	3,143	3,779
Overnight stays and length of stay							
Overnight stays in H&S	Thousand nights	(5.1)	12,463	14,652	16,215	17,493	21,296
Overnight stays in CE	Thousand nights	(5.2)	..	..	..	..	..
ALS of non resident tourists	Nights	(5.5)	5.40	5.30	5.50	6.04	5.76
Tourism expenditure							
in the country of reference	US$ Million	(8.1)	4,447	2,702	2,456	3,540	4,936
DOMESTIC TOURISM							
Overnight stays							
Overnight stays in H&S	Thousand nights	(5.3)	13,473	15,635	14,182	16,166	19,344
Overnight stays in CE	Thousand nights	(5.4)	..	..	..	..	..
OUTBOUND TOURISM							
Departures	Thousands	(6.1)	23,333	26,165	25,631	26,067	30,532
Tourism expenditure in other countries	US$ Million	(8.2)	2,569	2,590	1,785	1,973	..
TOURISM ACTIVITIES							
Hotels and similar establishments							
Number of rooms	H&S	(7.1)	85,514	98,440	107,791	109,413	134,503
Number of bed-places	H&S	(7.2)	..	..	..	..	..
Occupancy rate	Percent	(7.3)	62.30	58.00	49.90	51.70	57.70
Average length of stay	Nights	(5.6)	..	..	..	1.50	..
ECONOMIC AGGREGATES							
Gross National Product (GNP)	US$ Million	(9.1)	94,613	99,728	80,688	76,597	78,529
Exports (F.O.B.)	US$ Million	(9.2)	78,318	78,741	73,305	84,451	98,136
Imports (C.I.F.)	US$ Million	(9.3)	78,408	79,030	58,325	64,962	82,199

Abbreviations used in tables and notes:
H&S: Hotels and similar establishments; **CE:** All types of tourism accommodation establishments; **ALS:** Average length of stay; **THS:** Non-resident tourists staying in H&S; **TCE:** Non-resident tourists staying in CE; **TF:** Arrivals of international (or non-resident) tourists; **VF:** Arrivals of international (or non-resident) visitors; **NHS:** Overnight stays at H&S; **NCE:** Overnight stays at CE.

.. data not available
incl including
excl excluding
nra nationals residing abroad

Notes:
(1.2,2.1-2.6) TF, foreign tourist departures; incl Singapore residents crossing the frontier by road through Johore Causeway; (3.1-4.3) Peninsular Malaysia only; (6.1) Outgoing Peninsular Malaysians, incl departures via Johore Causeway by road; (7.1) Hotels with 10 rooms and above; (7.3) Rooms; (8.2) International Monetary Fund.

MALDIVES

Basic Indicators	Units	Code	1996	1997	1998	1999	2000
INBOUND TOURISM							
Arrivals							
Visitors	Thousands	(1.1)	..	..	..	..	..
Tourists (overnight visitors)	Thousands	(1.2)	339	366	396	430	467
Same-day visitors	Thousands	(1.3)	..	..	..	..	..
Cruise passengers	Thousands	(1.4)	..	..	..	..	..
Arrivals by region							
Africa	Thousands	(2.1)	8	8	7	2	2
Americas	Thousands	(2.2)	4	6	6	6	7
Europe	Thousands	(2.3)	253	273	305	340	362
East Asia and the Pacific	Thousands	(2.4)	53	61	57	61	73
South Asia	Thousands	(2.5)	20	16	19	19	21
Middle East	Thousands	(2.6)	1	1	1	1	1
Arrivals by mode of transport							
Air	Thousands	(3.1)	339	366	396	430	467
Rail	Thousands	(3.2)	..	..	..	..	..
Road	Thousands	(3.3)	..	..	..	..	..
Sea	Thousands	(3.4)	..	..	..	..	..
Arrivals by purpose of visit							
Leisure, recreation and holidays	Thousands	(4.1)	339	366	396	430	467
Business and professional	Thousands	(4.2)	..	..	..	..	..
Other	Thousands	(4.3)	..	..	..	..	..
Overnight stays and length of stay							
Overnight stays in H&S	Thousand nights	(5.1)	3,039	3,271	3,467	3,718	3,937
Overnight stays in CE	Thousand nights	(5.2)	..	..	..	..	..
ALS of non resident tourists	Nights	(5.5)	..	..	..	..	..
Tourism expenditure **in the country of reference**	US$ Million	(8.1)	266	286	303	325	344
DOMESTIC TOURISM							
Overnight stays							
Overnight stays in H&S	Thousand nights	(5.3)	..	..	..	..	..
Overnight stays in CE	Thousand nights	(5.4)	..	..	..	..	..
OUTBOUND TOURISM							
Departures	Thousands	(6.1)	32	33	37	42	42
Tourism expenditure in other countries	US$ Million	(8.2)	38	39	42	45	46
TOURISM ACTIVITIES							
Hotels and similar establishments							
Number of rooms	H&S	(7.1)	5,892	6,117	7,079	7,751	8,329
Number of bed-places	H&S	(7.2)	11,784	12,234	14,158	15,502	16,658
Occupancy rate	Percent	(7.3)	72.80	77.40	76.20	69.70	68.16
Average length of stay	Nights	(5.6)	9.00	8.90	8.80	8.70	8.43
ECONOMIC AGGREGATES							
Gross National Product (GNP)	US$ Million	(9.1)	279	306	334	366	403
Exports (F.O.B.)	US$ Million	(9.2)	59	73	74	64	76
Imports (C.I.F.)	US$ Million	(9.3)	302	349	354	402	389

Abbreviations used in tables and notes:
H&S: Hotels and similar establishments; **CE:** All types of tourism accommodation establishments; **ALS:** Average length of stay; **THS:** Non-resident tourists staying in H&S; **TCE:** Non-resident tourists staying in CE; **TF:** Arrivals of international (or non-resident) tourists; **VF:** Arrivals of international (or non-resident) visitors; **NHS:** Overnight stays at H&S; **NCE:** Overnight stays at CE.

..   data not available
incl   including
excl   excluding
nra   nationals residing abroad

Notes:
(1.2,2.1-2.6) Air arrivals; (5.1,5.6,7.1-7.3) Tourist resorts and hotels; (5.6) Days; (8.2) International Monetary Fund.

MALI

Basic Indicators	Units	Code	1996	1997	1998	1999	2000
INBOUND TOURISM							
Arrivals							
Visitors	Thousands	(1.1)	..	..	..	..	
Tourists (overnight visitors)	Thousands	(1.2)	98	75	83	82	86
Same-day visitors	Thousands	(1.3)	..	..	..	..	..
Cruise passengers	Thousands	(1.4)	..	..	..	..	..
Arrivals by region							
Africa	Thousands	(2.1)	12	14	18	16	19
Americas	Thousands	(2.2)	6	7	8	9	9
Europe	Thousands	(2.3)	31	38	49	50	48
East Asia and the Pacific	Thousands	(2.4)	1	2	2	1	1
South Asia	Thousands	(2.5)	..	..	..	..	..
Middle East	Thousands	(2.6)	..	..	..	1	2
Arrivals by mode of transport							
Air	Thousands	(3.1)	98	75	83	82	86
Rail	Thousands	(3.2)	..	..	..	..	..
Road	Thousands	(3.3)	..	..	..	..	..
Sea	Thousands	(3.4)	..	..	..	..	..
Arrivals by purpose of visit							
Leisure, recreation and holidays	Thousands	(4.1)	..	..	..	..	..
Business and professional	Thousands	(4.2)	..	..	..	..	..
Other	Thousands	(4.3)	..	..	..	..	..
Overnight stays and length of stay							
Overnight stays in H&S	Thousand nights	(5.1)	194	148	163	165	174
Overnight stays in CE	Thousand nights	(5.2)	..	..	..	..	..
ALS of non resident tourists	Nights	(5.5)	..	..	..	..	..
Tourism expenditure in the country of reference	US$ Million	(8.1)	29	26	89	77	71
DOMESTIC TOURISM							
Overnight stays							
Overnight stays in H&S	Thousand nights	(5.3)	..	..	..	5	6
Overnight stays in CE	Thousand nights	(5.4)	..	..	..	..	..
OUTBOUND TOURISM							
Departures	Thousands	(6.1)	..	..	..	..	..
Tourism expenditure in other countries	US$ Million	(8.2)	46	42	52	44	41
TOURISM ACTIVITIES							
Hotels and similar establishments							
Number of rooms	H&S	(7.1)	1,744	1,912	1,988	2,271	2,748
Number of bed-places	H&S	(7.2)	2,165	2,278	2,544	2,875	3,076
Occupancy rate	Percent	(7.3)	50.94	43.94	35.71	..	..
Average length of stay	Nights	(5.6)	2.00	1.97	1.96	3.00	2.00
ECONOMIC AGGREGATES							
Gross National Product (GNP)	US$ Million	(9.1)	2,361	2,625	2,571	2,588	2,568
Exports (F.O.B.)	US$ Million	(9.2)	433	561	556	571	378
Imports (C.I.F.)	US$ Million	(9.3)	772	738	761	753	689

Abbreviations used in tables and notes:
H&S: Hotels and similar establishments; **CE:** All types of tourism accommodation establishments; **ALS:** Average length of stay; **THS:** Non-resident tourists staying in H&S; **TCE:** Non-resident tourists staying in CE; **TF:** Arrivals of international (or non-resident) tourists; **VF:** Arrivals of international (or non-resident) visitors; **NHS:** Overnight stays at H&S; **NCE:** Overnight stays at CE.

..   data not available
incl   including
excl   excluding
nra   nationals residing abroad

Notes:
(1.2) Arrivals by air; (2.1-2.4) THS; (7.3) Rooms; (8.1,8.2/96/97) International Monetary Fund.

MALTA

Basic Indicators	Units	Code	1996	1997	1998	1999	2000
INBOUND TOURISM							
Arrivals							
Visitors	Thousands	(1.1)	1,123	1,238	1,326	1,402	1,387
Tourists (overnight visitors)	Thousands	(1.2)	1,054	1,111	1,182	1,214	1,216
Same-day visitors	Thousands	(1.3)	..	..	..	..	..
Cruise passengers	Thousands	(1.4)	69	127	144	188	171
Arrivals by region							
Africa	Thousands	(2.1)	4	6	6	7	10
Americas	Thousands	(2.2)	18	21	25	26	27
Europe	Thousands	(2.3)	953	1,023	1,088	1,108	1,104
East Asia and the Pacific	Thousands	(2.4)	12	14	16	18	21
South Asia	Thousands	(2.5)	1	1	2	2	2
Middle East	Thousands	(2.6)	53	42	41	48	46
Arrivals by mode of transport							
Air	Thousands	(3.1)	973	1,040	1,102	1,143	1,177
Rail	Thousands	(3.2)	..	..	..	..	..
Road	Thousands	(3.3)	..	..	..	..	..
Sea	Thousands	(3.4)	81	71	80	71	39
Arrivals by purpose of visit							
Leisure, recreation and holidays	Thousands	(4.1)	..	..	..	..	..
Business and professional	Thousands	(4.2)	..	..	..	..	..
Other	Thousands	(4.3)	..	..	..	..	..
Overnight stays and length of stay							
Overnight stays in H&S	Thousand nights	(5.1)	7,311	7,730	8,046	8,150	6,978
Overnight stays in CE	Thousand nights	(5.2)	10,665	11,187	11,326	11,658	10,266
ALS of non resident tourists	Nights	(5.5)	10.00	9.60	9.50	9.50	8.40
Tourism expenditure							
in the country of reference	US$ Million	(8.1)	635	648	656	679	614
DOMESTIC TOURISM							
Overnight stays							
Overnight stays in H&S	Thousand nights	(5.3)	..	..	..	..	..
Overnight stays in CE	Thousand nights	(5.4)	..	..	..	..	..
OUTBOUND TOURISM							
Departures	Thousands	(6.1)	168	172	167	179	200
Tourism expenditure in other countries	US$ Million	(8.2)	219	191	193	201	201
TOURISM ACTIVITIES							
Hotels and similar establishments							
Number of rooms	H&S	(7.1)	..	..	..	..	..
Number of bed-places	H&S	(7.2)	38,152	39,183	38,932	40,890	40,688
Occupancy rate	Percent	(7.3)	54.72	54.05	56.62	55.00	46.99
Average length of stay	Nights	(5.6)	..	..	..	..	..
ECONOMIC AGGREGATES							
Gross National Product (GNP)	US$ Million	(9.1)	3,347	3,501	3,384	3,566	..
Exports (F.O.B.)	US$ Million	(9.2)	1,731	1,630	1,833	1,783	2,337
Imports (C.I.F.)	US$ Million	(9.3)	2,796	2,552	2,666	2,841	3,417

Abbreviations used in tables and notes:
H&S: Hotels and similar establishments; **CE:** All types of tourism accommodation establishments; **ALS:** Average length of stay; **THS:** Non-resident tourists staying in H&S; **TCE:** Non-resident tourists staying in CE; **TF:** Arrivals of international (or non-resident) tourists; **VF:** Arrivals of international (or non-resident) visitors; **NHS:** Overnight stays at H&S; **NCE:** Overnight stays at CE.

..   data not available
incl   including
excl   excluding
nra   nationals residing abroad

Notes:
(1.2-3.4/96-99) Departures; (1.2-3.4) Arrivals; (7.2) Hotels, tourist complexes, guest houses and holiday flats; (7.3) Bed-places in H&S; (8.1,8.2/2000) Provisional data.

MARSHALL ISLANDS

Basic Indicators	Units	Code	1996	1997	1998	1999	2000
INBOUND TOURISM							
Arrivals							
Visitors	Thousands	(1.1)	..	..	..	..	..
Tourists (overnight visitors)	Thousands	(1.2)	6.2	6.4	6.4	4.6	5.2
Same-day visitors	Thousands	(1.3)	..	..	..	..	..
Cruise passengers	Thousands	(1.4)	..	..	..	..	..
Arrivals by region							
Africa	Thousands	(2.1)	..	..	..	..	..
Americas	Thousands	(2.2)	2.1	2.5	2.4	2.1	2.0
Europe	Thousands	(2.3)	0.4	0.4	0.3	0.2	0.1
East Asia and the Pacific	Thousands	(2.4)	3.7	3.4	3.5	2.2	2.7
South Asia	Thousands	(2.5)	..	..	..	..	..
Middle East	Thousands	(2.6)	..	..	..	..	..
Arrivals by mode of transport							
Air	Thousands	(3.1)	6.2	6.4	6.4	4.6	5.2
Rail	Thousands	(3.2)	..	..	..	..	..
Road	Thousands	(3.3)	..	..	..	..	..
Sea	Thousands	(3.4)	..	..	..	..	..
Arrivals by purpose of visit							
Leisure, recreation and holidays	Thousands	(4.1)	1.1	0.9	0.9	1.1	1.3
Business and professional	Thousands	(4.2)	2.5	2.5	1.9	2.0	2.1
Other	Thousands	(4.3)	2.6	3.0	3.6	1.5	1.8
Overnight stays and length of stay							
Overnight stays in H&S	Thousand nights	(5.1)	..	..	..	..	..
Overnight stays in CE	Thousand nights	(5.2)	..	..	..	..	..
ALS of non resident tourists	Nights	(5.5)	..	5.60	..	..	..
Tourism expenditure							
in the country of reference	US$ Million	(8.1)	3	3	3	4	4
DOMESTIC TOURISM							
Overnight stays							
Overnight stays in H&S	Thousand nights	(5.3)	..	..	..	..	..
Overnight stays in CE	Thousand nights	(5.4)	..	..	..	..	..
OUTBOUND TOURISM							
Departures	Thousands	(6.1)	..	..	..	..	..
Tourism expenditure in other countries	US$ Million	(8.2)	..	..	..	..	..
TOURISM ACTIVITIES							
Hotels and similar establishments							
Number of rooms	H&S	(7.1)	300	300	300	..	305
Number of bed-places	H&S	(7.2)	658	658	658	..	665
Occupancy rate	Percent	(7.3)	30.00	..	..	..	..
Average length of stay	Nights	(5.6)	..	..	..	..	..
ECONOMIC AGGREGATES							
Gross National Product (GNP)	US$ Million	(9.1)	..	..	..	99	102
Exports (F.O.B.)	US$ Million	(9.2)	..	..	..	..	..
Imports (C.I.F.)	US$ Million	(9.3)	..	..	..	..	..

Abbreviations used in tables and notes:
H&S: Hotels and similar establishments; **CE:** All types of tourism accommodation establishments; **ALS:** Average length of stay; **THS:** Non-resident tourists staying in H&S; **TCE:** Non-resident tourists staying in CE; **TF:** Arrivals of international (or non-resident) tourists; **VF:** Arrivals of international (or non-resident) visitors; **NHS:** Overnight stays at H&S; **NCE:** Overnight stays at CE.

..   data not available
incl   including
excl   excluding
nra   nationals residing abroad

Notes:
(1.2,2.2,2.4,4.1-4.3) Air arrivals; (5.5) Days.

Basic Indicators	Units	Code	1996	1997	1998	1999	2000
INBOUND TOURISM							
Arrivals							
Visitors	Thousands	(1.1)	885	900	964	903	816
Tourists (overnight visitors)	Thousands	(1.2)	477	513	549	564	526
Same-day visitors	Thousands	(1.3)	..	..	..	..	..
Cruise passengers	Thousands	(1.4)	408	387	415	339	290
Arrivals by region							
Africa	Thousands	(2.1)	..	..	..	..	..
Americas	Thousands	(2.2)	66	78	77	85	80
Europe	Thousands	(2.3)	406	431	467	474	443
East Asia and the Pacific	Thousands	(2.4)	..	..	..	..	..
South Asia	Thousands	(2.5)	..	..	..	..	..
Middle East	Thousands	(2.6)	..	..	..	..	..
Arrivals by mode of transport							
Air	Thousands	(3.1)	425	464	498	511	475
Rail	Thousands	(3.2)	..	..	..	..	..
Road	Thousands	(3.3)	..	..	..	..	..
Sea	Thousands	(3.4)	52	49	51	53	51
Arrivals by purpose of visit							
Leisure, recreation and holidays	Thousands	(4.1)	410	418	455	462	422
Business and professional	Thousands	(4.2)	51	74	64	76	74
Other	Thousands	(4.3)	16	21	30	26	30
Overnight stays and length of stay							
Overnight stays in H&S	Thousand nights	(5.1)	2,102	2,497	2,625	2,573	2,441
Overnight stays in CE	Thousand nights	(5.2)	6,220	6,644	8,133	7,497	6,956
ALS of non resident tourists	Nights	(5.5)	13.00	12.90	14.40	13.00	13.20
Tourism expenditure							
in the country of reference	US$ Million	(8.1)	382	400	415	404	302
DOMESTIC TOURISM							
Overnight stays							
Overnight stays in H&S	Thousand nights	(5.3)	..	..	..	..	..
Overnight stays in CE	Thousand nights	(5.4)	..	..	..	..	..
OUTBOUND TOURISM							
Departures	Thousands	(6.1)					
Tourism expenditure in other countries	US$ Million	(8.2)	..	..	..	..	..
TOURISM ACTIVITIES							
Hotels and similar establishments							
Number of rooms	H&S	(7.1)	5,090	5,690	6,049	6,766	6,766
Number of bed-places	H&S	(7.2)	10,994	12,275	13,005	14,566	14,566
Occupancy rate	Percent	(7.3)	54.20	55.80	58.00	58.10	52.00
Average length of stay	Nights	(5.6)	8.00	9.40	8.80	8.50	..
ECONOMIC AGGREGATES							
Gross National Product (GNP)	US$ Million	(9.1)	..	..	..	..	..
Exports (F.O.B.)	US$ Million	(9.2)	212	212	227	..	..
Imports (C.I.F.)	US$ Million	(9.3)	1,970	1,703	1,265	..	..

Abbreviations used in tables and notes:
H&S: Hotels and similar establishments; **CE:** All types of tourism accommodation establishments; **ALS:** Average length of stay; **THS:** Non-resident tourists staying in H&S; **TCE:** Non-resident tourists staying in CE; **TF:** Arrivals of international (or non-resident) tourists; **VF:** Arrivals of international (or non-resident) visitors; **NHS:** Overnight stays at H&S; **NCE:** Overnight stays at CE.

..   data not available
incl   including
excl   excluding
nra   nationals residing abroad

Notes:
(1.2,2.2,2.3,4.1-4.3) TF; (7.1) Hotels and holiday villages (Club Méditerranée); (7.3) Rooms in H&S.

MAURITANIA

Basic Indicators	Units	Code	1996	1997	1998	1999	2000
INBOUND TOURISM							
Arrivals							
Visitors	Thousands	(1.1)	..	..	..	..	
Tourists (overnight visitors)	Thousands	(1.2)	..	..	..	24	30
Same-day visitors	Thousands	(1.3)	..	..	..	..	..
Cruise passengers	Thousands	(1.4)	..	..	..	..	..
Arrivals by region							
Africa	Thousands	(2.1)	..	..	..	..	
Americas	Thousands	(2.2)	..	..	..	..	..
Europe	Thousands	(2.3)	..	..	..	..	
East Asia and the Pacific	Thousands	(2.4)	..	..	..	..	
South Asia	Thousands	(2.5)	..	..	..	..	
Middle East	Thousands	(2.6)	..	..	..	..	
Arrivals by mode of transport							
Air	Thousands	(3.1)	..	..	..	..	
Rail	Thousands	(3.2)	..	..	..	..	..
Road	Thousands	(3.3)	..	..	..	..	
Sea	Thousands	(3.4)	..	..	..	..	..
Arrivals by purpose of visit							
Leisure, recreation and holidays	Thousands	(4.1)	..	..	..	..	
Business and professional	Thousands	(4.2)	..	..	..	..	..
Other	Thousands	(4.3)	..	..	..	..	
Overnight stays and length of stay							
Overnight stays in H&S	Thousand nights	(5.1)	..	..	..	168	162
Overnight stays in CE	Thousand nights	(5.2)	..	..	..	..	
ALS of non resident tourists	Nights	(5.5)	..	..	..	..	5.32
Tourism expenditure							
in the country of reference	US$ Million	(8.1)	19	21	20	28	..
DOMESTIC TOURISM							
Overnight stays							
Overnight stays in H&S	Thousand nights	(5.3)	..	..	..	..	
Overnight stays in CE	Thousand nights	(5.4)	..	..	..	..	..
OUTBOUND TOURISM							
Departures	Thousands	(6.1)	..	..	..	..	
Tourism expenditure in other countries	US$ Million	(8.2)	36	48	42	55	..
TOURISM ACTIVITIES							
Hotels and similar establishments							
Number of rooms	H&S	(7.1)	..	..	..	2,000	
Number of bed-places	H&S	(7.2)	..	..	..	4,000	
Occupancy rate	Percent	(7.3)	..	..	..	47.00	49.50
Average length of stay	Nights	(5.6)	..	..	..	..	..
ECONOMIC AGGREGATES							
Gross National Product (GNP)	US$ Million	(9.1)	1,104	1,093	1,041	1,001	978
Exports (F.O.B.)	US$ Million	(9.2)	..	..	..	..	..
Imports (C.I.F.)	US$ Million	(9.3)	..	..	..	..	

Abbreviations used in tables and notes:
H&S: Hotels and similar establishments; **CE:** All types of tourism accommodation establishments; **ALS:** Average length of stay; **THS:** Non-resident tourists staying in H&S; **TCE:** Non-resident tourists staying in CE; **TF:** Arrivals of international (or non-resident) tourists; **VF:** Arrivals of international (or non-resident) visitors; **NHS:** Overnight stays at H&S; **NCE:** Overnight stays at CE.

..	data not available
incl	including
excl	excluding
nra	nationals residing abroad

MAURITIUS

Basic Indicators	Units	Code	1996	1997	1998	1999	2000
INBOUND TOURISM							
Arrivals							
Visitors	Thousands	(1.1)	509	558	579	600	678
Tourists (overnight visitors)	Thousands	(1.2)	487	536	558	578	656
Same-day visitors	Thousands	(1.3)	10	9	8	11	11
Cruise passengers	Thousands	(1.4)	12	13	13	11	11
Arrivals by region							
Africa	Thousands	(2.1)	163	164	163	156	164
Americas	Thousands	(2.2)	4	6	6	6	8
Europe	Thousands	(2.3)	282	326	352	379	440
East Asia and the Pacific	Thousands	(2.4)	23	25	23	21	24
South Asia	Thousands	(2.5)	13	14	13	15	20
Middle East	Thousands	(2.6)	1	1	1	1	1
Arrivals by mode of transport							
Air	Thousands	(3.1)	480	529	541	564	646
Rail	Thousands	(3.2)	..	..	..	..	..
Road	Thousands	(3.3)	..	..	..	..	..
Sea	Thousands	(3.4)	6	7	17	14	10
Arrivals by purpose of visit							
Leisure, recreation and holidays	Thousands	(4.1)	451	494	513	531	603
Business and professional	Thousands	(4.2)	21	23	25	27	27
Other	Thousands	(4.3)	37	41	41	42	48
Overnight stays and length of stay							
Overnight stays in H&S	Thousand nights	(5.1)	4,958	5,451	5,568	5,729	6,413
Overnight stays in CE	Thousand nights	(5.2)	..	..	..	..	..
ALS of non resident tourists	Nights	(5.5)	10.60	10.50	10.30	10.40	10.40
Tourism expenditure in the country of reference	US$ Million	(8.1)	452	485	503	545	542
DOMESTIC TOURISM							
Overnight stays							
Overnight stays in H&S	Thousand nights	(5.3)	..	..	..	..	..
Overnight stays in CE	Thousand nights	(5.4)	..	..	..	..	..
OUTBOUND TOURISM							
Departures	Thousands	(6.1)	120	132	143	154	163
Tourism expenditure in other countries	US$ Million	(8.2)	179	173	185	187	182
TOURISM ACTIVITIES							
Hotels and similar establishments							
Number of rooms	H&S	(7.1)	6,668	6,809	7,267	8,255	8,657
Number of bed-places	H&S	(7.2)	13,833	14,126	14,995	16,947	17,776
Occupancy rate	Percent	(7.3)	68.00	72.00	72.00	71.00	70.00
Average length of stay	Nights	(5.6)	..	..	..	..	..
ECONOMIC AGGREGATES							
Gross National Product (GNP)	US$ Million	(9.1)	4,217	4,364	4,163	4,156	4,512
Exports (F.O.B.)	US$ Million	(9.2)	1,802	1,592	1,645	1,554	..
Imports (C.I.F.)	US$ Million	(9.3)	2,289	2,181	2,073	2,248	..

Abbreviations used in tables and notes:
H&S: Hotels and similar establishments; **CE:** All types of tourism accommodation establishments; **ALS:** Average length of stay; **THS:** Non-resident tourists staying in H&S; **TCE:** Non-resident tourists staying in CE; **TF:** Arrivals of international (or non-resident) tourists; **VF:** Arrivals of international (or non-resident) visitors; **NHS:** Overnight stays at H&S; **NCE:** Overnight stays at CE.

.. data not available
incl including
excl excluding
nra nationals residing abroad

Notes:
(1.1,4.1-4.3) VF; (1.2,2.1-3.4) TF; (5.5) Large hotels; (7.3) Rooms; (8.2) International Monetary Fund.

123

MEXICO

Basic Indicators	Units	Code	1996	1997	1998	1999	2000
INBOUND TOURISM							
Arrivals							
Visitors	Thousands	(1.1)	90,404	92,915	95,214	99,869	105,673
Tourists (overnight visitors)	Thousands	(1.2)	21,405	19,351	19,392	19,043	20,641
Same-day visitors	Thousands	(1.3)	66,857	71,311	73,576	77,778	81,565
Cruise passengers	Thousands	(1.4)	2,142	2,253	2,246	3,048	3,467
Arrivals by region							
Africa	Thousands	(2.1)	..	..	..	..	
Americas	Thousands	(2.2)	21,020	18,941	18,550	18,183	19,950
Europe	Thousands	(2.3)	341	347	477	563	401
East Asia and the Pacific	Thousands	(2.4)	..	..	..	..	..
South Asia	Thousands	(2.5)	..	..	..	..	..
Middle East	Thousands	(2.6)	..	..	..	..	..
Arrivals by mode of transport							
Air	Thousands	(3.1)	6,317	6,978	7,086	7,301	7,973
Rail	Thousands	(3.2)	..	..	..	..	..
Road	Thousands	(3.3)	15,088	12,373	12,306	11,742	12,668
Sea	Thousands	(3.4)	..	..	..	..	..
Arrivals by purpose of visit							
Leisure, recreation and holidays	Thousands	(4.1)	5,298	5,994	6,145	6,189	6,682
Business and professional	Thousands	(4.2)	802	774	545	523	584
Other	Thousands	(4.3)	15,305	12,583	12,702	12,331	13,375
Overnight stays and length of stay							
Overnight stays in H&S	Thousand nights	(5.1)	28,278	30,574	29,723	34,361	33,970
Overnight stays in CE	Thousand nights	(5.2)	..	..	..	..	..
ALS of non resident tourists	Nights	(5.5)	10.20	10.12	9.60	9.70	9.90
Tourism expenditure in the country of reference	US$ Million	(8.1)	6,934	7,593	7,493	7,223	8,295
DOMESTIC TOURISM							
Overnight stays							
Overnight stays in H&S	Thousand nights	(5.3)	42,604	45,581	48,763	63,082	69,377
Overnight stays in CE	Thousand nights	(5.4)	..	..	..	..	..
OUTBOUND TOURISM							
Departures	Thousands	(6.1)	8,848	8,910	9,637	10,352	11,081
Tourism expenditure in other countries	US$ Million	(8.2)	3,387	3,891	4,209	4,541	5,499
TOURISM ACTIVITIES							
Hotels and similar establishments							
Number of rooms	H&S	(7.1)	381,522	382,364	396,968	419,608	421,850
Number of bed-places	H&S	(7.2)	..	..	..	..	..
Occupancy rate	Percent	(7.3)	53.34	56.42	56.44	50.53	54.78
Average length of stay	Nights	(5.6)	3.77	3.75	3.65	3.62	3.44
ECONOMIC AGGREGATES							
Gross National Product (GNP)	US$ Million	(9.1)	338,598	348,643	381,267	428,414	498,018
Exports (F.O.B.)	US$ Million	(9.2)	96,000	110,431	117,460	136,391	..
Imports (C.I.F.)	US$ Million	(9.3)	89,469	109,808	125,373	141,975	..

Abbreviations used in tables and notes:
H&S: Hotels and similar establishments; **CE:** All types of tourism accommodation establishments; **ALS:** Average length of stay; **THS:** Non-resident tourists staying in H&S; **TCE:** Non-resident tourists staying in CE; **TF:** Arrivals of international (or non-resident) tourists; **VF:** Arrivals of international (or non-resident) visitors; **NHS:** Overnight stays at H&S; **NCE:** Overnight stays at CE.

.. data not available
incl including
excl excluding
nra nationals residing abroad

Notes:
(1.2,2.2-4.3) TF, incl nra; (1.3) Incl visitors of the US border zone with a length of stay under 24 hours; (3.3) Incl rail; (5.1) Selected tourism resorts; (5.1/2000); Preliminary figure; (5.6) Foreign tourism only; (7.3) Rooms; (8.1) Incl receipts from cruise passengers; (8.1,8.2) Incl receipts/expenditure from frontier visitors (staying <24h, 24-72h and over).

MICRONESIA (FEDERATED STATES OF)

Basic Indicators	Units	Code	1996	1997	1998	1999	2000
INBOUND TOURISM							
Arrivals							
Visitors	Thousands	(1.1)	..	..	..	..	..
Tourists (overnight visitors)	Thousands	(1.2)	..	28	27	28	33
Same-day visitors	Thousands	(1.3)	..	..	..	..	..
Cruise passengers	Thousands	(1.4)	..	..	..	..	..
Arrivals by region							
Africa	Thousands	(2.1)	..	..	..	..	..
Americas	Thousands	(2.2)	..	8	7	8	9
Europe	Thousands	(2.3)	..	..	..	..	..
East Asia and the Pacific	Thousands	(2.4)	..	17	16	15	18
South Asia	Thousands	(2.5)	..	..	..	..	..
Middle East	Thousands	(2.6)	..	..	..	..	..
Arrivals by mode of transport							
Air	Thousands	(3.1)	..	..	..	..	..
Rail	Thousands	(3.2)	..	..	..	..	..
Road	Thousands	(3.3)	..	..	..	..	..
Sea	Thousands	(3.4)	..	..	..	..	..
Arrivals by purpose of visit							
Leisure, recreation and holidays	Thousands	(4.1)	..	..	..	..	..
Business and professional	Thousands	(4.2)	..	..	..	..	..
Other	Thousands	(4.3)	..	..	..	..	..
Overnight stays and length of stay							
Overnight stays in H&S	Thousand nights	(5.1)	..	..	..	..	..
Overnight stays in CE	Thousand nights	(5.2)	..	..	..	..	..
ALS of non resident tourists	Nights	(5.5)	..	..	..	..	..
Tourism expenditure in the country of reference	US$ Million	(8.1)	..	..	..	..	..
DOMESTIC TOURISM							
Overnight stays							
Overnight stays in H&S	Thousand nights	(5.3)	..	..	..	..	..
Overnight stays in CE	Thousand nights	(5.4)	..	..	..	..	..
OUTBOUND TOURISM							
Departures	Thousands	(6.1)	..	..	..	..	..
Tourism expenditure in other countries	US$ Million	(8.2)	..	..	..	..	..
TOURISM ACTIVITIES							
Hotels and similar establishments							
Number of rooms	H&S	(7.1)	..	..	..	..	..
Number of bed-places	H&S	(7.2)	..	..	..	..	..
Occupancy rate	Percent	(7.3)	..	..	..	..	..
Average length of stay	Nights	(5.6)	..	..	..	..	..
ECONOMIC AGGREGATES							
Gross National Product (GNP)	US$ Million	(9.1)	238	226	220	232	250
Exports (F.O.B.)	US$ Million	(9.2)	..	..	..	..	..
Imports (C.I.F.)	US$ Million	(9.3)	..	..	..	..	..

Abbreviations used in tables and notes:
H&S: Hotels and similar establishments; **CE:** All types of tourism accommodation establishments; **ALS:** Average length of stay; **THS:** Non-resident tourists staying in H&S; **TCE:** Non-resident tourists staying in CE; **TF:** Arrivals of international (or non-resident) tourists; **VF:** Arrivals of international (or non-resident) visitors; **NHS:** Overnight stays at H&S; **NCE:** Overnight stays at CE.

..   data not available
incl   including
excl   excluding
nra   nationals residing abroad

Notes:
(1.2,2.2,2.4) Arrivals in the States of Kosrae, Chuuk, Pohnpei and Yap.

MONACO

Basic Indicators	Units	Code	1996	1997	1998	1999	2000
INBOUND TOURISM							
Arrivals							
Visitors	Thousands	(1.1)	..	..	..	..	..
Tourists (overnight visitors)	Thousands	(1.2)	226	259	278	278	300
Same-day visitors	Thousands	(1.3)	..	..	..	..	..
Cruise passengers	Thousands	(1.4)	..	..	..	..	..
Arrivals by region							
Africa	Thousands	(2.1)	..	1	1	2	2
Americas	Thousands	(2.2)	31	46	43	42	44
Europe	Thousands	(2.3)	159	172	194	202	210
East Asia and the Pacific	Thousands	(2.4)	12	14	12	12	19
South Asia	Thousands	(2.5)	..	..	..	..	..
Middle East	Thousands	(2.6)	4	4	5	4	4
Arrivals by mode of transport							
Air	Thousands	(3.1)	..	..	..	..	..
Rail	Thousands	(3.2)	..	..	..	..	..
Road	Thousands	(3.3)	..	..	..	..	..
Sea	Thousands	(3.4)	..	..	..	..	..
Arrivals by purpose of visit							
Leisure, recreation and holidays	Thousands	(4.1)	161	174	194	201	196
Business and professional	Thousands	(4.2)	65	85	84	77	104
Other	Thousands	(4.3)	..	..	..	..	..
Overnight stays and length of stay							
Overnight stays in H&S	Thousand nights	(5.1)	643	782	829	814	861
Overnight stays in CE	Thousand nights	(5.2)	..	..	..	..	..
ALS of non resident tourists	Nights	(5.5)	..	..	..	..	..
Tourism expenditure							
in the country of reference	US$ Million	(8.1)	..	..	..	..	..
DOMESTIC TOURISM							
Overnight stays							
Overnight stays in H&S	Thousand nights	(5.3)	..	..	..	..	..
Overnight stays in CE	Thousand nights	(5.4)	..	..	..	..	..
OUTBOUND TOURISM							
Departures	Thousands	(6.1)	..	..	..	..	..
Tourism expenditure in other countries	US$ Million	(8.2)	..	..	..	..	..
TOURISM ACTIVITIES							
Hotels and similar establishments							
Number of rooms	H&S	(7.1)	2,247	2,203	2,231	2,219	2,240
Number of bed-places	H&S	(7.2)	..	..	..	..	..
Occupancy rate	Percent	(7.3)	51.00	62.00	65.00	65.00	71.50
Average length of stay	Nights	(5.6)	2.84	3.02	2.98	2.92	2.87
ECONOMIC AGGREGATES							
Gross National Product (GNP)	US$ Million	(9.1)	..	..	..	..	..
Exports (F.O.B.)	US$ Million	(9.2)	..	..	..	..	..
Imports (C.I.F.)	US$ Million	(9.3)	..	..	..	..	..

Abbreviations used in tables and notes:
H&S: Hotels and similar establishments; **CE:** All types of tourism accommodation establishments; **ALS:** Average length of stay; **THS:** Non-resident tourists staying in H&S; **TCE:** Non-resident tourists staying in CE; **TF:** Arrivals of international (or non-resident) tourists; **VF:** Arrivals of international (or non-resident) visitors; **NHS:** Overnight stays at H&S; **NCE:** Overnight stays at CE.

Notes:
(1.2-2.6) THS.

..	data not available
incl	including
excl	excluding
nra	nationals residing abroad

Basic Indicators	Units	Code	1996	1997	1998	1999	2000
INBOUND TOURISM							
Arrivals							
Visitors	Thousands	(1.1)	..	..	..	..	..
Tourists (overnight visitors)	Thousands	(1.2)	71	82	197	159	158
Same-day visitors	Thousands	(1.3)	..	..	..	..	..
Cruise passengers	Thousands	(1.4)	..	..	..	..	..
Arrivals by region							
Africa	Thousands	(2.1)	..	..	..	..	..
Americas	Thousands	(2.2)	4	5	5	6	7
Europe	Thousands	(2.3)	22	26	80	72	69
East Asia and the Pacific	Thousands	(2.4)	45	50	111	79	81
South Asia	Thousands	(2.5)	..	1	1	1	1
Middle East	Thousands	(2.6)	..	..	..	..	..
Arrivals by mode of transport							
Air	Thousands	(3.1)	..	..	..	..	..
Rail	Thousands	(3.2)	..	..	..	..	..
Road	Thousands	(3.3)	..	..	..	..	..
Sea	Thousands	(3.4)	..	..	..	..	..
Arrivals by purpose of visit							
Leisure, recreation and holidays	Thousands	(4.1)	..	..	42	34	..
Business and professional	Thousands	(4.2)	..	..	32	18	..
Other	Thousands	(4.3)	..	..	123	107	..
Overnight stays and length of stay							
Overnight stays in H&S	Thousand nights	(5.1)	..	..	..	..	..
Overnight stays in CE	Thousand nights	(5.2)	..	..	..	..	..
ALS of non resident tourists	Nights	(5.5)	..	..	..	..	..
Tourism expenditure							
in the country of reference	US$ Million	(8.1)	10	13	35	36	..
DOMESTIC TOURISM							
Overnight stays							
Overnight stays in H&S	Thousand nights	(5.3)	..	..	..	..	..
Overnight stays in CE	Thousand nights	(5.4)	..	..	..	..	..
OUTBOUND TOURISM							
Departures	Thousands	(6.1)	..	..	..	..	..
Tourism expenditure in other countries	US$ Million	(8.2)	19	14	45	41	..
TOURISM ACTIVITIES							
Hotels and similar establishments							
Number of rooms	H&S	(7.1)	..	..	..	..	..
Number of bed-places	H&S	(7.2)	..	..	..	..	..
Occupancy rate	Percent	(7.3)	..	..	..	..	..
Average length of stay	Nights	(5.6)	..	..	..	..	..
ECONOMIC AGGREGATES							
Gross National Product (GNP)	US$ Million	(9.1)	931	980	985	925	926
Exports (F.O.B.)	US$ Million	(9.2)	424	452	345	233	..
Imports (C.I.F.)	US$ Million	(9.3)	451	468	503	426	..

Abbreviations used in tables and notes:
H&S: Hotels and similar establishments; **CE:** All types of tourism accommodation establishments; **ALS:** Average length of stay; **THS:** Non-resident tourists staying in H&S; **TCE:** Non-resident tourists staying in CE; **TF:** Arrivals of international (or non-resident) tourists; **VF:** Arrivals of international (or non-resident) visitors; **NHS:** Overnight stays at H&S; **NCE:** Overnight stays at CE.

..	data not available
incl	including
excl	excluding
nra	nationals residing abroad

Notes:
(8.1,8.2) International Monetary Fund.

MONTSERRAT

Basic Indicators	Units	Code	1996	1997	1998	1999	2000
INBOUND TOURISM							
Arrivals							
Visitors	Thousands	(1.1)	17	..	..	..	
Tourists (overnight visitors)	Thousands	(1.2)	9	5	7	10	10
Same-day visitors	Thousands	(1.3)	1	1	..	..	..
Cruise passengers	Thousands	(1.4)	7	..	..	..	..
Arrivals by region							
Africa	Thousands	(2.1)	..	..	..	..	
Americas	Thousands	(2.2)	7	4	6	7	..
Europe	Thousands	(2.3)	2	1	1	2	3
East Asia and the Pacific	Thousands	(2.4)	..	..	..	..	..
South Asia	Thousands	(2.5)	..	..	..	..	..
Middle East	Thousands	(2.6)	..	..	..	..	..
Arrivals by mode of transport							
Air	Thousands	(3.1)	10	5	7	10	10
Rail	Thousands	(3.2)	..	..	..	..	..
Road	Thousands	(3.3)	..	..	..	..	..
Sea	Thousands	(3.4)	7	..	..	..	..
Arrivals by purpose of visit							
Leisure, recreation and holidays	Thousands	(4.1)	7	4	..	..	..
Business and professional	Thousands	(4.2)	2	1	..	..	..
Other	Thousands	(4.3)	..	..	..	..	..
Overnight stays and length of stay							
Overnight stays in H&S	Thousand nights	(5.1)	..	..	..	..	..
Overnight stays in CE	Thousand nights	(5.2)	..	..	..	..	..
ALS of non resident tourists	Nights	(5.5)	..	..	..	..	..
Tourism expenditure							
in the country of reference	US$ Million	(8.1)	10	5	8	11	9
DOMESTIC TOURISM							
Overnight stays							
Overnight stays in H&S	Thousand nights	(5.3)	..	..	..	..	..
Overnight stays in CE	Thousand nights	(5.4)	..	..	..	..	..
OUTBOUND TOURISM							
Departures	Thousands	(6.1)	..	..	..	..	..
Tourism expenditure in other countries	US$ Million	(8.2)	..	..	..	..	..
TOURISM ACTIVITIES							
Hotels and similar establishments							
Number of rooms	H&S	(7.1)	..	..	221	243	..
Number of bed-places	H&S	(7.2)	..	..	..	..	..
Occupancy rate	Percent	(7.3)	..	..	..	..	..
Average length of stay	Nights	(5.6)	..	..	..	..	..
ECONOMIC AGGREGATES							
Gross National Product (GNP)	US$ Million	(9.1)	42	33	32	34	..
Exports (F.O.B.)	US$ Million	(9.2)	..	..	..	..	..
Imports (C.I.F.)	US$ Million	(9.3)	..	..	..	..	..

Abbreviations used in tables and notes:
H&S: Hotels and similar establishments; **CE:** All types of tourism accommodation establishments; **ALS:** Average length of stay; **THS:** Non-resident tourists staying in H&S; **TCE:** Non-resident tourists staying in CE; **TF:** Arrivals of international (or non-resident) tourists; **VF:** Arrivals of international (or non-resident) visitors; **NHS:** Overnight stays at H&S; **NCE:** Overnight stays at CE.

.. data not available
incl including
excl excluding
nra nationals residing abroad

Notes:
(1.2,2.2,2.3) TF; (1.3) Air same-day visitors only; (2.2,2.3,4.1,4.2) TF, air arrivals only; (3.1,3.4) VF; (4.2) Business and other purposes; (7.1) Hotels and villas; (9.1) GDP.

Basic Indicators	Units	Code	1996	1997	1998	1999	2000
INBOUND TOURISM							
Arrivals							
Visitors	Thousands	(1.1)	2,856	3,203	3,414	4,088	4,293
Tourists (overnight visitors)	Thousands	(1.2)	2,693	3,072	3,242	3,817	4,113
Same-day visitors	Thousands	(1.3)	..	..	..	..	..
Cruise passengers	Thousands	(1.4)	163	131	172	271	180
Arrivals by region							
Africa	Thousands	(2.1)	76	78	81	88	100
Americas	Thousands	(2.2)	120	130	142	179	179
Europe	Thousands	(2.3)	1,337	1,508	1,656	1,876	2,056
East Asia and the Pacific	Thousands	(2.4)	32	36	39	45	35
South Asia	Thousands	(2.5)	3	3	4	5	5
Middle East	Thousands	(2.6)	63	66	77	78	67
Arrivals by mode of transport							
Air	Thousands	(3.1)	1,277	1,431	1,581	1,853	1,994
Rail	Thousands	(3.2)	..	..	..	..	..
Road	Thousands	(3.3)	395	454	525	508	502
Sea	Thousands	(3.4)	1,021	1,187	1,136	1,456	1,617
Arrivals by purpose of visit							
Leisure, recreation and holidays	Thousands	(4.1)	1,481	1,690	1,783	2,100	2,205
Business and professional	Thousands	(4.2)	216	246	259	305	272
Other	Thousands	(4.3)	996	1,136	1,200	1,412	1,636
Overnight stays and length of stay							
Overnight stays in H&S	Thousand nights	(5.1)	8,719	9,560	10,676	11,891	12,313
Overnight stays in CE	Thousand nights	(5.2)	18,719	19,676	21,021	22,486	23,234
ALS of non resident tourists	Nights	(5.5)	12.00	10.70	10.40	10.00	9.43
Tourism expenditure							
in the country of reference	US$ Million	(8.1)	1,674	1,449	1,712	1,880	2,040
DOMESTIC TOURISM							
Overnight stays							
Overnight stays in H&S	Thousand nights	(5.3)	3,876	4,062	4,114	4,088	4,211
Overnight stays in CE	Thousand nights	(5.4)	9,876	10,116	10,247	9,513	10,599
OUTBOUND TOURISM							
Departures	Thousands	(6.1)	1,212	1,203	1,359	1,612	1,595
Tourism expenditure in other countries	US$ Million	(8.2)	300	316	424	440	430
TOURISM ACTIVITIES							
Hotels and similar establishments							
Number of rooms	H&S	(7.1)	63,981	63,037	64,946	66,077	66,823
Number of bed-places	H&S	(7.2)	124,411	122,941	125,091	127,537	128,357
Occupancy rate	Percent	(7.3)	41.00	43.90	48.20	51.60	47.62
Average length of stay	Nights	(5.6)	7.00	7.10	7.30	7.00	6.34
ECONOMIC AGGREGATES							
Gross National Product (GNP)	US$ Million	(9.1)	34,904	34,198	34,749	33,715	33,820
Exports (F.O.B.)	US$ Million	(9.2)	6,881	7,033	7,153	7,367	7,429
Imports (C.I.F.)	US$ Million	(9.3)	9,704	9,526	10,290	9,925	11,534

Abbreviations used in tables and notes:
H&S: Hotels and similar establishments; **CE:** All types of tourism accommodation establishments; **ALS:** Average length of stay; **THS:** Non-resident tourists staying in H&S; **TCE:** Non-resident tourists staying in CE; **TF:** Arrivals of international (or non-resident) tourists; **VF:** Arrivals of international (or non-resident) visitors; **NHS:** Overnight stays at H&S; **NCE:** Overnight stays at CE.

.. data not available
incl including
excl excluding
nra nationals residing abroad

Notes:
(1.2,3.1-4.3) TF, incl nra; (2.1-2.6) TF, excl nra; (5.1,5.3) Overnight stays in classified and unclassified hotels, holiday villages and tourist residences; (7.3) Rooms (classified hotels).

MYANMAR

Basic Indicators	Units	Code	1996	1997	1998	1999	2000
INBOUND TOURISM							
Arrivals							
Visitors	Thousands	(1.1)	490	491	478	434	416
Tourists (overnight visitors)	Thousands	(1.2)	172	189	201	198	206
Same-day visitors	Thousands	(1.3)	315	299	274	235	209
Cruise passengers	Thousands	(1.4)	3	3	3	1	1
Arrivals by region							
Africa	Thousands	(2.1)	..	..	..	..	..
Americas	Thousands	(2.2)	14	15	13	13	14
Europe	Thousands	(2.3)	51	55	52	52	55
East Asia and the Pacific	Thousands	(2.4)	98	114	120	126	129
South Asia	Thousands	(2.5)	2	2	11	6	6
Middle East	Thousands	(2.6)	..	..	..	1	1
Arrivals by mode of transport							
Air	Thousands	(3.1)	172	189	201	198	206
Rail	Thousands	(3.2)	..	..	..	..	..
Road	Thousands	(3.3)	315	299	274	235	209
Sea	Thousands	(3.4)	3	3	3	1	1
Arrivals by purpose of visit							
Leisure, recreation and holidays	Thousands	(4.1)	100	122	125	118	126
Business and professional	Thousands	(4.2)	43	42	35	37	37
Other	Thousands	(4.3)	347	327	318	279	253
Overnight stays and length of stay							
Overnight stays in H&S	Thousand nights	(5.1)	1,225	1,323	1,407	1,386	1,442
Overnight stays in CE	Thousand nights	(5.2)	..	..	..	..	..
ALS of non resident tourists	Nights	(5.5)	7.00	7.00	7.00	7.00	7.00
Tourism expenditure							
in the country of reference	US$ Million	(8.1)	33	34	35	35	42
DOMESTIC TOURISM							
Overnight stays							
Overnight stays in H&S	Thousand nights	(5.3)	..	..	..	..	..
Overnight stays in CE	Thousand nights	(5.4)	..	..	..	..	..
OUTBOUND TOURISM							
Departures	Thousands	(6.1)	..	..	..	..	..
Tourism expenditure in other countries	US$ Million	(8.2)	28	33	27	21	25
TOURISM ACTIVITIES							
Hotels and similar establishments							
Number of rooms	H&S	(7.1)	11,916	13,338	14,891	14,706	16,157
Number of bed-places	H&S	(7.2)	23,732	26,676	29,782	29,412	32,314
Occupancy rate	Percent	(7.3)	32.00	26.00	28.00	30.00	26.60
Average length of stay	Nights	(5.6)	4.00	4.00	4.00	4.00	4.00
ECONOMIC AGGREGATES							
Gross National Product (GNP)	US$ Million	(9.1)	..	..	..	..	..
Exports (F.O.B.)	US$ Million	(9.2)	744	866	1,066	1,125	1,621
Imports (C.I.F.)	US$ Million	(9.3)	1,355	2,037	2,667	2,301	2,371

Abbreviations used in tables and notes:
H&S: Hotels and similar establishments; **CE:** All types of tourism accommodation establishments; **ALS:** Average length of stay; **THS:** Non-resident tourists staying in H&S; **TCE:** Non-resident tourists staying in CE; **TF:** Arrivals of international (or non-resident) tourists; **VF:** Arrivals of international (or non-resident) visitors; **NHS:** Overnight stays at H&S; **NCE:** Overnight stays at CE.

Notes:
(1.2,2.2-2.5,3.1) Arrivals at Yangon by air; (4.1-4.3) VF; (5.1,5.3,5.6) State-run H&S establishments only; (7.1,7.2) State-run hotels and private registered guest houses; (7.3) Rooms; (8.2) International Monetary Fund.

..	data not available
incl	including
excl	excluding
nra	nationals residing abroad

Basic Indicators	Units	Code	1996	1997	1998	1999	2000
INBOUND TOURISM							
Arrivals							
Visitors	Thousands	(1.1)	525	571	..	..	..
Tourists (overnight visitors)	Thousands	(1.2)	461	502	614	..	..
Same-day visitors	Thousands	(1.3)	64	69	..	..	..
Cruise passengers	Thousands	(1.4)	..	..	..	..	..
Arrivals by region							
Africa	Thousands	(2.1)	351	384	430	..	..
Americas	Thousands	(2.2)	8	9	10	..	..
Europe	Thousands	(2.3)	94	101	111	..	..
East Asia and the Pacific	Thousands	(2.4)	..	..	..	..	..
South Asia	Thousands	(2.5)	..	..	..	..	..
Middle East	Thousands	(2.6)	..	..	..	..	..
Arrivals by mode of transport							
Air	Thousands	(3.1)	112	121	..	..	..
Rail	Thousands	(3.2)	..	..	..	..	..
Road	Thousands	(3.3)	..	..	..	..	..
Sea	Thousands	(3.4)	..	..	..	..	..
Arrivals by purpose of visit							
Leisure, recreation and holidays	Thousands	(4.1)	369	402	..	..	..
Business and professional	Thousands	(4.2)	64	70	..	..	..
Other	Thousands	(4.3)	28	30	..	..	..
Overnight stays and length of stay							
Overnight stays in H&S	Thousand nights	(5.1)	..	393	497	..	..
Overnight stays in CE	Thousand nights	(5.2)	..	764	925	..	..
ALS of non resident tourists	Nights	(5.5)	..	19.60	..	..	..
Tourism expenditure							
in the country of reference	US$ Million	(8.1)	293	333	288	..	..
DOMESTIC TOURISM							
Overnight stays							
Overnight stays in H&S	Thousand nights	(5.3)	..	194	224	..	..
Overnight stays in CE	Thousand nights	(5.4)	..	403	473	..	..
OUTBOUND TOURISM							
Departures	Thousands	(6.1)	..	..	..	..	..
Tourism expenditure in other countries	US$ Million	(8.2)	89	99	88	..	..
TOURISM ACTIVITIES							
Hotels and similar establishments							
Number of rooms	H&S	(7.1)	..	2,652	2,779	..	..
Number of bed-places	H&S	(7.2)	..	5,501	5,767	..	..
Occupancy rate	Percent	(7.3)	38.20	32.90	35.90	..	..
Average length of stay	Nights	(5.6)	..	1.80	1.90	..	..
ECONOMIC AGGREGATES							
Gross National Product (GNP)	US$ Million	(9.1)	3,723	3,795	3,664	3,565	3,569
Exports (F.O.B.)	US$ Million	(9.2)	1,352	..	..	..	..
Imports (C.I.F.)	US$ Million	(9.3)	1,511	..	..	..	..

Abbreviations used in tables and notes:
H&S: Hotels and similar establishments; **CE:** All types of tourism accommodation establishments; **ALS:** Average length of stay; **THS:** Non-resident tourists staying in H&S; **TCE:** Non-resident tourists staying in CE; **TF:** Arrivals of international (or non-resident) tourists; **VF:** Arrivals of international (or non-resident) visitors; **NHS:** Overnight stays at H&S; **NCE:** Overnight stays at CE.

..   data not available
incl   including
excl   excluding
nra   nationals residing abroad

Notes:
(2.1-2.3) TF; (3.1) Arrivals at Windhoek airport; (4.1-4.3) TF; (7.3) Bed-places; (8.1,8.2) International Monetary Fund.

NEPAL

Basic Indicators	Units	Code	1996	1997	1998	1999	2000
INBOUND TOURISM							
Arrivals							
Visitors	Thousands	(1.1)	..	..	..	..	..
Tourists (overnight visitors)	Thousands	(1.2)	394	422	464	492	464
Same-day visitors	Thousands	(1.3)	..	..	..	..	..
Cruise passengers	Thousands	(1.4)	..	..	..	..	..
Arrivals by region							
Africa	Thousands	(2.1)	2	2	2	2	2
Americas	Thousands	(2.2)	33	39	47	51	53
Europe	Thousands	(2.3)	138	146	159	173	168
East Asia and the Pacific	Thousands	(2.4)	79	85	88	96	112
South Asia	Thousands	(2.5)	140	149	166	169	128
Middle East	Thousands	(2.6)	..	..	..	..	..
Arrivals by mode of transport							
Air	Thousands	(3.1)	343	371	398	421	377
Rail	Thousands	(3.2)	..	..	..	..	..
Road	Thousands	(3.3)	50	51	66	70	87
Sea	Thousands	(3.4)	..	..	..	..	..
Arrivals by purpose of visit							
Leisure, recreation and holidays	Thousands	(4.1)	298	341	374	399	375
Business and professional	Thousands	(4.2)	51	57	52	54	56
Other	Thousands	(4.3)	44	24	38	39	33
Overnight stays and length of stay							
Overnight stays in H&S	Thousand nights	(5.1)	1,017	..	..	..	..
Overnight stays in CE	Thousand nights	(5.2)	..	..	..	..	..
ALS of non resident tourists	Nights	(5.5)	13.50	10.49	10.76	12.28	11.88
Tourism expenditure in the country of reference	US$ Million	(8.1)	117	116	153	168	167
DOMESTIC TOURISM							
Overnight stays							
Overnight stays in H&S	Thousand nights	(5.3)	..	..	..	..	..
Overnight stays in CE	Thousand nights	(5.4)	..	..	..	..	..
OUTBOUND TOURISM							
Departures	Thousands	(6.1)	119	132	122	125	155
Tourism expenditure in other countries	US$ Million	(8.2)	125	103	78	71	73
TOURISM ACTIVITIES							
Hotels and similar establishments							
Number of rooms	H&S	(7.1)	13,084	14,214	14,871	16,719	18,203
Number of bed-places	H&S	(7.2)	25,638	27,612	28,878	32,214	34,958
Occupancy rate	Percent	(7.3)	50.00	..	..	..	..
Average length of stay	Nights	(5.6)	..	..	..	..	..
ECONOMIC AGGREGATES							
Gross National Product (GNP)	US$ Million	(9.1)	4,727	4,967	4,930	5,173	5,324
Exports (F.O.B.)	US$ Million	(9.2)	385	406	474	600	804
Imports (C.I.F.)	US$ Million	(9.3)	1,398	1,693	1,245	1,418	1,572

Abbreviations used in tables and notes:
H&S: Hotels and similar establishments; **CE:** All types of tourism accommodation establishments; **ALS:** Average length of stay; **THS:** Non-resident tourists staying in H&S; **TCE:** Non-resident tourists staying in CE; **TF:** Arrivals of international (or non-resident) tourists; **VF:** Arrivals of international (or non-resident) visitors; **NHS:** Overnight stays at H&S; **NCE:** Overnight stays at CE.

.. data not available
incl including
excl excluding
nra nationals residing abroad

Notes:
(1.2) Incl arrivals from India; (3.3) Land; (7.1,7.2) Hotels in Kathmandu and in the interior of the country; (8.2) International Monetary Fund.

Basic Indicators	Units	Code	1996	1997	1998	1999	2000
INBOUND TOURISM							
Arrivals							
Visitors	Thousands	(1.1)	..	..	..	..	..
Tourists (overnight visitors)	Thousands	(1.2)	6,580	7,841	9,312	9,874	10,003
Same-day visitors	Thousands	(1.3)	..	..	..	..	..
Cruise passengers	Thousands	(1.4)	..	..	..	..	..
Arrivals by region							
Africa	Thousands	(2.1)	55	72	80	107	108
Americas	Thousands	(2.2)	664	900	1,144	1,162	1,216
Europe	Thousands	(2.3)	5,340	6,149	7,371	7,905	7,956
East Asia and the Pacific	Thousands	(2.4)	521	720	717	700	723
South Asia	Thousands	(2.5)	..	..	..	..	..
Middle East	Thousands	(2.6)	..	..	..	..	..
Arrivals by mode of transport							
Air	Thousands	(3.1)	..	..	..	3,787	..
Rail	Thousands	(3.2)	..	..	..	836	..
Road	Thousands	(3.3)	..	..	..	5,172	..
Sea	Thousands	(3.4)	..	..	..	287	..
Arrivals by purpose of visit							
Leisure, recreation and holidays	Thousands	(4.1)	..	..	..	5,490	..
Business and professional	Thousands	(4.2)	..	..	..	2,946	..
Other	Thousands	(4.3)	..	..	..	1,438	..
Overnight stays and length of stay							
Overnight stays in H&S	Thousand nights	(5.1)	9,922	11,569	14,693	15,218	15,695
Overnight stays in CE	Thousand nights	(5.2)	19,042	21,422	24,967	27,433	27,261
ALS of non resident tourists	Nights	(5.5)	2.90	2.70	2.70	2.80	2.70
Tourism expenditure in the country of reference	US$ Million	(8.1)	6,548	6,319	6,792	6,998	7,206
DOMESTIC TOURISM							
Overnight stays							
Overnight stays in H&S	Thousand nights	(5.3)	9,074	10,427	12,488	13,829	14,027
Overnight stays in CE	Thousand nights	(5.4)	42,354	42,927	51,828	55,531	55,310
OUTBOUND TOURISM							
Departures	Thousands	(6.1)	12,813	12,855	13,549	14,186	13,891
Tourism expenditure in other countries	US$ Million	(8.2)	11,528	11,285	11,996	12,045	12,198
TOURISM ACTIVITIES							
Hotels and similar establishments							
Number of rooms	H&S	(7.1)	..	..	..	..	..
Number of bed-places	H&S	(7.2)	143,000	144,000	169,000	170,000	173,000
Occupancy rate	Percent	(7.3)	37.80	42.90	46.40	48.30	48.50
Average length of stay	Nights	(5.6)	3.48	3.27	3.25	3.25	3.19
ECONOMIC AGGREGATES							
Gross National Product (GNP)	US$ Million	(9.1)	417,756	425,227	403,336	397,393	400,280
Exports (F.O.B.)	US$ Million	(9.2)	197,420	194,909	201,382	200,290	208,896
Imports (C.I.F.)	US$ Million	(9.3)	180,642	178,133	187,754	187,488	197,290

Abbreviations used in tables and notes:
H&S: Hotels and similar establishments; **CE:** All types of tourism accommodation establishments; **ALS:** Average length of stay; **THS:** Non-resident tourists staying in H&S; **TCE:** Non-resident tourists staying in CE; **TF:** Arrivals of international (or non-resident) tourists; **VF:** Arrivals of international (or non-resident) visitors; **NHS:** Overnight stays at H&S; **NCE:** Overnight stays at CE.

.. data not available
incl including
excl excluding
nra nationals residing abroad

Notes:
(1.2-2.4) TCE; (5.1,5.3) Hotels and boarding houses; (6.1) Holiday departures of nationals; (7.2) Hotels; (7.3) Bed-places.

NEW CALEDONIA

Basic Indicators	Units	Code	1996	1997	1998	1999	2000
INBOUND TOURISM							
Arrivals							
Visitors	Thousands	(1.1)	138	139	129	147	160
Tourists (overnight visitors)	Thousands	(1.2)	91	105	104	100	110
Same-day visitors	Thousands	(1.3)	1	2	2	1	1
Cruise passengers	Thousands	(1.4)	46	32	23	46	49
Arrivals by region							
Africa	Thousands	(2.1)	..	..	1	1	1
Americas	Thousands	(2.2)	1	1	2	2	2
Europe	Thousands	(2.3)	30	33	31	32	34
East Asia and the Pacific	Thousands	(2.4)	59	70	70	65	72
South Asia	Thousands	(2.5)	..	..	..	..	..
Middle East	Thousands	(2.6)	..	..	..	..	..
Arrivals by mode of transport							
Air	Thousands	(3.1)	89	103	104	100	110
Rail	Thousands	(3.2)	..	..	..	..	..
Road	Thousands	(3.3)	..	..	..	..	..
Sea	Thousands	(3.4)	2	2	2	1	1
Arrivals by purpose of visit							
Leisure, recreation and holidays	Thousands	(4.1)	64	76	76	76	77
Business and professional	Thousands	(4.2)	9	10	11	10	10
Other	Thousands	(4.3)	18	19	17	14	26
Overnight stays and length of stay							
Overnight stays in H&S	Thousand nights	(5.1)	321	385	391	350	372
Overnight stays in CE	Thousand nights	(5.2)	..	..	..	..	..
ALS of non resident tourists	Nights	(5.5)	17.00	16.00	16.00	16.00	16.00
Tourism expenditure							
in the country of reference	US$ Million	(8.1)	114	117	110	112	110
DOMESTIC TOURISM							
Overnight stays							
Overnight stays in H&S	Thousand nights	(5.3)	167	159	140	166	181
Overnight stays in CE	Thousand nights	(5.4)	..	..	..	..	..
OUTBOUND TOURISM							
Departures	Thousands	(6.1)	64	64	68	69	69
Tourism expenditure in other countries	US$ Million	(8.2)	..	..	..	..	..
TOURISM ACTIVITIES							
Hotels and similar establishments							
Number of rooms	H&S	(7.1)	2,075	2,058	2,061	2,398	2,401
Number of bed-places	H&S	(7.2)	..	..	..	..	..
Occupancy rate	Percent	(7.3)	50.50	57.00	56.60	54.00	51.60
Average length of stay	Nights	(5.6)	4.60	4.70	4.50	4.40	4.40
ECONOMIC AGGREGATES							
Gross National Product (GNP)	US$ Million	(9.1)	3,604	3,587	3,305	3,169	3,203
Exports (F.O.B.)	US$ Million	(9.2)	487	522	..	..	..
Imports (C.I.F.)	US$ Million	(9.3)	995	928	..	..	..

Abbreviations used in tables and notes:
H&S: Hotels and similar establishments; **CE:** All types of tourism accommodation establishments; **ALS:** Average length of stay; **THS:** Non-resident tourists staying in H&S; **TCE:** Non-resident tourists staying in CE; **TF:** Arrivals of international (or non-resident) tourists; **VF:** Arrivals of international (or non-resident) visitors; **NHS:** Overnight stays at H&S; **NCE:** Overnight stays at CE.

.. data not available
incl including
excl excluding
nra nationals residing abroad

Notes:
(1.2,2.1-4.3) Incl nra; (5.6) Days, hotels in Noumea; (6.1) As from 2000, this figure relates to returning residents; (7.1) Source: "Nouvelle-Calédonie Tourisme"; (7.3) Rooms in Noumea; (8.1) Expenditure in the receiving country by international visitors; excluding international transport; (9.1) GDP.

Basic Indicators	Units	Code	1996	1997	1998	1999	2000
INBOUND TOURISM							
Arrivals							
Visitors	Thousands	(1.1)	1,529	1,497	1,485	1,607	1,787
Tourists (overnight visitors)	Thousands	(1.2)	..	..	..	..	..
Same-day visitors	Thousands	(1.3)	..	..	..	..	..
Cruise passengers	Thousands	(1.4)	..	..	..	..	..
Arrivals by region							
Africa	Thousands	(2.1)	14	16	17	17	19
Americas	Thousands	(2.2)	187	185	206	229	245
Europe	Thousands	(2.3)	270	281	295	318	372
East Asia and the Pacific	Thousands	(2.4)	983	942	887	958	1,069
South Asia	Thousands	(2.5)	6	6	7	8	10
Middle East	Thousands	(2.6)	4	4	4	5	5
Arrivals by mode of transport							
Air	Thousands	(3.1)	1,518	1,488	1,470	1,592	1,776
Rail	Thousands	(3.2)	..	..	..	..	..
Road	Thousands	(3.3)	..	..	..	..	..
Sea	Thousands	(3.4)	11	9	15	15	11
Arrivals by purpose of visit							
Leisure, recreation and holidays	Thousands	(4.1)	849	806	742	820	929
Business and professional	Thousands	(4.2)	194	200	212	227	235
Other	Thousands	(4.3)	486	491	531	560	623
Overnight stays and length of stay							
Overnight stays in H&S	Thousand nights	(5.1)	..	..	..	..	..
Overnight stays in CE	Thousand nights	(5.2)	..	7,637	7,470	8,230	9,115
ALS of non resident tourists	Nights	(5.5)	19.30	20.00	19.60	20.00	20.10
Tourism expenditure in the country of reference	US$ Million	(8.1)	2,432	1,762	1,692	2,030	2,100
DOMESTIC TOURISM							
Overnight stays							
Overnight stays in H&S	Thousand nights	(5.3)	..	..	..	5,718	5,056
Overnight stays in CE	Thousand nights	(5.4)	..	..	..	26,100	24,300
OUTBOUND TOURISM							
Departures	Thousands	(6.1)	1,093	1,132	1,166	1,185	1,283
Tourism expenditure in other countries	US$ Million	(8.2)	1,529	1,497	1,484	1,607	1,786
TOURISM ACTIVITIES							
Hotels and similar establishments							
Number of rooms	H&S	(7.1)	..	22,826	23,853	24,899	25,911
Number of bed-places	H&S	(7.2)	..	..	..	..	..
Occupancy rate	Percent	(7.3)	..	49.70	47.80	50.80	52.00
Average length of stay	Nights	(5.6)	..	1.74	1.79	1.80	1.75
ECONOMIC AGGREGATES							
Gross National Product (GNP)	US$ Million	(9.1)	57,079	60,810	55,091	53,337	50,120
Exports (F.O.B.)	US$ Million	(9.2)	14,360	14,215	12,071	12,455	13,266
Imports (C.I.F.)	US$ Million	(9.3)	14,724	14,519	12,496	14,299	13,906

Abbreviations used in tables and notes:
H&S: Hotels and similar establishments; **CE:** All types of tourism accommodation establishments; **ALS:** Average length of stay; **THS:** Non-resident tourists staying in H&S; **TCE:** Non-resident tourists staying in CE; **TF:** Arrivals of international (or non-resident) tourists; **VF:** Arrivals of international (or non-resident) visitors; **NHS:** Overnight stays at H&S; **NCE:** Overnight stays at CE.

..   data not available
incl   including
excl   excluding
nra   nationals residing abroad

Notes:
(1.1,3.1-4.3) VF, Incl nra; (2.1-2.6) VF, Excl nra; (5.2) Estimated from total guest nights based on average percentage of international guests in Jan, Apr, Jul and Oct; (5.3) Licensed hotels/motels; (6.1) Short-term departures of NZ residents (calendar year); (7.1) Hotels only; (7.1,7.3) Data relate to calendar year supplied by the Accommodation Survey which began in July 1996.

NICARAGUA

Basic Indicators	Units	Code	1996	1997	1998	1999	2000
INBOUND TOURISM							
Arrivals							
Visitors	Thousands	(1.1)	388	456	484	532	579
Tourists (overnight visitors)	Thousands	(1.2)	303	358	406	468	486
Same-day visitors	Thousands	(1.3)	84	95	77	62	80
Cruise passengers	Thousands	(1.4)	..	..	..	..	13
Arrivals by region							
Africa	Thousands	(2.1)	..	..	..	..	1
Americas	Thousands	(2.2)	267	322	365	424	437
Europe	Thousands	(2.3)	30	30	34	35	38
East Asia and the Pacific	Thousands	(2.4)	5	5	6	8	9
South Asia	Thousands	(2.5)	..	..	1	1	1
Middle East	Thousands	(2.6)	..	..	..	..	..
Arrivals by mode of transport							
Air	Thousands	(3.1)	105	123	136	153	172
Rail	Thousands	(3.2)	..	..	..	..	..
Road	Thousands	(3.3)	182	223	257	301	297
Sea	Thousands	(3.4)	15	12	13	14	17
Arrivals by purpose of visit							
Leisure, recreation and holidays	Thousands	(4.1)	82	109	125	150	191
Business and professional	Thousands	(4.2)	220	248	264	307	282
Other	Thousands	(4.3)	1	1	17	11	12
Overnight stays and length of stay							
Overnight stays in H&S	Thousand nights	(5.1)	170	260	280	247	300
Overnight stays in CE	Thousand nights	(5.2)	201	305	335	301	375
ALS of non resident tourists	Nights	(5.5)	..	..	..	..	..
Tourism expenditure							
in the country of reference	US$ Million	(8.1)	54	74	90	107	111
DOMESTIC TOURISM							
Overnight stays							
Overnight stays in H&S	Thousand nights	(5.3)	66	56	63	89	96
Overnight stays in CE	Thousand nights	(5.4)	87	84	104	143	182
OUTBOUND TOURISM							
Departures	Thousands	(6.1)	282	330	422	452	486
Tourism expenditure in other countries	US$ Million	(8.2)	60	65	70	78	79
TOURISM ACTIVITIES							
Hotels and similar establishments							
Number of rooms	H&S	(7.1)	2,119	2,217	2,566	2,764	3,320
Number of bed-places	H&S	(7.2)	3,813	4,002	4,507	4,856	5,819
Occupancy rate	Percent	(7.3)	..	..	..	..	..
Average length of stay	Nights	(5.6)	2.80	3.00	3.20	3.30	3.30
ECONOMIC AGGREGATES							
Gross National Product (GNP)	US$ Million	(9.1)	1,658	1,767	1,788	1,955	2,126
Exports (F.O.B.)	US$ Million	(9.2)	466	577	573	545	631
Imports (C.I.F.)	US$ Million	(9.3)	1,154	1,450	1,492	1,862	1,759

Abbreviations used in tables and notes:
H&S: Hotels and similar establishments; **CE:** All types of tourism accommodation establishments; **ALS:** Average length of stay; **THS:** Non-resident tourists staying in H&S; **TCE:** Non-resident tourists staying in CE; **TF:** Arrivals of international (or non-resident) tourists; **VF:** Arrivals of international (or non-resident) visitors; **NHS:** Overnight stays at H&S; **NCE:** Overnight stays at CE.

..	data not available
incl	including
excl	excluding
nra	nationals residing abroad

Notes:
(1.2,2.2-4.3) TF; (5.1,5.3) Main accommodation establishments in the country (7); (5.2,5.4) Total number of establishments in the country; (5.6) CE, inbound tourism; ALS for internal tourism are as follows (Nights): 96=1.7; 97=1.5; 98=1.8; 99=1.6; 2000=2.0; (7.1,7.2) H&S classified in higher categories.

NIGER

Basic Indicators	Units	Code	1996	1997	1998	1999	2000
INBOUND TOURISM							
Arrivals							
Visitors	Thousands	(1.1)	..	..	..	..	..
Tourists (overnight visitors)	Thousands	(1.2)	38	44	42	43	50
Same-day visitors	Thousands	(1.3)	..	..	..	..	..
Cruise passengers	Thousands	(1.4)	..	..	..	..	..
Arrivals by region							
Africa	Thousands	(2.1)	7	7	8	27	28
Americas	Thousands	(2.2)	2	2	3	1	2
Europe	Thousands	(2.3)	7	8	8	9	14
East Asia and the Pacific	Thousands	(2.4)	1	1	1	1	..
South Asia	Thousands	(2.5)	..	..	..	..	..
Middle East	Thousands	(2.6)	..	1	..	..	..
Arrivals by mode of transport							
Air	Thousands	(3.1)	38	44	42	43	50
Rail	Thousands	(3.2)	..	..	..	..	..
Road	Thousands	(3.3)	..	..	..	..	..
Sea	Thousands	(3.4)	..	..	..	..	..
Arrivals by purpose of visit							
Leisure, recreation and holidays	Thousands	(4.1)	5	6	6	13	..
Business and professional	Thousands	(4.2)	8	8	9	15	..
Other	Thousands	(4.3)	25	30	27	15	..
Overnight stays and length of stay							
Overnight stays in H&S	Thousand nights	(5.1)	..	..	..	..	..
Overnight stays in CE	Thousand nights	(5.2)	180	195	198	208	..
ALS of non resident tourists	Nights	(5.5)	10.00	10.00	10.00	10.00	..
Tourism expenditure in the country of reference	US$ Million	(8.1)	17	18	18	24	..
DOMESTIC TOURISM							
Overnight stays							
Overnight stays in H&S	Thousand nights	(5.3)	16	18	20	112	..
Overnight stays in CE	Thousand nights	(5.4)	..	..	..	..	..
OUTBOUND TOURISM							
Departures	Thousands	(6.1)	10	10	10	10	..
Tourism expenditure in other countries	US$ Million	(8.2)	23	24	25	26	28
TOURISM ACTIVITIES							
Hotels and similar establishments							
Number of rooms	H&S	(7.1)	1,519	1,519	1,519	1,233	..
Number of bed-places	H&S	(7.2)	3,037	3,037	3,037	2,336	..
Occupancy rate	Percent	(7.3)	37.50	37.80	45.00	39.26	..
Average length of stay	Nights	(5.6)	5.00	5.00	5.00	5.00	..
ECONOMIC AGGREGATES							
Gross National Product (GNP)	US$ Million	(9.1)	1,889	1,952	2,049	1,974	1,988
Exports (F.O.B.)	US$ Million	(9.2)	325	272	334	288	262
Imports (C.I.F.)	US$ Million	(9.3)	448	391	376	390	363

Abbreviations used in tables and notes:
H&S: Hotels and similar establishments; CE: All types of tourism accommodation establishments; ALS: Average length of stay; THS: Non-resident tourists staying in H&S; TCE: Non-resident tourists staying in CE; TF: Arrivals of international (or non-resident) tourists; VF: Arrivals of international (or non-resident) visitors; NHS: Overnight stays at H&S; NCE: Overnight stays at CE.

.. data not available
incl including
excl excluding
nra nationals residing abroad

Notes:
(1.2,4.1-4.3) Air arrivals (Niamey airport); (5.5) Days; (7.1,7.2) Hotels, inns and bungalows.

NIGERIA

Basic Indicators	Units	Code	1996	1997	1998	1999	2000
INBOUND TOURISM							
Arrivals							
Visitors	Thousands	(1.1)	1,230	1,292	1,357	1,425	1,492
Tourists (overnight visitors)	Thousands	(1.2)	822	611	739	776	813
Same-day visitors	Thousands	(1.3)	..	..	..	..	..
Cruise passengers	Thousands	(1.4)	..	..	..	..	..
Arrivals by region							
Africa	Thousands	(2.1)	867	910	955	1,003	1,051
Americas	Thousands	(2.2)	48	50	53	56	58
Europe	Thousands	(2.3)	190	200	210	221	230
East Asia and the Pacific	Thousands	(2.4)	76	80	84	88	92
South Asia	Thousands	(2.5)	28	29	31	32	34
Middle East	Thousands	(2.6)	21	22	23	24	25
Arrivals by mode of transport							
Air	Thousands	(3.1)	418	439	461	484	507
Rail	Thousands	(3.2)	..	..	..	..	..
Road	Thousands	(3.3)	61	64	67	70	73
Sea	Thousands	(3.4)	272	14	17	17	18
Arrivals by purpose of visit							
Leisure, recreation and holidays	Thousands	(4.1)	274	204	246	259	271
Business and professional	Thousands	(4.2)	411	306	369	388	407
Other	Thousands	(4.3)	137	101	124	129	135
Overnight stays and length of stay							
Overnight stays in H&S	Thousand nights	(5.1)	..	..	..	..	..
Overnight stays in CE	Thousand nights	(5.2)	..	..	..	..	..
ALS of non resident tourists	Nights	(5.5)	..	..	..	..	..
Tourism expenditure							
in the country of reference	US$ Million	(8.1)	85	118	142	171	200
DOMESTIC TOURISM							
Overnight stays							
Overnight stays in H&S	Thousand nights	(5.3)	..	..	..	..	..
Overnight stays in CE	Thousand nights	(5.4)	..	..	..	..	..
OUTBOUND TOURISM							
Departures	Thousands	(6.1)	..	..	..	..	..
Tourism expenditure in other countries	US$ Million	(8.2)	1,304	1,816	1,567	620	730
TOURISM ACTIVITIES							
Hotels and similar establishments							
Number of rooms	H&S	(7.1)	..	..	..	..	..
Number of bed-places	H&S	(7.2)	..	..	..	..	..
Occupancy rate	Percent	(7.3)	..	..	..	..	..
Average length of stay	Nights	(5.6)	..	..	..	..	..
ECONOMIC AGGREGATES							
Gross National Product (GNP)	US$ Million	(9.1)	28,570	32,204	31,679	30,903	32,814
Exports (F.O.B.)	US$ Million	(9.2)	16,154	15,207	9,855	13,856	20,975
Imports (C.I.F.)	US$ Million	(9.3)	6,438	9,501	9,211	8,588	8,721

Abbreviations used in tables and notes:
H&S: Hotels and similar establishments; **CE:** All types of tourism accommodation establishments; **ALS:** Average length of stay; **THS:** Non-resident tourists staying in H&S; **TCE:** Non-resident tourists staying in CE; **TF:** Arrivals of international (or non-resident) tourists; **VF:** Arrivals of international (or non-resident) visitors; **NHS:** Overnight stays at H&S; **NCE:** Overnight stays at CE.

..   data not available
incl   including
excl   excluding
nra   nationals residing abroad

Notes:
(1.1,2.1-2.6) VF; (1.2,4.1-4.3) TF.

Basic Indicators	Units	Code	1996	1997	1998	1999	2000
INBOUND TOURISM							
Arrivals							
Visitors	Thousands	(1.1)	..	2.0	2.0	3.3	..
Tourists (overnight visitors)	Thousands	(1.2)	1.5	1.8	1.7	2.3	2.0
Same-day visitors	Thousands	(1.3)	..	..	..	..	..
Cruise passengers	Thousands	(1.4)	..	0.2	0.3	..	..
Arrivals by region							
Africa	Thousands	(2.1)	..	..	..	..	..
Americas	Thousands	(2.2)	0.1	0.1	0.1	0.2	0.2
Europe	Thousands	(2.3)	0.1	0.1	0.1	0.2	0.1
East Asia and the Pacific	Thousands	(2.4)	1.4	1.6	1.5	1.6	1.4
South Asia	Thousands	(2.5)	..	..	..	..	..
Middle East	Thousands	(2.6)	..	..	..	..	..
Arrivals by mode of transport							
Air	Thousands	(3.1)	1.5	1.8	1.7	2.3	2.0
Rail	Thousands	(3.2)	..	..	..	..	..
Road	Thousands	(3.3)	..	..	..	..	..
Sea	Thousands	(3.4)	..	..	..	..	..
Arrivals by purpose of visit							
Leisure, recreation and holidays	Thousands	(4.1)	0.7	0.8	1.0	1.3	..
Business and professional	Thousands	(4.2)	0.4	0.5	0.3	0.5	..
Other	Thousands	(4.3)	0.4	0.5	0.4	0.5	..
Overnight stays and length of stay							
Overnight stays in H&S	Thousand nights	(5.1)	18.0	..	..	..	..
Overnight stays in CE	Thousand nights	(5.2)	..	..	..	..	..
ALS of non resident tourists	Nights	(5.5)	..	..	..	..	..
Tourism expenditure **in the country of reference**	US$ Million	(8.1)	1.0	1.5	1.1	..	..
DOMESTIC TOURISM							
Overnight stays							
Overnight stays in H&S	Thousand nights	(5.3)	..	..	..	..	..
Overnight stays in CE	Thousand nights	(5.4)	..	..	..	..	..
OUTBOUND TOURISM							
Departures	Thousands	(6.1)	..	..	..	..	..
Tourism expenditure in other countries	US$ Million	(8.2)	..	..	..	..	..
TOURISM ACTIVITIES							
Hotels and similar establishments							
Number of rooms	H&S	(7.1)	..	88	84	84	..
Number of bed-places	H&S	(7.2)	..	..	235	235	..
Occupancy rate	Percent	(7.3)	30.00	..	..	..	..
Average length of stay	Nights	(5.6)	..	..	..	..	..
ECONOMIC AGGREGATES							
Gross National Product (GNP)	US$ Million	(9.1)	..	..	..	..	..
Exports (F.O.B.)	US$ Million	(9.2)	..	..	..	..	..
Imports (C.I.F.)	US$ Million	(9.3)	..	..	..	..	..

Abbreviations used in tables and notes:
H&S: Hotels and similar establishments; **CE:** All types of tourism accommodation establishments; **ALS:** Average length of stay; **THS:** Non-resident tourists staying in H&S; **TCE:** Non-resident tourists staying in CE; **TF:** Arrivals of international (or non-resident) tourists; **VF:** Arrivals of international (or non-resident) visitors; **NHS:** Overnight stays at H&S; **NCE:** Overnight stays at CE.

..   data not available
incl   including
excl   excluding
nra   nationals residing abroad

Notes:
(1.2) Arrivals by air; incl Niueans residing usually in New Zealand.

NORTHERN MARIANA ISLANDS

Basic Indicators	Units	Code	1996	1997	1998	1999	2000
INBOUND TOURISM							
Arrivals							
Visitors	Thousands	(1.1)	736	695	490	502	529
Tourists (overnight visitors)	Thousands	(1.2)	728	685	481	493	517
Same-day visitors	Thousands	(1.3)	..	..	..	..	..
Cruise passengers	Thousands	(1.4)	8	10	9	8	12
Arrivals by region							
Africa	Thousands	(2.1)	..	..	..	..	..
Americas	Thousands	(2.2)	85	76	61	50	52
Europe	Thousands	(2.3)	2	3	3	2	2
East Asia and the Pacific	Thousands	(2.4)	648	615	425	449	474
South Asia	Thousands	(2.5)				..	..
Middle East	Thousands	(2.6)	..	..	..	..	..
Arrivals by mode of transport							
Air	Thousands	(3.1)	728	685	481	493	517
Rail	Thousands	(3.2)	..	..	..	..	..
Road	Thousands	(3.3)	..	..	..	..	..
Sea	Thousands	(3.4)	8	10	9	8	12
Arrivals by purpose of visit							
Leisure, recreation and holidays	Thousands	(4.1)	725	687	480	502	529
Business and professional	Thousands	(4.2)	11	8	10	..	..
Other	Thousands	(4.3)	..	..	..	..	..
Overnight stays and length of stay							
Overnight stays in H&S	Thousand nights	(5.1)	..	..	..	..	..
Overnight stays in CE	Thousand nights	(5.2)	..	..	..	..	..
ALS of non resident tourists	Nights	(5.5)	..	..	..	..	..
Tourism expenditure							
in the country of reference	US$ Million	(8.1)	..	..	..	..	..
DOMESTIC TOURISM							
Overnight stays							
Overnight stays in H&S	Thousand nights	(5.3)	..	..	..	..	..
Overnight stays in CE	Thousand nights	(5.4)	..	..	..	..	..
OUTBOUND TOURISM							
Departures	Thousands	(6.1)	..	..	..	..	..
Tourism expenditure in other countries	US$ Million	(8.2)	..	..	..	..	..
TOURISM ACTIVITIES							
Hotels and similar establishments							
Number of rooms	H&S	(7.1)	3,583	3,881	4,642	4,556	4,551
Number of bed-places	H&S	(7.2)	..	..	..	..	..
Occupancy rate	Percent	(7.3)	86.00	81.00	58.05	60.44	61.23
Average length of stay	Nights	(5.6)	..	..	..	..	..
ECONOMIC AGGREGATES							
Gross National Product (GNP)	US$ Million	(9.1)	..	..	..	..	..
Exports (F.O.B.)	US$ Million	(9.2)	..	..	..	..	..
Imports (C.I.F.)	US$ Million	(9.3)	..	..	..	..	..

Abbreviations used in tables and notes:
H&S: Hotels and similar establishments; CE: All types of tourism accommodation establishments; ALS: Average length of stay; THS: Non-resident tourists staying in H&S; TCE: Non-resident tourists staying in CE; TF: Arrivals of international (or non-resident) tourists; VF: Arrivals of international (or non-resident) visitors; NHS: Overnight stays at H&S; NCE: Overnight stays at CE.

..   data not available
incl   including
excl   excluding
nra   nationals residing abroad

Notes:
(1.1,2.2-2.4) VF; (1.2) Arrivals by air; (2.2) Incl Guam; (7.1) Covers 68 per cent of the total hotel room inventory.

NORWAY

Basic Indicators	Units	Code	1996	1997	1998	1999	2000
INBOUND TOURISM							
Arrivals							
Visitors	Thousands	(1.1)	..	..	..	..	..
Tourists (overnight visitors)	Thousands	(1.2)	2,746	2,702	4,538	4,481	4,348
Same-day visitors	Thousands	(1.3)	..	..	..	..	..
Cruise passengers	Thousands	(1.4)	..	..	..	..	..
Arrivals by region							
Africa	Thousands	(2.1)	..	..	9	8	8
Americas	Thousands	(2.2)	..	..	278	303	296
Europe	Thousands	(2.3)	..	..	3,960	3,846	3,697
East Asia and the Pacific	Thousands	(2.4)	..	..	187	210	243
South Asia	Thousands	(2.5)	..	..	..	..	..
Middle East	Thousands	(2.6)	..	..	..	..	..
Arrivals by mode of transport							
Air	Thousands	(3.1)	..	..	..	..	..
Rail	Thousands	(3.2)	..	..	..	..	..
Road	Thousands	(3.3)	..	..	..	..	..
Sea	Thousands	(3.4)	..	..	..	..	..
Arrivals by purpose of visit							
Leisure, recreation and holidays	Thousands	(4.1)	..	..	..	..	..
Business and professional	Thousands	(4.2)	..	..	..	..	..
Other	Thousands	(4.3)	..	..	..	..	..
Overnight stays and length of stay							
Overnight stays in H&S	Thousand nights	(5.1)	5,050	5,039	5,168	5,208	4,967
Overnight stays in CE	Thousand nights	(5.2)	6,986	7,005	7,869	7,815	7,469
ALS of non resident tourists	Nights	(5.5)	..	..	..	..	..
Tourism expenditure							
in the country of reference	US$ Million	(8.1)	2,402	2,183	2,172	2,115	1,937
DOMESTIC TOURISM							
Overnight stays							
Overnight stays in H&S	Thousand nights	(5.3)	10,261	10,680	11,252	11,319	11,398
Overnight stays in CE	Thousand nights	(5.4)	12,357	12,815	16,514	16,628	16,801
OUTBOUND TOURISM							
Departures	Thousands	(6.1)	692	753	..	..	..
Tourism expenditure in other countries	US$ Million	(8.2)	4,536	4,306	4,551	4,609	4,335
TOURISM ACTIVITIES							
Hotels and similar establishments							
Number of rooms	H&S	(7.1)	61,187	62,233	63,236	63,916	65,200
Number of bed-places	H&S	(7.2)	133,521	135,605	137,188	137,653	140,580
Occupancy rate	Percent	(7.3)	37.30	37.70	39.00	38.80	37.50
Average length of stay	Nights	(5.6)	1.67	1.71	..	..	..
ECONOMIC AGGREGATES							
Gross National Product (GNP)	US$ Million	(9.1)	151,040	160,221	153,250	149,298	151,153
Exports (F.O.B.)	US$ Million	(9.2)	49,646	48,547	39,649	44,892	57,519
Imports (C.I.F.)	US$ Million	(9.3)	35,616	35,713	36,196	34,047	32,655

Abbreviations used in tables and notes:
H&S: Hotels and similar establishments; **CE:** All types of tourism accommodation establishments; **ALS:** Average length of stay; **THS:** Non-resident tourists staying in H&S; **TCE:** Non-resident tourists staying in CE; **TF:** Arrivals of international (or non-resident) tourists; **VF:** Arrivals of international (or non-resident) visitors; **NHS:** Overnight stays at H&S; **NCE:** Overnight stays at CE.

..   data not available
incl   including
excl   excluding
nra   nationals residing abroad

Notes:
(1.2/96/97) THS in registered hotels; (1.2,2.1-2.4/98-2000) TCE, new series; (5.1) Nights in registered establishments; (5.1,7.1,7.2) As from 1988, figures for H&S relate to establishments with 20 or more beds the whole year; (6.1) Inclusive tour charter only; (7.3) Bed-places.

OMAN

Basic Indicators	Units	Code	1996	1997	1998	1999	2000
INBOUND TOURISM							
Arrivals							
Visitors	Thousands	(1.1)	..	..	..	..	..
Tourists (overnight visitors)	Thousands	(1.2)	349	376	424	503	571
Same-day visitors	Thousands	(1.3)	..	..	..	..	..
Cruise passengers	Thousands	(1.4)	..	..	..	..	..
Arrivals by region							
Africa	Thousands	(2.1)	22	22	27	37	20
Americas	Thousands	(2.2)	25	12	50	59	34
Europe	Thousands	(2.3)	110	159	176	172	227
East Asia and the Pacific	Thousands	(2.4)	65	70	55	84	98
South Asia	Thousands	(2.5)	..	31	39	54	66
Middle East	Thousands	(2.6)	58	81	77	96	126
Arrivals by mode of transport							
Air	Thousands	(3.1)	..	..	..	..	..
Rail	Thousands	(3.2)	..	..	..	..	..
Road	Thousands	(3.3)	..	..	..	..	..
Sea	Thousands	(3.4)	..	..	..	..	..
Arrivals by purpose of visit							
Leisure, recreation and holidays	Thousands	(4.1)	129	133	..	..	..
Business and professional	Thousands	(4.2)	..	..	..	..	..
Other	Thousands	(4.3)	..	..	..	..	..
Overnight stays and length of stay							
Overnight stays in H&S	Thousand nights	(5.1)	873	939	1,122	1,092	..
Overnight stays in CE	Thousand nights	(5.2)	..	..	..	..	..
ALS of non resident tourists	Nights	(5.5)	..	..	..	..	..
Tourism expenditure							
in the country of reference	US$ Million	(8.1)	105	111	114	106	120
DOMESTIC TOURISM							
Overnight stays							
Overnight stays in H&S	Thousand nights	(5.3)	215	218	263	247	..
Overnight stays in CE	Thousand nights	(5.4)	..	..	..	..	..
OUTBOUND TOURISM							
Departures	Thousands	(6.1)	..	..	..	..	..
Tourism expenditure in other countries	US$ Million	(8.2)	255	252	289	323	341
TOURISM ACTIVITIES							
Hotels and similar establishments							
Number of rooms	H&S	(7.1)	3,065	3,476	4,657	5,138	5,312
Number of bed-places	H&S	(7.2)	4,460	5,000	6,501	7,573	7,858
Occupancy rate	Percent	(7.3)	49.00	51.00	47.00	41.00	42.00
Average length of stay	Nights	(5.6)	..	..	..	..	..
ECONOMIC AGGREGATES							
Gross National Product (GNP)	US$ Million	(9.1)	..	..	..	..	..
Exports (F.O.B.)	US$ Million	(9.2)	7,346	7,630	5,508	..	..
Imports (C.I.F.)	US$ Million	(9.3)	4,578	5,026	5,682	4,674	5,040

Abbreviations used in tables and notes:
H&S: Hotels and similar establishments; **CE:** All types of tourism accommodation establishments; **ALS:** Average length of stay; **THS:** Non-resident tourists staying in H&S; **TCE:** Non-resident tourists staying in CE; **TF:** Arrivals of international (or non-resident) tourists; **VF:** Arrivals of international (or non-resident) visitors; **NHS:** Overnight stays at H&S; **NCE:** Overnight stays at CE.

..	data not available
incl	including
excl	excluding
nra	nationals residing abroad

Notes:
(1.2,2.1-2.6) THS; (7.3) Rooms; (8.1) Hotel sales; (8.2) International Monetary Fund.

Basic Indicators	Units	Code	1996	1997	1998	1999	2000
INBOUND TOURISM							
Arrivals							
Visitors	Thousands	(1.1)	..	..	..	..	..
Tourists (overnight visitors)	Thousands	(1.2)	369	375	429	432	557
Same-day visitors	Thousands	(1.3)	..	..	..	..	..
Cruise passengers	Thousands	(1.4)	..	..	..	..	..
Arrivals by region							
Africa	Thousands	(2.1)	10	8	8	10	16
Americas	Thousands	(2.2)	54	54	61	61	90
Europe	Thousands	(2.3)	153	154	184	190	258
East Asia and the Pacific	Thousands	(2.4)	44	42	49	44	50
South Asia	Thousands	(2.5)	88	97	107	107	109
Middle East	Thousands	(2.6)	20	20	19	20	33
Arrivals by mode of transport							
Air	Thousands	(3.1)	317	313	354	354	475
Rail	Thousands	(3.2)	25	40	54	47	45
Road	Thousands	(3.3)	26	22	20	29	34
Sea	Thousands	(3.4)	1	..	1	2	3
Arrivals by purpose of visit							
Leisure, recreation and holidays	Thousands	(4.1)	72	70	116	66	82
Business and professional	Thousands	(4.2)	105	102	110	108	139
Other	Thousands	(4.3)	192	203	203	258	336
Overnight stays and length of stay							
Overnight stays in H&S	Thousand nights	(5.1)	640	567	623	706	620
Overnight stays in CE	Thousand nights	(5.2)	..	..	..	..	..
ALS of non resident tourists	Nights	(5.5)	30.00	30.00	30.00	25.00	25.00
Tourism expenditure							
in the country of reference	US$ Million	(8.1)	146	117	98	76	84
DOMESTIC TOURISM							
Overnight stays							
Overnight stays in H&S	Thousand nights	(5.3)	3,457	2,710	2,470	3,036	3,574
Overnight stays in CE	Thousand nights	(5.4)	..	..	..	..	..
OUTBOUND TOURISM							
Departures	Thousands	(6.1)	..	..	..	..	..
Tourism expenditure in other countries	US$ Million	(8.2)	900	364	352	180	252
TOURISM ACTIVITIES							
Hotels and similar establishments							
Number of rooms	H&S	(7.1)	31,550	32,021	34,853	35,149	35,524
Number of bed-places	H&S	(7.2)	47,325	48,032	52,280	52,724	53,286
Occupancy rate	Percent	(7.3)	52.00	47.10	46.40	41.10	..
Average length of stay	Nights	(5.6)	1.10	1.01	1.21	1.17	1.18
ECONOMIC AGGREGATES							
Gross National Product (GNP)	US$ Million	(9.1)	64,103	65,469	63,781	62,101	64,550
Exports (F.O.B.)	US$ Million	(9.2)	9,367	8,760	8,515	8,387	9,174
Imports (C.I.F.)	US$ Million	(9.3)	12,191	11,652	9,331	10,163	11,486

Abbreviations used in tables and notes:
H&S: Hotels and similar establishments; **CE:** All types of tourism accommodation establishments; **ALS:** Average length of stay; **THS:** Non-resident tourists staying in H&S; **TCE:** Non-resident tourists staying in CE; **TF:** Arrivals of international (or non-resident) tourists; **VF:** Arrivals of international (or non-resident) visitors; **NHS:** Overnight stays at H&S; **NCE:** Overnight stays at CE.

..   data not available
incl   including
excl   excluding
nra   nationals residing abroad

Notes:
(5.5) Days; (8.1) State Bank of Pakistan.

PALAU

Basic Indicators	Units	Code	1996	1997	1998	1999	2000
INBOUND TOURISM							
Arrivals							
Visitors	Thousands	(1.1)	..	..	..	..	..
Tourists (overnight visitors)	Thousands	(1.2)	69	74	64	55	58
Same-day visitors	Thousands	(1.3)	..	..	..	..	..
Cruise passengers	Thousands	(1.4)	..	..	..	..	..
Arrivals by region							
Africa	Thousands	(2.1)	..	..	..	..	..
Americas	Thousands	(2.2)	10	10	12	6	..
Europe	Thousands	(2.3)	3	2	2	2	..
East Asia and the Pacific	Thousands	(2.4)	56	60	46	47	..
South Asia	Thousands	(2.5)	..	..	..	..	..
Middle East	Thousands	(2.6)	..	..	..	..	..
Arrivals by mode of transport							
Air	Thousands	(3.1)	69	74	64	55	58
Rail	Thousands	(3.2)	..	..	..	..	..
Road	Thousands	(3.3)	..	..	..	..	..
Sea	Thousands	(3.4)	..	..	..	..	..
Arrivals by purpose of visit							
Leisure, recreation and holidays	Thousands	(4.1)	58	64	55	..	..
Business and professional	Thousands	(4.2)	3	3	4	..	..
Other	Thousands	(4.3)	8	7	5	..	..
Overnight stays and length of stay							
Overnight stays in H&S	Thousand nights	(5.1)	..	..	..	..	..
Overnight stays in CE	Thousand nights	(5.2)	..	..	..	..	..
ALS of non resident tourists	Nights	(5.5)	6.02	..	..	..	..
Tourism expenditure **in the country of reference**	US$ Million	(8.1)	..	..	..	..	..
DOMESTIC TOURISM							
Overnight stays							
Overnight stays in H&S	Thousand nights	(5.3)	..	..	..	..	..
Overnight stays in CE	Thousand nights	(5.4)	..	..	..	..	..
OUTBOUND TOURISM							
Departures	Thousands	(6.1)	..	..	9	..	..
Tourism expenditure in other countries	US$ Million	(8.2)	..	..	..	..	..
TOURISM ACTIVITIES							
Hotels and similar establishments							
Number of rooms	H&S	(7.1)	716	726	973	..	..
Number of bed-places	H&S	(7.2)	..	..	..	..	..
Occupancy rate	Percent	(7.3)	..	..	..	..	..
Average length of stay	Nights	(5.6)	..	..	..	..	..
ECONOMIC AGGREGATES							
Gross National Product (GNP)	US$ Million	(9.1)	..	..	..	..	..
Exports (F.O.B.)	US$ Million	(9.2)	14	..	..	..	..
Imports (C.I.F.)	US$ Million	(9.3)	72	..	..	..	..

Abbreviations used in tables and notes:
H&S: Hotels and similar establishments; **CE:** All types of tourism accommodation establishments; **ALS:** Average length of stay; **THS:** Non-resident tourists staying in H&S; **TCE:** Non-resident tourists staying in CE; **TF:** Arrivals of international (or non-resident) tourists; **VF:** Arrivals of international (or non-resident) visitors; **NHS:** Overnight stays at H&S; **NCE:** Overnight stays at CE.

.. data not available
incl including
excl excluding
nra nationals residing abroad

Notes:
(1.2,2.2-2.4,3.1) Air arrivals (Palau International Airport).

Basic Indicators	Units	Code	1996	1997	1998	1999	2000
INBOUND TOURISM							
Arrivals							
Visitors	Thousands	(1.1)	795	685	767	907	1,055
Tourists (overnight visitors)	Thousands	(1.2)	..	..	201	271	330
Same-day visitors	Thousands	(1.3)	..	..	..	..	..
Cruise passengers	Thousands	(1.4)	..	..	..	..	..
Arrivals by region							
Africa	Thousands	(2.1)	..	21	15	18	21
Americas	Thousands	(2.2)	..	143	176	181	211
Europe	Thousands	(2.3)	..	418	499	608	717
East Asia and the Pacific	Thousands	(2.4)	..	41	33	38	43
South Asia	Thousands	(2.5)	..	14	13	17	21
Middle East	Thousands	(2.6)	..	48	31	45	42
Arrivals by mode of transport							
Air	Thousands	(3.1)	..	..	..	..	..
Rail	Thousands	(3.2)	..	..	..	..	..
Road	Thousands	(3.3)	..	..	..	..	..
Sea	Thousands	(3.4)	..	..	..	..	..
Arrivals by purpose of visit							
Leisure, recreation and holidays	Thousands	(4.1)	318	267	299	327	353
Business and professional	Thousands	(4.2)	..	..	..	..	..
Other	Thousands	(4.3)	477	418	468	580	702
Overnight stays and length of stay							
Overnight stays in H&S	Thousand nights	(5.1)	..	..	560	772	976
Overnight stays in CE	Thousand nights	(5.2)	..	..	675	907	1,106
ALS of non resident tourists	Nights	(5.5)	..	..	3.35	3.40	3.50
Tourism expenditure **in the country of reference**	US$ Million	(8.1)	104	96	114	132	155
DOMESTIC TOURISM							
Overnight stays							
Overnight stays in H&S	Thousand nights	(5.3)	..	..	..	..	..
Overnight stays in CE	Thousand nights	(5.4)	..	..	75	101	123
OUTBOUND TOURISM							
Departures	Thousands	(6.1)	..	..	..	..	..
Tourism expenditure in other countries	US$ Million	(8.2)	..	..	..	..	..
TOURISM ACTIVITIES							
Hotels and similar establishments							
Number of rooms	H&S	(7.1)	2,926	3,425	3,682	4,436	5,848
Number of bed-places	H&S	(7.2)	6,434	7,419	7,986	9,191	12,158
Occupancy rate	Percent	(7.3)	..	36.60	32.50	40.50	55.00
Average length of stay	Nights	(5.6)	..	..	3.35	3.40	3.50
ECONOMIC AGGREGATES							
Gross National Product (GNP)	US$ Million	(9.1)	3,977	4,375	4,826	5,115	4,745
Exports (F.O.B.)	US$ Million	(9.2)	..	..	..	..	..
Imports (C.I.F.)	US$ Million	(9.3)	..	..	..	..	..

Abbreviations used in tables and notes:
H&S: Hotels and similar establishments; **CE:** All types of tourism accommodation establishments; **ALS:** Average length of stay; **THS:** Non-resident tourists staying in H&S; **TCE:** Non-resident tourists staying in CE; **TF:** Arrivals of international (or non-resident) tourists; **VF:** Arrivals of international (or non-resident) visitors; **NHS:** Overnight stays at H&S; **NCE:** Overnight stays at CE.

..	data not available
incl	including
excl	excluding
nra	nationals residing abroad

PANAMA

Basic Indicators	Units	Code	1996	1997	1998	1999	2000
INBOUND TOURISM							
Arrivals							
Visitors	Thousands	(1.1)	443	504	529	555	600
Tourists (overnight visitors)	Thousands	(1.2)	362	421	431	457	484
Same-day visitors	Thousands	(1.3)	80	83	98	98	117
Cruise passengers	Thousands	(1.4)	14	18	30	27	25
Arrivals by region							
Africa	Thousands	(2.1)	..	..	..	..	..
Americas	Thousands	(2.2)	332	371	378	399	419
Europe	Thousands	(2.3)	30	32	31	34	35
East Asia and the Pacific	Thousands	(2.4)	15	15	13	13	12
South Asia	Thousands	(2.5)	..	..	..	..	..
Middle East	Thousands	(2.6)	..	..	..	..	..
Arrivals by mode of transport							
Air	Thousands	(3.1)	308	344	343	359	375
Rail	Thousands	(3.2)	..	..	..	..	..
Road	Thousands	(3.3)	48	51	59	68	72
Sea	Thousands	(3.4)	6	7	8	9	9
Arrivals by purpose of visit							
Leisure, recreation and holidays	Thousands	(4.1)	162	182	177	189	200
Business and professional	Thousands	(4.2)	129	140	139	141	147
Other	Thousands	(4.3)	17	22	27	29	28
Overnight stays and length of stay							
Overnight stays in H&S	Thousand nights	(5.1)	956	1,035	1,074	1,094	1,161
Overnight stays in CE	Thousand nights	(5.2)	..	..	..	..	..
ALS of non resident tourists	Nights	(5.5)	8.20	9.40	10.60	10.00	9.70
Tourism expenditure							
in the country of reference	US$ Million	(8.1)	425	457	494	538	576
DOMESTIC TOURISM							
Overnight stays							
Overnight stays in H&S	Thousand nights	(5.3)	..	..	..	..	..
Overnight stays in CE	Thousand nights	(5.4)	..	..	..	..	..
OUTBOUND TOURISM							
Departures	Thousands	(6.1)	188	194	211	221	216
Tourism expenditure in other countries	US$ Million	(8.2)	136	164	176	184	187
TOURISM ACTIVITIES							
Hotels and similar establishments							
Number of rooms	H&S	(7.1)	9,869	11,452	12,198	12,476	13,663
Number of bed-places	H&S	(7.2)	19,738	22,904	24,396	24,952	27,326
Occupancy rate	Percent	(7.3)	54.30	52.48	49.50	43.60	40.10
Average length of stay	Nights	(5.6)	2.42	2.29	2.24	2.30	2.50
ECONOMIC AGGREGATES							
Gross National Product (GNP)	US$ Million	(9.1)	8,062	8,252	8,373	8,602	9,316
Exports (F.O.B.)	US$ Million	(9.2)	623	723	784	822	859
Imports (C.I.F.)	US$ Million	(9.3)	2,780	3,002	3,398	3,516	3,379

Abbreviations used in tables and notes:
H&S: Hotels and similar establishments; **CE:** All types of tourism accommodation establishments; **ALS:** Average length of stay; **THS:** Non-resident tourists staying in H&S; **TCE:** Non-resident tourists staying in CE; **TF:** Arrivals of international (or non-resident) tourists; **VF:** Arrivals of international (or non-resident) visitors; **NHS:** Overnight stays at H&S; **NCE:** Overnight stays at CE.

.. data not available
incl including
excl excluding
nra nationals residing abroad

Notes:
(1.1) VF, Tocúmen International Airport (TIA), Paso Canoa frontier (PCF), the ports of Cristóbal and Balboa (PCB) and IPAT stat.; (2.2-2.4) VF, TIA, PCF and IPAT stat.; (3.1-3.4) TF, TIA, PCF, PCB and IPAT stat. Excl arrivals to other ports of entry (non specified) (000)= 97:19; 98:23; 99:20; 2000:28; (4.1-4.3) TF, TIA and IPAT stat.; (5.1) Hotels in Panama City and IPAT statistics; (7.1,7.2) Rooms/bed-places recorded for international tourism; (7.3) Rooms.

Basic Indicators	Units	Code	1996	1997	1998	1999	2000
INBOUND TOURISM							
Arrivals							
Visitors	Thousands	(1.1)	..	..	..	..	..
Tourists (overnight visitors)	Thousands	(1.2)	61	66	67	67	58
Same-day visitors	Thousands	(1.3)	..	..	..	..	..
Cruise passengers	Thousands	(1.4)	..	..	..	..	..
Arrivals by region							
Africa	Thousands	(2.1)	..	..	..	..	..
Americas	Thousands	(2.2)	6	7	7	7	7
Europe	Thousands	(2.3)	6	6	7	7	5
East Asia and the Pacific	Thousands	(2.4)	44	53	53	53	46
South Asia	Thousands	(2.5)	..	..	..	..	..
Middle East	Thousands	(2.6)	..	..	..	..	..
Arrivals by mode of transport							
Air	Thousands	(3.1)	..	..	..	63	58
Rail	Thousands	(3.2)	..	..	..	..	..
Road	Thousands	(3.3)	..	..	..	..	..
Sea	Thousands	(3.4)	..	..	..	4	..
Arrivals by purpose of visit							
Leisure, recreation and holidays	Thousands	(4.1)	22	21	23	19	14
Business and professional	Thousands	(4.2)	32	38	37	42	37
Other	Thousands	(4.3)	7	7	7	6	7
Overnight stays and length of stay							
Overnight stays in H&S	Thousand nights	(5.1)	115	..	..	..	..
Overnight stays in CE	Thousand nights	(5.2)	145	..	..	..	..
ALS of non resident tourists	Nights	(5.5)	11.00	10.00	..	8.00	10.20
Tourism expenditure							
in the country of reference	US$ Million	(8.1)	68	71	75	76	..
DOMESTIC TOURISM							
Overnight stays							
Overnight stays in H&S	Thousand nights	(5.3)	..	..	..	..	..
Overnight stays in CE	Thousand nights	(5.4)	..	..	..	..	..
OUTBOUND TOURISM							
Departures	Thousands	(6.1)	..	63	..	..	106
Tourism expenditure in other countries	US$ Million	(8.2)	72	78	52	53	..
TOURISM ACTIVITIES							
Hotels and similar establishments							
Number of rooms	H&S	(7.1)	..	..	..	..	..
Number of bed-places	H&S	(7.2)	..	..	..	..	..
Occupancy rate	Percent	(7.3)	60.00	..	..	..	..
Average length of stay	Nights	(5.6)	..	..	..	..	..
ECONOMIC AGGREGATES							
Gross National Product (GNP)	US$ Million	(9.1)	5,169	4,738	4,144	3,834	3,665
Exports (F.O.B.)	US$ Million	(9.2)	2,531	2,160	1,772	1,927	2,021
Imports (C.I.F.)	US$ Million	(9.3)	1,741	1,709	1,240	1,236	1,151

Abbreviations used in tables and notes:
H&S: Hotels and similar establishments; **CE:** All types of tourism accommodation establishments; **ALS:** Average length of stay; **THS:** Non-resident tourists staying in H&S; **TCE:** Non-resident tourists staying in CE; **TF:** Arrivals of international (or non-resident) tourists; **VF:** Arrivals of international (or non-resident) visitors; **NHS:** Overnight stays at H&S; **NCE:** Overnight stays at CE.

..   data not available
incl   including
excl   excluding
nra   nationals residing abroad

Notes:
(8.2) International Monetary Fund.

PARAGUAY

Basic Indicators	Units	Code	1996	1997	1998	1999	2000
INBOUND TOURISM							
Arrivals							
Visitors	Thousands	(1.1)	12,868	10,955	9,818	6,569	4,131
Tourists (overnight visitors)	Thousands	(1.2)	426	395	350	269	323
Same-day visitors	Thousands	(1.3)	12,442	10,560	9,468	6,300	3,808
Cruise passengers	Thousands	(1.4)	..	..	..	..	..
Arrivals by region							
Africa	Thousands	(2.1)	..	2	1	..	..
Americas	Thousands	(2.2)	349	316	283	214	265
Europe	Thousands	(2.3)	40	42	33	32	37
East Asia and the Pacific	Thousands	(2.4)	8	11	4	4	5
South Asia	Thousands	(2.5)	..	..	..	..	..
Middle East	Thousands	(2.6)	..	..	..	..	..
Arrivals by mode of transport							
Air	Thousands	(3.1)	168	208	189	121	67
Rail	Thousands	(3.2)	..	..	..	..	..
Road	Thousands	(3.3)	238	170	149	136	256
Sea	Thousands	(3.4)	19	17	12	12	..
Arrivals by purpose of visit							
Leisure, recreation and holidays	Thousands	(4.1)	204	185	184	141	156
Business and professional	Thousands	(4.2)	70	50	66	51	61
Other	Thousands	(4.3)	152	160	100	77	106
Overnight stays and length of stay							
Overnight stays in H&S	Thousand nights	(5.1)	921	851	641	560	755
Overnight stays in CE	Thousand nights	(5.2)	..	..	..	..	..
ALS of non resident tourists	Nights	(5.5)	3.26	3.26	4.00	3.50	6.00
Tourism expenditure in the country of reference	US$ Million	(8.1)	140	128	111	81	101
DOMESTIC TOURISM							
Overnight stays							
Overnight stays in H&S	Thousand nights	(5.3)	..	..	..	..	..
Overnight stays in CE	Thousand nights	(5.4)	..	..	..	..	..
OUTBOUND TOURISM							
Departures	Thousands	(6.1)	418	369	318	281	181
Tourism expenditure in other countries	US$ Million	(8.2)	139	139	143	109	97
TOURISM ACTIVITIES							
Hotels and similar establishments							
Number of rooms	H&S	(7.1)	5,048	4,843	5,129	4,894	4,894
Number of bed-places	H&S	(7.2)	10,396	10,388	10,827	10,748	10,748
Occupancy rate	Percent	(7.3)	61.00	58.00	52.00	47.00	45.00
Average length of stay	Nights	(5.6)	3.00	2.50	2.50	3.00	4.00
ECONOMIC AGGREGATES							
Gross National Product (GNP)	US$ Million	(9.1)	9,405	9,748	9,136	8,394	7,991
Exports (F.O.B.)	US$ Million	(9.2)	1,044	1,089	1,014	741	..
Imports (C.I.F.)	US$ Million	(9.3)	2,850	3,099	2,471	1,725	..

Abbreviations used in tables and notes:
H&S: Hotels and similar establishments; **CE:** All types of tourism accommodation establishments; **ALS:** Average length of stay; **THS:** Non-resident tourists staying in H&S; **TCE:** Non-resident tourists staying in CE; **TF:** Arrivals of international (or non-resident) tourists; **VF:** Arrivals of international (or non-resident) visitors; **NHS:** Overnight stays at H&S; **NCE:** Overnight stays at CE.

.. data not available
incl including
excl excluding
nra nationals residing abroad

Notes:
(1.2,2.1-4.3) Excl nra and crew members; (3.4) River; (7.3) Bed-places; (8.1,8.2) The Central Bank of Paraguay changed the methodology of calculation of tourism receipts and expenditure since the corresponding figures were considered overestimated. The data reported on tourism receipts and expenditure relate only to expenditure by tourists. Expenditure by same-day visitors (excursionists) are not included in the Balance of Payments and, consequently, this information was no longer included.

Basic Indicators	Units	Code	1996	1997	1998	1999	2000
INBOUND TOURISM							
Arrivals							
Visitors	Thousands	(1.1)	898	1,039	1,107	1,274	..
Tourists (overnight visitors)	Thousands	(1.2)	663	747	820	944	1,027
Same-day visitors	Thousands	(1.3)	235	292	288	330	..
Cruise passengers	Thousands	(1.4)	..	..	..	..	..
Arrivals by region							
Africa	Thousands	(2.1)	1	1	2	..	..
Americas	Thousands	(2.2)	372	436	483	..	..
Europe	Thousands	(2.3)	167	172	199	..	..
East Asia and the Pacific	Thousands	(2.4)	43	37	36	..	..
South Asia	Thousands	(2.5)	1	2	3	..	..
Middle East	Thousands	(2.6)	..	..	..	..	..
Arrivals by mode of transport							
Air	Thousands	(3.1)	425	459	517	..	..
Rail	Thousands	(3.2)	..	..	..	..	..
Road	Thousands	(3.3)	154	185	202	..	..
Sea	Thousands	(3.4)	5	6	5	..	..
Arrivals by purpose of visit							
Leisure, recreation and holidays	Thousands	(4.1)	486	525	583	..	..
Business and professional	Thousands	(4.2)	26	35	42	..	..
Other	Thousands	(4.3)	72	89	99	..	..
Overnight stays and length of stay							
Overnight stays in H&S	Thousand nights	(5.1)	2,035	2,099	2,173	2,703	..
Overnight stays in CE	Thousand nights	(5.2)	..	..	..	..	..
ALS of non resident tourists	Nights	(5.5)	9.50	9.50	10.20	..	..
Tourism expenditure in the country of reference	US$ Million	(8.1)	670	817	845	889	911
DOMESTIC TOURISM							
Overnight stays							
Overnight stays in H&S	Thousand nights	(5.3)	10,130	10,326	10,964	11,516	..
Overnight stays in CE	Thousand nights	(5.4)	..	..	..	..	..
OUTBOUND TOURISM							
Departures	Thousands	(6.1)	510	577	616	681	781
Tourism expenditure in other countries	US$ Million	(8.2)	350	434	453	444	531
TOURISM ACTIVITIES							
Hotels and similar establishments							
Number of rooms	H&S	(7.1)	..	..	98,106	..	..
Number of bed-places	H&S	(7.2)	..	..	156,796	..	..
Occupancy rate	Percent	(7.3)	33.11	32.30	29.93	28.86	..
Average length of stay	Nights	(5.6)	1.40	1.41	1.42	..	..
ECONOMIC AGGREGATES							
Gross National Product (GNP)	US$ Million	(9.1)	53,811	58,380	55,711	53,687	53,898
Exports (F.O.B.)	US$ Million	(9.2)	5,897	6,841	5,757	6,113	7,002
Imports (C.I.F.)	US$ Million	(9.3)	9,473	10,264	9,867	8,075	8,797

Abbreviations used in tables and notes:
H&S: Hotels and similar establishments; **CE:** All types of tourism accommodation establishments; **ALS:** Average length of stay; **THS:** Non-resident tourists staying in H&S; **TCE:** Non-resident tourists staying in CE; **TF:** Arrivals of international (or non-resident) tourists; **VF:** Arrivals of international (or non-resident) visitors; **NHS:** Overnight stays at H&S; **NCE:** Overnight stays at CE.

Notes:
(1.2) With passport and safe conduct; (2.1-2.5,3.1-3.4,4.1-4.3) TF, with passport only; (3.4) Incl river; (5.5) With passport and safe conduct; (8.1,8.2) International Monetary Fund.

.. data not available
incl including
excl excluding
nra nationals residing abroad

PHILIPPINES

Basic Indicators	Units	Code	1996	1997	1998	1999	2000
INBOUND TOURISM							
Arrivals							
Visitors	Thousands	(1.1)	..	..	..	..	..
Tourists (overnight visitors)	Thousands	(1.2)	2,049	2,223	2,149	2,171	1,992
Same-day visitors	Thousands	(1.3)	..	..	..	..	..
Cruise passengers	Thousands	(1.4)	10	18	30	18	7
Arrivals by region							
Africa	Thousands	(2.1)	2	2	2	2	1
Americas	Thousands	(2.2)	435	496	541	534	511
Europe	Thousands	(2.3)	273	295	311	294	252
East Asia and the Pacific	Thousands	(2.4)	1,134	1,232	1,051	1,077	1,022
South Asia	Thousands	(2.5)	26	27	31	26	24
Middle East	Thousands	(2.6)	18	15	16	16	15
Arrivals by mode of transport							
Air	Thousands	(3.1)	2,019	2,178	2,092	2,129	1,964
Rail	Thousands	(3.2)	..	..	..	..	..
Road	Thousands	(3.3)	..	..	..	..	..
Sea	Thousands	(3.4)	30	45	57	42	28
Arrivals by purpose of visit							
Leisure, recreation and holidays	Thousands	(4.1)	1,057	994	835	839	788
Business and professional	Thousands	(4.2)	418	472	442	445	393
Other	Thousands	(4.3)	544	712	815	845	783
Overnight stays and length of stay							
Overnight stays in H&S	Thousand nights	(5.1)	..	..	13,577	13,731	13,063
Overnight stays in CE	Thousand nights	(5.2)	..	..	..	..	..
ALS of non resident tourists	Nights	(5.5)	9.92	9.48	9.05	8.91	8.79
Tourism expenditure							
in the country of reference	US$ Million	(8.1)	2,701	2,831	2,413	2,531	2,134
DOMESTIC TOURISM							
Overnight stays							
Overnight stays in H&S	Thousand nights	(5.3)	..	..	..	..	..
Overnight stays in CE	Thousand nights	(5.4)	..	..	..	..	..
OUTBOUND TOURISM							
Departures	Thousands	(6.1)	2,121	1,930	1,817	1,755	..
Tourism expenditure in other countries	US$ Million	(8.2)	1,266	1,935	1,950	1,308	1,005
TOURISM ACTIVITIES							
Hotels and similar establishments							
Number of rooms	H&S	(7.1)	20,915	29,661	38,263	36,539	29,841
Number of bed-places	H&S	(7.2)	41,830	59,322	76,526	73,078	53,752
Occupancy rate	Percent	(7.3)	70.03	69.13	56.92	59.20	58.77
Average length of stay	Nights	(5.6)	2.88	2.64	2.65	2.85	2.73
ECONOMIC AGGREGATES							
Gross National Product (GNP)	US$ Million	(9.1)	83,066	88,169	79,337	78,398	78,705
Exports (F.O.B.)	US$ Million	(9.2)	20,408	24,895	29,449	36,577	39,794
Imports (C.I.F.)	US$ Million	(9.3)	34,127	38,604	31,542	32,569	33,808

Abbreviations used in tables and notes:
H&S: Hotels and similar establishments; **CE:** All types of tourism accommodation establishments; **ALS:** Average length of stay; **THS:** Non-resident tourists staying in H&S; **TCE:** Non-resident tourists staying in CE; **TF:** Arrivals of international (or non-resident) tourists; **VF:** Arrivals of international (or non-resident) visitors; **NHS:** Overnight stays at H&S; **NCE:** Overnight stays at CE.

..   data not available
incl   including
excl   excluding
nra   nationals residing abroad

Notes:
(1.2,3.1-4.3) TF incl nra; (2.1-2.6) TF excl nra; (4.1-4.3) Air arrivals; (5.6,7.3) Classified hotels in Metro Manila; (6.1) Incl overseas contract workers; (7.1,7.2) Classified hotels only.

Basic Indicators	Units	Code	1996	1997	1998	1999	2000
INBOUND TOURISM							
Arrivals							
Visitors	Thousands	(1.1)	87,439	87,817	88,592	89,118	84,515
Tourists (overnight visitors)	Thousands	(1.2)	19,410	19,520	18,780	17,950	17,400
Same-day visitors	Thousands	(1.3)	68,029	68,297	69,812	71,168	67,115
Cruise passengers	Thousands	(1.4)	..	..	..	..	..
Arrivals by region							
Africa	Thousands	(2.1)	6	6	8	8	9
Americas	Thousands	(2.2)	251	276	307	298	330
Europe	Thousands	(2.3)	87,023	87,369	88,145	88,678	84,043
East Asia and the Pacific	Thousands	(2.4)	67	75	71	78	88
South Asia	Thousands	(2.5)	12	11	9	9	9
Middle East	Thousands	(2.6)	8	8	7	7	7
Arrivals by mode of transport							
Air	Thousands	(3.1)	772	927	1,011	1,069	1,161
Rail	Thousands	(3.2)	2,755	2,464	1,821	2,502	2,952
Road	Thousands	(3.3)	83,357	83,146	84,186	83,891	78,638
Sea	Thousands	(3.4)	551	1,280	1,574	1,656	1,764
Arrivals by purpose of visit							
Leisure, recreation and holidays	Thousands	(4.1)	4,500	4,290	4,950	5,210	4,460
Business and professional	Thousands	(4.2)	6,360	7,010	5,180	4,520	4,850
Other	Thousands	(4.3)	8,550	8,220	8,650	8,220	8,090
Overnight stays and length of stay							
Overnight stays in H&S	Thousand nights	(5.1)	3,432	5,595	5,325	4,899	4,944
Overnight stays in CE	Thousand nights	(5.2)	5,650	7,580	7,230	7,182	6,891
ALS of non resident tourists	Nights	(5.5)	4.90	5.10	5.00	4.50	4.80
Tourism expenditure							
in the country of reference	US$ Million	(8.1)	8,444	8,679	7,946	6,100	6,100
DOMESTIC TOURISM							
Overnight stays							
Overnight stays in H&S	Thousand nights	(5.3)	4,546	9,359	10,169	9,842	9,352
Overnight stays in CE	Thousand nights	(5.4)	37,333	43,880	48,430	50,442	41,902
OUTBOUND TOURISM							
Departures	Thousands	(6.1)	44,713	48,610	49,328	55,097	56,677
Tourism expenditure in other countries	US$ Million	(8.2)	6,240	5,750	4,430	3,600	3,600
TOURISM ACTIVITIES							
Hotels and similar establishments							
Number of rooms	H&S	(7.1)	52,163	55,492	59,641	59,704	60,853
Number of bed-places	H&S	(7.2)	100,425	111,316	120,589	120,285	120,280
Occupancy rate	Percent	(7.3)	44.60	46.10	43.40	43.60	39.60
Average length of stay	Nights	(5.6)	2.50	3.32	3.50	3.48	3.35
ECONOMIC AGGREGATES							
Gross National Product (GNP)	US$ Million	(9.1)	123,676	137,633	149,091	156,876	162,169
Exports (F.O.B.)	US$ Million	(9.2)	24,389	25,708	27,370	27,323	31,684
Imports (C.I.F.)	US$ Million	(9.3)	37,045	42,237	46,803	45,778	48,970

Abbreviations used in tables and notes:
H&S: Hotels and similar establishments; **CE:** All types of tourism accommodation establishments; **ALS:** Average length of stay; **THS:** Non-resident tourists staying in H&S; **TCE:** Non-resident tourists staying in CE; **TF:** Arrivals of international (or non-resident) tourists; **VF:** Arrivals of international (or non-resident) visitors; **NHS:** Overnight stays at H&S; **NCE:** Overnight stays at CE.

.. data not available
incl including
excl excluding
nra nationals residing abroad

Notes:
(1.1,2.1-3.4) VF; (4.1-4.3) TF, based on surveys by Institute of Tourism; (5.1,5.3/96) Rented rooms; (5.6) CE; (6.1) Outbound trips registered at frontiers; (7.3) Rooms; (7.3/99) Rooms, hotels only; (8.1,8.2) Based on surveys and estimations by Institute of Tourism.

PORTUGAL

Basic Indicators	Units	Code	1996	1997	1998	1999	2000
INBOUND TOURISM							
Arrivals							
Visitors	Thousands	(1.1)	23,252	24,244	26,560	27,016	28,014
Tourists (overnight visitors)	Thousands	(1.2)	9,730	10,172	11,295	11,632	12,097
Same-day visitors	Thousands	(1.3)	13,301	13,842	15,030	15,120	15,691
Cruise passengers	Thousands	(1.4)	221	230	235	264	226
Arrivals by region							
Africa	Thousands	(2.1)	..	..	..	..	..
Americas	Thousands	(2.2)	337	374	409	417	479
Europe	Thousands	(2.3)	9,151	9,551	10,589	10,870	11,192
East Asia and the Pacific	Thousands	(2.4)	38	38	44	41	46
South Asia	Thousands	(2.5)	..	..	..	..	..
Middle East	Thousands	(2.6)	..	..	..	..	..
Arrivals by mode of transport							
Air	Thousands	(3.1)	4,116	4,344	4,752	4,947	5,238
Rail	Thousands	(3.2)	102	106	117	106	94
Road	Thousands	(3.3)	18,792	19,543	21,432	21,669	22,410
Sea	Thousands	(3.4)	242	251	260	293	272
Arrivals by purpose of visit							
Leisure, recreation and holidays	Thousands	(4.1)	6,286	6,439	7,466	7,840	..
Business and professional	Thousands	(4.2)	1,664	1,953	1,864	2,198	..
Other	Thousands	(4.3)	1,780	1,780	1,965	1,594	..
Overnight stays and length of stay							
Overnight stays in H&S	Thousand nights	(5.1)	19,962	20,851	23,241	23,331	24,102
Overnight stays in CE	Thousand nights	(5.2)	21,708	22,601	25,273	25,080	25,785
ALS of non resident tourists	Nights	(5.5)	7.00	6.90	7.00	6.80	6.70
Tourism expenditure							
in the country of reference	US$ Million	(8.1)	4,265	4,619	5,302	5,261	5,257
DOMESTIC TOURISM							
Overnight stays							
Overnight stays in H&S	Thousand nights	(5.3)	8,101	8,499	9,164	9,397	9,693
Overnight stays in CE	Thousand nights	(5.4)	14,528	14,707	15,326	16,243	16,171
OUTBOUND TOURISM							
Departures	Thousands	(6.1)	..	..	..	..	..
Tourism expenditure in other countries	US$ Million	(8.2)	2,283	2,161	2,319	2,260	2,230
TOURISM ACTIVITIES							
Hotels and similar establishments							
Number of rooms	H&S	(7.1)	91,094	93,460	94,788	95,401	97,709
Number of bed-places	H&S	(7.2)	208,205	211,315	215,572	216,828	222,958
Occupancy rate	Percent	(7.3)	38.20	39.50	42.50	43.00	42.20
Average length of stay	Nights	(5.6)	3.60	3.40	3.60	3.30	3.60
ECONOMIC AGGREGATES							
Gross National Product (GNP)	US$ Million	(9.1)	108,746	111,892	109,857	109,991	110,674
Exports (F.O.B.)	US$ Million	(9.2)	24,606	23,974	24,816	25,228	23,314
Imports (C.I.F.)	US$ Million	(9.3)	35,179	35,066	38,539	39,826	38,257

Abbreviations used in tables and notes:
H&S: Hotels and similar establishments; **CE:** All types of tourism accommodation establishments; **ALS:** Average length of stay; **THS:** Non-resident tourists staying in H&S; **TCE:** Non-resident tourists staying in CE; **TF:** Arrivals of international (or non-resident) tourists; **VF:** Arrivals of international (or non-resident) visitors; **NHS:** Overnight stays at H&S; **NCE:** Overnight stays at CE.

..   data not available
incl   including
excl   excluding
nra   nationals residing abroad

Notes:
(1.1,3.1-3.4) VF; (1.2,2.1-2.4,4.1-4.3) TF, excl nra; incl arrivals from abroad in Madeira/Azores; (1.4) Incl transit sea passengers; (5.2) Incl nights in accommodation establishments in Madeira and Azores; (5.6) CE; (7.1,7.3) Hotels, motels, inns, boarding houses & "pousadas" (July-June); (7.3) Bed-places (classified hotels).

Basic Indicators	Units	Code	1996	1997	1998	1999	2000
INBOUND TOURISM							
Arrivals							
Visitors	Thousands	(1.1)	4,110	4,350	4,671	4,221	4,566
Tourists (overnight visitors)	Thousands	(1.2)	3,065	3,242	3,396	3,024	3,341
Same-day visitors	Thousands	(1.3)	..	2	9	2	4
Cruise passengers	Thousands	(1.4)	1,045	1,106	1,266	1,196	1,221
Arrivals by region							
Africa	Thousands	(2.1)	..	..	..	..	..
Americas	Thousands	(2.2)	2,238	2,474	2,570	2,284	2,501
Europe	Thousands	(2.3)	..	..	..	..	..
East Asia and the Pacific	Thousands	(2.4)	..	..	..	..	..
South Asia	Thousands	(2.5)	..	..	..	..	..
Middle East	Thousands	(2.6)	..	..	..	..	..
Arrivals by mode of transport							
Air	Thousands	(3.1)	3,065	3,242	3,396	3,024	3,341
Rail	Thousands	(3.2)	..	..	..	..	..
Road	Thousands	(3.3)	..	..	..	..	..
Sea	Thousands	(3.4)	1,045	1,108	1,275	1,197	1,225
Arrivals by purpose of visit							
Leisure, recreation and holidays	Thousands	(4.1)	..	..	..	..	..
Business and professional	Thousands	(4.2)	..	..	..	..	..
Other	Thousands	(4.3)	..	..	..	..	..
Overnight stays and length of stay							
Overnight stays in H&S	Thousand nights	(5.1)	893	949	1,065	1,095	1,103
Overnight stays in CE	Thousand nights	(5.2)	..	..	..	0	0
ALS of non resident tourists	Nights	(5.5)	..	..	..	..	..
Tourism expenditure **in the country of reference**	US$ Million	(8.1)	1,898	2,046	2,233	2,138	2,388
DOMESTIC TOURISM							
Overnight stays							
Overnight stays in H&S	Thousand nights	(5.3)	..	..	..	..	..
Overnight stays in CE	Thousand nights	(5.4)	508	512	505	543	571
OUTBOUND TOURISM							
Departures	Thousands	(6.1)	1,184	1,251	1,250	1,134	1,259
Tourism expenditure in other countries	US$ Million	(8.2)	821	869	874	815	931
TOURISM ACTIVITIES							
Hotels and similar establishments							
Number of rooms	H&S	(7.1)	10,265	10,869	11,848	11,102	11,928
Number of bed-places	H&S	(7.2)	20,530	21,738	23,696	22,204	23,856
Occupancy rate	Percent	(7.3)	69.00	69.80	67.30	71.90	70.70
Average length of stay	Nights	(5.6)	2.60	2.70	2.70	3.00	2.50
ECONOMIC AGGREGATES							
Gross National Product (GNP)	US$ Million	(9.1)	30,099	31,478	..	..	..
Exports (F.O.B.)	US$ Million	(9.2)	22,944	23,947	30,273	34,902	..
Imports (C.I.F.)	US$ Million	(9.3)	19,061	21,387	21,798	..	..

Abbreviations used in tables and notes:
H&S: Hotels and similar establishments; **CE:** All types of tourism accommodation establishments; **ALS:** Average length of stay; **THS:** Non-resident tourists staying in H&S; **TCE:** Non-resident tourists staying in CE; **TF:** Arrivals of international (or non-resident) tourists; **VF:** Arrivals of international (or non-resident) visitors; **NHS:** Overnight stays at H&S; **NCE:** Overnight stays at CE.

..   data not available
incl   including
excl   excluding
nra   nationals residing abroad

Notes:
(1.2) TF, air arrivals (Fiscal year: July-June); (2.2) Incl U.S. Virgin Islands and USA only; (7.1) Rooms classified by the "Compañia de Turismo" of Puerto Rico; (7.3) Rooms; Fiscal year (July-June); Incl rooms occupied by residents of Puerto Rico.

QATAR

Basic Indicators	Units	Code	1996	1997	1998	1999	2000
INBOUND TOURISM							
Arrivals							
Visitors	Thousands	(1.1)	..	..	..	..	..
Tourists (overnight visitors)	Thousands	(1.2)	327	435	..	..	..
Same-day visitors	Thousands	(1.3)	..	..	..	..	..
Cruise passengers	Thousands	(1.4)	..	..	..	..	..
Arrivals by region							
Africa	Thousands	(2.1)	..	..	..	..	..
Americas	Thousands	(2.2)	..	110	..	..	..
Europe	Thousands	(2.3)	..	300	..	..	..
East Asia and the Pacific	Thousands	(2.4)	..	25	..	..	..
South Asia	Thousands	(2.5)	..	..	..	..	..
Middle East	Thousands	(2.6)	..	..	..	..	..
Arrivals by mode of transport							
Air	Thousands	(3.1)	..	..	..	..	..
Rail	Thousands	(3.2)	..	..	..	..	..
Road	Thousands	(3.3)	..	..	..	..	..
Sea	Thousands	(3.4)	..	..	..	..	..
Arrivals by purpose of visit							
Leisure, recreation and holidays	Thousands	(4.1)	..	..	..	..	..
Business and professional	Thousands	(4.2)	..	..	..	..	..
Other	Thousands	(4.3)	..	..	..	..	..
Overnight stays and length of stay							
Overnight stays in H&S	Thousand nights	(5.1)	..	..	..	..	..
Overnight stays in CE	Thousand nights	(5.2)	386	502	403	..	..
ALS of non resident tourists	Nights	(5.5)	..	..	..	..	..
Tourism expenditure **in the country of reference**	US$ Million	(8.1)	..	..	..	..	..
DOMESTIC TOURISM							
Overnight stays							
Overnight stays in H&S	Thousand nights	(5.3)	..	..	..	..	..
Overnight stays in CE	Thousand nights	(5.4)	..	..	..	..	..
OUTBOUND TOURISM							
Departures	Thousands	(6.1)	..	..	..	..	..
Tourism expenditure in other countries	US$ Million	(8.2)	..	..	..	..	..
TOURISM ACTIVITIES							
Hotels and similar establishments							
Number of rooms	H&S	(7.1)	2,978	1,998	1,842	..	..
Number of bed-places	H&S	(7.2)	2,646	2,710	2,743	..	..
Occupancy rate	Percent	(7.3)	65.80	78.30	79.00	..	..
Average length of stay	Nights	(5.6)	..	..	..	..	..
ECONOMIC AGGREGATES							
Gross National Product (GNP)	US$ Million	(9.1)	9,059	9,193	9,217	..	..
Exports (F.O.B.)	US$ Million	(9.2)	3,752	4,474	4,355	..	..
Imports (C.I.F.)	US$ Million	(9.3)	2,868	3,322	3,409	2,499	..

Abbreviations used in tables and notes:
H&S: Hotels and similar establishments; **CE:** All types of tourism accommodation establishments; **ALS:** Average length of stay; **THS:** Non-resident tourists staying in H&S; **TCE:** Non-resident tourists staying in CE; **TF:** Arrivals of international (or non-resident) tourists; **VF:** Arrivals of international (or non-resident) visitors; **NHS:** Overnight stays at H&S; **NCE:** Overnight stays at CE.

..   data not available
incl   including
excl   excluding
nra   nationals residing abroad

Notes:
(1.2) Arrivals in hotels; (9.1) GDP.

Basic Indicators	Units	Code	1996	1997	1998	1999	2000
INBOUND TOURISM							
Arrivals							
Visitors	Thousands	(1.1)	29	21	20	14	19
Tourists (overnight visitors)	Thousands	(1.2)	29	21	19	14	18
Same-day visitors	Thousands	(1.3)	0.1	..	0.5	0.3	0.8
Cruise passengers	Thousands	(1.4)	..	..	..	..	..
Arrivals by region							
Africa	Thousands	(2.1)	..	..	..	..	..
Americas	Thousands	(2.2)	0.8	1.0	0.9	0.9	1.1
Europe	Thousands	(2.3)	27.6	19.7	18.6	12.8	17.2
East Asia and the Pacific	Thousands	(2.4)	0.2	0.3	0.2	0.2	0.4
South Asia	Thousands	(2.5)	0.1	0.1	0.1	..	0.1
Middle East	Thousands	(2.6)	0.2	0.1	0.1	0.1	0.2
Arrivals by mode of transport							
Air	Thousands	(3.1)	..	..	..	..	..
Rail	Thousands	(3.2)	..	..	..	..	..
Road	Thousands	(3.3)	..	..	..	..	..
Sea	Thousands	(3.4)	..	..	..	..	..
Arrivals by purpose of visit							
Leisure, recreation and holidays	Thousands	(4.1)	4.6	2.7	3.2	1.6	7.1
Business and professional	Thousands	(4.2)	22.0	17.4	15.8	11.9	11.6
Other	Thousands	(4.3)	2.3	1.0	0.9	0.6	0.3
Overnight stays and length of stay							
Overnight stays in H&S	Thousand nights	(5.1)	82	62	78	59	85
Overnight stays in CE	Thousand nights	(5.2)	..	..	..	..	..
ALS of non resident tourists	Nights	(5.5)	..	..	..	..	..
Tourism expenditure in the country of reference	US$ Million	(8.1)	33	50	40	38	46
DOMESTIC TOURISM							
Overnight stays							
Overnight stays in H&S	Thousand nights	(5.3)	26	45	46	62	212
Overnight stays in CE	Thousand nights	(5.4)	..	..	..	..	..
OUTBOUND TOURISM							
Departures	Thousands	(6.1)	54	35	28	37	32
Tourism expenditure in other countries	US$ Million	(8.2)	52	65	59	58	78
TOURISM ACTIVITIES							
Hotels and similar establishments							
Number of rooms	H&S	(7.1)	4,060	3,500	3,170	3,148	2,954
Number of bed-places	H&S	(7.2)	8,174	6,708	5,868	5,679	5,562
Occupancy rate	Percent	(7.3)	18.30	20.50	19.00	20.90	19.80
Average length of stay	Nights	(5.6)	..	..	..	..	..
ECONOMIC AGGREGATES							
Gross National Product (GNP)	US$ Million	(9.1)	2,395	2,155	1,707	1,495	1,413
Exports (F.O.B.)	US$ Million	(9.2)	805	890	644	465	..
Imports (C.I.F.)	US$ Million	(9.3)	1,079	1,200	1,018	567	..

Abbreviations used in tables and notes:
H&S: Hotels and similar establishments; **CE:** All types of tourism accommodation establishments; **ALS:** Average length of stay; **THS:** Non-resident tourists staying in H&S; **TCE:** Non-resident tourists staying in CE; **TF:** Arrivals of international (or non-resident) tourists; **VF:** Arrivals of international (or non-resident) visitors; **NHS:** Overnight stays at H&S; **NCE:** Overnight stays at CE.

..   data not available
incl   including
excl   excluding
nra   nationals residing abroad

Notes:
(1.1-6.1) Visitors who enjoyed the services of the economic agents officially registered under tourism activity and accommodation (excluding the regions of the left bank of the Dniestr and the municipality of Bender).

REUNION

Basic Indicators	Units	Code	1996	1997	1998	1999	2000
INBOUND TOURISM							
Arrivals							
Visitors	Thousands	(1.1)	..	..	..	..	..
Tourists (overnight visitors)	Thousands	(1.2)	350	374	400	394	430
Same-day visitors	Thousands	(1.3)	..	..	..	..	..
Cruise passengers	Thousands	(1.4)	..	..	..	..	..
Arrivals by region							
Africa	Thousands	(2.1)	40	41	43	53	..
Americas	Thousands	(2.2)	1	1	1	1	..
Europe	Thousands	(2.3)	304	325	345	338	359
East Asia and the Pacific	Thousands	(2.4)	1	1	1	1	..
South Asia	Thousands	(2.5)	1	1	1	1	..
Middle East	Thousands	(2.6)	..	..	..	..	..
Arrivals by mode of transport							
Air	Thousands	(3.1)	347	370	391	387	425
Rail	Thousands	(3.2)	..	..	..	..	..
Road	Thousands	(3.3)	..	..	..	..	..
Sea	Thousands	(3.4)	3	4	9	7	5
Arrivals by purpose of visit							
Leisure, recreation and holidays	Thousands	(4.1)	176	186	222	201	220
Business and professional	Thousands	(4.2)	30	33	31	41	44
Other	Thousands	(4.3)	141	151	138	152	166
Overnight stays and length of stay							
Overnight stays in H&S	Thousand nights	(5.1)	690	715	912	1,032	1,081
Overnight stays in CE	Thousand nights	(5.2)	..	..	..	..	..
ALS of non resident tourists	Nights	(5.5)	17.00	15.80	16.40	15.70	15.70
Tourism expenditure							
in the country of reference	US$ Million	(8.1)	258	249	265	270	276
DOMESTIC TOURISM							
Overnight stays							
Overnight stays in H&S	Thousand nights	(5.3)	..	..	..	..	..
Overnight stays in CE	Thousand nights	(5.4)	..	..	..	..	..
OUTBOUND TOURISM							
Departures	Thousands	(6.1)	258	267	262	319	322
Tourism expenditure in other countries	US$ Million	(8.2)	..	..	..	..	..
TOURISM ACTIVITIES							
Hotels and similar establishments							
Number of rooms	H&S	(7.1)	1,884	1,831	2,174	2,527	2,719
Number of bed-places	H&S	(7.2)	3,768	3,662	4,348	5,054	5,438
Occupancy rate	Percent	(7.3)	59.30	61.50	64.00	63.90	64.80
Average length of stay	Nights	(5.6)	6.30	6.70	7.20	7.10	6.70
ECONOMIC AGGREGATES							
Gross National Product (GNP)	US$ Million	(9.1)	..	..	..	..	..
Exports (F.O.B.)	US$ Million	(9.2)	208	214	..	..	..
Imports (C.I.F.)	US$ Million	(9.3)	2,760	2,443	..	..	..

Abbreviations used in tables and notes:
H&S: Hotels and similar establishments; **CE:** All types of tourism accommodation establishments; **ALS:** Average length of stay; **THS:** Non-resident tourists staying in H&S; **TCE:** Non-resident tourists staying in CE; **TF:** Arrivals of international (or non-resident) tourists; **VF:** Arrivals of international (or non-resident) visitors; **NHS:** Overnight stays at H&S; **NCE:** Overnight stays at CE.

..   data not available
incl   including
excl   excluding
nra   nationals residing abroad

Notes:
(2.1-2.5,4.1-4.3/96-98) Air arrivals; (5.5) Days.

Basic Indicators	Units	Code	1996	1997	1998	1999	2000
INBOUND TOURISM							
Arrivals							
Visitors	Thousands	(1.1)	5,205	5,149	4,831	5,224	5,264
Tourists (overnight visitors)	Thousands	(1.2)	3,028	2,957	2,966	3,209	3,274
Same-day visitors	Thousands	(1.3)	2,177	2,192	1,865	2,015	1,990
Cruise passengers	Thousands	(1.4)	..	..	..	..	..
Arrivals by region							
Africa	Thousands	(2.1)	5	5	5	5	5
Americas	Thousands	(2.2)	73	81	90	84	95
Europe	Thousands	(2.3)	5,023	4,971	4,650	5,049	5,074
East Asia and the Pacific	Thousands	(2.4)	41	41	41	36	37
South Asia	Thousands	(2.5)	14	14	14	16	17
Middle East	Thousands	(2.6)	38	36	30	32	34
Arrivals by mode of transport							
Air	Thousands	(3.1)	479	533	553	566	655
Rail	Thousands	(3.2)	492	596	589	586	660
Road	Thousands	(3.3)	4,073	3,850	3,530	3,930	3,808
Sea	Thousands	(3.4)	161	171	160	141	141
Arrivals by purpose of visit							
Leisure, recreation and holidays	Thousands	(4.1)	2,834	2,774	2,783	..	..
Business and professional	Thousands	(4.2)	194	183	182	..	..
Other	Thousands	(4.3)	2,177	2,192	1,866	..	..
Overnight stays and length of stay							
Overnight stays in H&S	Thousand nights	(5.1)	2,201	2,366	2,117	1,960	2,085
Overnight stays in CE	Thousand nights	(5.2)	2,288	2,506	2,207	1,981	2,149
ALS of non resident tourists	Nights	(5.5)	..	3.01	2.72	2.49	2.48
Tourism expenditure in the country of reference	US$ Million	(8.1)	529	526	260	254	359
DOMESTIC TOURISM							
Overnight stays							
Overnight stays in H&S	Thousand nights	(5.3)	16,246	14,147	14,696	15,681	13,862
Overnight stays in CE	Thousand nights	(5.4)	19,550	17,106	16,976	15,689	15,497
OUTBOUND TOURISM							
Departures	Thousands	(6.1)	5,748	6,243	6,893	6,274	6,388
Tourism expenditure in other countries	US$ Million	(8.2)	666	783	451	395	420
TOURISM ACTIVITIES							
Hotels and similar establishments							
Number of rooms	H&S	(7.1)	97,317	97,075	97,247	96,830	95,404
Number of bed-places	H&S	(7.2)	211,694	204,124	204,499	202,867	199,333
Occupancy rate	Percent	(7.3)	40.70	37.70	36.10	34.50	35.20
Average length of stay	Nights	(5.6)	3.30	3.40	3.50	3.50	3.20
ECONOMIC AGGREGATES							
Gross National Product (GNP)	US$ Million	(9.1)	33,319	31,575	32,245	33,840	37,370
Exports (F.O.B.)	US$ Million	(9.2)	8,085	8,431	8,300	8,505	10,367
Imports (C.I.F.)	US$ Million	(9.3)	11,435	11,280	11,821	10,392	13,055

Abbreviations used in tables and notes:
H&S: Hotels and similar establishments; **CE:** All types of tourism accommodation establishments; **ALS:** Average length of stay; **THS:** Non-resident tourists staying in H&S; **TCE:** Non-resident tourists staying in CE; **TF:** Arrivals of international (or non-resident) tourists; **VF:** Arrivals of international (or non-resident) visitors; **NHS:** Overnight stays at H&S; **NCE:** Overnight stays at CE.

..   data not available
incl   including
excl   excluding
nra   nationals residing abroad

Notes:
(1.1,2.1-2.6,3.1-4.3) VF; (4.1-4.3/99) As from 1999 data on international arrivals by purpose of visit have not been registered.

RUSSIAN FEDERATION

Basic Indicators	Units	Code	1996	1997	1998	1999	2000
INBOUND TOURISM							
Arrivals							
Visitors	Thousands	(1.1)	16,208	17,463	15,805	18,496	21,169
Tourists (overnight visitors)	Thousands	(1.2)	..	..	..	..	..
Same-day visitors	Thousands	(1.3)	..	..	..	..	..
Cruise passengers	Thousands	(1.4)	..	..	..	..	..
Arrivals by region							
Africa	Thousands	(2.1)	25	34	31	29	..
Americas	Thousands	(2.2)	246	293	292	255	..
Europe	Thousands	(2.3)	15,197	16,034	14,287	16,780	..
East Asia and the Pacific	Thousands	(2.4)	652	757	754	748	..
South Asia	Thousands	(2.5)	35	51	52	43	..
Middle East	Thousands	(2.6)	45	39	64	28	..
Arrivals by mode of transport							
Air	Thousands	(3.1)	2,194	2,977	2,685	2,225	..
Rail	Thousands	(3.2)	5,375	6,156	5,533	6,977	..
Road	Thousands	(3.3)	8,066	7,612	6,767	8,504	..
Sea	Thousands	(3.4)	573	718	820	787	..
Arrivals by purpose of visit							
Leisure, recreation and holidays	Thousands	(4.1)	1,889	2,515	2,885	3,059	2,598
Business and professional	Thousands	(4.2)	4,814	3,375	3,011	4,009	3,218
Other	Thousands	(4.3)	9,505	11,573	9,909	11,427	15,353
Overnight stays and length of stay							
Overnight stays in H&S	Thousand nights	(5.1)	..	..	..	..	..
Overnight stays in CE	Thousand nights	(5.2)	..	..	..	..	..
ALS of non resident tourists	Nights	(5.5)	..	..	..	..	..
Tourism expenditure							
in the country of reference	US$ Million	(8.1)	6,868	7,164	6,508	7,510	..
DOMESTIC TOURISM							
Overnight stays							
Overnight stays in H&S	Thousand nights	(5.3)	..	..	..	..	..
Overnight stays in CE	Thousand nights	(5.4)	..	..	..	..	..
OUTBOUND TOURISM							
Departures	Thousands	(6.1)	12,261	11,182	11,711	12,631	18,371
Tourism expenditure in other countries	US$ Million	(8.2)	10,270	9,363	8,279	7,434	..
TOURISM ACTIVITIES							
Hotels and similar establishments							
Number of rooms	H&S	(7.1)	207,362	202,033	194,262	188,255	..
Number of bed-places	H&S	(7.2)	410,592	390,931	372,810	358,142	..
Occupancy rate	Percent	(7.3)	33.00	31.00	32.00	33.00	..
Average length of stay	Nights	(5.6)	..	..	..	..	..
ECONOMIC AGGREGATES							
Gross National Product (GNP)	US$ Million	(9.1)	348,305	383,520	332,905	256,010	241,110
Exports (F.O.B.)	US$ Million	(9.2)	85,107	85,036	71,265	71,817	103,070
Imports (C.I.F.)	US$ Million	(9.3)	46,034	53,039	43,530	30,185	33,884

Abbreviations used in tables and notes:
H&S: Hotels and similar establishments; **CE:** All types of tourism accommodation establishments; **ALS:** Average length of stay; **THS:** Non-resident tourists staying in H&S; **TCE:** Non-resident tourists staying in CE; **TF:** Arrivals of international (or non-resident) tourists; **VF:** Arrivals of international (or non-resident) visitors; **NHS:** Overnight stays at H&S; **NCE:** Overnight stays at CE.

..	data not available
incl	including
excl	excluding
nra	nationals residing abroad

Notes:
(7.1,7.2) Accommodation in hotels and other tourist establishments.

SABA

Basic Indicators	Units	Code	1996	1997	1998	1999	2000
INBOUND TOURISM							
Arrivals							
Visitors	Thousands	(1.1)	24.3	28.6	25.4	24.3	24.4
Tourists (overnight visitors)	Thousands	(1.2)	9.8	10.6	10.6	9.3	9.0
Same-day visitors	Thousands	(1.3)	14.5	18.0	14.8	15.0	..
Cruise passengers	Thousands	(1.4)	..	..	..	..	..
Arrivals by region							
Africa	Thousands	(2.1)	..	..	..	..	..
Americas	Thousands	(2.2)	7.5	8.3	8.2	6.9	..
Europe	Thousands	(2.3)	1.0	1.0	1.1	0.9	..
East Asia and the Pacific	Thousands	(2.4)	..	..	..	..	..
South Asia	Thousands	(2.5)	..	..	..	..	..
Middle East	Thousands	(2.6)	..	..	..	..	..
Arrivals by mode of transport							
Air	Thousands	(3.1)	7.3	8.1	7.8	6.9	..
Rail	Thousands	(3.2)	..	..	..	..	..
Road	Thousands	(3.3)	..	..	..	..	..
Sea	Thousands	(3.4)	2.5	2.5	2.8	2.3	..
Arrivals by purpose of visit							
Leisure, recreation and holidays	Thousands	(4.1)	..	..	..	..	..
Business and professional	Thousands	(4.2)	..	..	..	..	..
Other	Thousands	(4.3)	..	..	..	..	..
Overnight stays and length of stay							
Overnight stays in H&S	Thousand nights	(5.1)	..	..	..	..	..
Overnight stays in CE	Thousand nights	(5.2)	..	..	..	..	..
ALS of non resident tourists	Nights	(5.5)	..	..	..	..	..
Tourism expenditure in the country of reference	US$ Million	(8.1)	..	..	..	..	..
DOMESTIC TOURISM							
Overnight stays							
Overnight stays in H&S	Thousand nights	(5.3)	..	..	..	..	..
Overnight stays in CE	Thousand nights	(5.4)	..	..	..	..	..
OUTBOUND TOURISM							
Departures	Thousands	(6.1)	..	..	..	..	..
Tourism expenditure in other countries	US$ Million	(8.2)	..	..	..	..	..
TOURISM ACTIVITIES							
Hotels and similar establishments							
Number of rooms	H&S	(7.1)	186	186	91	87	..
Number of bed-places	H&S	(7.2)	..	..	..	..	..
Occupancy rate	Percent	(7.3)	..	..	..	..	..
Average length of stay	Nights	(5.6)	..	..	..	..	..
ECONOMIC AGGREGATES							
Gross National Product (GNP)	US$ Million	(9.1)	..	..	..	..	..
Exports (F.O.B.)	US$ Million	(9.2)	..	..	..	..	..
Imports (C.I.F.)	US$ Million	(9.3)	..	..	..	..	..

Abbreviations used in tables and notes:
H&S: Hotels and similar establishments; **CE:** All types of tourism accommodation establishments; **ALS:** Average length of stay; **THS:** Non-resident tourists staying in H&S; **TCE:** Non-resident tourists staying in CE; **TF:** Arrivals of international (or non-resident) tourists; **VF:** Arrivals of international (or non-resident) visitors; **NHS:** Overnight stays at H&S; **NCE:** Overnight stays at CE.

..	data not available
incl	including
excl	excluding
nra	nationals residing abroad

Notes:
(1.3) Mainly from St. Maarten; (7.1) Hotels.

SAINT EUSTATIUS

Basic Indicators	Units	Code	1996	1997	1998	1999	2000
INBOUND TOURISM							
Arrivals							
Visitors	Thousands	(1.1)	24	25	25	25	..
Tourists (overnight visitors)	Thousands	(1.2)	..	..	..	..	..
Same-day visitors	Thousands	(1.3)	..	..	..	..	..
Cruise passengers	Thousands	(1.4)	..	..	..	..	..
Arrivals by region							
Africa	Thousands	(2.1)	..	..	..		..
Americas	Thousands	(2.2)	15	14	14	14	..
Europe	Thousands	(2.3)	4	4	4	4	..
East Asia and the Pacific	Thousands	(2.4)	..	..	..	..	..
South Asia	Thousands	(2.5)	..	..	..	..	..
Middle East	Thousands	(2.6)	..	..	..	..	..
Arrivals by mode of transport							
Air	Thousands	(3.1)	20	19	19	19	..
Rail	Thousands	(3.2)	..	..	..	..	..
Road	Thousands	(3.3)	..	..	..	..	..
Sea	Thousands	(3.4)	4	6	6	6	..
Arrivals by purpose of visit							
Leisure, recreation and holidays	Thousands	(4.1)	..	..	..	..	..
Business and professional	Thousands	(4.2)	..	..	..	..	..
Other	Thousands	(4.3)	..	..	..	..	..
Overnight stays and length of stay							
Overnight stays in H&S	Thousand nights	(5.1)	..	..	..	..	..
Overnight stays in CE	Thousand nights	(5.2)	..	..	..	..	..
ALS of non resident tourists	Nights	(5.5)	..	..	..	..	..
Tourism expenditure							
in the country of reference	US$ Million	(8.1)	..	..	..	..	..
DOMESTIC TOURISM							
Overnight stays							
Overnight stays in H&S	Thousand nights	(5.3)	..	..	..	..	..
Overnight stays in CE	Thousand nights	(5.4)	..	..	..	..	..
OUTBOUND TOURISM							
Departures	Thousands	(6.1)	..	..	..	..	..
Tourism expenditure in other countries	US$ Million	(8.2)	..	..	..	..	..
TOURISM ACTIVITIES							
Hotels and similar establishments							
Number of rooms	H&S	(7.1)	77	77	63	63	..
Number of bed-places	H&S	(7.2)	..	..	..	..	..
Occupancy rate	Percent	(7.3)	..	45.00	..	..	..
Average length of stay	Nights	(5.6)	..	..	..	..	..
ECONOMIC AGGREGATES							
Gross National Product (GNP)	US$ Million	(9.1)	..	..	..	..	..
Exports (F.O.B.)	US$ Million	(9.2)	..	..	..	..	..
Imports (C.I.F.)	US$ Million	(9.3)	..	..	..	..	..

Abbreviations used in tables and notes:
H&S: Hotels and similar establishments; CE: All types of tourism accommodation establishments; ALS: Average length of stay; THS: Non-resident tourists staying in H&S; TCE: Non-resident tourists staying in CE; TF: Arrivals of international (or non-resident) tourists; VF: Arrivals of international (or non-resident) visitors; NHS: Overnight stays at H&S; NCE: Overnight stays at CE.

..   data not available
incl   including
excl   excluding
nra   nationals residing abroad

Notes:
(1.1) air and sea arrivals, incl nra.

Basic Indicators	Units	Code	1996	1997	1998	1999	2000
INBOUND TOURISM							
Arrivals							
Visitors	Thousands	(1.1)	172	194	250	224	..
Tourists (overnight visitors)	Thousands	(1.2)	84	88	93	84	69
Same-day visitors	Thousands	(1.3)	2	3	3	3	..
Cruise passengers	Thousands	(1.4)	86	103	154	137	164
Arrivals by region							
Africa	Thousands	(2.1)	..	..	..	..	..
Americas	Thousands	(2.2)	71	75	77	68	..
Europe	Thousands	(2.3)	12	13	15	16	..
East Asia and the Pacific	Thousands	(2.4)	..	..	..	..	..
South Asia	Thousands	(2.5)	..	..	..	..	..
Middle East	Thousands	(2.6)	..	..	..	..	..
Arrivals by mode of transport							
Air	Thousands	(3.1)	86	92	96	87	..
Rail	Thousands	(3.2)	..	..	..	..	..
Road	Thousands	(3.3)	..	..	..	..	..
Sea	Thousands	(3.4)	86	103	154	137	..
Arrivals by purpose of visit							
Leisure, recreation and holidays	Thousands	(4.1)	78	82	86	78	..
Business and professional	Thousands	(4.2)	6	6	7	5	..
Other	Thousands	(4.3)	..	..	..	..	..
Overnight stays and length of stay							
Overnight stays in H&S	Thousand nights	(5.1)	..	..	..	..	..
Overnight stays in CE	Thousand nights	(5.2)	..	..	..	..	..
ALS of non resident tourists	Nights	(5.5)	8.80	8.30	8.70	8.70	..
Tourism expenditure **in the country of reference**	US$ Million	(8.1)	67	67	76	70	58
DOMESTIC TOURISM							
Overnight stays							
Overnight stays in H&S	Thousand nights	(5.3)	..	..	..	..	..
Overnight stays in CE	Thousand nights	(5.4)	..	..	..	..	..
OUTBOUND TOURISM							
Departures	Thousands	(6.1)	..	..	..	..	..
Tourism expenditure in other countries	US$ Million	(8.2)	6	6	6	..	..
TOURISM ACTIVITIES							
Hotels and similar establishments							
Number of rooms	H&S	(7.1)	1,610	1,759	1,762	1,754	..
Number of bed-places	H&S	(7.2)	..	..	..	..	..
Occupancy rate	Percent	(7.3)	..	..	..	..	..
Average length of stay	Nights	(5.6)	..	..	..	..	..
ECONOMIC AGGREGATES							
Gross National Product (GNP)	US$ Million	(9.1)	232	245	242	259	273
Exports (F.O.B.)	US$ Million	(9.2)	22	36	31	..	..
Imports (C.I.F.)	US$ Million	(9.3)	149	148	148	..	..

Abbreviations used in tables and notes:
H&S: Hotels and similar establishments; **CE:** All types of tourism accommodation establishments; **ALS:** Average length of stay; **THS:** Non-resident tourists staying in H&S; **TCE:** Non-resident tourists staying in CE; **TF:** Arrivals of international (or non-resident) tourists; **VF:** Arrivals of international (or non-resident) visitors; **NHS:** Overnight stays at H&S; **NCE:** Overnight stays at CE.

Notes:
(1.2) TF, air and sea arrivals; (1.4) Yacht and cruise ship arrivals; (2.2,2.3) TF, air arrivals.

..   data not available
incl   including
excl   excluding
nra   nationals residing abroad

SAINT LUCIA

Basic Indicators	Units	Code	1996	1997	1998	1999	2000
INBOUND TOURISM							
Arrivals							
Visitors	Thousands	(1.1)	423	563	629	636	727
Tourists (overnight visitors)	Thousands	(1.2)	236	248	252	264	270
Same-day visitors	Thousands	(1.3)	6	5	5	21	13
Cruise passengers	Thousands	(1.4)	181	310	372	351	444
Arrivals by region							
Africa	Thousands	(2.1)	..	..	..	..	..
Americas	Thousands	(2.2)	148	149	161	159	168
Europe	Thousands	(2.3)	84	96	89	99	99
East Asia and the Pacific	Thousands	(2.4)	..	..	..	..	..
South Asia	Thousands	(2.5)	..	..	..	..	..
Middle East	Thousands	(2.6)	..	..	..	..	..
Arrivals by mode of transport							
Air	Thousands	(3.1)	226	235	241	260	272
Rail	Thousands	(3.2)	..	..	..	..	..
Road	Thousands	(3.3)	..	..	..	..	..
Sea	Thousands	(3.4)	196	328	388	376	455
Arrivals by purpose of visit							
Leisure, recreation and holidays	Thousands	(4.1)	225	237	242	251	237
Business and professional	Thousands	(4.2)	10	11	10	11	14
Other	Thousands	(4.3)	1	..	..	2	19
Overnight stays and length of stay							
Overnight stays in H&S	Thousand nights	(5.1)	..	..	..	..	..
Overnight stays in CE	Thousand nights	(5.2)	..	..	..	..	..
ALS of non resident tourists	Nights	(5.5)	..	..	..	..	..
Tourism expenditure							
in the country of reference	US$ Million	(8.1)	269	284	291	311	277
DOMESTIC TOURISM							
Overnight stays							
Overnight stays in H&S	Thousand nights	(5.3)	..	..	..	..	..
Overnight stays in CE	Thousand nights	(5.4)	..	..	..	..	..
OUTBOUND TOURISM							
Departures	Thousands	(6.1)	..	..	..	..	..
Tourism expenditure in other countries	US$ Million	(8.2)	29	..	..	..	..
TOURISM ACTIVITIES							
Hotels and similar establishments							
Number of rooms	H&S	(7.1)	3,986	3,701	3,769	4,125	4,428
Number of bed-places	H&S	(7.2)	7,435	6,382	..	..	8,236
Occupancy rate	Percent	(7.3)	66.60	71.40	75.30	72.50	67.00
Average length of stay	Nights	(5.6)	8.70	8.80	8.70	8.70	9.60
ECONOMIC AGGREGATES							
Gross National Product (GNP)	US$ Million	(9.1)	541	546	558	599	634
Exports (F.O.B.)	US$ Million	(9.2)	82	66	..	..	..
Imports (C.I.F.)	US$ Million	(9.3)	304	332	335	..	..

Abbreviations used in tables and notes:
H&S: Hotels and similar establishments; **CE:** All types of tourism accommodation establishments; **ALS:** Average length of stay; **THS:** Non-resident tourists staying in H&S; **TCE:** Non-resident tourists staying in CE; **TF:** Arrivals of international (or non-resident) tourists; **VF:** Arrivals of international (or non-resident) visitors; **NHS:** Overnight stays at H&S; **NCE:** Overnight stays at CE.

..   data not available
incl   including
excl   excluding
nra   nationals residing abroad

Notes:
(1.2,2.2,2.3,3.1,4.1-4.3) TF, excl nra; (3.4) Incl cruise passengers; (7.3) Rooms.

Basic Indicators	Units	Code	1996	1997	1998	1999	2000
INBOUND TOURISM							
Arrivals							
Visitors	Thousands	(1.1)	1,008	1,304	1,344	1,061	1,300
Tourists (overnight visitors)	Thousands	(1.2)	351	418	458	445	432
Same-day visitors	Thousands	(1.3)	..	..	..	..	..
Cruise passengers	Thousands	(1.4)	657	886	886	616	868
Arrivals by region							
Africa	Thousands	(2.1)	..	..	..	..	..
Americas	Thousands	(2.2)	215	272	290	281	..
Europe	Thousands	(2.3)	101	110	133	126	..
East Asia and the Pacific	Thousands	(2.4)	..	..	..	..	..
South Asia	Thousands	(2.5)	..	..	..	..	..
Middle East	Thousands	(2.6)	..	..	..	..	..
Arrivals by mode of transport							
Air	Thousands	(3.1)	351	418	458	445	432
Rail	Thousands	(3.2)	..	..	..	..	..
Road	Thousands	(3.3)	..	..	..	..	..
Sea	Thousands	(3.4)	657	886	882	616	868
Arrivals by purpose of visit							
Leisure, recreation and holidays	Thousands	(4.1)	..	..	..	..	..
Business and professional	Thousands	(4.2)	..	..	..	..	..
Other	Thousands	(4.3)	..	..	..	..	..
Overnight stays and length of stay							
Overnight stays in H&S	Thousand nights	(5.1)	..	..	..	..	..
Overnight stays in CE	Thousand nights	(5.2)	..	2,168	2,248	2,238	..
ALS of non resident tourists	Nights	(5.5)	..	..	..	..	..
Tourism expenditure							
in the country of reference	US$ Million	(8.1)	322	379	413	449	482
DOMESTIC TOURISM							
Overnight stays							
Overnight stays in H&S	Thousand nights	(5.3)	..	..	..	..	..
Overnight stays in CE	Thousand nights	(5.4)	..	..	..	..	..
OUTBOUND TOURISM							
Departures	Thousands	(6.1)	..	..	..	..	..
Tourism expenditure in other countries	US$ Million	(8.2)	..	65	128	141	..
TOURISM ACTIVITIES							
Hotels and similar establishments							
Number of rooms	H&S	(7.1)	4,043	4,049	4,174	3,065	..
Number of bed-places	H&S	(7.2)	8,086	8,098	8,348	6,130	..
Occupancy rate	Percent	(7.3)	54.80	54.80	57.90	59.30	..
Average length of stay	Nights	(5.6)	..	..	5.00	..	..
ECONOMIC AGGREGATES							
Gross National Product (GNP)	US$ Million	(9.1)	..	..	..	..	..
Exports (F.O.B.)	US$ Million	(9.2)	43	24	25	..	..
Imports (C.I.F.)	US$ Million	(9.3)	..	..	..	..	..

Abbreviations used in tables and notes:

H&S: Hotels and similar establishments; **CE:** All types of tourism accommodation establishments; **ALS:** Average length of stay; **THS:** Non-resident tourists staying in H&S; **TCE:** Non-resident tourists staying in CE; **TF:** Arrivals of international (or non-resident) tourists; **VF:** Arrivals of international (or non-resident) visitors; **NHS:** Overnight stays at H&S; **NCE:** Overnight stays at CE.

..   data not available
incl   including
excl   excluding
nra   nationals residing abroad

Notes:

(1.2,2.2,2.3) By air, incl arrivals to Saint Maarten (the French side of the island); (3.1) Arrivals at Juliana Airport (incl visitors destined to Saint Maarten, French side); (7.1,7.2) Hotels, guest houses and apartments; (8.1) Central Bank estimates, incl estimates for Saba and Saint Eustatius.

SAINT VINCENT AND THE GRENADINES

Basic Indicators	Units	Code	1996	1997	1998	1999	2000
INBOUND TOURISM							
Arrivals							
Visitors	Thousands	(1.1)	216	200	202	223	256
Tourists (overnight visitors)	Thousands	(1.2)	58	65	67	68	73
Same-day visitors	Thousands	(1.3)	30	28	21	18	21
Cruise passengers	Thousands	(1.4)	128	107	114	137	162
Arrivals by region							
Africa	Thousands	(2.1)	..	..	..	..	..
Americas	Thousands	(2.2)	39	46	46	47	..
Europe	Thousands	(2.3)	18	19	20	20	..
East Asia and the Pacific	Thousands	(2.4)	..	..	..	..	..
South Asia	Thousands	(2.5)	..	..	..	..	..
Middle East	Thousands	(2.6)	..	..	..	..	..
Arrivals by mode of transport							
Air	Thousands	(3.1)	88	93	88	86	94
Rail	Thousands	(3.2)	..	..	..	..	..
Road	Thousands	(3.3)	..	..	..	..	..
Sea	Thousands	(3.4)	128	107	114	137	162
Arrivals by purpose of visit							
Leisure, recreation and holidays	Thousands	(4.1)	45	49	45	50	..
Business and professional	Thousands	(4.2)	6	8	7	8	..
Other	Thousands	(4.3)	7	8	15	10	..
Overnight stays and length of stay							
Overnight stays in H&S	Thousand nights	(5.1)	..	..	33	35	..
Overnight stays in CE	Thousand nights	(5.2)	..	..	..	..	..
ALS of non resident tourists	Nights	(5.5)	10.70	10.30	11.10	10.60	..
Tourism expenditure							
in the country of reference	US$ Million	(8.1)	64	70	72	77	74
DOMESTIC TOURISM							
Overnight stays							
Overnight stays in H&S	Thousand nights	(5.3)	..	..	12	11	..
Overnight stays in CE	Thousand nights	(5.4)	..	..	..	..	..
OUTBOUND TOURISM							
Departures	Thousands	(6.1)	..	..	..	..	..
Tourism expenditure in other countries	US$ Million	(8.2)	8	7	8	..	..
TOURISM ACTIVITIES							
Hotels and similar establishments							
Number of rooms	H&S	(7.1)	1,254	1,272	1,550	1,540	1,747
Number of bed-places	H&S	(7.2)	2,508	2,544	3,100	3,080	3,494
Occupancy rate	Percent	(7.3)	..	..	..	..	..
Average length of stay	Nights	(5.6)	..	..	..	..	..
ECONOMIC AGGREGATES							
Gross National Product (GNP)	US$ Million	(9.1)	273	279	291	299	309
Exports (F.O.B.)	US$ Million	(9.2)	46	46	50	49	47
Imports (C.I.F.)	US$ Million	(9.3)	132	182	193	201	163

Abbreviations used in tables and notes:
H&S: Hotels and similar establishments; **CE:** All types of tourism accommodation establishments; **ALS:** Average length of stay; **THS:** Non-resident tourists staying in H&S; **TCE:** Non-resident tourists staying in CE; **TF:** Arrivals of international (or non-resident) tourists; **VF:** Arrivals of international (or non-resident) visitors; **NHS:** Overnight stays at H&S; **NCE:** Overnight stays at CE.

.. data not available
incl including
excl excluding
nra nationals residing abroad

Notes:
(1.2,2.2-2.3,4.1-4.3) TF; (3.4) Incl cruise ship and yacht passengers; (7.1) Hotels, apartments, cottages, villas and guest houses.

Basic Indicators	Units	Code	1996	1997	1998	1999	2000
INBOUND TOURISM							
Arrivals							
Visitors	Thousands	(1.1)	..	..	..	..	..
Tourists (overnight visitors)	Thousands	(1.2)	73	68	78	85	88
Same-day visitors	Thousands	(1.3)	..	..	..	..	..
Cruise passengers	Thousands	(1.4)	..	..	..	..	..
Arrivals by region							
Africa	Thousands	(2.1)	..	..	..	..	..
Americas	Thousands	(2.2)	8	7	8	8	9
Europe	Thousands	(2.3)	5	4	5	5	6
East Asia and the Pacific	Thousands	(2.4)	58	55	65	71	71
South Asia	Thousands	(2.5)	..	..	..	..	..
Middle East	Thousands	(2.6)	..	..	..	..	..
Arrivals by mode of transport							
Air	Thousands	(3.1)	..	..	76	81	85
Rail	Thousands	(3.2)	..	..	..	..	..
Road	Thousands	(3.3)	..	..	..	..	..
Sea	Thousands	(3.4)	..	..	2	4	3
Arrivals by purpose of visit							
Leisure, recreation and holidays	Thousands	(4.1)	22	21	27	28	30
Business and professional	Thousands	(4.2)	9	8	9	11	11
Other	Thousands	(4.3)	42	39	42	46	46
Overnight stays and length of stay							
Overnight stays in H&S	Thousand nights	(5.1)	..	..	..	..	..
Overnight stays in CE	Thousand nights	(5.2)	..	..	..	..	..
ALS of non resident tourists	Nights	(5.5)	..	7.60	..	..	..
Tourism expenditure in the country of reference	US$ Million	(8.1)	41	37	38	42	40
DOMESTIC TOURISM							
Overnight stays							
Overnight stays in H&S	Thousand nights	(5.3)	..	..	..	..	..
Overnight stays in CE	Thousand nights	(5.4)	..	..	..	..	..
OUTBOUND TOURISM							
Departures	Thousands	(6.1)	..	..	..	..	..
Tourism expenditure in other countries	US$ Million	(8.2)	4	5	4	4	..
TOURISM ACTIVITIES							
Hotels and similar establishments							
Number of rooms	H&S	(7.1)	777	747	710	757	763
Number of bed-places	H&S	(7.2)	..	1,614	..	..	..
Occupancy rate	Percent	(7.3)	..	..	..	..	..
Average length of stay	Nights	(5.6)	..	..	..	..	..
ECONOMIC AGGREGATES							
Gross National Product (GNP)	US$ Million	(9.1)	223	225	229	239	246
Exports (F.O.B.)	US$ Million	(9.2)	10	15	15	20	14
Imports (C.I.F.)	US$ Million	(9.3)	100	97	97	115	106

Abbreviations used in tables and notes:
H&S: Hotels and similar establishments; **CE:** All types of tourism accommodation establishments; **ALS:** Average length of stay; **THS:** Non-resident tourists staying in H&S; **TCE:** Non-resident tourists staying in CE; **TF:** Arrivals of international (or non-resident) tourists; **VF:** Arrivals of international (or non-resident) visitors; **NHS:** Overnight stays at H&S; **NCE:** Overnight stays at CE.

..   data not available
incl   including
excl   excluding
nra   nationals residing abroad

Notes:
(8.2) International Monetary Fund.

SAN MARINO

Basic Indicators	Units	Code	1996	1997	1998	1999	2000
INBOUND TOURISM							
Arrivals							
Visitors	Thousands	(1.1)	3,345	3,308	3,264	3,148	3,071
Tourists (overnight visitors)	Thousands	(1.2)	..	..	..	..	..
Same-day visitors	Thousands	(1.3)	..	..	..	..	..
Cruise passengers	Thousands	(1.4)	..	..	..	..	..
Arrivals by region							
Africa	Thousands	(2.1)	..	..	..	..	..
Americas	Thousands	(2.2)	..	..	..	..	..
Europe	Thousands	(2.3)	..	..	..	..	..
East Asia and the Pacific	Thousands	(2.4)	..	..	..	..	..
South Asia	Thousands	(2.5)	..	..	..	..	..
Middle East	Thousands	(2.6)	..	..	..	..	..
Arrivals by mode of transport							
Air	Thousands	(3.1)	..	..	..	..	..
Rail	Thousands	(3.2)	..	..	..	..	..
Road	Thousands	(3.3)	..	..	..	..	..
Sea	Thousands	(3.4)	..	..	..	..	..
Arrivals by purpose of visit							
Leisure, recreation and holidays	Thousands	(4.1)	..	..	..	..	..
Business and professional	Thousands	(4.2)	..	..	..	..	..
Other	Thousands	(4.3)	..	..	..	..	..
Overnight stays and length of stay							
Overnight stays in H&S	Thousand nights	(5.1)	7	8	9	8	10
Overnight stays in CE	Thousand nights	(5.2)	..	..	..	..	..
ALS of non resident tourists	Nights	(5.5)	..	..	..	..	..
Tourism expenditure							
in the country of reference	US$ Million	(8.1)	..	..	..	..	..
DOMESTIC TOURISM							
Overnight stays							
Overnight stays in H&S	Thousand nights	(5.3)	33	49	44	45	52
Overnight stays in CE	Thousand nights	(5.4)	..	..	..	..	..
OUTBOUND TOURISM							
Departures	Thousands	(6.1)	..	..	..	..	..
Tourism expenditure in other countries	US$ Million	(8.2)	..	..	..	..	..
TOURISM ACTIVITIES							
Hotels and similar establishments							
Number of rooms	H&S	(7.1)	481	521	521	638	631
Number of bed-places	H&S	(7.2)	1,163	1,219	1,219	1,584	1,625
Occupancy rate	Percent	(7.3)	20.90	35.30	32.70	33.00	38.60
Average length of stay	Nights	(5.6)	1.30	2.10	1.50	1.50	1.40
ECONOMIC AGGREGATES							
Gross National Product (GNP)	US$ Million	(9.1)	..	..	..	..	..
Exports (F.O.B.)	US$ Million	(9.2)	..	..	..	..	..
Imports (C.I.F.)	US$ Million	(9.3)	..	..	..	..	..

Abbreviations used in tables and notes:
H&S: Hotels and similar establishments; **CE:** All types of tourism accommodation establishments; **ALS:** Average length of stay; **THS:** Non-resident tourists staying in H&S; **TCE:** Non-resident tourists staying in CE; **TF:** Arrivals of international (or non-resident) tourists; **VF:** Arrivals of international (or non-resident) visitors; **NHS:** Overnight stays at H&S; **NCE:** Overnight stays at CE.

..	data not available
incl	including
excl	excluding
nra	nationals residing abroad

Notes:
(1.1) Incl Italian visitors; (7.1,7.2) Hotels only.

Basic Indicators	Units	Code	1996	1997	1998	1999	2000
INBOUND TOURISM							
Arrivals							
Visitors	Thousands	(1.1)	..	..	..	..	..
Tourists (overnight visitors)	Thousands	(1.2)	6.4	4.8	..	..	..
Same-day visitors	Thousands	(1.3)	..	..	..	..	..
Cruise passengers	Thousands	(1.4)	..	..	..	..	..
Arrivals by region							
Africa	Thousands	(2.1)	1.7	1.1	..	..	..
Americas	Thousands	(2.2)	0.3	0.2	..	..	..
Europe	Thousands	(2.3)	4.1	3.4	..	..	..
East Asia and the Pacific	Thousands	(2.4)	0.2	0.1	..	..	..
South Asia	Thousands	(2.5)	..	..	..	..	..
Middle East	Thousands	(2.6)	..	..	..	..	..
Arrivals by mode of transport							
Air	Thousands	(3.1)	6.4	4.8	..	..	..
Rail	Thousands	(3.2)	..	..	..	..	..
Road	Thousands	(3.3)	..	..	..	..	..
Sea	Thousands	(3.4)	..	..	..	..	..
Arrivals by purpose of visit							
Leisure, recreation and holidays	Thousands	(4.1)	2.7	2.9	..	..	..
Business and professional	Thousands	(4.2)	2.7	1.2	..	..	..
Other	Thousands	(4.3)	1.0	0.7	..	..	..
Overnight stays and length of stay							
Overnight stays in H&S	Thousand nights	(5.1)	9	..	..	..	..
Overnight stays in CE	Thousand nights	(5.2)	..	..	..	..	..
ALS of non resident tourists	Nights	(5.5)	..	..	..	..	..
Tourism expenditure in the country of reference	US$ Million	(8.1)	..	..	..	..	..
DOMESTIC TOURISM							
Overnight stays							
Overnight stays in H&S	Thousand nights	(5.3)	..	..	..	..	..
Overnight stays in CE	Thousand nights	(5.4)	..	..	..	..	..
OUTBOUND TOURISM							
Departures	Thousands	(6.1)	..	..	..	..	..
Tourism expenditure in other countries	US$ Million	(8.2)	..	..	..	..	..
TOURISM ACTIVITIES							
Hotels and similar establishments							
Number of rooms	H&S	(7.1)	227	236	259	..	..
Number of bed-places	H&S	(7.2)	312	396	465	..	..
Occupancy rate	Percent	(7.3)	..	..	..	..	..
Average length of stay	Nights	(5.6)	..	..	..	..	..
ECONOMIC AGGREGATES							
Gross National Product (GNP)	US$ Million	(9.1)	44	41	38	40	43
Exports (F.O.B.)	US$ Million	(9.2)	..	..	..	..	..
Imports (C.I.F.)	US$ Million	(9.3)	..	..	..	..	..

Abbreviations used in tables and notes:
H&S: Hotels and similar establishments; **CE:** All types of tourism accommodation establishments; **ALS:** Average length of stay; **THS:** Non-resident tourists staying in H&S; **TCE:** Non-resident tourists staying in CE; **TF:** Arrivals of international (or non-resident) tourists; **VF:** Arrivals of international (or non-resident) visitors; **NHS:** Overnight stays at H&S; **NCE:** Overnight stays at CE.

..	data not available
incl	including
excl	excluding
nra	nationals residing abroad

SAUDI ARABIA

Basic Indicators	Units	Code	1996	1997	1998	1999	2000
INBOUND TOURISM							
Arrivals							
Visitors	Thousands	(1.1)	..	..	..	..	..
Tourists (overnight visitors)	Thousands	(1.2)	..	..	..	..	6,296
Same-day visitors	Thousands	(1.3)	..	..	..	..	..
Cruise passengers	Thousands	(1.4)	..	..	..	..	..
Arrivals by region							
Africa	Thousands	(2.1)	..	..	..	..	..
Americas	Thousands	(2.2)	..	..	..	..	..
Europe	Thousands	(2.3)	..	..	..	..	..
East Asia and the Pacific	Thousands	(2.4)	..	..	..	..	..
South Asia	Thousands	(2.5)	..	..	..	..	..
Middle East	Thousands	(2.6)	..	..	..	..	..
Arrivals by mode of transport							
Air	Thousands	(3.1)	..	..	..	..	..
Rail	Thousands	(3.2)	..	..	..	..	..
Road	Thousands	(3.3)	..	..	..	..	..
Sea	Thousands	(3.4)	..	..	..	..	..
Arrivals by purpose of visit							
Leisure, recreation and holidays	Thousands	(4.1)	..	..	..	..	262
Business and professional	Thousands	(4.2)	..	..	..	..	688
Other	Thousands	(4.3)	..	..	..	..	5,345
Overnight stays and length of stay							
Overnight stays in H&S	Thousand nights	(5.1)	..	..	..	..	..
Overnight stays in CE	Thousand nights	(5.2)	..	..	..	..	..
ALS of non resident tourists	Nights	(5.5)	..	..	..	..	..
Tourism expenditure							
in the country of reference	US$ Million	(8.1)	..	..	..	..	..
DOMESTIC TOURISM							
Overnight stays							
Overnight stays in H&S	Thousand nights	(5.3)	..	..	..	..	..
Overnight stays in CE	Thousand nights	(5.4)	..	..	..	..	14,540
OUTBOUND TOURISM							
Departures	Thousands	(6.1)	..	..	..	..	..
Tourism expenditure in other countries	US$ Million	(8.2)	..	..	..	..	..
TOURISM ACTIVITIES							
Hotels and similar establishments							
Number of rooms	H&S	(7.1)	..	..	..	..	55,893
Number of bed-places	H&S	(7.2)	..	..	..	..	..
Occupancy rate	Percent	(7.3)	..	..	..	..	42.00
Average length of stay	Nights	(5.6)	..	..	..	..	..
ECONOMIC AGGREGATES							
Gross National Product (GNP)	US$ Million	(9.1)	137,469	145,524	141,202	139,365	..
Exports (F.O.B.)	US$ Million	(9.2)	60,729	60,732	38,822	50,760	..
Imports (C.I.F.)	US$ Million	(9.3)	27,744	28,732	30,013	28,010	30,267

Abbreviations used in tables and notes:
H&S: Hotels and similar establishments; **CE:** All types of tourism accommodation establishments; **ALS:** Average length of stay; **THS:** Non-resident tourists staying in H&S; **TCE:** Non-resident tourists staying in CE; **TF:** Arrivals of international (or non-resident) tourists; **VF:** Arrivals of international (or non-resident) visitors; **NHS:** Overnight stays at H&S; **NCE:** Overnight stays at CE.

..   data not available
incl   including
excl   excluding
nra   nationals residing abroad

Basic Indicators	Units	Code	1996	1997	1998	1999	2000
INBOUND TOURISM							
Arrivals							
Visitors	Thousands	(1.1)	..	..	..	..	..
Tourists (overnight visitors)	Thousands	(1.2)	282	314	352	369	389
Same-day visitors	Thousands	(1.3)	..	..	..	..	..
Cruise passengers	Thousands	(1.4)	6	6	13	9	11
Arrivals by region							
Africa	Thousands	(2.1)	67	70	84	81	97
Americas	Thousands	(2.2)	13	12	12	10	13
Europe	Thousands	(2.3)	195	225	248	270	274
East Asia and the Pacific	Thousands	(2.4)	4	3	3	3	3
South Asia	Thousands	(2.5)	..	..	..	..	..
Middle East	Thousands	(2.6)	2	1	2	1	1
Arrivals by mode of transport							
Air	Thousands	(3.1)	282	314	352	369	389
Rail	Thousands	(3.2)	..	..	..	..	..
Road	Thousands	(3.3)	..	..	..	..	..
Sea	Thousands	(3.4)	6	6	13	9	11
Arrivals by purpose of visit							
Leisure, recreation and holidays	Thousands	(4.1)	..	..	..	..	..
Business and professional	Thousands	(4.2)	..	..	..	..	..
Other	Thousands	(4.3)	..	..	..	..	..
Overnight stays and length of stay							
Overnight stays in H&S	Thousand nights	(5.1)	..	..	..	..	..
Overnight stays in CE	Thousand nights	(5.2)	1,127	1,329	1,449	1,469	1,401
ALS of non resident tourists	Nights	(5.5)	..	..	..	..	..
Tourism expenditure							
in the country of reference	US$ Million	(8.1)	149	153	178	166	140
DOMESTIC TOURISM							
Overnight stays							
Overnight stays in H&S	Thousand nights	(5.3)	..	..	..	..	..
Overnight stays in CE	Thousand nights	(5.4)	79	100	77	91	106
OUTBOUND TOURISM							
Departures	Thousands	(6.1)	..	..	..	..	..
Tourism expenditure in other countries	US$ Million	(8.2)	53	53	54	54	..
TOURISM ACTIVITIES							
Hotels and similar establishments							
Number of rooms	H&S	(7.1)	7,829	8,184	8,239	8,472	9,835
Number of bed-places	H&S	(7.2)	16,095	17,032	17,147	17,586	18,340
Occupancy rate	Percent	(7.3)	34.40	38.00	40.00	42.80	35.40
Average length of stay	Nights	(5.6)	3.80	4.00	4.10	4.10	3.60
ECONOMIC AGGREGATES							
Gross National Product (GNP)	US$ Million	(9.1)	4,508	4,684	4,632	4,685	4,726
Exports (F.O.B.)	US$ Million	(9.2)	987	904	968	1,025	998
Imports (C.I.F.)	US$ Million	(9.3)	1,435	1,446	1,406	1,468	1,365

Abbreviations used in tables and notes:
H&S: Hotels and similar establishments; **CE:** All types of tourism accommodation establishments; **ALS:** Average length of stay; **THS:** Non-resident tourists staying in H&S; **TCE:** Non-resident tourists staying in CE; **TF:** Arrivals of international (or non-resident) tourists; **VF:** Arrivals of international (or non-resident) visitors; **NHS:** Overnight stays at H&S; **NCE:** Overnight stays at CE.

.. data not available
incl including
excl excluding
nra nationals residing abroad

Notes:
(1.2,2.1-2.6) THS; (5.2,5.4) Hotels and holiday villages; (5.6) H&S; (7.3) Bed-places; (8.2) International Monetary Fund.

SEYCHELLES

Basic Indicators	Units	Code	1996	1997	1998	1999	2000
INBOUND TOURISM							
Arrivals							
Visitors	Thousands	(1.1)	142	136	134	130	140
Tourists (overnight visitors)	Thousands	(1.2)	131	130	128	125	130
Same-day visitors	Thousands	(1.3)	..	..	..	..	..
Cruise passengers	Thousands	(1.4)	11	6	6	5	10
Arrivals by region							
Africa	Thousands	(2.1)	13	14	12	14	14
Americas	Thousands	(2.2)	7	7	7	4	6
Europe	Thousands	(2.3)	103	103	103	101	105
East Asia and the Pacific	Thousands	(2.4)	4	3	3	3	3
South Asia	Thousands	(2.5)	2	2	2	1	1
Middle East	Thousands	(2.6)	1	1	1	1	2
Arrivals by mode of transport							
Air	Thousands	(3.1)	126	125	124	121	127
Rail	Thousands	(3.2)	..	..	..	..	..
Road	Thousands	(3.3)	..	..	..	..	..
Sea	Thousands	(3.4)	5	5	4	3	3
Arrivals by purpose of visit							
Leisure, recreation and holidays	Thousands	(4.1)	112	111	111	110	118
Business and professional	Thousands	(4.2)	6	6	6	7	6
Other	Thousands	(4.3)	13	13	11	8	6
Overnight stays and length of stay							
Overnight stays in H&S	Thousand nights	(5.1)	933	948	910	904	933
Overnight stays in CE	Thousand nights	(5.2)	1,270	1,340	..	..	..
ALS of non resident tourists	Nights	(5.5)	9.70	10.30	10.50	10.40	10.40
Tourism expenditure							
in the country of reference	US$ Million	(8.1)	107	122	111	112	..
DOMESTIC TOURISM							
Overnight stays							
Overnight stays in H&S	Thousand nights	(5.3)	6	7	9	11	12
Overnight stays in CE	Thousand nights	(5.4)	..	..	..	..	..
OUTBOUND TOURISM							
Departures	Thousands	(6.1)	29	30	31	32	36
Tourism expenditure in other countries	US$ Million	(8.2)	30	30	26	21	..
TOURISM ACTIVITIES							
Hotels and similar establishments							
Number of rooms	H&S	(7.1)	2,204	2,276	2,347	2,376	2,479
Number of bed-places	H&S	(7.2)	4,478	4,600	4,732	4,777	5,010
Occupancy rate	Percent	(7.3)	57.00	56.00	53.00	53.00	52.00
Average length of stay	Nights	(5.6)	..	..	..	..	..
ECONOMIC AGGREGATES							
Gross National Product (GNP)	US$ Million	(9.1)	531	572	574	561	593
Exports (F.O.B.)	US$ Million	(9.2)	139	113	122	145	..
Imports (C.I.F.)	US$ Million	(9.3)	379	340	384	434	..

Abbreviations used in tables and notes:
H&S: Hotels and similar establishments; **CE:** All types of tourism accommodation establishments; **ALS:** Average length of stay; **THS:** Non-resident tourists staying in H&S; **TCE:** Non-resident tourists staying in CE; **TF:** Arrivals of international (or non-resident) tourists; **VF:** Arrivals of international (or non-resident) visitors; **NHS:** Overnight stays at H&S; **NCE:** Overnight stays at CE.

.. data not available
incl including
excl excluding
nra nationals residing abroad

Notes:
(1.2,2.1-4.3) TF; (5.5) Nights based on departures; (7.1,7.2) Hotels and guest houses; (7.3) Bed-places.

Basic Indicators	Units	Code	1996	1997	1998	1999	2000
INBOUND TOURISM							
Arrivals							
Visitors	Thousands	(1.1)	..	..	..	..	..
Tourists (overnight visitors)	Thousands	(1.2)	22	23	6	6	..
Same-day visitors	Thousands	(1.3)	..	..	..	..	..
Cruise passengers	Thousands	(1.4)	..	..	..	..	..
Arrivals by region							
Africa	Thousands	(2.1)	7	..	..	..	..
Americas	Thousands	(2.2)	4	..	..	..	..
Europe	Thousands	(2.3)	4	..	..	..	..
East Asia and the Pacific	Thousands	(2.4)	..	..	..	..	..
South Asia	Thousands	(2.5)	..	..	..	..	..
Middle East	Thousands	(2.6)	..	..	..	..	..
Arrivals by mode of transport							
Air	Thousands	(3.1)	22	7	6	6	..
Rail	Thousands	(3.2)	..	..	..	..	..
Road	Thousands	(3.3)	..	16	..	..	..
Sea	Thousands	(3.4)	..	..	..	..	..
Arrivals by purpose of visit							
Leisure, recreation and holidays	Thousands	(4.1)	..	..	..	..	..
Business and professional	Thousands	(4.2)	..	..	..	..	..
Other	Thousands	(4.3)	..	..	..	..	..
Overnight stays and length of stay							
Overnight stays in H&S	Thousand nights	(5.1)	374	448	..	..	..
Overnight stays in CE	Thousand nights	(5.2)	..	..	..	..	..
ALS of non resident tourists	Nights	(5.5)	..	..	..	..	..
Tourism expenditure in the country of reference	US$ Million	(8.1)	10	..	8	8	..
DOMESTIC TOURISM							
Overnight stays							
Overnight stays in H&S	Thousand nights	(5.3)	..	..	..	..	..
Overnight stays in CE	Thousand nights	(5.4)	..	..	..	..	..
OUTBOUND TOURISM							
Departures	Thousands	(6.1)	..	..	..	..	..
Tourism expenditure in other countries	US$ Million	(8.2)	2	..	4	4	..
TOURISM ACTIVITIES							
Hotels and similar establishments							
Number of rooms	H&S	(7.1)	709	704	312	..	..
Number of bed-places	H&S	(7.2)	1,419	1,409	625	..	..
Occupancy rate	Percent	(7.3)	17.00	20.00	..	..	..
Average length of stay	Nights	(5.6)	..	..	..	..	..
ECONOMIC AGGREGATES							
Gross National Product (GNP)	US$ Million	(9.1)	915	781	722	653	633
Exports (F.O.B.)	US$ Million	(9.2)	47	17	7	6	13
Imports (C.I.F.)	US$ Million	(9.3)	211	92	95	80	149

Abbreviations used in tables and notes:
H&S: Hotels and similar establishments; **CE:** All types of tourism accommodation establishments; **ALS:** Average length of stay; **THS:** Non-resident tourists staying in H&S; **TCE:** Non-resident tourists staying in CE; **TF:** Arrivals of international (or non-resident) tourists; **VF:** Arrivals of international (or non-resident) visitors; **NHS:** Overnight stays at H&S; **NCE:** Overnight stays at CE.

..   data not available
incl   including
excl   excluding
nra   nationals residing abroad

Notes:
(2.1) Western Africa only; (2.2) North America only; (2.3) France/United Kingdom only; (7.1,7.2) Hotels only; (7.1,7.2/96) Drastic reduction in number of rooms and bed-places recorded, due to increased hostilities leading the destruction of a number of hotels and similar establishments.

SINGAPORE

Basic Indicators	Units	Code	1996	1997	1998	1999	2000
INBOUND TOURISM							
Arrivals							
Visitors	Thousands	(1.1)	7,292	7,198	6,242	6,958	7,691
Tourists (overnight visitors)	Thousands	(1.2)	6,608	6,531	5,631	6,258	6,917
Same-day visitors	Thousands	(1.3)	685	667	611	700	774
Cruise passengers	Thousands	(1.4)	..	..	..	..	..
Arrivals by region							
Africa	Thousands	(2.1)	75	65	72	84	92
Americas	Thousands	(2.2)	459	460	425	444	483
Europe	Thousands	(2.3)	1,011	997	991	1,058	1,139
East Asia and the Pacific	Thousands	(2.4)	5,329	5,216	4,288	4,850	5,347
South Asia	Thousands	(2.5)	367	396	395	444	516
Middle East	Thousands	(2.6)	50	48	60	66	71
Arrivals by mode of transport							
Air	Thousands	(3.1)	5,463	5,362	4,687	5,142	5,658
Rail	Thousands	(3.2)	..	..	..	..	..
Road	Thousands	(3.3)	933	864	724	798	877
Sea	Thousands	(3.4)	896	972	830	1,018	1,157
Arrivals by purpose of visit							
Leisure, recreation and holidays	Thousands	(4.1)	3,880	3,442	2,829	3,411	3,702
Business and professional	Thousands	(4.2)	1,385	1,579	1,385	1,523	1,715
Other	Thousands	(4.3)	2,027	2,176	2,028	2,024	2,274
Overnight stays and length of stay							
Overnight stays in H&S	Thousand nights	(5.1)	..	..	..	..	..
Overnight stays in CE	Thousand nights	(5.2)	..	..	..	..	..
ALS of non resident tourists	Nights	(5.5)	3.29	3.27	3.43	3.18	3.16
Tourism expenditure							
in the country of reference	US$ Million	(8.1)	8,012	6,073	5,402	5,859	6,018
DOMESTIC TOURISM							
Overnight stays							
Overnight stays in H&S	Thousand nights	(5.3)	..	..	..	..	..
Overnight stays in CE	Thousand nights	(5.4)	..	..	..	..	..
OUTBOUND TOURISM							
Departures	Thousands	(6.1)	3,305	3,671	3,745	3,971	4,444
Tourism expenditure in other countries	US$ Million	(8.2)	5,797	4,605	4,707	4,666	4,970
TOURISM ACTIVITIES							
Hotels and similar establishments							
Number of rooms	H&S	(7.1)	32,348	33,199	35,126	34,886	35,625
Number of bed-places	H&S	(7.2)	..	..	..	..	..
Occupancy rate	Percent	(7.3)	82.30	79.40	71.30	74.90	83.50
Average length of stay	Nights	(5.6)	2.84	2.82	2.87	2.72	2.71
ECONOMIC AGGREGATES							
Gross National Product (GNP)	US$ Million	(9.1)	92,858	104,114	96,447	95,604	99,404
Exports (F.O.B.)	US$ Million	(9.2)	125,016	124,990	109,905	114,682	137,806
Imports (C.I.F.)	US$ Million	(9.3)	131,340	132,443	104,728	111,062	134,546

Abbreviations used in tables and notes:
H&S: Hotels and similar establishments; **CE:** All types of tourism accommodation establishments; **ALS:** Average length of stay; **THS:** Non-resident tourists staying in H&S; **TCE:** Non-resident tourists staying in CE; **TF:** Arrivals of international (or non-resident) tourists; **VF:** Arrivals of international (or non-resident) visitors; **NHS:** Overnight stays at H&S; **NCE:** Overnight stays at CE.

..   data not available
incl   including
excl   excluding
nra   nationals residing abroad

Notes:
(1.1) Excl arrivals of Malaysian citizens by land but incl same-day visitors; (1.3) Transit and cruise passengers; (5.5,5.6) Days; (7.1) Hotels (gazetted and non-gazetted); (7.3) Rooms; classified hotels only.

SLOVAKIA

Basic Indicators	Units	Code	1996	1997	1998	1999	2000
INBOUND TOURISM							
Arrivals							
Visitors	Thousands	(1.1)	33,113	31,742	32,735	30,757	28,769
Tourists (overnight visitors)	Thousands	(1.2)	951	814	896	975	1,053
Same-day visitors	Thousands	(1.3)	..	..	..	..	..
Cruise passengers	Thousands	(1.4)	..	..	..	..	..
Arrivals by region							
Africa	Thousands	(2.1)	2	2	3	3	3
Americas	Thousands	(2.2)	28	26	30	31	36
Europe	Thousands	(2.3)	898	762	839	918	980
East Asia and the Pacific	Thousands	(2.4)	23	21	23	23	25
South Asia	Thousands	(2.5)	..	..	..	..	1
Middle East	Thousands	(2.6)	..	..	..	..	..
Arrivals by mode of transport							
Air	Thousands	(3.1)	6	7	7	6	6
Rail	Thousands	(3.2)	76	75	78	58	58
Road	Thousands	(3.3)	15,383	14,611	15,759	13,390	12,151
Sea	Thousands	(3.4)	10	9	10	2	2
Arrivals by purpose of visit							
Leisure, recreation and holidays	Thousands	(4.1)	..	..	..	..	..
Business and professional	Thousands	(4.2)	..	..	..	..	..
Other	Thousands	(4.3)	..	..	..	..	..
Overnight stays and length of stay							
Overnight stays in H&S	Thousand nights	(5.1)	2,865	2,454	2,798	2,922	3,138
Overnight stays in CE	Thousand nights	(5.2)	3,309	2,836	3,311	3,524	3,743
ALS of non resident tourists	Nights	(5.5)	3.50	3.50	3.70	3.60	3.60
Tourism expenditure **in the country of reference**	US$ Million	(8.1)	673	546	489	461	432
DOMESTIC TOURISM							
Overnight stays							
Overnight stays in H&S	Thousand nights	(5.3)	3,989	2,923	3,924	4,042	3,768
Overnight stays in CE	Thousand nights	(5.4)	5,374	5,469	7,145	7,414	6,798
OUTBOUND TOURISM							
Departures	Thousands	(6.1)	318	403	414	343	388
Tourism expenditure in other countries	US$ Million	(8.2)	483	439	475	339	295
TOURISM ACTIVITIES							
Hotels and similar establishments							
Number of rooms	H&S	(7.1)	25,234	19,503	27,344	27,983	28,387
Number of bed-places	H&S	(7.2)	58,433	47,854	70,748	72,449	73,008
Occupancy rate	Percent	(7.3)	36.20	31.40	30.60	29.60	29.20
Average length of stay	Nights	(5.6)	3.70	3.80	3.90	3.90	3.80
ECONOMIC AGGREGATES							
Gross National Product (GNP)	US$ Million	(9.1)	19,070	20,795	20,888	20,317	19,995
Exports (F.O.B.)	US$ Million	(9.2)	8,818	8,251	10,721	10,062	11,885
Imports (C.I.F.)	US$ Million	(9.3)	11,431	10,770	13,725	11,688	13,423

Abbreviations used in tables and notes:
H&S: Hotels and similar establishments; **CE:** All types of tourism accommodation establishments; **ALS:** Average length of stay; **THS:** Non-resident tourists staying in H&S; **TCE:** Non-resident tourists staying in CE; **TF:** Arrivals of international (or non-resident) tourists; **VF:** Arrivals of international (or non-resident) visitors; **NHS:** Overnight stays at H&S; **NCE:** Overnight stays at CE.

..   data not available
incl   including
excl   excluding
nra   nationals residing abroad

Notes:
(1.1) Incl the border with Czech Rep.; (1.2,2.1-2.4) TCE; (5.5,5.6) Inbound tourism in all types of tourism accommodation establishments; (6.1) Tourism organized through Slovak travel agencies; (8.1,8.2) Estimates.

SLOVENIA

Basic Indicators	Units	Code	1996	1997	1998	1999	2000
INBOUND TOURISM							
Arrivals							
Visitors	Thousands	(1.1)	71,876	76,568	65,587	60,009	63,580
Tourists (overnight visitors)	Thousands	(1.2)	832	974	977	884	1,090
Same-day visitors	Thousands	(1.3)	..	..	..	..	..
Cruise passengers	Thousands	(1.4)	..	..	..	..	..
Arrivals by region							
Africa	Thousands	(2.1)	3	3	2	2	3
Americas	Thousands	(2.2)	17	17	21	22	30
Europe	Thousands	(2.3)	800	942	940	845	1,038
East Asia and the Pacific	Thousands	(2.4)	5	6	8	8	12
South Asia	Thousands	(2.5)	3	3	2	2	3
Middle East	Thousands	(2.6)	4	3	2	2	3
Arrivals by mode of transport							
Air	Thousands	(3.1)	75	90	88	80	202
Rail	Thousands	(3.2)	17	18	19	18	21
Road	Thousands	(3.3)	739	864	868	785	865
Sea	Thousands	(3.4)	1	2	2	2	2
Arrivals by purpose of visit							
Leisure, recreation and holidays	Thousands	(4.1)	557	598	599	543	669
Business and professional	Thousands	(4.2)	116	156	156	141	191
Other	Thousands	(4.3)	159	220	222	200	230
Overnight stays and length of stay							
Overnight stays in H&S	Thousand nights	(5.1)	2,167	2,500	2,478	2,267	2,758
Overnight stays in CE	Thousand nights	(5.2)	2,437	2,945	2,934	2,627	3,277
ALS of non resident tourists	Nights	(5.5)	3.07	3.16	3.14	3.10	3.12
Tourism expenditure							
in the country of reference	US$ Million	(8.1)	1,240	1,187	1,088	954	961
DOMESTIC TOURISM							
Overnight stays							
Overnight stays in H&S	Thousand nights	(5.3)	2,004	1,787	1,728	1,852	1,860
Overnight stays in CE	Thousand nights	(5.4)	3,214	3,236	3,161	3,243	3,332
OUTBOUND TOURISM							
Departures	Thousands	(6.1)	..	..	..	..	1,965
Tourism expenditure in other countries	US$ Million	(8.2)	602	518	558	539	461
TOURISM ACTIVITIES							
Hotels and similar establishments							
Number of rooms	H&S	(7.1)	16,847	16,350	16,195	15,753	16,265
Number of bed-places	H&S	(7.2)	36,028	33,714	33,771	32,272	33,502
Occupancy rate	Percent	(7.3)	34.60	37.20	36.50	36.60	39.40
Average length of stay	Nights	(5.6)	3.26	3.31	3.30	3.27	3.31
ECONOMIC AGGREGATES							
Gross National Product (GNP)	US$ Million	(9.1)	18,502	19,604	19,277	19,806	20,022
Exports (F.O.B.)	US$ Million	(9.2)	8,312	8,372	9,048	8,604	8,733
Imports (C.I.F.)	US$ Million	(9.3)	9,423	9,357	10,110	9,952	10,107

Abbreviations used in tables and notes:

H&S: Hotels and similar establishments; **CE:** All types of tourism accommodation establishments; **ALS:** Average length of stay; **THS:** Non-resident tourists staying in H&S; **TCE:** Non-resident tourists staying in CE; **TF:** Arrivals of international (or non-resident) tourists; **VF:** Arrivals of international (or non-resident) visitors; **NHS:** Overnight stays at H&S; **NCE:** Overnight stays at CE.

..   data not available
incl   including
excl   excluding
nra   nationals residing abroad

Notes:

(1.1) Incl all categories of travellers irrespective of purpose of visit; (1.2,2.1-2.6) TCE; (2.1,2.5,2.6) Estimates; (3.1-3.4,4.1-4.3) TCE, data from 3 yearly survey on foreign tourists in Slovenia in Summer; (6.1) Quarterly survey on travels of domestic population; (8.1,8.2) Source: Central Bank of Slovenia; data refer to item "travel" of Balance of Payments.

SOLOMON ISLANDS

Basic Indicators	Units	Code	1996	1997	1998	1999	2000
INBOUND TOURISM							
Arrivals							
Visitors	Thousands	(1.1)	..	..	..	..	..
Tourists (overnight visitors)	Thousands	(1.2)	11	16	13	21	..
Same-day visitors	Thousands	(1.3)	..	..	..	..	..
Cruise passengers	Thousands	(1.4)	..	..	..	..	..
Arrivals by region							
Africa	Thousands	(2.1)	..	..	..	..	..
Americas	Thousands	(2.2)	1	1	1	2	..
Europe	Thousands	(2.3)	1	1	1	2	..
East Asia and the Pacific	Thousands	(2.4)	9	13	11	16	..
South Asia	Thousands	(2.5)	..	..	..	..	..
Middle East	Thousands	(2.6)	..	..	..	..	..
Arrivals by mode of transport							
Air	Thousands	(3.1)	..	..	..	10	..
Rail	Thousands	(3.2)	..	..	..	..	..
Road	Thousands	(3.3)	..	..	..	..	..
Sea	Thousands	(3.4)	..	..	..	11	..
Arrivals by purpose of visit							
Leisure, recreation and holidays	Thousands	(4.1)	..	7	5	..	..
Business and professional	Thousands	(4.2)	..	6	4	..	..
Other	Thousands	(4.3)	..	3	4	..	..
Overnight stays and length of stay							
Overnight stays in H&S	Thousand nights	(5.1)	..	..	..	..	..
Overnight stays in CE	Thousand nights	(5.2)	..	..	..	..	..
ALS of non resident tourists	Nights	(5.5)	..	..	..	..	..
Tourism expenditure							
in the country of reference	US$ Million	(8.1)	14	7	7	6	..
DOMESTIC TOURISM							
Overnight stays							
Overnight stays in H&S	Thousand nights	(5.3)	..	..	..	..	..
Overnight stays in CE	Thousand nights	(5.4)	..	..	..	..	..
OUTBOUND TOURISM							
Departures	Thousands	(6.1)	..	..	..	..	..
Tourism expenditure in other countries	US$ Million	(8.2)	15	9	6	7	..
TOURISM ACTIVITIES							
Hotels and similar establishments							
Number of rooms	H&S	(7.1)	..	860	860	..	..
Number of bed-places	H&S	(7.2)	..	..	..	..	..
Occupancy rate	Percent	(7.3)	..	..	..	..	..
Average length of stay	Nights	(5.6)	..	..	..	..	..
ECONOMIC AGGREGATES							
Gross National Product (GNP)	US$ Million	(9.1)	333	337	347	333	278
Exports (F.O.B.)	US$ Million	(9.2)	162	173	126	..	..
Imports (C.I.F.)	US$ Million	(9.3)	151	170	..	..	..

Abbreviations used in tables and notes:
H&S: Hotels and similar establishments; **CE:** All types of tourism accommodation establishments; **ALS:** Average length of stay; **THS:** Non-resident tourists staying in H&S; **TCE:** Non-resident tourists staying in CE; **TF:** Arrivals of international (or non-resident) tourists; **VF:** Arrivals of international (or non-resident) visitors; **NHS:** Overnight stays at H&S; **NCE:** Overnight stays at CE.

..   data not available
incl   including
excl   excluding
nra   nationals residing abroad

Notes:
(8.1,8.2) International Monetary Fund.

SOUTH AFRICA

Basic Indicators	Units	Code	1996	1997	1998	1999	2000
INBOUND TOURISM							
Arrivals							
Visitors	Thousands	(1.1)	5,186	5,170	5,898	6,026	6,000
Tourists (overnight visitors)	Thousands	(1.2)	..	..	..	..	..
Same-day visitors	Thousands	(1.3)	..	..	..	..	..
Cruise passengers	Thousands	(1.4)	..	..	..	..	..
Arrivals by region							
Africa	Thousands	(2.1)	3,790	3,677	4,305	4,363	4,282
Americas	Thousands	(2.2)	178	208	255	245	258
Europe	Thousands	(2.3)	817	924	1,016	1,049	1,070
East Asia and the Pacific	Thousands	(2.4)	180	190	199	188	190
South Asia	Thousands	(2.5)	27	30	34	39	39
Middle East	Thousands	(2.6)	8	7	11	11	10
Arrivals by mode of transport							
Air	Thousands	(3.1)	1,230	1,329	1,463	1,523	1,597
Rail	Thousands	(3.2)	4	..	1	1	8
Road	Thousands	(3.3)	3,922	3,804	4,396	4,453	4,369
Sea	Thousands	(3.4)	30	37	38	49	26
Arrivals by purpose of visit							
Leisure, recreation and holidays	Thousands	(4.1)	3,938	4,002	4,731	4,990	4,988
Business and professional	Thousands	(4.2)	661	646	728	627	629
Other	Thousands	(4.3)	587	522	439	409	383
Overnight stays and length of stay							
Overnight stays in H&S	Thousand nights	(5.1)	2,790	..	..	..	..
Overnight stays in CE	Thousand nights	(5.2)	..	..	..	..	..
ALS of non resident tourists	Nights	(5.5)	..	..	..	..	..
Tourism expenditure							
in the country of reference	US$ Million	(8.1)	2,575	2,769	2,717	2,637	2,707
DOMESTIC TOURISM							
Overnight stays							
Overnight stays in H&S	Thousand nights	(5.3)	12,100	13,415	14,006	14,098	..
Overnight stays in CE	Thousand nights	(5.4)	..	..	..	..	..
OUTBOUND TOURISM							
Departures	Thousands	(6.1)	2,882	2,926	3,363	5,299	5,466
Tourism expenditure in other countries	US$ Million	(8.2)	1,754	1,961	1,908	2,028	2,004
TOURISM ACTIVITIES							
Hotels and similar establishments							
Number of rooms	H&S	(7.1)	47,214	49,768	52,207	53,345	51,913
Number of bed-places	H&S	(7.2)	96,340	103,267	107,477	110,383	108,027
Occupancy rate	Percent	(7.3)	56.44	53.50	52.50	52.40	..
Average length of stay	Nights	(5.6)	..	..	..	..	..
ECONOMIC AGGREGATES							
Gross National Product (GNP)	US$ Million	(9.1)	150,303	150,261	137,154	133,092	129,171
Exports (F.O.B.)	US$ Million	(9.2)	28,145	29,964	25,396	25,901	29,267
Imports (C.I.F.)	US$ Million	(9.3)	29,105	31,939	28,277	25,890	28,980

Abbreviations used in tables and notes:
H&S: Hotels and similar establishments; **CE:** All types of tourism accommodation establishments; **ALS:** Average length of stay; **THS:** Non-resident tourists staying in H&S; **TCE:** Non-resident tourists staying in CE; **TF:** Arrivals of international (or non-resident) tourists; **VF:** Arrivals of international (or non-resident) visitors; **NHS:** Overnight stays at H&S; **NCE:** Overnight stays at CE.

..   data not available
incl   including
excl   excluding
nra   nationals residing abroad

Notes:
(1.1,3.1-4.2) Excl nra; (7.1,7.2) Hotels only; (7.3) Rooms (hotels); (8.1,8.2) International Monetary Fund.
Note: South Africa, incl the former Republics of Transkei, Bophuthatswana, Venda and Ciskei.

Basic Indicators	Units	Code	1996	1997	1998	1999	2000
INBOUND TOURISM							
Arrivals							
Visitors	Thousands	(1.1)	57,271	62,415	67,762	72,060	74,462
Tourists (overnight visitors)	Thousands	(1.2)	36,221	39,553	43,396	46,776	47,898
Same-day visitors	Thousands	(1.3)	21,049	22,862	24,366	25,284	26,564
Cruise passengers	Thousands	(1.4)	..	..	..	..	..
Arrivals by region							
Africa	Thousands	(2.1)	..	..	..	..	39
Americas	Thousands	(2.2)	..	1,904	2,165	2,238	2,172
Europe	Thousands	(2.3)	..	36,743	40,262	43,587	44,499
East Asia and the Pacific	Thousands	(2.4)	..	299	388	359	301
South Asia	Thousands	(2.5)	..	..	..	..	..
Middle East	Thousands	(2.6)	..	..	..	..	..
Arrivals by mode of transport							
Air	Thousands	(3.1)	24,658	27,677	30,457	32,574	34,380
Rail	Thousands	(3.2)	379	409	422	428	445
Road	Thousands	(3.3)	9,369	9,454	10,581	11,522	10,669
Sea	Thousands	(3.4)	1,815	2,012	1,936	2,252	2,403
Arrivals by purpose of visit							
Leisure, recreation and holidays	Thousands	(4.1)	..	34,854	38,230	40,801	40,832
Business and professional	Thousands	(4.2)	..	2,638	3,126	3,544	4,132
Other	Thousands	(4.3)	..	2,061	2,040	2,431	2,934
Overnight stays and length of stay							
Overnight stays in H&S	Thousand nights	(5.1)	100,215	105,435	111,803	149,036	143,762
Overnight stays in CE	Thousand nights	(5.2)	106,658	113,270	122,486	160,424	233,897
ALS of non resident tourists	Nights	(5.5)	12.30	12.00	12.90	..	..
Tourism expenditure							
in the country of reference	US$ Million	(8.1)	26,690	26,651	29,839	32,497	31,454
DOMESTIC TOURISM							
Overnight stays							
Overnight stays in H&S	Thousand nights	(5.3)	58,043	61,298	66,552	81,504	83,382
Overnight stays in CE	Thousand nights	(5.4)	71,762	75,012	77,931	95,878	110,750
OUTBOUND TOURISM							
Departures	Thousands	(6.1)	4,224	3,980	4,794	..	..
Tourism expenditure in other countries	US$ Million	(8.2)	4,919	4,467	5,001	5,523	5,572
TOURISM ACTIVITIES							
Hotels and similar establishments							
Number of rooms	H&S	(7.1)	569,802	576,514	585,606	..	676,672
Number of bed-places	H&S	(7.2)	1,087,529	1,102,424	1,121,217	1,282,013	1,314,491
Occupancy rate	Percent	(7.3)	59.60	61.73	63.55	60.00	58.85
Average length of stay	Nights	(5.6)	4.09	4.02	3.87	3.93	3.83
ECONOMIC AGGREGATES							
Gross National Product (GNP)	US$ Million	(9.1)	593,230	603,160	587,681	583,093	590,150
Exports (F.O.B.)	US$ Million	(9.2)	102,003	104,368	109,240	109,966	113,348
Imports (C.I.F.)	US$ Million	(9.3)	121,792	122,721	133,164	144,438	152,900

Abbreviations used in tables and notes:
H&S: Hotels and similar establishments; **CE:** All types of tourism accommodation establishments; **ALS:** Average length of stay; **THS:** Non-resident tourists staying in H&S; **TCE:** Non-resident tourists staying in CE; **TF:** Arrivals of international (or non-resident) tourists; **VF:** Arrivals of international (or non-resident) visitors; **NHS:** Overnight stays at H&S; **NCE:** Overnight stays at CE.

.. data not available
incl including
excl excluding
nra nationals residing abroad

Notes:
(1.1) VF, incl nra; (2.2-4.3) TF, incl nra; (2.4) Japan only; (5.1,5.3) Nights in hotels and "hostales" (accommodation establishments providing limited services); (5.2,5.4/96-99) Nights in hotels, "hostales" and camping sites; (5.2,5.4/2000) Nights in hotels, "hostales", camping sites and tourism apartments; (7.1,7.2) Hotels and "hostales" only; (7.3) Bed-places.

SRI LANKA

Basic Indicators	Units	Code	1996	1997	1998	1999	2000
INBOUND TOURISM							
Arrivals							
Visitors	Thousands	(1.1)	315	384	409	465	445
Tourists (overnight visitors)	Thousands	(1.2)	302	366	381	436	400
Same-day visitors	Thousands	(1.3)	13	18	28	28	45
Cruise passengers	Thousands	(1.4)	..	..	..	..	..
Arrivals by region							
Africa	Thousands	(2.1)	2	2	1	1	1
Americas	Thousands	(2.2)	13	16	18	19	18
Europe	Thousands	(2.3)	172	218	246	282	268
East Asia and the Pacific	Thousands	(2.4)	50	58	54	66	58
South Asia	Thousands	(2.5)	61	67	58	63	52
Middle East	Thousands	(2.6)	4	4	4	5	4
Arrivals by mode of transport							
Air	Thousands	(3.1)	302	366	381	436	400
Rail	Thousands	(3.2)	..	..	..	..	..
Road	Thousands	(3.3)	..	..	..	..	..
Sea	Thousands	(3.4)	0.2	0.4	0.3	0.2	0.3
Arrivals by purpose of visit							
Leisure, recreation and holidays	Thousands	(4.1)	287	349	355	384	361
Business and professional	Thousands	(4.2)	11	14	19	23	19
Other	Thousands	(4.3)	4	4	7	29	20
Overnight stays and length of stay							
Overnight stays in H&S	Thousand nights	(5.1)	2,399	3,123	3,455	4,048	3,735
Overnight stays in CE	Thousand nights	(5.2)	2,947	3,680	3,944	4,479	4,056
ALS of non resident tourists	Nights	(5.5)	9.80	10.10	10.40	10.30	10.10
Tourism expenditure							
in the country of reference	US$ Million	(8.1)	173	217	231	275	253
DOMESTIC TOURISM							
Overnight stays							
Overnight stays in H&S	Thousand nights	(5.3)	678	769	857	874	952
Overnight stays in CE	Thousand nights	(5.4)	..	..	..	..	..
OUTBOUND TOURISM							
Departures	Thousands	(6.1)	494	531	518	497	524
Tourism expenditure in other countries	US$ Million	(8.2)	176	180	202	219	244
TOURISM ACTIVITIES							
Hotels and similar establishments							
Number of rooms	H&S	(7.1)	14,109	15,005	15,412	15,618	15,860
Number of bed-places	H&S	(7.2)	26,614	27,528	28,563	28,887	29,363
Occupancy rate	Percent	(7.3)	40.30	49.10	52.80	57.60	52.30
Average length of stay	Nights	(5.6)	..	..	..	..	..
ECONOMIC AGGREGATES							
Gross National Product (GNP)	US$ Million	(9.1)	13,650	14,746	15,204	15,688	16,632
Exports (F.O.B.)	US$ Million	(9.2)	4,095	4,639	4,787	4,594	5,416
Imports (C.I.F.)	US$ Million	(9.3)	5,442	5,864	5,877	5,961	7,210

Abbreviations used in tables and notes:
H&S: Hotels and similar establishments; **CE:** All types of tourism accommodation establishments; **ALS:** Average length of stay; **THS:** Non-resident tourists staying in H&S; **TCE:** Non-resident tourists staying in CE; **TF:** Arrivals of international (or non-resident) tourists; **VF:** Arrivals of international (or non-resident) visitors; **NHS:** Overnight stays at H&S; **NCE:** Overnight stays at CE.

..   data not available
incl   including
excl   excluding
nra   nationals residing abroad

Notes:
(1.2,2.1-4.3) TF, excl nra; (7.1,7.2) Hotels, motels, inns, guest houses and apart-hotels; (7.3) Rooms.

Basic Indicators	Units	Code	1996	1997	1998	1999	2000
INBOUND TOURISM							
Arrivals							
Visitors	Thousands	(1.1)	..	..	..	..	..
Tourists (overnight visitors)	Thousands	(1.2)	57	30	25	29	38
Same-day visitors	Thousands	(1.3)	..	..	..	..	..
Cruise passengers	Thousands	(1.4)	..	..	..	..	..
Arrivals by region							
Africa	Thousands	(2.1)	..	..	5	7	5
Americas	Thousands	(2.2)	..	..	..	..	..
Europe	Thousands	(2.3)	..	..	5	7	9
East Asia and the Pacific	Thousands	(2.4)	..	..	5	4	7
South Asia	Thousands	(2.5)	..	..	..	..	..
Middle East	Thousands	(2.6)	..	..	6	8	10
Arrivals by mode of transport							
Air	Thousands	(3.1)	..	29	25	29	38
Rail	Thousands	(3.2)	..	..	..	..	..
Road	Thousands	(3.3)	..	..	..	..	..
Sea	Thousands	(3.4)	..	..	..	..	..
Arrivals by purpose of visit							
Leisure, recreation and holidays	Thousands	(4.1)	..	..	..	..	..
Business and professional	Thousands	(4.2)	..	..	..	..	..
Other	Thousands	(4.3)	..	..	..	..	..
Overnight stays and length of stay							
Overnight stays in H&S	Thousand nights	(5.1)	..	..	..	..	..
Overnight stays in CE	Thousand nights	(5.2)	..	..	..	..	..
ALS of non resident tourists	Nights	(5.5)	..	..	..	..	..
Tourism expenditure in the country of reference	US$ Million	(8.1)	8	4	2	2	5
DOMESTIC TOURISM							
Overnight stays							
Overnight stays in H&S	Thousand nights	(5.3)	..	..	..	..	..
Overnight stays in CE	Thousand nights	(5.4)	..	..	..	..	..
OUTBOUND TOURISM							
Departures	Thousands	(6.1)	..	..	..	..	..
Tourism expenditure in other countries	US$ Million	(8.2)	28	33	29	35	55
TOURISM ACTIVITIES							
Hotels and similar establishments							
Number of rooms	H&S	(7.1)	..	3,667	3,491	4,545	..
Number of bed-places	H&S	(7.2)	..	8,692	7,963	7,907	..
Occupancy rate	Percent	(7.3)	..	..	..	..	..
Average length of stay	Nights	(5.6)	..	..	..	..	..
ECONOMIC AGGREGATES							
Gross National Product (GNP)	US$ Million	(9.1)	..	..	8,219	9,046	9,596
Exports (F.O.B.)	US$ Million	(9.2)	620	594	596	616	..
Imports (C.I.F.)	US$ Million	(9.3)	1,548	1,580	1,915	1,988	..

Abbreviations used in tables and notes:
H&S: Hotels and similar establishments; **CE:** All types of tourism accommodation establishments; **ALS:** Average length of stay; **THS:** Non-resident tourists staying in H&S; **TCE:** Non-resident tourists staying in CE; **TF:** Arrivals of international (or non-resident) tourists; **VF:** Arrivals of international (or non-resident) visitors; **NHS:** Overnight stays at H&S; **NCE:** Overnight stays at CE.

..	data not available
incl	including
excl	excluding
nra	nationals residing abroad

Notes:
(1.2,2.1-2.6,3.1/98-2000) Arrivals at Khartoum airport; (7.1,7.2) Hotels, inns and resorts; (8.1,8.2) International Monetary Fund.

SURINAME

Basic Indicators	Units	Code	1996	1997	1998	1999	2000
INBOUND TOURISM							
Arrivals							
Visitors	Thousands	(1.1)	74	78	69	..	..
Tourists (overnight visitors)	Thousands	(1.2)	53	61	54	57	58
Same-day visitors	Thousands	(1.3)	..	..	..	..	..
Cruise passengers	Thousands	(1.4)	21	17	15	..	..
Arrivals by region							
Africa	Thousands	(2.1)	..	..	..	..	..
Americas	Thousands	(2.2)	10	9	6	..	..
Europe	Thousands	(2.3)	39	50	46	..	..
East Asia and the Pacific	Thousands	(2.4)	3	2	2	..	..
South Asia	Thousands	(2.5)	..	..	..	..	..
Middle East	Thousands	(2.6)	..	..	..	..	..
Arrivals by mode of transport							
Air	Thousands	(3.1)	53	61	54	57	58
Rail	Thousands	(3.2)	..	..	..	..	..
Road	Thousands	(3.3)	..	..	..	..	..
Sea	Thousands	(3.4)	21	17	15	..	..
Arrivals by purpose of visit							
Leisure, recreation and holidays	Thousands	(4.1)	19	21	34	..	..
Business and professional	Thousands	(4.2)	5	5	3	..	..
Other	Thousands	(4.3)	29	35	17	..	..
Overnight stays and length of stay							
Overnight stays in H&S	Thousand nights	(5.1)	..	..	..	..	..
Overnight stays in CE	Thousand nights	(5.2)	..	..	..	..	..
ALS of non resident tourists	Nights	(5.5)	..	..	..	..	..
Tourism expenditure							
in the country of reference	US$ Million	(8.1)	14	9	2	9	16
DOMESTIC TOURISM							
Overnight stays							
Overnight stays in H&S	Thousand nights	(5.3)	..	..	..	..	..
Overnight stays in CE	Thousand nights	(5.4)	..	..	..	..	..
OUTBOUND TOURISM							
Departures	Thousands	(6.1)	..	..	..	..	..
Tourism expenditure in other countries	US$ Million	(8.2)	8	11	11	13	23
TOURISM ACTIVITIES							
Hotels and similar establishments							
Number of rooms	H&S	(7.1)	1,088	1,276	1,276	1,276	1,276
Number of bed-places	H&S	(7.2)	..	..	..	..	..
Occupancy rate	Percent	(7.3)	..	..	..	..	..
Average length of stay	Nights	(5.6)	..	..	..	..	..
ECONOMIC AGGREGATES							
Gross National Product (GNP)	US$ Million	(9.1)	391	490	558	..	..
Exports (F.O.B.)	US$ Million	(9.2)	433	700	435	..	..
Imports (C.I.F.)	US$ Million	(9.3)	501	657	551	..	..

Abbreviations used in tables and notes:
H&S: Hotels and similar establishments; **CE:** All types of tourism accommodation establishments; **ALS:** Average length of stay; **THS:** Non-resident tourists staying in H&S; **TCE:** Non-resident tourists staying in CE; **TF:** Arrivals of international (or non-resident) tourists; **VF:** Arrivals of international (or non-resident) visitors; **NHS:** Overnight stays at H&S; **NCE:** Overnight stays at CE.

.. data not available
incl including
excl excluding
nra nationals residing abroad

Notes:
(1.2,2.2-2.4,3.1,4.1-43) Arrivals at Zanderij airport; (2.3) Incl persons of Surinamese origin from Holland; (8.1,8.2) International Monetary Fund.

Basic Indicators	Units	Code	1996	1997	1998	1999	2000
INBOUND TOURISM							
Arrivals							
Visitors	Thousands	(1.1)	1,337	1,635	986	1,253	1,151
Tourists (overnight visitors)	Thousands	(1.2)	315	269	284	289	281
Same-day visitors	Thousands	(1.3)	..	..	..	..	..
Cruise passengers	Thousands	(1.4)	..	..	..	..	..
Arrivals by region							
Africa	Thousands	(2.1)	264	131	201	199	177
Americas	Thousands	(2.2)	6	17	5	10	11
Europe	Thousands	(2.3)	38	104	76	73	85
East Asia and the Pacific	Thousands	(2.4)	4	13	1	6	7
South Asia	Thousands	(2.5)	..	..	..	..	..
Middle East	Thousands	(2.6)	..	..	..	..	..
Arrivals by mode of transport							
Air	Thousands	(3.1)	22	20	21	17	20
Rail	Thousands	(3.2)	..	..	1	1	..
Road	Thousands	(3.3)	1,315	1,615	964	1,235	1,131
Sea	Thousands	(3.4)	..	..	..	..	..
Arrivals by purpose of visit							
Leisure, recreation and holidays	Thousands	(4.1)	162	154	147	154	152
Business and professional	Thousands	(4.2)	93	54	93	81	77
Other	Thousands	(4.3)	60	61	44	54	52
Overnight stays and length of stay							
Overnight stays in H&S	Thousand nights	(5.1)	..	..	..	..	..
Overnight stays in CE	Thousand nights	(5.2)	..	..	..	..	..
ALS of non resident tourists	Nights	(5.5)	1.10	1.10	1.00	1.00	0.80
Tourism expenditure							
in the country of reference	US$ Million	(8.1)	38	40	47	50	34
DOMESTIC TOURISM							
Overnight stays							
Overnight stays in H&S	Thousand nights	(5.3)	22	26	22	23	24
Overnight stays in CE	Thousand nights	(5.4)	..	..	..	..	..
OUTBOUND TOURISM							
Departures	Thousands	(6.1)	..	..	..	..	..
Tourism expenditure in other countries	US$ Million	(8.2)	42	38	40	40	36
TOURISM ACTIVITIES							
Hotels and similar establishments							
Number of rooms	H&S	(7.1)	1,212	1,212	1,212	1,068	1,162
Number of bed-places	H&S	(7.2)	2,284	2,284	2,284	1,989	2,193
Occupancy rate	Percent	(7.3)	40.93	36.89	34.32	36.89	46.99
Average length of stay	Nights	(5.6)	1.10	1.10	1.00	1.00	0.80
ECONOMIC AGGREGATES							
Gross National Product (GNP)	US$ Million	(9.1)	1,386	1,512	1,321	1,360	1,350
Exports (F.O.B.)	US$ Million	(9.2)	781	818	744	..	..
Imports (C.I.F.)	US$ Million	(9.3)	917	936	838	..	..

Abbreviations used in tables and notes:
H&S: Hotels and similar establishments; **CE:** All types of tourism accommodation establishments; **ALS:** Average length of stay; **THS:** Non-resident tourists staying in H&S; **TCE:** Non-resident tourists staying in CE; **TF:** Arrivals of international (or non-resident) tourists; **VF:** Arrivals of international (or non-resident) visitors; **NHS:** Overnight stays at H&S; **NCE:** Overnight stays at CE.

..   data not available
incl   including
excl   excluding
nra   nationals residing abroad

Notes:
(1.2) Arrivals in hotels only; (7.3) Bed-places; (8.1,8.2) International Monetary Fund.

SWEDEN

Basic Indicators	Units	Code	1996	1997	1998	1999	2000
INBOUND TOURISM							
Arrivals							
Visitors	Thousands	(1.1)	..	..	..	..	..
Tourists (overnight visitors)	Thousands	(1.2)	2,376	2,388	2,573	2,595	2,746
Same-day visitors	Thousands	(1.3)	..	..	..	..	..
Cruise passengers	Thousands	(1.4)	..	..	..	..	..
Arrivals by region							
Africa	Thousands	(2.1)	..	..	..	..	..
Americas	Thousands	(2.2)	..	..	..	..	..
Europe	Thousands	(2.3)	..	..	..	..	..
East Asia and the Pacific	Thousands	(2.4)	..	..	..	..	..
South Asia	Thousands	(2.5)	..	..	..	..	..
Middle East	Thousands	(2.6)	..	..	..	..	..
Arrivals by mode of transport							
Air	Thousands	(3.1)	..	..	..	..	..
Rail	Thousands	(3.2)	..	..	..	..	..
Road	Thousands	(3.3)	..	..	..	..	..
Sea	Thousands	(3.4)	..	..	..	..	..
Arrivals by purpose of visit							
Leisure, recreation and holidays	Thousands	(4.1)	..	..	..	..	..
Business and professional	Thousands	(4.2)	..	..	..	..	..
Other	Thousands	(4.3)	..	..	..	..	..
Overnight stays and length of stay							
Overnight stays in H&S	Thousand nights	(5.1)	3,930	4,051	4,409	4,516	4,675
Overnight stays in CE	Thousand nights	(5.2)	7,701	7,659	8,029	8,601	8,650
ALS of non resident tourists	Nights	(5.5)	..	..	..	..	..
Tourism expenditure							
in the country of reference	US$ Million	(8.1)	3,657	3,730	4,189	3,894	4,034
DOMESTIC TOURISM							
Overnight stays							
Overnight stays in H&S	Thousand nights	(5.3)	14,668	14,815	15,643	16,192	16,614
Overnight stays in CE	Thousand nights	(5.4)	28,848	29,270	29,469	31,254	31,190
OUTBOUND TOURISM							
Departures	Thousands	(6.1)	10,390	10,818	11,422	10,500	10,400
Tourism expenditure in other countries	US$ Million	(8.2)	6,448	6,898	7,723	7,557	8,015
TOURISM ACTIVITIES							
Hotels and similar establishments							
Number of rooms	H&S	(7.1)	91,467	93,629	94,266	94,509	96,109
Number of bed-places	H&S	(7.2)	177,620	182,604	184,545	184,970	188,319
Occupancy rate	Percent	(7.3)	32.00	32.00	33.00	34.00	35.00
Average length of stay	Nights	(5.6)	..	..	..	..	..
ECONOMIC AGGREGATES							
Gross National Product (GNP)	US$ Million	(9.1)	239,433	245,505	241,626	236,911	237,473
Exports (F.O.B.)	US$ Million	(9.2)	84,904	82,956	85,003	84,796	86,920
Imports (C.I.F.)	US$ Million	(9.3)	66,932	65,710	68,634	68,586	72,643

Abbreviations used in tables and notes:
H&S: Hotels and similar establishments; **CE:** All types of tourism accommodation establishments; **ALS:** Average length of stay; **THS:** Non-resident tourists staying in H&S; **TCE:** Non-resident tourists staying in CE; **TF:** Arrivals of international (or non-resident) tourists; **VF:** Arrivals of international (or non-resident) visitors; **NHS:** Overnight stays at H&S; **NCE:** Overnight stays at CE.

..   data not available
incl   including
excl   excluding
nra   nationals residing abroad

Notes:
(1.2) TCE, camping excluding; (5.1,5.3) Hotels only; (7.3) Bed-places.

Basic Indicators	Units	Code	1996	1997	1998	1999	2000
INBOUND TOURISM							
Arrivals							
Visitors	Thousands	(1.1)	126,300	132,300	142,000	141,700	141,700
Tourists (overnight visitors)	Thousands	(1.2)	10,600	10,600	10,900	10,700	11,000
Same-day visitors	Thousands	(1.3)	115,700	121,700	131,100	131,000	130,700
Cruise passengers	Thousands	(1.4)	..	..	..	..	..
Arrivals by region							
Africa	Thousands	(2.1)	80	81	82	73	77
Americas	Thousands	(2.2)	946	990	1,074	1,020	1,199
Europe	Thousands	(2.3)	4,557	4,847	5,050	5,030	5,343
East Asia and the Pacific	Thousands	(2.4)	1,058	1,027	880	924	1,079
South Asia	Thousands	(2.5)	37	42	55	65	72
Middle East	Thousands	(2.6)	52	52	44	43	51
Arrivals by mode of transport							
Air	Thousands	(3.1)	..	..	..	..	..
Rail	Thousands	(3.2)	..	..	..	..	..
Road	Thousands	(3.3)	..	..	..	..	..
Sea	Thousands	(3.4)	..	..	..	..	..
Arrivals by purpose of visit							
Leisure, recreation and holidays	Thousands	(4.1)	..	..	..	..	..
Business and professional	Thousands	(4.2)	..	..	..	..	..
Other	Thousands	(4.3)	..	..	..	..	..
Overnight stays and length of stay							
Overnight stays in H&S	Thousand nights	(5.1)	17,284	18,034	18,712	18,544	19,914
Overnight stays in CE	Thousand nights	(5.2)	31,461	31,324	32,237	31,863	32,794
ALS of non resident tourists	Nights	(5.5)	..	..	..	..	..
Tourism expenditure							
in the country of reference	US$ Million	(8.1)	8,826	7,915	7,973	7,769	7,500
DOMESTIC TOURISM							
Overnight stays							
Overnight stays in H&S	Thousand nights	(5.3)	11,958	12,363	12,670	13,134	13,558
Overnight stays in CE	Thousand nights	(5.4)	35,166	34,841	35,557	35,477	35,785
OUTBOUND TOURISM							
Departures	Thousands	(6.1)	12,061	12,515	11,891	12,012	..
Tourism expenditure in other countries	US$ Million	(8.2)	7,570	6,960	6,798	6,718	6,238
TOURISM ACTIVITIES							
Hotels and similar establishments							
Number of rooms	H&S	(7.1)	142,375	141,826	141,056	141,243	141,422
Number of bed-places	H&S	(7.2)	262,471	261,482	260,290	260,592	261,387
Occupancy rate	Percent	(7.3)	36.80	38.50	39.70	40.10	42.30
Average length of stay	Nights	(5.6)	2.60	2.60	2.60	2.60	2.50
ECONOMIC AGGREGATES							
Gross National Product (GNP)	US$ Million	(9.1)	311,702	307,639	285,759	272,843	273,690
Exports (F.O.B.)	US$ Million	(9.2)	76,205	72,506	75,439	76,124	74,876
Imports (C.I.F.)	US$ Million	(9.3)	74,471	71,075	73,885	75,440	76,082

Abbreviations used in tables and notes:
H&S: Hotels and similar establishments; **CE:** All types of tourism accommodation establishments; **ALS:** Average length of stay; **THS:** Non-resident tourists staying in H&S; **TCE:** Non-resident tourists staying in CE; **TF:** Arrivals of international (or non-resident) tourists; **VF:** Arrivals of international (or non-resident) visitors; **NHS:** Overnight stays at H&S; **NCE:** Overnight stays at CE.

Notes:
(1.1,1.2) Estimates; (1.3) Incl persons in transit; (2.1-2.6) THS; (5.6) THS (foreign tourists); (7.1,7.2) Registered hotels, motels and inns; (7.3) Net occupancy rates (bed-places available).

..	data not available
incl	including
excl	excluding
nra	nationals residing abroad

SYRIAN ARAB REPUBLIC

Basic Indicators	Units	Code	1996	1997	1998	1999	2000
INBOUND TOURISM							
Arrivals							
Visitors	Thousands	(1.1)	2,435	2,332	2,464	2,682	3,015
Tourists (overnight visitors)	Thousands	(1.2)	830	891	1,267	1,386	1,416
Same-day visitors	Thousands	(1.3)	1,605	1,441	1,197	1,296	1,599
Cruise passengers	Thousands	(1.4)	9	10	11	12	9
Arrivals by region							
Africa	Thousands	(2.1)	72	76	71	65	66
Americas	Thousands	(2.2)	21	26	28	31	38
Europe	Thousands	(2.3)	332	343	343	369	398
East Asia and the Pacific	Thousands	(2.4)	13	18	16	22	26
South Asia	Thousands	(2.5)	199	140	170	221	243
Middle East	Thousands	(2.6)	1,746	1,697	1,800	1,929	2,196
Arrivals by mode of transport							
Air	Thousands	(3.1)	325	355	343	344	394
Rail	Thousands	(3.2)	..	..	..	..	..
Road	Thousands	(3.3)	2,101	1,965	2,108	2,322	2,600
Sea	Thousands	(3.4)	9	12	12	15	20
Arrivals by purpose of visit							
Leisure, recreation and holidays	Thousands	(4.1)	1,371	1,869	2,031	2,100	2,200
Business and professional	Thousands	(4.2)	110	158	200	300	400
Other	Thousands	(4.3)	954	305	233	282	415
Overnight stays and length of stay							
Overnight stays in H&S	Thousand nights	(5.1)	1,851	1,837	1,804	1,845	1,837
Overnight stays in CE	Thousand nights	(5.2)	3,098	2,961	4,454	5,130	5,997
ALS of non resident tourists	Nights	(5.5)	1.91	1.83	3.50	4.41	4.54
Tourism expenditure							
in the country of reference	US$ Million	(8.1)	1,165	1,013	1,017	1,031	1,082
DOMESTIC TOURISM							
Overnight stays							
Overnight stays in H&S	Thousand nights	(5.3)	1,247	1,124	1,158	1,133	1,081
Overnight stays in CE	Thousand nights	(5.4)	..	..	..	..	..
OUTBOUND TOURISM							
Departures	Thousands	(6.1)	1,871	2,299	2,411	2,994	3,863
Tourism expenditure in other countries	US$ Million	(8.2)	513	545	580	630	640
TOURISM ACTIVITIES							
Hotels and similar establishments							
Number of rooms	H&S	(7.1)	14,692	14,820	14,717	15,375	15,461
Number of bed-places	H&S	(7.2)	31,244	31,412	31,528	33,412	34,209
Occupancy rate	Percent	(7.3)	28.00	32.00	34.00	28.00	23.00
Average length of stay	Nights	(5.6)	2.23	3.56	2.45	2.00	1.60
ECONOMIC AGGREGATES							
Gross National Product (GNP)	US$ Million	(9.1)	15,829	15,497	16,548	16,043	16,014
Exports (F.O.B.)	US$ Million	(9.2)	3,999	3,916	2,890	3,464	19,260
Imports (C.I.F.)	US$ Million	(9.3)	5,380	4,028	3,895	3,832	16,706

Abbreviations used in tables and notes:
H&S: Hotels and similar establishments; **CE:** All types of tourism accommodation establishments; **ALS:** Average length of stay; **THS:** Non-resident tourists staying in H&S; **TCE:** Non-resident tourists staying in CE; **TF:** Arrivals of international (or non-resident) tourists; **VF:** Arrivals of international (or non-resident) visitors; **NHS:** Overnight stays at H&S; **NCE:** Overnight stays at CE.

.. data not available
incl including
excl excluding
nra nationals residing abroad

Notes:
(1.1,2.1-3.4) VF, excl arrivals of nra; (1.2/96/97) THS; (1.2/98-2000) TCE; (1.2,5.2/98) Change in methodology; (7.3) Rooms; (8.1) International Monetary Fund.

TAIWAN (PROVINCE OF CHINA)

Basic Indicators	Units	Code	1996	1997	1998	1999	2000
INBOUND TOURISM							
Arrivals							
Visitors	Thousands	(1.1)	2,358	2,372	2,299	2,411	2,624
Tourists (overnight visitors)	Thousands	(1.2)	..	..	..	..	..
Same-day visitors	Thousands	(1.3)	..	..	..	..	..
Cruise passengers	Thousands	(1.4)	..	..	..	..	..
Arrivals by region							
Africa	Thousands	(2.1)	9	9	8	8	9
Americas	Thousands	(2.2)	318	338	346	357	406
Europe	Thousands	(2.3)	152	158	160	161	161
East Asia and the Pacific	Thousands	(2.4)	1,585	1,583	1,490	1,560	1,704
South Asia	Thousands	(2.5)	10	11	12	11	13
Middle East	Thousands	(2.6)	10	11	11	11	11
Arrivals by mode of transport							
Air	Thousands	(3.1)	2,344	2,358	2,284	2,397	2,611
Rail	Thousands	(3.2)	..	..	..	..	..
Road	Thousands	(3.3)	..	..	..	..	..
Sea	Thousands	(3.4)	14	14	14	14	13
Arrivals by purpose of visit							
Leisure, recreation and holidays	Thousands	(4.1)	904	843	762	783	871
Business and professional	Thousands	(4.2)	758	804	825	864	963
Other	Thousands	(4.3)	696	725	712	764	790
Overnight stays and length of stay							
Overnight stays in H&S	Thousand nights	(5.1)	..	..	..	..	..
Overnight stays in CE	Thousand nights	(5.2)	15,145	15,199	15,058	15,966	16,487
ALS of non resident tourists	Nights	(5.5)	7.40	7.41	7.71	7.74	7.40
Tourism expenditure							
in the country of reference	US$ Million	(8.1)	3,636	3,402	3,372	3,571	3,738
DOMESTIC TOURISM							
Overnight stays							
Overnight stays in H&S	Thousand nights	(5.3)	..	..	..	..	..
Overnight stays in CE	Thousand nights	(5.4)	..	..	..	..	..
OUTBOUND TOURISM							
Departures	Thousands	(6.1)	5,714	6,162	5,912	6,559	7,329
Tourism expenditure in other countries	US$ Million	(8.2)	6,493	5,670	5,050	5,635	6,376
TOURISM ACTIVITIES							
Hotels and similar establishments							
Number of rooms	H&S	(7.1)	19,783	19,402	19,211	20,274	19,928
Number of bed-places	H&S	(7.2)	..	..	..	..	..
Occupancy rate	Percent	(7.3)	62.26	63.51	62.18	60.65	63.89
Average length of stay	Nights	(5.6)	..	..	..	..	..
ECONOMIC AGGREGATES							
Gross National Product (GNP)	US$ Million	(9.1)	291,314	301,479	288,665	292,830	..
Exports (F.O.B.)	US$ Million	(9.2)	..	..	..	..	..
Imports (C.I.F.)	US$ Million	(9.3)	..	..	..	..	..

Abbreviations used in tables and notes:
H&S: Hotels and similar establishments; CE: All types of tourism accommodation establishments; ALS: Average length of stay; THS: Non-resident tourists staying in H&S; TCE: Non-resident tourists staying in CE; TF: Arrivals of international (or non-resident) tourists; VF: Arrivals of international (or non-resident) visitors; NHS: Overnight stays at H&S; NCE: Overnight stays at CE.

.. data not available
incl including
excl excluding
nra nationals residing abroad

Notes:
(1.1) Incl. nra; (2.1-2.6) Excl. nra.

THAILAND

Basic Indicators	Units	Code	1996	1997	1998	1999	2000
INBOUND TOURISM							
Arrivals							
Visitors	Thousands	(1.1)	7,434	7,530	8,204	9,151	10,096
Tourists (overnight visitors)	Thousands	(1.2)	7,244	7,294	7,843	8,651	9,579
Same-day visitors	Thousands	(1.3)	189	236	361	500	517
Cruise passengers	Thousands	(1.4)	..	..	..	..	..
Arrivals by region							
Africa	Thousands	(2.1)	47	51	72	73	80
Americas	Thousands	(2.2)	384	388	449	515	585
Europe	Thousands	(2.3)	1,652	1,636	1,946	2,055	2,242
East Asia and the Pacific	Thousands	(2.4)	4,765	4,840	4,932	5,547	6,134
South Asia	Thousands	(2.5)	276	236	259	280	339
Middle East	Thousands	(2.6)	68	71	108	110	127
Arrivals by mode of transport							
Air	Thousands	(3.1)	6,124	6,205	6,678	7,263	8,077
Rail	Thousands	(3.2)	..	..	..	..	..
Road	Thousands	(3.3)	983	973	987	1,154	1,254
Sea	Thousands	(3.4)	137	116	178	234	248
Arrivals by purpose of visit							
Leisure, recreation and holidays	Thousands	(4.1)	6,251	6,268	6,833	7,561	8,369
Business and professional	Thousands	(4.2)	809	821	772	818	973
Other	Thousands	(4.3)	132	132	160	201	167
Overnight stays and length of stay							
Overnight stays in H&S	Thousand nights	(5.1)	59,212	60,120	65,232	68,293	73,855
Overnight stays in CE	Thousand nights	(5.2)	..	..	..	..	..
ALS of non resident tourists	Nights	(5.5)	8.23	8.33	8.40	7.98	7.77
Tourism expenditure							
in the country of reference	US$ Million	(8.1)	8,664	7,048	5,934	6,695	7,112
DOMESTIC TOURISM							
Overnight stays							
Overnight stays in H&S	Thousand nights	(5.3)	..	89,674	89,158	95,590	97,341
Overnight stays in CE	Thousand nights	(5.4)	..	..	..	..	..
OUTBOUND TOURISM							
Departures	Thousands	(6.1)	1,845	1,660	1,412	1,686	1,909
Tourism expenditure in other countries	US$ Million	(8.2)	4,171	1,888	1,448	1,843	2,068
TOURISM ACTIVITIES							
Hotels and similar establishments							
Number of rooms	H&S	(7.1)	265,542	272,993	279,070	279,943	318,812
Number of bed-places	H&S	(7.2)	..	..	..	..	..
Occupancy rate	Percent	(7.3)	51.43	46.58	47.50	49.50	50.84
Average length of stay	Nights	(5.6)	..	..	..	..	..
ECONOMIC AGGREGATES							
Gross National Product (GNP)	US$ Million	(9.1)	177,622	165,062	125,926	120,216	121,760
Exports (F.O.B.)	US$ Million	(9.2)	55,721	57,402	54,458	58,440	69,057
Imports (C.I.F.)	US$ Million	(9.3)	72,336	62,880	42,971	50,343	61,924

Abbreviations used in tables and notes:
H&S: Hotels and similar establishments; **CE:** All types of tourism accommodation establishments; **ALS:** Average length of stay; **THS:** Non-resident tourists staying in H&S; **TCE:** Non-resident tourists staying in CE; **TF:** Arrivals of international (or non-resident) tourists; **VF:** Arrivals of international (or non-resident) visitors; **NHS:** Overnight stays at H&S; **NCE:** Overnight stays at CE.

.. data not available
incl including
excl excluding
nra nationals residing abroad

Notes:
(1.2,3.1-3.4) Incl arrivals of nra; (2.1-2.6,4.1-4.3) Excl arrivals of nra; (3.3) Incl rail; (5.5) Days; (7.3) In main tourist destinations only.

THE FORMER YUGOSLAV REP. OF MACEDONIA

Basic Indicators	Units	Code	1996	1997	1998	1999	2000
INBOUND TOURISM							
Arrivals							
Visitors	Thousands	(1.1)	2,156	2,078	1,848	2,223	2,865
Tourists (overnight visitors)	Thousands	(1.2)	136	121	157	181	224
Same-day visitors	Thousands	(1.3)	..	..	..	..	..
Cruise passengers	Thousands	(1.4)	..	..	..	..	..
Arrivals by region							
Africa	Thousands	(2.1)	..	..	..	..	..
Americas	Thousands	(2.2)	6	5	9	15	17
Europe	Thousands	(2.3)	127	113	144	159	198
East Asia and the Pacific	Thousands	(2.4)	2	2	2	2	3
South Asia	Thousands	(2.5)	..	..	..	..	..
Middle East	Thousands	(2.6)	..	..	..	..	..
Arrivals by mode of transport							
Air	Thousands	(3.1)	74	72	87	223	263
Rail	Thousands	(3.2)	101	95	85	27	67
Road	Thousands	(3.3)	1,981	1,911	1,676	1,973	2,534
Sea	Thousands	(3.4)	..	..	..	..	..
Arrivals by purpose of visit							
Leisure, recreation and holidays	Thousands	(4.1)	..	..	..	..	..
Business and professional	Thousands	(4.2)	..	..	..	..	..
Other	Thousands	(4.3)	..	..	..	..	..
Overnight stays and length of stay							
Overnight stays in H&S	Thousand nights	(5.1)	234	236	310	439	439
Overnight stays in CE	Thousand nights	(5.2)	277	266	360	474	494
ALS of non resident tourists	Nights	(5.5)	..	..	..	..	..
Tourism expenditure **in the country of reference**	US$ Million	(8.1)	21	14	15	37	37
DOMESTIC TOURISM							
Overnight stays							
Overnight stays in H&S	Thousand nights	(5.3)	447	414	505	422	443
Overnight stays in CE	Thousand nights	(5.4)	1,420	1,322	2,067	1,839	1,941
OUTBOUND TOURISM							
Departures	Thousands	(6.1)	..	..	..	..	..
Tourism expenditure in other countries	US$ Million	(8.2)	26	27	30	32	34
TOURISM ACTIVITIES							
Hotels and similar establishments							
Number of rooms	H&S	(7.1)	6,253	6,356	6,514	6,758	6,636
Number of bed-places	H&S	(7.2)	15,063	15,476	15,955	16,418	16,147
Occupancy rate	Percent	(7.3)	12.40	11.50	14.00	14.40	15.00
Average length of stay	Nights	(5.6)	3.60	3.50	4.20	4.20	3.90
ECONOMIC AGGREGATES							
Gross National Product (GNP)	US$ Million	(9.1)	2,647	2,826	3,093	3,348	3,481
Exports (F.O.B.)	US$ Million	(9.2)	1,147	1,237	1,311	1,192	..
Imports (C.I.F.)	US$ Million	(9.3)	1,627	1,779	1,915	1,796	..

Abbreviations used in tables and notes:
H&S: Hotels and similar establishments; **CE:** All types of tourism accommodation establishments; **ALS:** Average length of stay; **THS:** Non-resident tourists staying in H&S; **TCE:** Non-resident tourists staying in CE; **TF:** Arrivals of international (or non-resident) tourists; **VF:** Arrivals of international (or non-resident) visitors; **NHS:** Overnight stays at H&S; **NCE:** Overnight stays at CE.

..   data not available
incl   including
excl   excluding
nra   nationals residing abroad

Notes:
(1.2,2.2-2.4) TCE; (3.1-3.3) VF.

TOGO

Basic Indicators	Units	Code	1996	1997	1998	1999	2000
INBOUND TOURISM							
Arrivals							
Visitors	Thousands	(1.1)	..	..	..	..	..
Tourists (overnight visitors)	Thousands	(1.2)	58	92	69	70	60
Same-day visitors	Thousands	(1.3)	..	..	..	..	..
Cruise passengers	Thousands	(1.4)	..	..	..	..	..
Arrivals by region							
Africa	Thousands	(2.1)	31	52	39	41	30
Americas	Thousands	(2.2)	3	4	5	3	2
Europe	Thousands	(2.3)	23	30	22	21	25
East Asia and the Pacific	Thousands	(2.4)	1	2	1	1	1
South Asia	Thousands	(2.5)	..	..	..	..	1
Middle East	Thousands	(2.6)	1	3	2	2	..
Arrivals by mode of transport							
Air	Thousands	(3.1)	..	..	..	..	..
Rail	Thousands	(3.2)	..	..	..	..	..
Road	Thousands	(3.3)	..	..	..	..	..
Sea	Thousands	(3.4)	..	..	..	..	..
Arrivals by purpose of visit							
Leisure, recreation and holidays	Thousands	(4.1)	..	..	..	..	..
Business and professional	Thousands	(4.2)	..	..	..	..	..
Other	Thousands	(4.3)	..	..	..	..	..
Overnight stays and length of stay							
Overnight stays in H&S	Thousand nights	(5.1)	145	154	153	162	132
Overnight stays in CE	Thousand nights	(5.2)	..	..	..	..	..
ALS of non resident tourists	Nights	(5.5)	..	..	..	..	..
Tourism expenditure							
in the country of reference	US$ Million	(8.1)	11	12	13	9	5
DOMESTIC TOURISM							
Overnight stays							
Overnight stays in H&S	Thousand nights	(5.3)	45	40	44	43	26
Overnight stays in CE	Thousand nights	(5.4)	..	..	..	..	..
OUTBOUND TOURISM							
Departures	Thousands	(6.1)	..	..	..	..	..
Tourism expenditure in other countries	US$ Million	(8.2)	3	5	3	3	..
TOURISM ACTIVITIES							
Hotels and similar establishments							
Number of rooms	H&S	(7.1)	2,062	2,463	2,268	2,258	2,358
Number of bed-places	H&S	(7.2)	4,077	4,679	4,289	4,289	4,405
Occupancy rate	Percent	(7.3)	21.90	23.10	20.00	21.40	19.10
Average length of stay	Nights	(5.6)	2.30	2.30	2.10	2.20	2.10
ECONOMIC AGGREGATES							
Gross National Product (GNP)	US$ Million	(9.1)	1,360	1,503	1,409	1,398	1,385
Exports (F.O.B.)	US$ Million	(9.2)	441	424	969	389	329
Imports (C.I.F.)	US$ Million	(9.3)	664	645	589	593	520

Abbreviations used in tables and notes:
H&S: Hotels and similar establishments; **CE:** All types of tourism accommodation establishments; **ALS:** Average length of stay; **THS:** Non-resident tourists staying in H&S; **TCE:** Non-resident tourists staying in CE; **TF:** Arrivals of international (or non-resident) tourists; **VF:** Arrivals of international (or non-resident) visitors; **NHS:** Overnight stays at H&S; **NCE:** Overnight stays at CE.

..	data not available
incl	including
excl	excluding
nra	nationals residing abroad

Notes:
(1.2) THS; (7.3) Rooms; (8.1) Hotel receipts; (8.2) International Monetary Fund.

Basic Indicators	Units	Code	1996	1997	1998	1999	2000
INBOUND TOURISM							
Arrivals							
Visitors	Thousands	(1.1)	31	29	35	44	43
Tourists (overnight visitors)	Thousands	(1.2)	27	26	27	31	35
Same-day visitors	Thousands	(1.3)	..	..	..	..	..
Cruise passengers	Thousands	(1.4)	4	3	8	13	8
Arrivals by region							
Africa	Thousands	(2.1)	..	..	..	..	..
Americas	Thousands	(2.2)	6	5	6	6	8
Europe	Thousands	(2.3)	4	4	4	5	6
East Asia and the Pacific	Thousands	(2.4)	16	17	17	20	21
South Asia	Thousands	(2.5)	..	..	..	..	..
Middle East	Thousands	(2.6)	..	..	..	..	..
Arrivals by mode of transport							
Air	Thousands	(3.1)	27	26	27	31	35
Rail	Thousands	(3.2)	..	..	..	..	..
Road	Thousands	(3.3)	..	..	..	..	..
Sea	Thousands	(3.4)	4	3	7	13	8
Arrivals by purpose of visit							
Leisure, recreation and holidays	Thousands	(4.1)	12	11	12	..	..
Business and professional	Thousands	(4.2)	6	3	6	..	..
Other	Thousands	(4.3)	9	12	9	..	..
Overnight stays and length of stay							
Overnight stays in H&S	Thousand nights	(5.1)	..	..	..	..	..
Overnight stays in CE	Thousand nights	(5.2)	..	..	..	..	..
ALS of non resident tourists	Nights	(5.5)	..	..	..	..	..
Tourism expenditure in the country of reference	US$ Million	(8.1)	13	16	8	9	7
DOMESTIC TOURISM							
Overnight stays							
Overnight stays in H&S	Thousand nights	(5.3)	..	..	..	..	..
Overnight stays in CE	Thousand nights	(5.4)	..	..	..	..	..
OUTBOUND TOURISM							
Departures	Thousands	(6.1)	..	..	..	..	..
Tourism expenditure in other countries	US$ Million	(8.2)	..	..	..	..	..
TOURISM ACTIVITIES							
Hotels and similar establishments							
Number of rooms	H&S	(7.1)	630	642	642	..	..
Number of bed-places	H&S	(7.2)	1,378	1,047	1,047	..	..
Occupancy rate	Percent	(7.3)	..	..	..	..	..
Average length of stay	Nights	(5.6)	..	..	..	..	..
ECONOMIC AGGREGATES							
Gross National Product (GNP)	US$ Million	(9.1)	171	171	169	167	166
Exports (F.O.B.)	US$ Million	(9.2)	13	10	8	12	9
Imports (C.I.F.)	US$ Million	(9.3)	75	73	69	73	70

Abbreviations used in tables and notes:
H&S: Hotels and similar establishments; **CE:** All types of tourism accommodation establishments; **ALS:** Average length of stay; **THS:** Non-resident tourists staying in H&S; **TCE:** Non-resident tourists staying in CE; **TF:** Arrivals of international (or non-resident) tourists; **VF:** Arrivals of international (or non-resident) visitors; **NHS:** Overnight stays at H&S; **NCE:** Overnight stays at CE.

.. data not available
incl including
excl excluding
nra nationals residing abroad

Notes:
(1.2) Arrivals by air.

TRINIDAD AND TOBAGO

Basic Indicators	Units	Code	1996	1997	1998	1999	2000
INBOUND TOURISM							
Arrivals							
Visitors	Thousands	(1.1)	317	360	377	421	481
Tourists (overnight visitors)	Thousands	(1.2)	266	324	334	358	399
Same-day visitors	Thousands	(1.3)	..	..	..	..	..
Cruise passengers	Thousands	(1.4)	51	36	43	63	82
Arrivals by region							
Africa	Thousands	(2.1)	..	1	1	1	1
Americas	Thousands	(2.2)	208	250	255	278	309
Europe	Thousands	(2.3)	53	70	74	74	83
East Asia and the Pacific	Thousands	(2.4)	2	2	2	3	4
South Asia	Thousands	(2.5)	1	1	1	1	1
Middle East	Thousands	(2.6)	..	..	..	..	..
Arrivals by mode of transport							
Air	Thousands	(3.1)	266	324	334	358	399
Rail	Thousands	(3.2)	..	..	..	..	..
Road	Thousands	(3.3)	..	..	..	..	..
Sea	Thousands	(3.4)	51	36	43	63	82
Arrivals by purpose of visit							
Leisure, recreation and holidays	Thousands	(4.1)	196	220	251	276	311
Business and professional	Thousands	(4.2)	48	65	60	61	68
Other	Thousands	(4.3)	21	39	22	21	20
Overnight stays and length of stay							
Overnight stays in H&S	Thousand nights	(5.1)	..	..	..	..	..
Overnight stays in CE	Thousand nights	(5.2)	..	..	..	..	..
ALS of non resident tourists	Nights	(5.5)	..	..	..	..	..
Tourism expenditure							
in the country of reference	US$ Million	(8.1)	110	193	201	210	..
DOMESTIC TOURISM							
Overnight stays							
Overnight stays in H&S	Thousand nights	(5.3)	..	..	..	..	..
Overnight stays in CE	Thousand nights	(5.4)	..	..	..	..	..
OUTBOUND TOURISM							
Departures	Thousands	(6.1)	248	..	..	..	..
Tourism expenditure in other countries	US$ Million	(8.2)	76	72	67	..	..
TOURISM ACTIVITIES							
Hotels and similar establishments							
Number of rooms	H&S	(7.1)	3,519	3,652	3,971	4,236	4,532
Number of bed-places	H&S	(7.2)	..	..	..	..	..
Occupancy rate	Percent	(7.3)	49.20	50.00	54.10	..	..
Average length of stay	Nights	(5.6)	..	..	..	..	..
ECONOMIC AGGREGATES							
Gross National Product (GNP)	US$ Million	(9.1)	5,209	5,508	5,696	6,142	6,477
Exports (F.O.B.)	US$ Million	(9.2)	2,500	2,542	2,258	2,803	4,654
Imports (C.I.F.)	US$ Million	(9.3)	2,144	2,990	2,999	2,740	3,308

Abbreviations used in tables and notes:
H&S: Hotels and similar establishments; **CE:** All types of tourism accommodation establishments; **ALS:** Average length of stay; **THS:** Non-resident tourists staying in H&S; **TCE:** Non-resident tourists staying in CE; **TF:** Arrivals of international (or non-resident) tourists; **VF:** Arrivals of international (or non-resident) visitors; **NHS:** Overnight stays at H&S; **NCE:** Overnight stays at CE.

..	data not available
incl	including
excl	excluding
nra	nationals residing abroad

Notes:
(1.2) Arrivals by air; (7.1/99/2000) Provisional data; (8.2) International Monetary Fund.

TUNISIA

Basic Indicators	Units	Code	1996	1997	1998	1999	2000
INBOUND TOURISM							
Arrivals							
Visitors	Thousands	(1.1)	3,986	4,392	4,831	5,000	..
Tourists (overnight visitors)	Thousands	(1.2)	3,885	4,263	4,718	4,832	5,057
Same-day visitors	Thousands	(1.3)	..	..	..	..	..
Cruise passengers	Thousands	(1.4)	101	129	113	168	..
Arrivals by region							
Africa	Thousands	(2.1)	719	672	751	672	666
Americas	Thousands	(2.2)	27	27	28	27	31
Europe	Thousands	(2.3)	2,523	2,846	3,011	3,461	3,616
East Asia and the Pacific	Thousands	(2.4)	5	6	8	9	8
South Asia	Thousands	(2.5)	..	..	..	..	..
Middle East	Thousands	(2.6)	571	675	879	635	713
Arrivals by mode of transport							
Air	Thousands	(3.1)	2,674	3,030	3,224	3,591	..
Rail	Thousands	(3.2)	..	..	..	..	..
Road	Thousands	(3.3)	1,155	1,176	1,439	1,173	..
Sea	Thousands	(3.4)	55	58	55	68	..
Arrivals by purpose of visit							
Leisure, recreation and holidays	Thousands	(4.1)	..	..	..	..	..
Business and professional	Thousands	(4.2)	..	..	..	..	..
Other	Thousands	(4.3)	..	..	..	..	..
Overnight stays and length of stay							
Overnight stays in H&S	Thousand nights	(5.1)	24,130	27,684	28,788	33,151	33,168
Overnight stays in CE	Thousand nights	(5.2)	..	..	..	..	..
ALS of non resident tourists	Nights	(5.5)	6.20	6.50	6.10	6.90	6.60
Tourism expenditure							
in the country of reference	US$ Million	(8.1)	1,411	1,361	1,557	1,560	1,496
DOMESTIC TOURISM							
Overnight stays							
Overnight stays in H&S	Thousand nights	(5.3)	1,995	2,112	2,194	2,169	2,255
Overnight stays in CE	Thousand nights	(5.4)	..	..	..	..	..
OUTBOUND TOURISM							
Departures	Thousands	(6.1)	1,428	1,381	1,526	1,480	..
Tourism expenditure in other countries	US$ Million	(8.2)	251	235	235	239	263
TOURISM ACTIVITIES							
Hotels and similar establishments							
Number of rooms	H&S	(7.1)	84,972	89,088	92,308	95,977	..
Number of bed-places	H&S	(7.2)	169,945	178,176	184,616	191,955	197,400
Occupancy rate	Percent	(7.3)	48.00	52.70	52.50	56.50	55.80
Average length of stay	Nights	(5.6)	6.50	6.40	6.20	6.40	..
ECONOMIC AGGREGATES							
Gross National Product (GNP)	US$ Million	(9.1)	18,212	19,159	19,120	19,768	20,057
Exports (F.O.B.)	US$ Million	(9.2)	5,517	5,559	5,738	5,872	5,850
Imports (C.I.F.)	US$ Million	(9.3)	7,700	7,914	8,350	8,474	8,567

Abbreviations used in tables and notes:
H&S: Hotels and similar establishments; CE: All types of tourism accommodation establishments; ALS: Average length of stay; THS: Non-resident tourists staying in H&S; TCE: Non-resident tourists staying in CE; TF: Arrivals of international (or non-resident) tourists; VF: Arrivals of international (or non-resident) visitors; NHS: Overnight stays at H&S; NCE: Overnight stays at CE.

..   data not available
incl   including
excl   excluding
nra   nationals residing abroad

Notes:
(1.2,2.1-3.4) TF, excl nra; (7.1,7.2) Classified and unclassified hotels, boarding houses and holiday villages; (7.3) Bed-places; (8.2) International Monetary Fund.

TURKEY

Basic Indicators	Units	Code	1996	1997	1998	1999	2000
INBOUND TOURISM							
Arrivals							
Visitors	Thousands	(1.1)	8,614	9,689	9,753	7,487	10,428
Tourists (overnight visitors)	Thousands	(1.2)	7,966	9,040	8,960	6,893	9,586
Same-day visitors	Thousands	(1.3)	648	649	793	594	842
Cruise passengers	Thousands	(1.4)	..	..	..	..	..
Arrivals by region							
Africa	Thousands	(2.1)	91	96	96	82	106
Americas	Thousands	(2.2)	220	268	317	283	361
Europe	Thousands	(2.3)	6,855	7,875	7,786	5,786	8,234
East Asia and the Pacific	Thousands	(2.4)	170	205	195	166	229
South Asia	Thousands	(2.5)	399	348	321	367	397
Middle East	Thousands	(2.6)	219	233	231	200	247
Arrivals by mode of transport							
Air	Thousands	(3.1)	6,240	7,020	6,699	4,687	7,274
Rail	Thousands	(3.2)	92	140	114	47	40
Road	Thousands	(3.3)	1,360	1,576	1,829	1,918	1,970
Sea	Thousands	(3.4)	922	953	1,111	835	1,145
Arrivals by purpose of visit							
Leisure, recreation and holidays	Thousands	(4.1)	5,924	7,111	6,825	..	..
Business and professional	Thousands	(4.2)	1,853	1,793	1,973	..	..
Other	Thousands	(4.3)	837	785	955	..	..
Overnight stays and length of stay							
Overnight stays in H&S	Thousand nights	(5.1)	25,518	35,967	30,159	20,358	28,377
Overnight stays in CE	Thousand nights	(5.2)	25,548	36,167	30,433	20,435	28,511
ALS of non resident tourists	Nights	(5.5)	8.00	10.00	9.00	..	..
Tourism expenditure							
in the country of reference	US$ Million	(8.1)	5,962	8,088	7,809	5,203	7,636
DOMESTIC TOURISM							
Overnight stays							
Overnight stays in H&S	Thousand nights	(5.3)	11,417	14,811	15,358	16,715	16,351
Overnight stays in CE	Thousand nights	(5.4)	11,490	14,941	15,514	16,783	16,476
OUTBOUND TOURISM							
Departures	Thousands	(6.1)	4,261	4,633	4,601	4,758	5,284
Tourism expenditure in other countries	US$ Million	(8.2)	1,265	1,716	1,754	1,471	1,711
TOURISM ACTIVITIES							
Hotels and similar establishments							
Number of rooms	H&S	(7.1)	143,552	149,317	149,659	152,638	155,441
Number of bed-places	H&S	(7.2)	295,743	308,096	309,013	315,932	322,334
Occupancy rate	Percent	(7.3)	51.20	54.50	46.10	37.10	36.82
Average length of stay	Nights	(5.6)	4.00	3.80	4.00	4.20	4.20
ECONOMIC AGGREGATES							
Gross National Product (GNP)	US$ Million	(9.1)	177,180	198,814	199,920	185,651	201,497
Exports (F.O.B.)	US$ Million	(9.2)	23,224	26,261	26,974	26,588	26,572
Imports (C.I.F.)	US$ Million	(9.3)	43,627	48,559	45,921	40,692	53,499

Abbreviations used in tables and notes:

H&S: Hotels and similar establishments; **CE:** All types of tourism accommodation establishments; **ALS:** Average length of stay; **THS:** Non-resident tourists staying in H&S; **TCE:** Non-resident tourists staying in CE; **TF:** Arrivals of international (or non-resident) tourists; **VF:** Arrivals of international (or non-resident) visitors; **NHS:** Overnight stays at H&S; **NCE:** Overnight stays at CE.

..   data not available
incl   including
excl   excluding
nra   nationals residing abroad

Notes:

(1.1,3.1-4.3) VF; (1.3) Sea arrivals (excl one land border from 1989); (2.1-2.6) TF; (3.4) Incl cruise passengers; (5.2) Survey in accommodation establishments licensed by Ministry of Tourism; (5.2,5.4) Incl camping sites; (5.5,8.1) Survey (departing foreign visitors); (5.6,7.3) Classified hotels, excl camping sites; (7.3) Bed-places.

Basic Indicators	Units	Code	1996	1997	1998	1999	2000
INBOUND TOURISM							
Arrivals							
Visitors	Thousands	(1.1)	282	332	380	..	..
Tourists (overnight visitors)	Thousands	(1.2)	217	257	300	..	..
Same-day visitors	Thousands	(1.3)	65	75	80	..	..
Cruise passengers	Thousands	(1.4)	..	..	..	..	..
Arrivals by region							
Africa	Thousands	(2.1)	..	..	..	..	..
Americas	Thousands	(2.2)	4	3	3	..	..
Europe	Thousands	(2.3)	163	151	33	..	..
East Asia and the Pacific	Thousands	(2.4)	3	2	9	..	..
South Asia	Thousands	(2.5)	108	175	99	..	..
Middle East	Thousands	(2.6)	4	1	..	..	..
Arrivals by mode of transport							
Air	Thousands	(3.1)	89	91	94	..	..
Rail	Thousands	(3.2)	..	..	..	..	..
Road	Thousands	(3.3)	182	241	286	..	..
Sea	Thousands	(3.4)	11	..	..	..	..
Arrivals by purpose of visit							
Leisure, recreation and holidays	Thousands	(4.1)	63	29	38	..	..
Business and professional	Thousands	(4.2)	84	154	90	..	..
Other	Thousands	(4.3)	134	149	252	..	..
Overnight stays and length of stay							
Overnight stays in H&S	Thousand nights	(5.1)	..	..	..	..	..
Overnight stays in CE	Thousand nights	(5.2)	..	..	..	..	..
ALS of non resident tourists	Nights	(5.5)	..	..	..	..	..
Tourism expenditure							
in the country of reference	US$ Million	(8.1)	66	74	192	..	..
DOMESTIC TOURISM							
Overnight stays							
Overnight stays in H&S	Thousand nights	(5.3)	..	..	..	..	..
Overnight stays in CE	Thousand nights	(5.4)	..	..	..	..	..
OUTBOUND TOURISM							
Departures	Thousands	(6.1)	29	31	357	..	..
Tourism expenditure in other countries	US$ Million	(8.2)	73	125	..	..	..
TOURISM ACTIVITIES							
Hotels and similar establishments							
Number of rooms	H&S	(7.1)	2,743	2,616	2,153	..	..
Number of bed-places	H&S	(7.2)	7,179	6,571	3,919	..	..
Occupancy rate	Percent	(7.3)	..	24.00	..	..	..
Average length of stay	Nights	(5.6)	..	..	..	..	..
ECONOMIC AGGREGATES							
Gross National Product (GNP)	US$ Million	(9.1)	3,629	2,959	2,605	3,274	4,049
Exports (F.O.B.)	US$ Million	(9.2)	..	..	..	..	..
Imports (C.I.F.)	US$ Million	(9.3)	..	..	..	..	..

Abbreviations used in tables and notes:
H&S: Hotels and similar establishments; **CE:** All types of tourism accommodation establishments; **ALS:** Average length of stay; **THS:** Non-resident tourists staying in H&S; **TCE:** Non-resident tourists staying in CE; **TF:** Arrivals of international (or non-resident) tourists; **VF:** Arrivals of international (or non-resident) visitors; **NHS:** Overnight stays at H&S; **NCE:** Overnight stays at CE.

.. data not available
incl including
excl excluding
nra nationals residing abroad

Notes:
(2.2-2.6,3.1-3.4,4.1-4.3) VF; (8.2) International Monetary Fund.

TURKS AND CAICOS ISLANDS

Basic Indicators	Units	Code	1996	1997	1998	1999	2000
INBOUND TOURISM							
Arrivals							
Visitors	Thousands	(1.1)	..	..	..	..	..
Tourists (overnight visitors)	Thousands	(1.2)	88	93	111	121	152
Same-day visitors	Thousands	(1.3)	..	..	..	..	..
Cruise passengers	Thousands	(1.4)	..	..	..	..	..
Arrivals by region							
Africa	Thousands	(2.1)	..	..	..	..	..
Americas	Thousands	(2.2)	73	79	90	98	134
Europe	Thousands	(2.3)	11	9	12	11	12
East Asia and the Pacific	Thousands	(2.4)	..	..	..	..	..
South Asia	Thousands	(2.5)	..	..	..	..	..
Middle East	Thousands	(2.6)	..	..	..	..	..
Arrivals by mode of transport							
Air	Thousands	(3.1)	86	91	111	120	139
Rail	Thousands	(3.2)	..	..	..	..	..
Road	Thousands	(3.3)	..	..	..	..	..
Sea	Thousands	(3.4)	2	2	..	1	13
Arrivals by purpose of visit							
Leisure, recreation and holidays	Thousands	(4.1)	73	85	98	88	83
Business and professional	Thousands	(4.2)	5	5	8	23	48
Other	Thousands	(4.3)	10	3	5	10	21
Overnight stays and length of stay							
Overnight stays in H&S	Thousand nights	(5.1)	..	584	651	762	..
Overnight stays in CE	Thousand nights	(5.2)	649	744	831	906	..
ALS of non resident tourists	Nights	(5.5)	7.50	7.70	7.40	..	..
Tourism expenditure							
in the country of reference	US$ Million	(8.1)	99	113	157	238	285
DOMESTIC TOURISM							
Overnight stays							
Overnight stays in H&S	Thousand nights	(5.3)	..	..	..	..	..
Overnight stays in CE	Thousand nights	(5.4)	..	..	..	..	..
OUTBOUND TOURISM							
Departures	Thousands	(6.1)	..	..	..	..	..
Tourism expenditure in other countries	US$ Million	(8.2)	174	235	194	244	..
TOURISM ACTIVITIES							
Hotels and similar establishments							
Number of rooms	H&S	(7.1)	1,201	1,482	1,562	1,674	2,023
Number of bed-places	H&S	(7.2)	2,402	2,594	2,734	2,930	3,540
Occupancy rate	Percent	(7.3)	68.00	70.00	72.00	72.00	76.00
Average length of stay	Nights	(5.6)	..	..	..	..	..
ECONOMIC AGGREGATES							
Gross National Product (GNP)	US$ Million	(9.1)	98	112	121	150	..
Exports (F.O.B.)	US$ Million	(9.2)	95	..	..	..	..
Imports (C.I.F.)	US$ Million	(9.3)	111	..	..	..	..

Abbreviations used in tables and notes:
H&S: Hotels and similar establishments; **CE:** All types of tourism accommodation establishments; **ALS:** Average length of stay; **THS:** Non-resident tourists staying in H&S; **TCE:** Non-resident tourists staying in CE; **TF:** Arrivals of international (or non-resident) tourists; **VF:** Arrivals of international (or non-resident) visitors; **NHS:** Overnight stays at H&S; **NCE:** Overnight stays at CE.

  ..   data not available
incl including
excl excluding
nra nationals residing abroad

Notes:
(9.1) GDP.

TUVALU

Basic Indicators	Units	Code	1996	1997	1998	1999	2000
INBOUND TOURISM							
Arrivals							
Visitors	Thousands	(1.1)	..	..	..	..	..
Tourists (overnight visitors)	Thousands	(1.2)	1.0	1.0	1.1	..	1.2
Same-day visitors	Thousands	(1.3)	..	..	..	..	..
Cruise passengers	Thousands	(1.4)	..	..	..	..	..
Arrivals by region							
Africa	Thousands	(2.1)	..	..	..	..	..
Americas	Thousands	(2.2)	0.1	0.1	0.1	..	..
Europe	Thousands	(2.3)	0.1	0.1	0.1	..	..
East Asia and the Pacific	Thousands	(2.4)	0.8	0.8	0.8	..	..
South Asia	Thousands	(2.5)	..	..	..	..	..
Middle East	Thousands	(2.6)	..	..	..	..	..
Arrivals by mode of transport							
Air	Thousands	(3.1)	..	..	..	..	..
Rail	Thousands	(3.2)	..	..	..	..	..
Road	Thousands	(3.3)	..	..	..	..	..
Sea	Thousands	(3.4)	..	..	..	..	..
Arrivals by purpose of visit							
Leisure, recreation and holidays	Thousands	(4.1)	0.2	0.3	0.2	..	0.1
Business and professional	Thousands	(4.2)	0.5	0.4	0.5	..	0.5
Other	Thousands	(4.3)	0.2	0.3	0.4	..	0.6
Overnight stays and length of stay							
Overnight stays in H&S	Thousand nights	(5.1)	..	..	..	..	..
Overnight stays in CE	Thousand nights	(5.2)	..	..	..	..	..
ALS of non resident tourists	Nights	(5.5)	..	..	..	..	..
Tourism expenditure **in the country of reference**	US$ Million	(8.1)	0.3	0.3	0.2	..	..
DOMESTIC TOURISM							
Overnight stays							
Overnight stays in H&S	Thousand nights	(5.3)	..	..	..	..	..
Overnight stays in CE	Thousand nights	(5.4)	..	..	..	..	..
OUTBOUND TOURISM							
Departures	Thousands	(6.1)	..	..	..	..	..
Tourism expenditure in other countries	US$ Million	(8.2)	..	..	..	..	..
TOURISM ACTIVITIES							
Hotels and similar establishments							
Number of rooms	H&S	(7.1)	65	59	59	..	..
Number of bed-places	H&S	(7.2)	..	..	..	..	..
Occupancy rate	Percent	(7.3)	..	..	..	..	..
Average length of stay	Nights	(5.6)	..	..	..	..	..
ECONOMIC AGGREGATES							
Gross National Product (GNP)	US$ Million	(9.1)	..	..	..	..	..
Exports (F.O.B.)	US$ Million	(9.2)	..	..	..	..	..
Imports (C.I.F.)	US$ Million	(9.3)	..	..	..	..	..

Abbreviations used in tables and notes:
H&S: Hotels and similar establishments; **CE:** All types of tourism accommodation establishments; **ALS:** Average length of stay; **THS:** Non-resident tourists staying in H&S; **TCE:** Non-resident tourists staying in CE; **TF:** Arrivals of international (or non-resident) tourists; **VF:** Arrivals of international (or non-resident) visitors; **NHS:** Overnight stays at H&S; **NCE:** Overnight stays at CE.

..   data not available
incl   including
excl   excluding
nra   nationals residing abroad

UGANDA

Basic Indicators	Units	Code	1996	1997	1998	1999	2000
INBOUND TOURISM							
Arrivals							
Visitors	Thousands	(1.1)	..	..	..	..	..
Tourists (overnight visitors)	Thousands	(1.2)	174	171	192	187	191
Same-day visitors	Thousands	(1.3)	..	..	..	..	..
Cruise passengers	Thousands	(1.4)	..	..	..	..	..
Arrivals by region							
Africa	Thousands	(2.1)	103	100	116	116	132
Americas	Thousands	(2.2)	12	14	15	13	12
Europe	Thousands	(2.3)	43	44	46	43	36
East Asia and the Pacific	Thousands	(2.4)	6	6	7	6	5
South Asia	Thousands	(2.5)	7	7	8	7	6
Middle East	Thousands	(2.6)	1	1	1	1	1
Arrivals by mode of transport							
Air	Thousands	(3.1)	..	..	..	..	..
Rail	Thousands	(3.2)	..	..	..	..	..
Road	Thousands	(3.3)	..	..	..	..	..
Sea	Thousands	(3.4)	..	..	..	..	..
Arrivals by purpose of visit							
Leisure, recreation and holidays	Thousands	(4.1)	..	..	..	..	..
Business and professional	Thousands	(4.2)	..	..	..	..	..
Other	Thousands	(4.3)	..	..	..	..	..
Overnight stays and length of stay							
Overnight stays in H&S	Thousand nights	(5.1)	1,647	..	..	..	..
Overnight stays in CE	Thousand nights	(5.2)	..	..	..	..	..
ALS of non resident tourists	Nights	(5.5)	14.00	..	..	..	..
Tourism expenditure							
in the country of reference	US$ Million	(8.1)	117	135	144	149	..
DOMESTIC TOURISM							
Overnight stays							
Overnight stays in H&S	Thousand nights	(5.3)	..	..	..	..	..
Overnight stays in CE	Thousand nights	(5.4)	..	..	..	..	..
OUTBOUND TOURISM							
Departures	Thousands	(6.1)	..	..	..	..	..
Tourism expenditure in other countries	US$ Million	(8.2)	135	113	95	141	..
TOURISM ACTIVITIES							
Hotels and similar establishments							
Number of rooms	H&S	(7.1)	3,887	..	..	..	..
Number of bed-places	H&S	(7.2)	6,608	..	..	..	..
Occupancy rate	Percent	(7.3)	63.00	..	..	..	..
Average length of stay	Nights	(5.6)	..	..	..	..	..
ECONOMIC AGGREGATES							
Gross National Product (GNP)	US$ Million	(9.1)	5,814	6,448	6,564	6,801	6,797
Exports (F.O.B.)	US$ Million	(9.2)	587	555	501	517	469
Imports (C.I.F.)	US$ Million	(9.3)	1,190	1,317	1,414	1,342	1,512

Abbreviations used in tables and notes:
H&S: Hotels and similar establishments; **CE:** All types of tourism accommodation establishments; **ALS:** Average length of stay; **THS:** Non-resident tourists staying in H&S; **TCE:** Non-resident tourists staying in CE; **TF:** Arrivals of international (or non-resident) tourists; **VF:** Arrivals of international (or non-resident) visitors; **NHS:** Overnight stays at H&S; **NCE:** Overnight stays at CE.

..	data not available
incl	including
excl	excluding
nra	nationals residing abroad

Notes:
(7.2) Hotels only; (8.1,8.2) International Monetary Fund.

Basic Indicators	Units	Code	1996	1997	1998	1999	2000
INBOUND TOURISM							
Arrivals							
Visitors	Thousands	(1.1)	5,391	10,298	8,352	10,994	11,690
Tourists (overnight visitors)	Thousands	(1.2)	3,854	7,658	6,208	4,232	4,406
Same-day visitors	Thousands	(1.3)	1,467	2,593	2,080	6,697	..
Cruise passengers	Thousands	(1.4)	70	47	64	65	..
Arrivals by region							
Africa	Thousands	(2.1)	1	10	4	7	15
Americas	Thousands	(2.2)	26	80	64	70	71
Europe	Thousands	(2.3)	3,612	7,466	6,091	4,098	4,258
East Asia and the Pacific	Thousands	(2.4)	4	28	22	24	27
South Asia	Thousands	(2.5)	3	36	13	11	11
Middle East	Thousands	(2.6)	205	29	9	14	18
Arrivals by mode of transport							
Air	Thousands	(3.1)	323	515	418	523	..
Rail	Thousands	(3.2)	3,494	6,631	6,013	6,786	..
Road	Thousands	(3.3)	1,044	1,981	1,670	3,379	..
Sea	Thousands	(3.4)	530	1,171	251	306	..
Arrivals by purpose of visit							
Leisure, recreation and holidays	Thousands	(4.1)	1,126	1,414	853	713	..
Business and professional	Thousands	(4.2)	948	1,194	1,478	1,538	..
Other	Thousands	(4.3)	3,317	7,690	6,021	8,739	..
Overnight stays and length of stay							
Overnight stays in H&S	Thousand nights	(5.1)	2,074	1,582	1,140	1,106	..
Overnight stays in CE	Thousand nights	(5.2)	..	..	..	..	..
ALS of non resident tourists	Nights	(5.5)	5.60	6.10	6.40	6.69	..
Tourism expenditure **in the country of reference**	US$ Million	(8.1)	3,416	3,865	3,317	2,124	..
DOMESTIC TOURISM							
Overnight stays							
Overnight stays in H&S	Thousand nights	(5.3)	8,853	7,836	7,589	3,807	..
Overnight stays in CE	Thousand nights	(5.4)	..	..	..	..	..
OUTBOUND TOURISM							
Departures	Thousands	(6.1)	14,913	10,074	7,773	7,399	8,654
Tourism expenditure in other countries	US$ Million	(8.2)	2,596	2,564	2,021	1,774	..
TOURISM ACTIVITIES							
Hotels and similar establishments							
Number of rooms	H&S	(7.1)	74,679	76,945	..	..	..
Number of bed-places	H&S	(7.2)	167,233	160,290	161,567	166,254	..
Occupancy rate	Percent	(7.3)	24.00	21.00	21.00	21.50	..
Average length of stay	Nights	(5.6)	4.60	5.50	3.15	3.13	..
ECONOMIC AGGREGATES							
Gross National Product (GNP)	US$ Million	(9.1)	48,917	51,242	48,901	38,364	34,693
Exports (F.O.B.)	US$ Million	(9.2)	14,441	14,232	12,637	11,582	..
Imports (C.I.F.)	US$ Million	(9.3)	18,639	17,114	14,676	11,846	..

Abbreviations used in tables and notes:
H&S: Hotels and similar establishments; **CE:** All types of tourism accommodation establishments; **ALS:** Average length of stay; **THS:** Non-resident tourists staying in H&S; **TCE:** Non-resident tourists staying in CE; **TF:** Arrivals of international (or non-resident) tourists; **VF:** Arrivals of international (or non-resident) visitors; **NHS:** Overnight stays at H&S; **NCE:** Overnight stays at CE.

..   data not available
incl including
excl excluding
nra   nationals residing abroad

Notes:
(2.1-2.6) TF; (3.1-4.3) VF.

UNITED ARAB EMIRATES

Basic Indicators	Units	Code	1996	1997	1998	1999	2000
INBOUND TOURISM							
Arrivals							
Visitors	Thousands	(1.1)	..	..	..	..	..
Tourists (overnight visitors)	Thousands	(1.2)	2,572	2,476	2,991	3,393	3,907
Same-day visitors	Thousands	(1.3)	..	..	..	..	..
Cruise passengers	Thousands	(1.4)	..	..	..	..	..
Arrivals by region							
Africa	Thousands	(2.1)	100	119	146	154	174
Americas	Thousands	(2.2)	84	80	111	130	139
Europe	Thousands	(2.3)	964	787	947	1,017	1,077
East Asia and the Pacific	Thousands	(2.4)	216	200	236	248	264
South Asia	Thousands	(2.5)	329	372	426	501	568
Middle East	Thousands	(2.6)	647	642	797	923	1,089
Arrivals by mode of transport							
Air	Thousands	(3.1)	..	..	..	..	..
Rail	Thousands	(3.2)	..	..	..	..	..
Road	Thousands	(3.3)	..	..	..	..	..
Sea	Thousands	(3.4)	..	..	..	..	..
Arrivals by purpose of visit							
Leisure, recreation and holidays	Thousands	(4.1)	..	..	..	..	..
Business and professional	Thousands	(4.2)	..	..	..	..	..
Other	Thousands	(4.3)	..	..	..	..	..
Overnight stays and length of stay							
Overnight stays in H&S	Thousand nights	(5.1)	7,004	7,009	7,984	8,554	10,313
Overnight stays in CE	Thousand nights	(5.2)	..	..	..	..	..
ALS of non resident tourists	Nights	(5.5)	..	..	..	..	..
Tourism expenditure							
in the country of reference	US$ Million	(8.1)	743	814	859	893	1,012
DOMESTIC TOURISM							
Overnight stays							
Overnight stays in H&S	Thousand nights	(5.3)	..	..	..	..	..
Overnight stays in CE	Thousand nights	(5.4)	..	..	..	..	..
OUTBOUND TOURISM							
Departures	Thousands	(6.1)	..	..	..	..	..
Tourism expenditure in other countries	US$ Million	(8.2)	..	..	..	..	..
TOURISM ACTIVITIES							
Hotels and similar establishments							
Number of rooms	H&S	(7.1)	21,630	23,170	26,487	28,343	30,241
Number of bed-places	H&S	(7.2)	36,639	39,052	44,378	45,847	49,301
Occupancy rate	Percent	(7.3)	64.00	61.00	58.00	58.00	62.00
Average length of stay	Nights	(5.6)	..	..	..	..	..
ECONOMIC AGGREGATES							
Gross National Product (GNP)	US$ Million	(9.1)	51,205	52,480	49,205	..	..
Exports (F.O.B.)	US$ Million	(9.2)	28,085	39,613	42,666	43,307	..
Imports (C.I.F.)	US$ Million	(9.3)	22,638	29,952	24,728	34,745	..

Abbreviations used in tables and notes:

H&S: Hotels and similar establishments; **CE:** All types of tourism accommodation establishments; **ALS:** Average length of stay; **THS:** Non-resident tourists staying in H&S; **TCE:** Non-resident tourists staying in CE; **TF:** Arrivals of international (or non-resident) tourists; **VF:** Arrivals of international (or non-resident) visitors; **NHS:** Overnight stays at H&S; **NCE:** Overnight stays at CE.

..   data not available
incl   including
excl   excluding
nra   nationals residing abroad

Notes:

(1.2) Arrivals in hotels only. Incl domestic tourism and nra; (2.1-2.6) Arrivals in hotels only. Excl domestic tourism and nra; (5.1) Nights in hotels only. Incl domestic tourism and nra; (7.1,7.2) Hotels only; (7.3) Rooms rented; (8.1) Hotel revenues. Incl domestic tourism and nra.

Basic Indicators	Units	Code	1996	1997	1998	1999	2000
INBOUND TOURISM							
Arrivals							
Visitors	Thousands	(1.1)	25,163	25,515	25,745	25,394	25,209
Tourists (overnight visitors)	Thousands	(1.2)	..	..	..	..	..
Same-day visitors	Thousands	(1.3)	2,430	2,520	2,240	2,053	1,996
Cruise passengers	Thousands	(1.4)	..	..	..	..	..
Arrivals by region							
Africa	Thousands	(2.1)	510	525	570	588	618
Americas	Thousands	(2.2)	4,017	4,509	5,053	5,000	5,287
Europe	Thousands	(2.3)	17,856	17,644	17,581	17,046	16,307
East Asia and the Pacific	Thousands	(2.4)	2,166	2,155	1,872	2,062	2,256
South Asia	Thousands	(2.5)	238	269	264	291	314
Middle East	Thousands	(2.6)	376	413	404	409	429
Arrivals by mode of transport							
Air	Thousands	(3.1)	16,279	16,858	17,479	17,284	17,831
Rail	Thousands	(3.2)	..	..	..	..	..
Road	Thousands	(3.3)	2,719	2,922	3,168	3,117	3,080
Sea	Thousands	(3.4)	6,165	5,734	5,098	4,993	4,298
Arrivals by purpose of visit							
Leisure, recreation and holidays	Thousands	(4.1)	10,987	10,803	10,475	9,826	9,302
Business and professional	Thousands	(4.2)	6,095	6,347	7,589	7,762	8,008
Other	Thousands	(4.3)	8,080	8,365	7,681	7,806	7,899
Overnight stays and length of stay							
Overnight stays in H&S	Thousand nights	(5.1)	..	..	..	..	..
Overnight stays in CE	Thousand nights	(5.2)	219,764	222,527	230,777	211,735	203,759
ALS of non resident tourists	Nights	(5.5)	8.70	8.70	9.00	8.30	8.08
Tourism expenditure							
in the country of reference	US$ Million	(8.1)	19,173	20,039	20,978	20,223	19,544
DOMESTIC TOURISM							
Overnight stays							
Overnight stays in H&S	Thousand nights	(5.3)	..	..	..	..	..
Overnight stays in CE	Thousand nights	(5.4)	454,600	473,600	438,000	540,445	..
OUTBOUND TOURISM							
Departures	Thousands	(6.1)	42,050	45,957	50,872	53,881	56,837
Tourism expenditure in other countries	US$ Million	(8.2)	25,309	27,710	32,267	35,631	36,267
TOURISM ACTIVITIES							
Hotels and similar establishments							
Number of rooms	H&S	(7.1)	..	..	..	..	..
Number of bed-places	H&S	(7.2)	1,040,677	1,072,762	..	..	..
Occupancy rate	Percent	(7.3)	..	44.00	44.00	..	..
Average length of stay	Nights	(5.6)	..	..	..	..	..
ECONOMIC AGGREGATES							
Gross National Product (GNP)	US$ Million	(9.1)	1,186,427	1,269,498	1,325,306	1,403,871	1,463,474
Exports (F.O.B.)	US$ Million	(9.2)	262,130	281,083	271,851	268,254	281,550
Imports (C.I.F.)	US$ Million	(9.3)	287,472	306,592	314,036	317,969	334,366

Abbreviations used in tables and notes:
H&S: Hotels and similar establishments; **CE:** All types of tourism accommodation establishments; **ALS:** Average length of stay; **THS:** Non-resident tourists staying in H&S; **TCE:** Non-resident tourists staying in CE; **TF:** Arrivals of international (or non-resident) tourists; **VF:** Arrivals of international (or non-resident) visitors; **NHS:** Overnight stays at H&S; **NCE:** Overnight stays at CE.

..	data not available
incl	including
excl	excluding
nra	nationals residing abroad

Notes:
(1.1-4.3) VF, departures; (3.3) Tunnel; (5.5) Days; (7.2) Hotels; (7.3) Bed-places (England only).

UNITED REPUBLIC OF TANZANIA

Basic Indicators	Units	Code	1996	1997	1998	1999	2000
INBOUND TOURISM							
Arrivals							
Visitors	Thousands	(1.1)	326	360	482	627	501
Tourists (overnight visitors)	Thousands	(1.2)	315	347	450	564	459
Same-day visitors	Thousands	(1.3)	11	13	32	63	42
Cruise passengers	Thousands	(1.4)	..	..	..	..	..
Arrivals by region							
Africa	Thousands	(2.1)	136	151	202	262	210
Americas	Thousands	(2.2)	32	35	47	62	49
Europe	Thousands	(2.3)	97	107	143	186	149
East Asia and the Pacific	Thousands	(2.4)	25	27	37	48	38
South Asia	Thousands	(2.5)	16	18	24	31	25
Middle East	Thousands	(2.6)	20	22	29	38	30
Arrivals by mode of transport							
Air	Thousands	(3.1)	146	160	311	365	311
Rail	Thousands	(3.2)	9	14	11	36	20
Road	Thousands	(3.3)	149	151	152	220	155
Sea	Thousands	(3.4)	22	35	8	6	15
Arrivals by purpose of visit							
Leisure, recreation and holidays	Thousands	(4.1)	219	246	300	383	339
Business and professional	Thousands	(4.2)	65	81	128	133	130
Other	Thousands	(4.3)	42	33	54	111	32
Overnight stays and length of stay							
Overnight stays in H&S	Thousand nights	(5.1)	..	..	..	..	..
Overnight stays in CE	Thousand nights	(5.2)	880	1,479	2,534	1,695	1,957
ALS of non resident tourists	Nights	(5.5)	..	..	..	..	..
Tourism expenditure							
in the country of reference	US$ Million	(8.1)	322	392	570	733	739
DOMESTIC TOURISM							
Overnight stays							
Overnight stays in H&S	Thousand nights	(5.3)	..	..	..	..	..
Overnight stays in CE	Thousand nights	(5.4)	1,403	1,645	1,888	1,686	1,880
OUTBOUND TOURISM							
Departures	Thousands	(6.1)	148	..	..	..	..
Tourism expenditure in other countries	US$ Million	(8.2)	412	407	493	368	337
TOURISM ACTIVITIES							
Hotels and similar establishments							
Number of rooms	H&S	(7.1)	6,970	7,470	7,500	9,575	10,025
Number of bed-places	H&S	(7.2)	12,348	13,248	13,400	17,235	17,303
Occupancy rate	Percent	(7.3)	57.00	56.30	59.90	63.70	54.20
Average length of stay	Nights	(5.6)	7.30	7.50	7.60	7.70	8.00
ECONOMIC AGGREGATES							
Gross National Product (GNP)	US$ Million	(9.1)	5,644	6,587	7,592	8,515	9,266
Exports (F.O.B.)	US$ Million	(9.2)	783	752	589	543	663
Imports (C.I.F.)	US$ Million	(9.3)	1,386	1,336	1,453	1,550	1,523

Abbreviations used in tables and notes:
H&S: Hotels and similar establishments; **CE:** All types of tourism accommodation establishments; **ALS:** Average length of stay; **THS:** Non-resident tourists staying in H&S; **TCE:** Non-resident tourists staying in CE; **TF:** Arrivals of international (or non-resident) tourists; **VF:** Arrivals of international (or non-resident) visitors; **NHS:** Overnight stays at H&S; **NCE:** Overnight stays at CE.

..   data not available
incl   including
excl   excluding
nra   nationals residing abroad

Notes:
(8.2) International Monetary Fund; (9.1) Data for GNP cover mainland Tanzania only.

Basic Indicators	Units	Code	1996	1997	1998	1999	2000
INBOUND TOURISM							
Arrivals							
Visitors	Thousands	(1.1)	..	..	..	..	..
Tourists (overnight visitors)	Thousands	(1.2)	46,489	47,766	46,395	48,491	50,891
Same-day visitors	Thousands	(1.3)	..	..	..	..	..
Cruise passengers	Thousands	(1.4)	..	..	..	..	..
Arrivals by region							
Africa	Thousands	(2.1)	204	234	258	274	295
Americas	Thousands	(2.2)	27,948	28,155	27,513	28,747	30,010
Europe	Thousands	(2.3)	10,028	10,735	11,041	11,634	12,052
East Asia and the Pacific	Thousands	(2.4)	7,929	8,201	7,082	7,302	7,921
South Asia	Thousands	(2.5)	202	235	282	301	363
Middle East	Thousands	(2.6)	178	206	220	234	249
Arrivals by mode of transport							
Air	Thousands	(3.1)	27,558	29,402	29,018	30,222	..
Rail	Thousands	(3.2)	..	..	..	..	..
Road	Thousands	(3.3)	11,303	12,356	11,012	11,543	..
Sea	Thousands	(3.4)	432	453	461	454	..
Arrivals by purpose of visit							
Leisure, recreation and holidays	Thousands	(4.1)	19,722	22,354	22,342	23,207	..
Business and professional	Thousands	(4.2)	4,272	4,728	4,728	4,833	..
Other	Thousands	(4.3)	..	..	..	..	..
Overnight stays and length of stay							
Overnight stays in H&S	Thousand nights	(5.1)	..	..	..	..	..
Overnight stays in CE	Thousand nights	(5.2)	..	..	..	..	..
ALS of non resident tourists	Nights	(5.5)	..	..	..	..	..
Tourism expenditure							
in the country of reference	US$ Million	(8.1)	69,809	74,426	71,286	74,881	85,153
DOMESTIC TOURISM							
Overnight stays							
Overnight stays in H&S	Thousand nights	(5.3)	..	..	..	..	..
Overnight stays in CE	Thousand nights	(5.4)	..	..	..	..	..
OUTBOUND TOURISM							
Departures	Thousands	(6.1)	52,311	52,944	56,287	58,386	..
Tourism expenditure in other countries	US$ Million	(8.2)	48,048	52,051	56,509	59,351	65,044
TOURISM ACTIVITIES							
Hotels and similar establishments							
Number of rooms	H&S	(7.1)	..	..	..	..	..
Number of bed-places	H&S	(7.2)	..	..	..	..	..
Occupancy rate	Percent	(7.3)	..	..	..	..	..
Average length of stay	Nights	(5.6)	..	..	..	..	..
ECONOMIC AGGREGATES							
Gross National Product (GNP)	US$ Million	(9.1)	7,830,157	8,179,517	8,446,141	8,880,152	9,645,556
Exports (F.O.B.)	US$ Million	(9.2)	625,073	688,696	682,138	702,098	781,125
Imports (C.I.F.)	US$ Million	(9.3)	822,025	899,019	944,353	1,059,430	1,257,640

Abbreviations used in tables and notes:
H&S: Hotels and similar establishments; **CE:** All types of tourism accommodation establishments; **ALS:** Average length of stay; **THS:** Non-resident tourists staying in H&S; **TCE:** Non-resident tourists staying in CE; **TF:** Arrivals of international (or non-resident) tourists; **VF:** Arrivals of international (or non-resident) visitors; **NHS:** Overnight stays at H&S; **NCE:** Overnight stays at CE.

.. data not available
incl including
excl excluding
nra nationals residing abroad

Notes:
(1.2,2.2) Incl Mexicans staying one or more nights in the US; (3.1-3.4,4.1,4.2) Does not incl the total of Mexicans but only those travelling beyond the 40km border zone; (3.3) Land; (3.4) Incl arrivals at the Great Lake ports and Puget Sound (Washington State); (4.1,4.2) By visa type. Canada data excl; (6.1) Incl Americans staying one or more nights in Mexico.

UNITED STATES VIRGIN ISLANDS

Basic Indicators	Units	Code	1996	1997	1998	1999	2000
INBOUND TOURISM							
Arrivals							
Visitors	Thousands	(1.1)	1,779	2,128	2,139	1,964	2,478
Tourists (overnight visitors)	Thousands	(1.2)	373	411	422	484	607
Same-day visitors	Thousands	(1.3)	90	116	101	77	102
Cruise passengers	Thousands	(1.4)	1,316	1,619	1,616	1,404	1,768
Arrivals by region							
Africa	Thousands	(2.1)	..	..	1	..	..
Americas	Thousands	(2.2)	213	361	453	452	436
Europe	Thousands	(2.3)	12	15	15	19	10
East Asia and the Pacific	Thousands	(2.4)	..	1	1	1	1
South Asia	Thousands	(2.5)	..	..	..	..	..
Middle East	Thousands	(2.6)	..	..	..	..	..
Arrivals by mode of transport							
Air	Thousands	(3.1)	462	509	523	560	709
Rail	Thousands	(3.2)	..	..	..	..	..
Road	Thousands	(3.3)	..	..	..	..	..
Sea	Thousands	(3.4)	1,316	1,619	1,616	1,404	1,768
Arrivals by purpose of visit							
Leisure, recreation and holidays	Thousands	(4.1)	71	..	..	..	..
Business and professional	Thousands	(4.2)	17	..	..	..	..
Other	Thousands	(4.3)	12	..	..	..	..
Overnight stays and length of stay							
Overnight stays in H&S	Thousand nights	(5.1)	..	..	..	..	..
Overnight stays in CE	Thousand nights	(5.2)	711	829	914	966	1,061
ALS of non resident tourists	Nights	(5.5)	..	..	..	..	..
Tourism expenditure							
in the country of reference	US$ Million	(8.1)	781	894	940	955	1,157
DOMESTIC TOURISM							
Overnight stays							
Overnight stays in H&S	Thousand nights	(5.3)	..	..	..	..	..
Overnight stays in CE	Thousand nights	(5.4)	..	..	..	..	..
OUTBOUND TOURISM							
Departures	Thousands	(6.1)	..	..	..	..	..
Tourism expenditure in other countries	US$ Million	(8.2)	..	..	..	..	..
TOURISM ACTIVITIES							
Hotels and similar establishments							
Number of rooms	H&S	(7.1)	4,087	4,406	4,929	4,849	4,997
Number of bed-places	H&S	(7.2)	..	..	..	..	..
Occupancy rate	Percent	(7.3)	51.60	53.30	52.50	55.70	58.60
Average length of stay	Nights	(5.6)	4.40	4.20	4.40	4.40	4.50
ECONOMIC AGGREGATES							
Gross National Product (GNP)	US$ Million	(9.1)	..	..	..	..	..
Exports (F.O.B.)	US$ Million	(9.2)	3,652	3,454	2,640	3,198	..
Imports (C.I.F.)	US$ Million	(9.3)	3,595	3,826	..	..	..

Abbreviations used in tables and notes:
H&S: Hotels and similar establishments; **CE:** All types of tourism accommodation establishments; **ALS:** Average length of stay; **THS:** Non-resident tourists staying in H&S; **TCE:** Non-resident tourists staying in CE; **TF:** Arrivals of international (or non-resident) tourists; **VF:** Arrivals of international (or non-resident) visitors; **NHS:** Overnight stays at H&S; **NCE:** Overnight stays at CE.

..	data not available
incl	including
excl	excluding
nra	nationals residing abroad

Notes:
(2.2,2.3) THS; (3.1) Visitor air arrivals excl resident arrivals and inter-island traffic but incl same-day visitors; (3.4) Cruise passengers; (5.2) Room nights incl domestic tourist nights (about 40% of total); (7.1,7.3) Hotel units and condominium or villa units; (7.3) Rooms.

Basic Indicators	Units	Code	1996	1997	1998	1999	2000
INBOUND TOURISM							
Arrivals							
Visitors	Thousands	(1.1)	2,258	2,463	2,324	2,273	2,236
Tourists (overnight visitors)	Thousands	(1.2)	2,152	2,316	2,163	2,073	1,968
Same-day visitors	Thousands	(1.3)	106	147	161	200	268
Cruise passengers	Thousands	(1.4)	..	..	..	..	..
Arrivals by region							
Africa	Thousands	(2.1)	..	..	..	..	..
Americas	Thousands	(2.2)	1,750	1,889	1,810	1,760	1,758
Europe	Thousands	(2.3)	60	84	96	86	85
East Asia and the Pacific	Thousands	(2.4)	..	..	..	..	7
South Asia	Thousands	(2.5)	..	..	..	..	..
Middle East	Thousands	(2.6)	..	..	..	..	..
Arrivals by mode of transport							
Air	Thousands	(3.1)	466	436	429	402	377
Rail	Thousands	(3.2)	..	..	..	..	..
Road	Thousands	(3.3)	877	922	938	962	841
Sea	Thousands	(3.4)	916	1,105	956	909	1,018
Arrivals by purpose of visit							
Leisure, recreation and holidays	Thousands	(4.1)	1,406	1,481	1,469	1,390	1,344
Business and professional	Thousands	(4.2)	171	155	127	117	109
Other	Thousands	(4.3)	681	826	728	766	783
Overnight stays and length of stay							
Overnight stays in H&S	Thousand nights	(5.1)	2,291	2,888	2,509	2,566	2,577
Overnight stays in CE	Thousand nights	(5.2)	3,914	4,250	3,478	3,488	3,314
ALS of non resident tourists	Nights	(5.5)	7.80	7.50	7.10	..	6.90
Tourism expenditure							
in the country of reference	US$ Million	(8.1)	717	759	695	653	652
DOMESTIC TOURISM							
Overnight stays							
Overnight stays in H&S	Thousand nights	(5.3)	..	..	..	..	..
Overnight stays in CE	Thousand nights	(5.4)	..	..	..	..	..
OUTBOUND TOURISM							
Departures	Thousands	(6.1)	..	562	654	778	667
Tourism expenditure in other countries	US$ Million	(8.2)	192	264	265	280	281
TOURISM ACTIVITIES							
Hotels and similar establishments							
Number of rooms	H&S	(7.1)	14,411	14,957	15,535	14,047	..
Number of bed-places	H&S	(7.2)	34,541	36,140	37,902	36,460	..
Occupancy rate	Percent	(7.3)	..	..	..	..	..
Average length of stay	Nights	(5.6)	..	..	7.10	..	4.43
ECONOMIC AGGREGATES							
Gross National Product (GNP)	US$ Million	(9.1)	19,155	20,890	21,532	20,663	20,307
Exports (F.O.B.)	US$ Million	(9.2)	2,397	2,726	2,771	2,237	2,295
Imports (C.I.F.)	US$ Million	(9.3)	3,323	3,727	3,811	3,357	3,466

Abbreviations used in tables and notes:
H&S: Hotels and similar establishments; **CE:** All types of tourism accommodation establishments; **ALS:** Average length of stay; **THS:** Non-resident tourists staying in H&S; **TCE:** Non-resident tourists staying in CE; **TF:** Arrivals of international (or non-resident) tourists; **VF:** Arrivals of international (or non-resident) visitors; **NHS:** Overnight stays at H&S; **NCE:** Overnight stays at CE.

..   data not available
incl   including
excl   excluding
nra   nationals residing abroad

Notes:
(1.1,4.1-4.3) Incl nra; (2.2-3.4) Excl nra; (3.3) Incl rail; (5.5) Days.

UZBEKISTAN

Basic Indicators	Units	Code	1996	1997	1998	1999	2000
INBOUND TOURISM							
Arrivals							
Visitors	Thousands	(1.1)	..	..	..	..	..
Tourists (overnight visitors)	Thousands	(1.2)	174	253	272	..	..
Same-day visitors	Thousands	(1.3)	..	..	..	..	..
Cruise passengers	Thousands	(1.4)	..	..	..	..	..
Arrivals by region							
Africa	Thousands	(2.1)	..	..	..	..	..
Americas	Thousands	(2.2)	..	..	30	..	..
Europe	Thousands	(2.3)	..	..	140	..	..
East Asia and the Pacific	Thousands	(2.4)	..	..	53	..	..
South Asia	Thousands	(2.5)	..	..	11	..	..
Middle East	Thousands	(2.6)	..	..	38	..	..
Arrivals by mode of transport							
Air	Thousands	(3.1)	168	232	250	..	..
Rail	Thousands	(3.2)	5	20	21	..	..
Road	Thousands	(3.3)	1	1	1	..	..
Sea	Thousands	(3.4)	..	..	..	..	..
Arrivals by purpose of visit							
Leisure, recreation and holidays	Thousands	(4.1)	..	..	188	..	..
Business and professional	Thousands	(4.2)	..	..	63	..	..
Other	Thousands	(4.3)	..	..	21	..	..
Overnight stays and length of stay							
Overnight stays in H&S	Thousand nights	(5.1)	..	..	..	..	..
Overnight stays in CE	Thousand nights	(5.2)	1,503	2,307	1,748	..	..
ALS of non resident tourists	Nights	(5.5)	..	..	..	..	..
Tourism expenditure							
in the country of reference	US$ Million	(8.1)	15	19	..	..	..
DOMESTIC TOURISM							
Overnight stays							
Overnight stays in H&S	Thousand nights	(5.3)	..	..	..	..	..
Overnight stays in CE	Thousand nights	(5.4)	1,126	1,857	1,240	..	..
OUTBOUND TOURISM							
Departures	Thousands	(6.1)	..	..	..	..	..
Tourism expenditure in other countries	US$ Million	(8.2)	..	..	..	..	..
TOURISM ACTIVITIES							
Hotels and similar establishments							
Number of rooms	H&S	(7.1)	..	..	..	..	..
Number of bed-places	H&S	(7.2)	..	..	..	..	..
Occupancy rate	Percent	(7.3)	35.70	44.80	..	..	..
Average length of stay	Nights	(5.6)	..	..	..	..	..
ECONOMIC AGGREGATES							
Gross National Product (GNP)	US$ Million	(9.1)	14,383	12,707	14,434	15,649	15,235
Exports (F.O.B.)	US$ Million	(9.2)	4,590	4,388	3,528	..	..
Imports (C.I.F.)	US$ Million	(9.3)	4,721	4,523	3,289	..	..

Abbreviations used in tables and notes:
H&S: Hotels and similar establishments; **CE:** All types of tourism accommodation establishments; **ALS:** Average length of stay; **THS:** Non-resident tourists staying in H&S; **TCE:** Non-resident tourists staying in CE; **TF:** Arrivals of international (or non-resident) tourists; **VF:** Arrivals of international (or non-resident) visitors; **NHS:** Overnight stays at H&S; **NCE:** Overnight stays at CE.

..   data not available
incl   including
excl   excluding
nra   nationals residing abroad

Basic Indicators	Units	Code	1996	1997	1998	1999	2000
INBOUND TOURISM							
Arrivals							
Visitors	Thousands	(1.1)	103	81	78	97	106
Tourists (overnight visitors)	Thousands	(1.2)	46	50	52	51	58
Same-day visitors	Thousands	(1.3)	1	1	1	1	1
Cruise passengers	Thousands	(1.4)	56	30	25	45	47
Arrivals by region							
Africa	Thousands	(2.1)	..	..	..	..	..
Americas	Thousands	(2.2)	1	1	1	1	2
Europe	Thousands	(2.3)	3	3	2	3	3
East Asia and the Pacific	Thousands	(2.4)	42	44	48	45	52
South Asia	Thousands	(2.5)	..	..	..	..	..
Middle East	Thousands	(2.6)	..	..	..	..	..
Arrivals by mode of transport							
Air	Thousands	(3.1)	45	49	51	50	57
Rail	Thousands	(3.2)	..	..	..	..	..
Road	Thousands	(3.3)	..	..	..	..	..
Sea	Thousands	(3.4)	57	32	27	47	49
Arrivals by purpose of visit							
Leisure, recreation and holidays	Thousands	(4.1)	34	36	39	38	45
Business and professional	Thousands	(4.2)	6	6	6	6	6
Other	Thousands	(4.3)	6	8	7	7	7
Overnight stays and length of stay							
Overnight stays in H&S	Thousand nights	(5.1)	..	..	465	343	..
Overnight stays in CE	Thousand nights	(5.2)	..	..	..	..	..
ALS of non resident tourists	Nights	(5.5)	9.10	8.80	8.20	7.20	7.60
Tourism expenditure in the country of reference	US$ Million	(8.1)	50	46	52	56	58
DOMESTIC TOURISM							
Overnight stays							
Overnight stays in H&S	Thousand nights	(5.3)	..	..	..	..	..
Overnight stays in CE	Thousand nights	(5.4)	..	..	..	..	..
OUTBOUND TOURISM							
Departures	Thousands	(6.1)	..	..	..	..	..
Tourism expenditure in other countries	US$ Million	(8.2)	5	5	8	9	9
TOURISM ACTIVITIES							
Hotels and similar establishments							
Number of rooms	H&S	(7.1)	717	717	663	..	1,060
Number of bed-places	H&S	(7.2)	..	..	..	..	2,911
Occupancy rate	Percent	(7.3)	50.70	55.30	59.10	51.90	52.00
Average length of stay	Nights	(5.6)	..	..	..	..	6.90
ECONOMIC AGGREGATES							
Gross National Product (GNP)	US$ Million	(9.1)	229	238	239	227	228
Exports (F.O.B.)	US$ Million	(9.2)	30	35	34	26	26
Imports (C.I.F.)	US$ Million	(9.3)	97	94	88	96	89

Abbreviations used in tables and notes:
H&S: Hotels and similar establishments; **CE:** All types of tourism accommodation establishments; **ALS:** Average length of stay; **THS:** Non-resident tourists staying in H&S; **TCE:** Non-resident tourists staying in CE; **TF:** Arrivals of international (or non-resident) tourists; **VF:** Arrivals of international (or non-resident) visitors; **NHS:** Overnight stays at H&S; **NCE:** Overnight stays at CE.

.. data not available
incl including
excl excluding
nra nationals residing abroad

Notes:
(3.4) Incl cruise passengers; (5.5) Days; (7.3) Rooms in Greater Vila.

VENEZUELA

Basic Indicators	Units	Code	1996	1997	1998	1999	2000
INBOUND TOURISM							
Arrivals							
Visitors	Thousands	(1.1)	960	933	813	702	604
Tourists (overnight visitors)	Thousands	(1.2)	759	814	685	587	469
Same-day visitors	Thousands	(1.3)	201	119	128	115	135
Cruise passengers	Thousands	(1.4)	..	..	..	..	..
Arrivals by region							
Africa	Thousands	(2.1)	1	1	3	1	..
Americas	Thousands	(2.2)	424	453	366	296	172
Europe	Thousands	(2.3)	323	344	302	277	288
East Asia and the Pacific	Thousands	(2.4)	7	7	9	5	3
South Asia	Thousands	(2.5)	1	1	1	1	..
Middle East	Thousands	(2.6)	1	2	1	1	1
Arrivals by mode of transport							
Air	Thousands	(3.1)	665	714	682	584	455
Rail	Thousands	(3.2)	..	..	..	..	..
Road	Thousands	(3.3)	90	97	..	..	6
Sea	Thousands	(3.4)	3	3	3	3	8
Arrivals by purpose of visit							
Leisure, recreation and holidays	Thousands	(4.1)	362	348	245	215	123
Business and professional	Thousands	(4.2)	313	356	302	275	249
Other	Thousands	(4.3)	84	110	138	97	97
Overnight stays and length of stay							
Overnight stays in H&S	Thousand nights	(5.1)	9,956	9,440	7,949	5,571	5,338
Overnight stays in CE	Thousand nights	(5.2)	14,407	14,487	12,821	9,126	8,456
ALS of non resident tourists	Nights	(5.5)	18.00	18.00	18.00	13.00	14.00
Tourism expenditure							
in the country of reference	US$ Million	(8.1)	944	1,086	961	673	563
DOMESTIC TOURISM							
Overnight stays							
Overnight stays in H&S	Thousand nights	(5.3)	..	..	..	..	..
Overnight stays in CE	Thousand nights	(5.4)	..	..	..	..	..
OUTBOUND TOURISM							
Departures	Thousands	(6.1)	511	460	752	754	954
Tourism expenditure in other countries	US$ Million	(8.2)	2,251	2,381	2,451	1,646	1,824
TOURISM ACTIVITIES							
Hotels and similar establishments							
Number of rooms	H&S	(7.1)	67,210	71,737	73,813	75,356	76,016
Number of bed-places	H&S	(7.2)	143,693	154,547	159,075	163,120	164,698
Occupancy rate	Percent	(7.3)	..	..	58.20	..	..
Average length of stay	Nights	(5.6)	..	10.00	10.00	7.00	7.00
ECONOMIC AGGREGATES							
Gross National Product (GNP)	US$ Million	(9.1)	69,423	80,174	82,262	88,518	104,075
Exports (F.O.B.)	US$ Million	(9.2)	23,053	21,073	17,175	20,880	31,738
Imports (C.I.F.)	US$ Million	(9.3)	9,794	14,577	15,749	13,835	16,142

Abbreviations used in tables and notes:
H&S: Hotels and similar establishments; **CE:** All types of tourism accommodation establishments; **ALS:** Average length of stay; **THS:** Non-resident tourists staying in H&S; **TCE:** Non-resident tourists staying in CE; **TF:** Arrivals of international (or non-resident) tourists; **VF:** Arrivals of international (or non-resident) visitors; **NHS:** Overnight stays at H&S; **NCE:** Overnight stays at CE.

..   data not available
incl   including
excl   excluding
nra   nationals residing abroad

Notes:
(1.2,2.1-4.3) TF.

VIET NAM

Basic Indicators	Units	Code	1996	1997	1998	1999	2000
INBOUND TOURISM							
Arrivals							
Visitors	Thousands	(1.1)	1,607	1,716	1,520	1,782	2,140
Tourists (overnight visitors)	Thousands	(1.2)	975	1,114	978	1,211	1,383
Same-day visitors	Thousands	(1.3)	470	471	385	383	501
Cruise passengers	Thousands	(1.4)	162	131	157	188	256
Arrivals by region							
Africa	Thousands	(2.1)	..	1	..	5	2
Americas	Thousands	(2.2)	..	176	..	244	242
Europe	Thousands	(2.3)	..	219	..	242	271
East Asia and the Pacific	Thousands	(2.4)	..	1,034	..	1,059	1,399
South Asia	Thousands	(2.5)	..	6	..	6	7
Middle East	Thousands	(2.6)	..	..	..	..	..
Arrivals by mode of transport							
Air	Thousands	(3.1)	940	1,034	874	1,022	1,113
Rail	Thousands	(3.2)	..	..	..	..	..
Road	Thousands	(3.3)	505	550	489	572	771
Sea	Thousands	(3.4)	162	131	157	188	256
Arrivals by purpose of visit							
Leisure, recreation and holidays	Thousands	(4.1)	662	691	599	838	1,139
Business and professional	Thousands	(4.2)	365	403	292	266	420
Other	Thousands	(4.3)	580	622	629	678	581
Overnight stays and length of stay							
Overnight stays in H&S	Thousand nights	(5.1)	4,157	4,642	4,104	4,816	6,307
Overnight stays in CE	Thousand nights	(5.2)	..	..	..	..	..
ALS of non resident tourists	Nights	(5.5)	4.50	4.50	5.60	5.60	6.00
Tourism expenditure in the country of reference	US$ Million	(8.1)	..	..	..	..	..
DOMESTIC TOURISM							
Overnight stays							
Overnight stays in H&S	Thousand nights	(5.3)	9,885	13,085	14,784	17,096	17,920
Overnight stays in CE	Thousand nights	(5.4)	..	..	..	..	..
OUTBOUND TOURISM							
Departures	Thousands	(6.1)	..	..	..	..	..
Tourism expenditure in other countries	US$ Million	(8.2)	..	..	..	..	..
TOURISM ACTIVITIES							
Hotels and similar establishments							
Number of rooms	H&S	(7.1)	55,600	56,000	60,300	63,580	66,700
Number of bed-places	H&S	(7.2)	107,944	106,421	113,670	116,300	120,800
Occupancy rate	Percent	(7.3)	43.10	43.00	42.70	45.20	50.10
Average length of stay	Nights	(5.6)	2.40	2.20	2.20	2.40	2.40
ECONOMIC AGGREGATES							
Gross National Product (GNP)	US$ Million	(9.1)	21,509	25,799	27,157	28,742	30,692
Exports (F.O.B.)	US$ Million	(9.2)	7,256	9,185	9,360	11,541	..
Imports (C.I.F.)	US$ Million	(9.3)	11,144	11,592	11,500	11,742	..

Abbreviations used in tables and notes:
H&S: Hotels and similar establishments; **CE:** All types of tourism accommodation establishments; **ALS:** Average length of stay; **THS:** Non-resident tourists staying in H&S; **TCE:** Non-resident tourists staying in CE; **TF:** Arrivals of international (or non-resident) tourists; **VF:** Arrivals of international (or non-resident) visitors; **NHS:** Overnight stays at H&S; **NCE:** Overnight stays at CE.

.. data not available
incl including
excl excluding
nra nationals residing abroad

Notes:
(1.1) Incl nra; (1.4,3.4) Incl cruise and sea passengers; (2.1-4.3) VF; (5.6) Non resident tourists. Domestic tourists: 96=1.36; 97=1.54; 98=1.54; 99=1.60; 2000=1.60.

YEMEN

Basic Indicators	Units	Code	1996	1997	1998	1999	2000
INBOUND TOURISM							
Arrivals							
Visitors	Thousands	(1.1)	..	..	..	..	..
Tourists (overnight visitors)	Thousands	(1.2)	74	80	88	58	73
Same-day visitors	Thousands	(1.3)	..	..	..	..	..
Cruise passengers	Thousands	(1.4)	..	..	..	..	..
Arrivals by region							
Africa	Thousands	(2.1)	2	2	3	4	6
Americas	Thousands	(2.2)	3	5	5	7	8
Europe	Thousands	(2.3)	49	51	54	22	25
East Asia and the Pacific	Thousands	(2.4)	5	8	7	5	9
South Asia	Thousands	(2.5)	..	..	..	..	..
Middle East	Thousands	(2.6)	15	15	18	20	25
Arrivals by mode of transport							
Air	Thousands	(3.1)	..	..	..	..	..
Rail	Thousands	(3.2)	..	..	..	..	..
Road	Thousands	(3.3)	..	..	..	..	..
Sea	Thousands	(3.4)	..	..	..	..	..
Arrivals by purpose of visit							
Leisure, recreation and holidays	Thousands	(4.1)	..	..	..	..	..
Business and professional	Thousands	(4.2)	..	..	..	..	..
Other	Thousands	(4.3)	..	..	..	..	..
Overnight stays and length of stay							
Overnight stays in H&S	Thousand nights	(5.1)	373	483	526	379	473
Overnight stays in CE	Thousand nights	(5.2)	..	..	..	..	..
ALS of non resident tourists	Nights	(5.5)	5.00	5.70	5.97	6.46	6.50
Tourism expenditure							
in the country of reference	US$ Million	(8.1)	56	70	84	61	76
DOMESTIC TOURISM							
Overnight stays							
Overnight stays in H&S	Thousand nights	(5.3)	..	..	..	..	1,170
Overnight stays in CE	Thousand nights	(5.4)	..	..	..	..	..
OUTBOUND TOURISM							
Departures	Thousands	(6.1)	..	..	..	..	..
Tourism expenditure in other countries	US$ Million	(8.2)	78	124	130	136	..
TOURISM ACTIVITIES							
Hotels and similar establishments							
Number of rooms	H&S	(7.1)	6,977	7,697	8,799	9,745	10,440
Number of bed-places	H&S	(7.2)	15,005	16,402	18,595	20,918	26,010
Occupancy rate	Percent	(7.3)	60.00	60.00	..	..	..
Average length of stay	Nights	(5.6)	..	..	..	..	..
ECONOMIC AGGREGATES							
Gross National Product (GNP)	US$ Million	(9.1)	4,127	5,046	5,989	6,088	6,674
Exports (F.O.B.)	US$ Million	(9.2)	3,206	2,509	1,501	2,438	4,078
Imports (C.I.F.)	US$ Million	(9.3)	2,442	2,017	2,172	2,006	2,326

Abbreviations used in tables and notes:
H&S: Hotels and similar establishments; **CE:** All types of tourism accommodation establishments; **ALS:** Average length of stay; **THS:** Non-resident tourists staying in H&S; **TCE:** Non-resident tourists staying in CE; **TF:** Arrivals of international (or non-resident) tourists; **VF:** Arrivals of international (or non-resident) visitors; **NHS:** Overnight stays at H&S; **NCE:** Overnight stays at CE.

..   data not available
incl   including
excl   excluding
nra   nationals residing abroad

Notes:
(1.2,2.1-2.6) THS; (7.3) Bed-places; (8.2) International Monetary Fund.

Basic Indicators	Units	Code	1996	1997	1998	1999	2000
INBOUND TOURISM							
Arrivals							
Visitors	Thousands	(1.1)	..	..	..	..	..
Tourists (overnight visitors)	Thousands	(1.2)	301	298	283	152	239
Same-day visitors	Thousands	(1.3)	..	..	..	..	..
Cruise passengers	Thousands	(1.4)	..	..	..	..	..
Arrivals by region							
Africa	Thousands	(2.1)	..	..	..	..	..
Americas	Thousands	(2.2)	6	6	10	3	4
Europe	Thousands	(2.3)	285	280	259	141	222
East Asia and the Pacific	Thousands	(2.4)	2	2	2	2	2
South Asia	Thousands	(2.5)	..	..	..	..	..
Middle East	Thousands	(2.6)	..	..	..	..	..
Arrivals by mode of transport							
Air	Thousands	(3.1)	..	..	..	..	..
Rail	Thousands	(3.2)	..	..	..	..	..
Road	Thousands	(3.3)	..	..	..	..	..
Sea	Thousands	(3.4)	..	..	..	..	..
Arrivals by purpose of visit							
Leisure, recreation and holidays	Thousands	(4.1)	..	..	..	..	..
Business and professional	Thousands	(4.2)	..	..	..	..	..
Other	Thousands	(4.3)	..	..	..	..	..
Overnight stays and length of stay							
Overnight stays in H&S	Thousand nights	(5.1)	872	825	833	410	716
Overnight stays in CE	Thousand nights	(5.2)	1,099	1,044	990	498	865
ALS of non resident tourists	Nights	(5.5)	..	..	..	..	..
Tourism expenditure in the country of reference	US$ Million	(8.1)	43	41	35	17	26
DOMESTIC TOURISM							
Overnight stays							
Overnight stays in H&S	Thousand nights	(5.3)	5,943	5,752	6,003	3,983	5,513
Overnight stays in CE	Thousand nights	(5.4)	11,150	11,038	11,515	7,004	10,008
OUTBOUND TOURISM							
Departures	Thousands	(6.1)	..	..	..	..	..
Tourism expenditure in other countries	US$ Million	(8.2)	..	..	..	..	..
TOURISM ACTIVITIES							
Hotels and similar establishments							
Number of rooms	H&S	(7.1)	37,841	38,013	38,290	36,182	37,371
Number of bed-places	H&S	(7.2)	79,180	79,902	80,579	76,897	78,608
Occupancy rate	Percent	(7.3)	23.57	22.53	23.21	14.89	21.70
Average length of stay	Nights	(5.6)	4.29	4.30	4.28	4.31	3.61
ECONOMIC AGGREGATES							
Gross National Product (GNP)	US$ Million	(9.1)	..	..	..	..	..
Exports (F.O.B.)	US$ Million	(9.2)	1,842	2,368	2,604	..	..
Imports (C.I.F.)	US$ Million	(9.3)	4,102	4,799	4,622	..	..

Abbreviations used in tables and notes:
H&S: Hotels and similar establishments; **CE:** All types of tourism accommodation establishments; **ALS:** Average length of stay; **THS:** Non-resident tourists staying in H&S; **TCE:** Non-resident tourists staying in CE; **TF:** Arrivals of international (or non-resident) tourists; **VF:** Arrivals of international (or non-resident) visitors; **NHS:** Overnight stays at H&S; **NCE:** Overnight stays at CE.

..   data not available
incl   including
excl   excluding
nra   nationals residing abroad

Notes:
(1.2,2.2-2.4) TCE, incl rented private rooms, houses and flats; (7.1,7.2) As of 31st August of each year; (7.2) Permanent bed-places; (7.3) Bed-places.

ZAMBIA

Basic Indicators	Units	Code	1996	1997	1998	1999	2000
INBOUND TOURISM							
Arrivals							
Visitors	Thousands	(1.1)	..	..	..	..	
Tourists (overnight visitors)	Thousands	(1.2)	264	341	362	404	457
Same-day visitors	Thousands	(1.3)	..	..	..	..	..
Cruise passengers	Thousands	(1.4)	..	..	..	..	..
Arrivals by region							
Africa	Thousands	(2.1)	187	204	260	302	294
Americas	Thousands	(2.2)	12	28	15	15	27
Europe	Thousands	(2.3)	44	71	67	67	105
East Asia and the Pacific	Thousands	(2.4)	16	34	17	17	28
South Asia	Thousands	(2.5)	5	3	2	2	2
Middle East	Thousands	(2.6)	..	..	..	..	..
Arrivals by mode of transport							
Air	Thousands	(3.1)	31	36	42	46	..
Rail	Thousands	(3.2)	8	8	16	22	..
Road	Thousands	(3.3)	225	297	304	388	..
Sea	Thousands	(3.4)	..	..	..	..	..
Arrivals by purpose of visit							
Leisure, recreation and holidays	Thousands	(4.1)	52	90	95	112	123
Business and professional	Thousands	(4.2)	109	140	166	184	201
Other	Thousands	(4.3)	103	111	100	108	133
Overnight stays and length of stay							
Overnight stays in H&S	Thousand nights	(5.1)	..	..	2,301	2,646	..
Overnight stays in CE	Thousand nights	(5.2)	..	..	2,820	3,046	..
ALS of non resident tourists	Nights	(5.5)	10.00	9.00	8.00	8.00	..
Tourism expenditure							
in the country of reference	US$ Million	(8.1)	60	75	75	85	..
DOMESTIC TOURISM							
Overnight stays							
Overnight stays in H&S	Thousand nights	(5.3)	..	..	..	..	..
Overnight stays in CE	Thousand nights	(5.4)	..	..	..	..	..
OUTBOUND TOURISM							
Departures	Thousands	(6.1)	..	..	..	..	..
Tourism expenditure in other countries	US$ Million	(8.2)	..	..	..	..	..
TOURISM ACTIVITIES							
Hotels and similar establishments							
Number of rooms	H&S	(7.1)	4,069	4,203	4,335	..	..
Number of bed-places	H&S	(7.2)	6,737	7,348	7,424	..	..
Occupancy rate	Percent	(7.3)	48.45	49.40	40.30	46.00	..
Average length of stay	Nights	(5.6)	..	..	..	..	..
ECONOMIC AGGREGATES							
Gross National Product (GNP)	US$ Million	(9.1)	3,360	3,530	3,154	3,186	3,004
Exports (F.O.B.)	US$ Million	(9.2)	1,049	914	..	..	..
Imports (C.I.F.)	US$ Million	(9.3)	836	819	..	..	..

Abbreviations used in tables and notes:
H&S: Hotels and similar establishments; **CE:** All types of tourism accommodation establishments; **ALS:** Average length of stay; **THS:** Non-resident tourists staying in H&S; **TCE:** Non-resident tourists staying in CE; **TF:** Arrivals of international (or non-resident) tourists; **VF:** Arrivals of international (or non-resident) visitors; **NHS:** Overnight stays at H&S; **NCE:** Overnight stays at CE.

..   data not available
incl   including
excl   excluding
nra   nationals residing abroad

Notes:
(3.4) River or lake; (5.5) Days; (7.3) Rooms.

Basic Indicators	Units	Code	1996	1997	1998	1999	2000
INBOUND TOURISM							
Arrivals							
Visitors	Thousands	(1.1)	1,597	1,336	2,090	2,250	1,967
Tourists (overnight visitors)	Thousands	(1.2)	1,577	1,281	1,986	2,101	1,868
Same-day visitors	Thousands	(1.3)	20	55	104	149	99
Cruise passengers	Thousands	(1.4)	..	..	..	..	..
Arrivals by region							
Africa	Thousands	(2.1)	1,242	935	1,486	1,508	1,404
Americas	Thousands	(2.2)	48	62	119	115	116
Europe	Thousands	(2.3)	230	228	302	377	269
East Asia and the Pacific	Thousands	(2.4)	57	56	79	100	79
South Asia	Thousands	(2.5)	..	..	..	..	..
Middle East	Thousands	(2.6)	..	..	..	..	..
Arrivals by mode of transport							
Air	Thousands	(3.1)	..	..	324	504	463
Rail	Thousands	(3.2)	..	..	49	86	108
Road	Thousands	(3.3)	..	..	1,714	1,660	1,396
Sea	Thousands	(3.4)	..	..	..	..	..
Arrivals by purpose of visit							
Leisure, recreation and holidays	Thousands	(4.1)	1,411	1,076	1,828	1,763	1,614
Business and professional	Thousands	(4.2)	186	260	262	487	352
Other	Thousands	(4.3)	..	..	..	..	..
Overnight stays and length of stay							
Overnight stays in H&S	Thousand nights	(5.1)	1,684	2,857	..	..	..
Overnight stays in CE	Thousand nights	(5.2)	7,769	..	..	..	..
ALS of non resident tourists	Nights	(5.5)	4.50	5.20	3.40	..	..
Tourism expenditure							
in the country of reference	US$ Million	(8.1)	232	205	158	202	125
DOMESTIC TOURISM							
Overnight stays							
Overnight stays in H&S	Thousand nights	(5.3)	..	..	..	..	..
Overnight stays in CE	Thousand nights	(5.4)	..	..	..	..	..
OUTBOUND TOURISM							
Departures	Thousands	(6.1)	69	123	213	331	..
Tourism expenditure in other countries	US$ Million	(8.2)	118	120	131	..	..
TOURISM ACTIVITIES							
Hotels and similar establishments							
Number of rooms	H&S	(7.1)	4,422	4,545	4,932	5,069	5,206
Number of bed-places	H&S	(7.2)	8,661	9,241	9,462	8,646	9,427
Occupancy rate	Percent	(7.3)	50.30	52.00	49.00	42.00	29.00
Average length of stay	Nights	(5.6)	..	..	..	..	..
ECONOMIC AGGREGATES							
Gross National Product (GNP)	US$ Million	(9.1)	7,994	8,202	7,511	6,348	5,801
Exports (F.O.B.)	US$ Million	(9.2)	2,397	2,508	1,864	..	..
Imports (C.I.F.)	US$ Million	(9.3)	2,817	3,092	2,701	..	..

Abbreviations used in tables and notes:
H&S: Hotels and similar establishments; **CE:** All types of tourism accommodation establishments; **ALS:** Average length of stay; **THS:** Non-resident tourists staying in H&S; **TCE:** Non-resident tourists staying in CE; **TF:** Arrivals of international (or non-resident) tourists; **VF:** Arrivals of international (or non-resident) visitors; **NHS:** Overnight stays at H&S; **NCE:** Overnight stays at CE.

.. data not available
incl including
excl excluding
nra nationals residing abroad

Notes:
(2.1-2.4) TF; (3.1-3.3,4.1,4.2) VF; (7.1,7.2) Graded hotels only; (7.3) Bed-places.

ANNEXES

BASIC METHODOLOGICAL REFERENCES

INBOUND TOURISM

Arrivals

When a person visits the same country several times a year, an equal number of arrivals is recorded. Likewise, if a person visits several countries during the course of a single trip, his/her arrival in each country is recorded separately. Consequently, *arrivals* cannot be assumed to be equal to the number of persons travelling.

Arrivals associated to inbound tourism correspond to those arrivals by *international (or non-resident) visitors* within the economic territory of the country of reference.

International visitors include:

(a) *Tourists (overnight visitors)*: "a visitor who stays at least one night in a collective or private accommodation in the country visited";

(b) *Same-day visitors*: "a visitor who does not spend the night in a collective or private accommodation in the country visited".

Data on arrivals may be obtained from different sources. In some cases data are obtained from border statistics derived from administrative records (police, immigration, traffic and other type of controls applied at national borders), and eventually, completed by means of border statistical surveys. In other cases, data are obtained from different types of tourism accommodation establishments (hotels and similar establishments and/or all types of tourism accommodation establishments).

Unless otherwise stated, basic indicators (1.1) on visitors correspond to the aggregation of basic indicators (1.2) and (1.3). In principle, basic indicators (1.3) should include basic indicators (1.4). However, in this publication, data on basic indicators (1.4) have been shown separately and are generally not included in basic indicators (1.3).

Arrivals by region

The aggregate of basic indicators (2.1) to (2.6) does not always correspond to the total of the basic indicators (1.1) or (1.2), due to the exclusion of "nationals residing abroad (nra)", and of "arrivals from other countries of the world".

Overnight stays and length of stay

Figures on *overnight stays* refer to the number of nights spent by non-resident tourists in hotels and similar establishments, or in all types of tourism accommodation establishments. If one person travels to a country and spends five nights there, that makes five tourist overnight stays.

ALS of non-resident tourists refers to the average length of trips of non-resident tourists in the country of reference.

Expenditure in the country of reference

Tourism expenditure data are obtained from the item "Travel receipts" of the Balance of Payments of each country and corresponds to the "expenditure of non-resident visitors (tourists and same-day visitors)" within the economic territory of the country of reference.

OUTBOUND TOURISM

Departures associated to outbound tourism correspond to the departures of resident visitors outside the economic territory of the country of reference.

Tourism expenditure data in other countries are obtained from the item "Travel expenditure" of the Balance of Payments of each country and corresponds to the "expenditure of resident visitors (tourists and same-day visitors)" outside the economic territory of the country of reference.

TOURISM ACTIVITIES

Hotels and similar establishments

The number of *rooms* and *bed-places* refers to the corresponding total capacity in this type of tourism accommodation establishments.

Occupancy rate: Relationship between available capacity and the extent to which it is used. This rate may refer either to use of rooms or of beds. Occupancy rate is based on the number of overnight stays of both resident and non-resident tourists.

Average length of stay refers to the average number of nights spent by tourists (overnight visitors) in all types of tourism accommodation establishments. This covers generally both resident and non-resident overnight stays.

**For additional references, visit
http://www.world-Tourism.org**

NOTES RELATIVES AUX INDICATEURS DE BASE

AFRIQUE DU SUD

(1.1,3.1-4.2) Excl nre; (7.1,7.2) Hôtels seulement; (7.3) Chambres (hôtels); (8.1,8.2) Fonds monétaire international.
Note: Afrique du Sud, incl des Républiques du Transkei, Bophuthatswana, Venda et Ciskei.

ALBANIE

(1.2,2.2-2.6,4.1-4.3) Arrivées dans les hôtels seulement; (3.1-3.4) VF; (8.1,8.2) Fonds Monétaire International.

ALGERIE

(1.1) Y compris les nationaux résidant à l'étranger; (2.1-2.6) A l'exclusion des nationaux résidant à l'étranger.

ALLEMAGNE

1.2,2.1-2.6) TEC; (5.6) Tourisme récepteur HA; DMS tourisme intérieur (nuitées): 96=3,36; 97=3,15; 98=3,09; 99=3,07; 2000=3.05; (7.3) Places-lit HA; (8.1,8.2) Y compris les transactions commerciales de marchandises aux frontières et les achats des travailleurs frontaliers à l'entrée et a la sortie du pays.

ANGOLA

(8.2) Fonds Monétaire International.

ANGUILLA

(1.1,3.1-4.2) VF; (1.2,2.2-2.3) TF, excl nre; (7.1) Hôtels, pensions de famille, appartements/ villas; (7.3) Chambres; (9.1) PIB.

ANTIGUA-ET-BARBUDA

(1.2) Arrivées par mer et voie aérienne, excl nre; (1.4) Incl arrivées en bateaux de croisière, "windjammer" et yachts; (4.1-4.3) Arrivées par voie aérienne; (6.1) Voyages à, l'étranger y compris départs de residents.

ARGENTINE

(1.2) Excl nre; (7.1/96) Données se rapportent aux hôtels de une à cinq étoiles et aux hôtels non classés.
Note: Les arrivées et les recettes économiques du tourisme international récepteur constituent une nouvelle série de 1990 à 1999. Source: données publiées par le Sous-secrétariat de Programmation Macro-économique du Ministère de l'économie et Travaux et Services Publics.

ARMENIE

(1.2,2.2-2.6) TEC.

ARUBA

(1.2,2.2-4.3) TF; (5.5) THA; (7.3) Chambres; (9.1) PIB.

AUSTRALIE

(1.1) Excl nre et membres des équipages; (5.5) Commercial; (5.6) Tourisme récepteur dans l'hébergement commercial; (7.1-7.3) Hôtels, motels et pensions de famille avec 15 chambres ou plus; (7.3) Chambres.

AUTRICHE

(1.2-2.6) TEC; (5.1,5.3/96/97) Hôtels seulement; (5.1,5.3/98/99) Incl villages de vacances; (5.2,5.4) Excl hébergement privé; (8.1,8.2) Incl transport international.

AZERBAIDJAN

(8.1,8.2) Fonds Monétaire International.

BAHAMAS

(1.2,2.2-2.4,4.1-4.3) TF; (5.2) Nuitées dans toutes formes d'hébergement commercial; (7.1,7.2) Hôtels, appartements, bungalows et villas - Etablissements homologués uniquement; (7.3) Chambres; (8.2) Fonds Monétaire International.

BAHREIN

(1.1,2.1-4.3) VF, Excl. nre; (3.3) Arrivées à travers le King Fahad Causeway; (5.1,7.1,7.2) Hôtels homologués seulement; (8.1,8.2) Fonds Monétaire International.

BARBADE

(1.2,2.2-4.3) TF; (7.1-7.2) Hôtels, hôtels-appartements, appartements et bungalows, pensions de famille; (7.3) Chambres; (8.2) Fonds Monétaire International.

BELARUS

(8.1,8.2) Fonds Monétaire International.

BOTSWANA

(8.1,8.2/96-99) Fonds Monétaire International.

BELGIQUE

(1.2,2.1-2.4,4.1-4.3) TEC; (6.1/96) Voyages de vacances de 4 nuitées et plus; (6.1/97) Voyages pour vacances et affaires; (8.1,8.2) Fonds Monétaire International; Belgique et Luxembourg.

BRESIL

(3.4) Incl arrivées par voie fluviale; (5.5) Jours; (7.1,7.2/96) Hôtels, hôtels- résidence, hôtels de villégiature et auberges de l'Etat ("pousadas") classés par EMBRATUR; (7.1,7.2/97) Hôtels homologués et non-homologués; (8.1) Données tirées de l'enquête par sondage réalisée par EMBRATUR.
Note 1998: Changement de méthodologie.

BELIZE

(1.1,2.2-4.3) VF; (1.3,4.3) Passagers en transit et passages aux frontières; (2.2) Incl passages aux frontières et résidents de retour de voyage; (2.4) Chine.

BULGARIE

(1.1,1.2/98-2000) A l'exclusion d'enfants sans passeports personnels; (3.4) Mer et voies d'eau intérieures; (5.1-5.6,7.2,7.3) Couvre principalement l'ancien hébergement du secteur public et celui propriété de l'Etat. Une partie considérable du secteur privé (plus du 70 pour cent en 1998) n'est pas inclus dans ces données; (7.2) Hôtels uniquement; (7.3) Places-lit dans les hôtels; (8.1,8.2/98-2000) Nouvelle méthodologie élaborée para la Banque Centrale de la Bulgarie et le Ministère de l'Economie.

BENIN

(1.2) THA. 1998: Estimations.

BURKINA FASO

(1.2,2.1-2.4) THA; (4.1-4.3) Y compris tourisme interne; (7.3) Chambres.

BERMUDES

(1.1) Excl nre; (1.2,2.2,2.3,4.1-4.3) Arrivées par voie aérienne; (5.2) Incl nuitées dans les résidences particulières; (7.3) Chambres; (9.1) PIB.

BURUNDI

(1.2,2.1-2.4,3.1-4.3) TF, incl nre; (3.4) Arrivées par voie lacustre; (5.6) Jours; (7.1,7.2) Hôtels; (8.1,8.2) Fonds Monétaire International.

BOLIVIE

(1.2-4.3) Données tirées d'enquêtes. A partir de l'an 2000 une nouvelle enquête a été appliquée; (1.2-4.3,8.1,8.2/99/2000) Données provisoires; (3.4) Arrivées par voie lacustre; (5.1,5.3,7.1,7.2) Capitales de Département seulement; (5.6) Jours, HA, tourisme récepteur; (7.3) Places-lit (hôtels).

CAMBODGE

(1.2/96/97) Arrivées par voie aérienne; (1.2/98-2000) Arrivées de touristes internationaux par tous moyens de transport; (1.3) Temple "Preah Vihear"; (2.2-2.6,4.1-4.3) Arrivées par voie aérienne; (3.3) Arrivées par terre ou par navier; (4.1/98,2000) Incl arrivées à l'aéroport de Siem Reap en vols directs; 1998: 10.423; 2000: 87.012; (5.5) Jours; (8.2) Fonds Monétaire International.

BONAIRE

8.1/2000) Le total des dépenses est obtenu à partir d'un nouveau taux de dépense par jour estimé en 2001. Ce chiffre est largement utilisé par le Département de l'Economie.

CAMEROUN

(1.2,2.1-2.6) THA.

BOSNIE-HERZEGOVINE

(8.1/96) Recettes touristiques: Mai-décembre 1996.

CANADA

(1.1,1.3) Données élaborées à partir des inventaires douaniers et ajustées en fonction des résultats d'enquêtes; (1.2,2.1-4.3) TF; (4.2) Incl congrès; (5.6) Tourisme récepteur; (6.1) Voyages- personnes (une/plusieurs nuits); (8.1,8.2) Incl frais médicaux, d'éducation et des membres des équipages. Excl transport international.
Note: Le "Statistics Canada's Tourism Program" utilise deux méthodes pour le rassemblement de statistiques concernant les voyageurs internationaux: le comptage aux frontières et les questionnaires de retour (caractéristiques). Cependant, suite à des différences méthodologiques, ces deux sources donnent lieu à des estimations différentes dans le nombre de visiteurs étrangers de la journée qui entrent au Canada par voie aérienne commerciale ou par bateau.

CAP-VERT

(1.2) Arrivées par voie aérienne; (5.5) Jours; (8.2) Fonds Monétaire International.

CHINE

(1.1,3.1-3.4) Incl arrivées de personnes d'origine ethnique chinoise en provenance de HK, Macao, Taïwan et chinois de l'étranger (1996= 44.383.182; 1997= 50.159.917; 1998= 56.370.654; 1999= 64.363.298; 2000= 73.283.449), la plupart visiteurs de la journée (excursionnistes) en provenance de HK et de Macao; (2.1-2.6) Excl arrivées de personnes d'origine chinoise de souche en provenance de HK, Macao, Taïwan et chinois de l'étranger; (5.6) Tourisme récepteur uniquement; (6.1/98-2000) Incl membres des équipages et autres membres des forces armées; (7.3) Chambres.

CHYPRE

(1.2,2.1-2.6) TF; (1.3) Incl passagers en croisière/transit; (3.4) Incl. passagers en croisière; (7.3) Places-lit.

COLOMBIE

(7.3) Chambres.
Source: "Departamento Administrativo de Seguridad (DAS), Banco de la República, COTELCO".

COMORES

(1.2,2.1-2.4,4.1-4.3) Arrivées par voie aérienne.

CONGO

(1.2-2.3) THA; (7.3) Chambres.

COREE, REPUBLIQUE DE

(1.1) Y compris nre et, à partir de juin 1988, également membres des équipages; (2.1-2.6) Excl nre; (3.1,3.4) Excl nre et membres des équipages; (7.1) Hôtels seulement; (7.3) Chambres; (8.1,8.2) Excl dépenses des étudiants qui font des études à l'étranger.

COSTA RICA

(4.1) Voyages d'agrément et visites aux parents; (5.5) Dans la zone centrale du pays; (7.3) Etablissements de catégorie "5 étoiles" dans la zone métropolitaine de San José (enquête).

COTE D'IVOIRE

(1.2,2.1-3.1,4.1-4.3) Arrivées par voie aérienne à l'aéroport international FHB de Port-Bouet. Les arrivées aux frontières terrestres, à l'aéroport de Bouaké, ainsi qu'à l'aéroport Air Ivoire d'Abidjan ne sont pas prises en compte; (1.2/97/98) Arrivées par voie aérienne à l'aéroport international FHB de Port-Bouet et arrivées aux frontières terrestres; (5.1,5.3) Hôtels; (7.3) Chambres; (8.1,8.2) Fonds Monétaire International.
1998: Données préliminaires.

CROATIE

(1.2,2.2-2.6) TEC, incl arrivées dans des ports à tourisme nautique; (3.1-3.4) VF; (5.2,5.4) Incl nuitées dans des ports à tourisme nautique; (5.6) Tourisme intérieur (interne et récepteur) dans l'ensemble des moyens d'hébergement (incl ports à tourisme nautique).

CUBA

(1.1,2.1-2.4) VF; (1.2,4.1-4.3) Arrivées par voie aérienne; (1.3) Incl passagers en croisière; (5.1,5.3,7.1,7.2) Hôtels, motels et apart-hôtels; (5.2,5.4) Hôtels, motels, apart-hôtels, terrains de camping/caravaning et autres; (6.1) Comprend seulement circuits contrôlés par l'Instituto de Turismo; (7.3) Chambres.

CURAÇAO

(1.2,2.2,2.3,3.1,4.1-4.3) Arrivées par voie aérienne; Incl nre; (3.4) Arrivées de passagers en croisière; (7.1) Hôtels, pensions de famille, appartements; (7.3) Chambres.

DANEMARK

(1.2,2.2-2.4) TEC; (7.1,7.2) Incl logements pour vacances; (7.3) Places-lit; (8.2) Incl les dépenses au titre des transports internationaux.

DOMINIQUE

(1.2,2.2-2.3,4.1-4.3) TF; (3.1-3.4) VF, excl des passagers en croisière; (7.1) Hôtels, pensions de famille, appartements et bungalows.

EGYPTE

(1.1,2.1-3.4) VF; (4.1-4.3) TF; (5.3) Hôtels seulement dans les principales régions: le Caire, Giza, le Sud du Sinaï, la Mer Rouge, Luxor, Aswan, Alexandrie; (6.1) Voyages à des fins de tourisme et de non-tourisme (plus de 50 % des départs ont lieu pour des motifs de travail); (7.3) Chambres.

EL SALVADOR

(1.2) Excl nre; (7.3) Places-lit; (8.2) Fonds Monétaire International.

NOTES RELATIVES AUX INDICATEURS DE BASE

EMIRATS ARABES UNIS

(1.2) Arrivées dans les hôtels seulement. Incl tourisme interne et nre; (2.1-2.6) Arrivées dans les hôtels seulement. Excl tourisme interne et nre; (5.1) Nuitées dans les hôtels seulement. Incl tourisme interne et nre; (7.1,7.2) Hôtels seulement; (7.3) Chambres louées; (8.1) Recettes des hôtels. Incl tourisme interne et nre.

FEDERATION DE RUSSIE

(7.1,7.2) Hébergement dans les hôtels et autres établissements touristiques.

EQUATEUR

(1.1) Excl nre.

FIDJI

(1.2,2.2-2.4,4.1-4.3) TF, excl nre; (3.4) Incl. les passagers en croisière; (5.6) Jours; (7.3) Chambres; (8.2) Fonds Monétaire International.

ERYTHREE

(1.1) Incl. nre; (2.1-2.6) Excl. nre.

FINLANDE

(1.1,3.1-3.4,4.1-4.3) VF, Enquête aux frontières; (1.2/96/97) TCE; (1.2/98-2000) TF, nouvelle série; (2.1-2.6) VF; (5.1,5.3,7.1,7.2) Hôtels et etablissements assimilés; (5.2,5.4) Etablissements collectifs touristiques; (6.1) Voyages à l'etranger; (7.3) Chambres (hôtels seulement); (8.1,8.2) Données rassemblées au moyen d'enquêtes aux voyageurs.

ESPAGNE

(1.1) VF, incl nre; (2.2-4.3) TF, incl nre; (2.4) Japon seulement; (5.1,5.3) Nuitées dans les hôtels et les "hostales" (établissements d'hébergement offrant des services limités); (5.2,5.4/96-99) Nuitées dans les hôtels, "hostales" et terrains de camping; (5.2,5.4/2000) Nuitées dans les hôtels, "hostales", terrains de camping et appartements touristiques; (7.1,7.2) Hôtels et "hostales" seulement; (7.3) Paces-lit.

FRANCE

(1.1-4.3/96/97) Enquêtes aux frontières; (1.1-4.3/98-2000) Estimation; (2.4) Incl Asie du Sud; (5.1,5.3,7.1-7.3) Hôtels uniquement; (5.2,5.4) Tous modes d'hébergement; (5.4) Série révisée et rétropolée; (5.5) DMS récepteur; (7.3) Taux net des chambres; (8.1,8.2) A partir de 1999 nouvelle série hors travailleurs frontaliers payés en devise (cf. 5ème édition du manuel du Fonds Monétaire International).

ESTONIE

(1.1,2.2-4.3) VF; (4.3) Achats, transit, visites à des amis.

GABON

(1.2,2.1-2.6,3.1,4.1-4.3) TF, arrivées à l'aéroport de Libreville. Note: 1996-1998: Estimations.

ETATS-UNIS

(1.2,2.2) Incl Mexicains passant 1 nuit ou plus aux EU; (3.1-3.4,4.1,4.2) Incl seulement les Mexicains voyageant 40 km au-delà de la frontière; (3.3) Terrestre; (3.4) Incl arrivées aux ports des Grands Lacs et à Puget Sound; (4.1,4.2) Par type de visa. Excl données Canada; (6.1) Incl Américains passant une nuit ou plus au Mexique.

GAMBIE

(1.2,2.1-2.3,3.1) Arrivées en vols à la demande seulement.

ETHIOPIE

(1.2,2.1-2.6,3.1,4.1-4.3/96-99) Arrivées à l'aéroport de Bole seulement; (1.2,2.1-2.6,3.1-3.3,4.1-4.3/2000) Arrivées à travers tous les ports d'entrée ; (1.2) Incl nre; (5.6) Années fiscales éthiopiennes; (7.1,7.2/97,2000) Incl. hôtels privés et de l'état; (7.3) Places-lit; (8.1/96-99) Incl recettes services hôteliers, opérateurs touristiques et agences de voyages, ventes hors-taxe, cadeaux et souvenirs; excl: recettes en devises du rapport de la Banque Nationale d'Ethiopie et revenus du secteur privé ; (8.1/2000) Comporte une estimation de toutes les recettes du secteur; (8.2) Fonds Monétaire International.

GEORGIE

(8.2) Fonds Monétaire International.

NOTES RELATIVES AUX INDICATEURS DE BASE

GHANA

(1.2) Incl nre; (2.1-2.6) Excl nre; (8.1,8.2) Fonds Monétaire International.

GUYANE

(7.1) Hôtels seulement.

GRECE

(1.1,3.1-4.3) VF; (1.2,2.1-2.6) Données tirées d'enquêtes; (3.4) Incl passagers en croisière; (8.1,8.2/98/99) Y compris les enregistrements à travers de nouvelles méthodologies; (8.1,8.2/2000) Fonds Monétaire International.

HAITI

(7.1) Hôtels, hôtels au bord de la plage et pensions de famille.

GRENADE

(1.2,2.2-4.3) TF; (7.1,7.2) Hôtels, bungalows/appartements et pensions de famille; (7.3) Chambres.

HAWAII (EU)

(4.1) Voyages de plaisir/distraction; (4.2) Convention, réunions corp., voyages de stimulation, autres voyages d'affaires, missions gouvernementales, études; (4.3) Y compris visites a des parents et amis; (5.2,5.5) Jours.

GUADELOUPE

(1.2) THA; (2.2,2.3,5.1/96-99) HA, arrivées et nuitées dans 21 établissements hôteliers; (2.2,2.3,5.1/2000) HA, arrivées et nuitées dans 83 établissements hôteliers; (7.1) Hôtels; (7.3) Chambres.

HONDURAS

(1.1,2.2-4.3) VF; (5.5) Jours; (8.2) Fonds Monétaire International.

GUAM

(1.2) Arrivées par voies aérienne et maritime; (2.2) Incl Hawaï; (7.3) Année fiscale au 30 septembre (valeur pondérée); (9.1) PIB.

HONG-KONG, CHINE

(1.4) Passagers en croisière (incl dans VF); (6.1) Excl résid. de HK voyageant à Macao et Chine; (7.1) Hôtels (tarifs élevés/moyens) et auberges/ pensions de famille; (7.3) Chambres; (8.1) Incl recettes des membres des forces armées, équipages et passagers en transit. Note: A partir de 1996, les chiffres incluent les arrivées de non-macanais arrivant via "Macao, Chine".

GUATEMALA

(5.5) Jours; (8.2) Fonds Monétaire International.

HONGRIE

(1.1,2.1-2.6,3.1-3.4) VF, départs; (1.2,4.1-4.3) TF, départs, excl nre; (3.4) Voie fluviale; (5.2,5.4/96/97) Y compris service de chambres organisé chez l'habitant; (7.3) Chambres, juillet-juin; (8.2) Fonds Monétaire International.

GUINEE

(1.2,2.1-2.6,4.1-4.3) Arrivées par voie aérienne à l'aéroport de Conakry.

ILES CAIMANES

(1.2,2.2-2.4,4.1-4.3) Arrivées par voie aérienne; (5.5,5.6) Jours; (7.1,7.2) Hôtels et appartements; (7.3) Hôtels (chambres); (8.1) Incl dépenses des passagers en croisière; (9.1) PIB.

NOTES RELATIVES AUX INDICATEURS DE BASE

ILES COOK

(1.2,2.2-2.4,4.1-4.3) Arrivées par voies aérienne et maritime; (7.3) Chambres.

ILES MARIANNES DU NORD

(1.1,2.2-2.4) VF; (1.2) Arrivées par voie aérienne; (2.2) Incl Guam; (7.1) Couvre le 68 pour cent du nombre total de chambres recensées.

ILES MARSHALL

(1.2,2.2,2.4,4.1-4.3) Arrivées par voie aérienne; (5.5) Jours.

ILES SALOMON

(8.1,8.2) Fonds Monétaire International.

ILES TURQUES ET CAIQUES

(9.1) PIB.

ILES VIERGES AMERICAINES

(2.2,2.3) THA; (3.1) Arrivées de visiteurs par voie aérienne, excl arrivées de résidents et le trafic entre les îles, mais incl les visiteurs de la journée (excursionnistes); (3.4) G221 (5.2) Nuitées incl celles de touristes nationaux (environ 40 pour cent de l'ensemble); (7.1,7.3) Hôtels et condominiums ou villas; (7.3) Chambres.

ILES VIERGES BRITANNIQUES

(7.1) Hôtels et pensions de famille; (7.3) Chambres; (9.1) PIB.

INDE

(1.2,2.1-4.3) TF, excl nre; (4.1-4.3) Excl arrivées de nationaux du Pakistan et du Bangladesh; (6.1) Départs de nationaux seulement, pour tous motifs de visite; (7.1,7.2) Hôtels homologués; (7.3) Chambres.

INDONESIE

(5.5) Jours; (5.6,7.3) Hôtels homologués seulement; (7.1,7.2) Toutes formes d'hébergement commercial; (7.3) Chambres; (8.2) Fonds monétaire international.

IRAN, REPUBLIQUE ISLAMIQUE D'

(1.2,2.1-3.4) TF; (3.3) Incl chemin de fer; (7.1,7.2) Hôtels seulement, 21 mars - 20 mars; (7.3) Estimations (Places-lit).

IRLANDE

(1.2,2.3,3.3,4.1,4.3,5.5) Incl touristes en provenance de l'Irlande du Nord; (3.3) Incl rail; (5.1-5.4) Excl touristes en provenance de l'Irlande du Nord; (6.1) Incl visiteurs de la journée (excursionnistes); (7.3) Chambres, hôtels seulement; (8.2) Excl. transport payé aux compagnies de transport nationales.

ISRAEL

(1.1) VF, excl nre; (1.2,2.1-2.6,3.1-3.4,4.1-4.3) TF, excl nre; (3.3) Incl nouvelle entrée de touristes après une visite au Sinaï d'un maximum de 7 jours; (3.4) Incl membres marine E.U. en visite de courtoisie; (4.3) Incl visite à des parents et amis et pélerinages; (5.1) Hôtels de touristes et aparthôtels; (5.6) Tourisme récepteur dans hôtels touristiques; (7.3) Taux d'occupation/lits dans HA ouverts.

ITALIE

(1.1,2.1-3.4,4.1,4.2) VF, à l'exclusion des travailleurs saisonniers et frontaliers; (1.1-4.2,6.1,8.1,8.2) A partir de 1996 : nouveau système de collecte (enquête aux frontières de l'"Ufficio Italiano dei Cambi"); (1.2) TF, à l'exclusion des travailleurs saisonniers et frontaliers; (1.3) Incl passagers en croisière; (5.1) Hôtels seulement; (6.1) Nombre de touristes résidents (visiteurs qui passent la nuit) voyageant à l'étranger; (7.3) Places-lit.

JAMAHIRIYA ARABE LIBYENNE

(1.1,2.1-2.6) Y compris tous voyageurs (visiteurs et autres voyageurs non définis comme visiteurs par l'OMT); (5.1,5.2,5.4,7.3,8.2) Estimations.

JAMAIQUE

(1.2,2.1-2.4,3.1,4.1-4.3) TF, arrivées par voie aérienne, incl nre, carts E/D; (5.2) Données obtenues en multipliant la DMS par le nombre d'escales dans chacun des pays d'origine; (5.5) Durée de séjour prévue; (5.6) Nuitées dans les hôtels seulement; (7.3) Chambres; (8.2) Fonds monétaire international.

JAPON

(1.2,2.1-2.6,4.1-4.3) TF, excl nre; (3.1,3.4) VF, incl résidents étrangers au Japon; (5.5) Jours; (7.1) Hôtels homologués et non homologués, ainsi que "ryokans" (Auberges); (7.3) Taux d'occupation des principaux hôtels gouvernementaux homologués (chambres).

NOTES RELATIVES AUX INDICATEURS DE BASE

JORDANIE

(1.1,2.1-3.4) VF; (5.5) Circuits organisés seulement; (7.3) Chambres; (8.2)Incl paiements en éducation; (9.1) Transjordanie seulement.

L'EX-REP. YOUGOSLAVE DE MACEDOINE

(1.2,2.2-2.4) TEC; (3.1-3.3) VF.

KAZAKHSTAN

(2.2-2.6) VF; (8.1,8.2) Fonds Monétaire International.

LIBAN

(1.2) Excl ressortissants syriens; (8.1/99-2000) Du fait d'un manque de données sur les recettes du tourisme international concernant les statistiques sur le tourisme récepteur, le Département « Internet et Service Statistique du Ministère du Tourisme » considère qu'un touriste dépense en moyenne 1.000$EU.

KENYA

(1.1-4.3) VF, excl nre, arrivées à travers tous les postes frontière; (1.1,2.1-2.5) Les données représentent des estimations, dont la projection a été faite sur la base des taux de marché de l'année 1989; (2.5) Inde seulement; (5.6) Jours; (7.2) Hôtels seulement (excl hôtels non-homologués); (7.3) Places-lit; (8.1,8.2) Fonds Monétaire International.
Source: Enquête économique de diverses années.

LIECHTENSTEIN

(1.2,2.2-2.4) THA; (7.3) Places-lit.

KIRGHIZISTAN

(8.1,8.2) Fonds Monétaire International.

LITUANIE

(2.2-2.4) TEC; (2.4) Asie/Pacifique; (3.1-3.4) VF; (4.1-4.3) TF; (5.6) EC; (7.3) Chambres, hôtels seulement.

KIRIBATI

(1.2) Arrivées par voie aérienne, Tarawa et Ile Christmas; (4.1-4.3) TF.

LUXEMBOURG

(1.2,2.1-2.4) TEC incl auberges de jeunesse, hébergement touristique privé et autres; (5.1,5.3) Nuitées dans hôtels, auberges et pensions de famille; (5.2,5.4) Incl hébergement touristique privé et autres; (7.3) Chambres.

KOWEIT

(1.1,2.1-2.6,3.1-3.4) VF; (1.2,4.1-4.3) THA; (8.1,8.2) Fonds Monétaire International.

MACAO, CHINE

(1.1,2.1-4.3) VF; (1.1-1.3,2.4,3.1-3.4) Incl Chinois de souche provenant de Hong-Kong; (1.2,1.3) Estimations; (3.1) Incl arrivées en hélicoptère; (6.1) Circuits organisés; (7.1,7.2) Hôtels, pensions de famille et "pousadas" (auberges); (7.3) Chambres; (8.1) Incl recettes en provenance du jeu; (9.1) PIB.

LESOTHO

(1.1,2.1-4.3) VF; (7.1,7.2) Hôtels seulement; (8.1,8.2) Fonds Monétaire International.

MADAGASCAR

(1.2,2.1-2.4,3.1,4.1-4.3) TF. Arrivées par voie aérienne; (7.3) Chambres.

LETTONIE

(1.1,3.1-3.4) VF, arrivées de non-résidents aux frontières. Données provenant de la Police d'Etat aux frontières; (1.2-1.4,2.2-2.5,4.1-4.3,5.5) Départs des no-résidents; Enquête auprès des personnes qui traversent les frontières du pays; (1.3) Incl passagers en croisière; (7.3) Places-lit.

MALAISIE

(1.2,2.1-2.6) TF, départs de touristes étrangers; incl résidents de Singapour qui traversent la frontière par le Johore Causeway; (3.1-4.3) Péninsule de Malaisie seulement; (6.1) Déplacement des Malaysiens péninsulaires, incl départs par voie terrestre utilisant le Johore Causeway; (7.1) Hôtels avec 10 chambres et plus; (7.3) Chambres; (8.2) Fonds Monétaire International.

NOTES RELATIVES AUX INDICATEURS DE BASE

MALAWI

(1.2-4.3) Départs; (7.1) Incl pavillons; (7.3) Places-lit.
Note: Tous les chiffres de 1999 et 2000 sont provisoires.

MICRONESIE (ETATS FEDERES DE)

(1.2,2.2,2.4) Arrivées dans les États de Kosrae, Chuuk, Pohnpei et Yap.

MALDIVES

(1.2,2.1-2.6) Arrivées par voie aérienne; (5.1,5.6,7.1-7.3) Centres touristiques et hôtels; (5.6) Jours; (8.2) Fonds Monétaire International.

MONACO

(1.2-2.6) THA.

MALI

(1.2) Arrivées par voie aérienne; (2.1-2.4) THA; (7.3) Chambres; (8.1,8.2/96/97) Fonds Monétaire International.

MONGOLIA

(8.1,8.2) Fonds Monétaire International.

MALTE

(1.2-3.4/96-99) Départs; (1.2-3.4/2000) Arrivées; (7.2) Hôtels, complexes touristiques, pensions de famille et appartements de vacances; (7.3) Places-lit dans HA; (8.1,8.2/2000) Données provisoires.

MONTSERRAT

(1.2,2.2,2.3) TF; (1.3) Arrivées visiteurs de la journée (excursionnistes) par voie aérienne seulement; (2.2,2.3,4.1,4.2) TF, arrivées par voie aérienne seulement; (3.1,3.4) VF; (4.2) Affaires et autres motivations; (7.1) Hôtels et villas; (9.1) PIB.

MAROC

(1.2,3.1-4.3) TF, incl nre; (2.1-2.6) TF, excl nre; (5.1,5.3) Nuitées dans Hôtels homologués et non homologués, villages de vacances et résidences touristiques; (7.3) Chambres (hôtels homologués).

MYANMAR

(1.2,2.2-2.5,3.1) Arrivées à Yangon par voie aérienne; (4.1-4.3) VF; (5.1,5.3,5.6) HA gérés uniquement par l'Etat; (7.1,7.2) Hôtels gérés par l'Etat et pensions de famille privées homologuées; (7.3) Chambres; (8.2) Fonds Monétaire International.

MARTINIQUE

(1.2,2.2,2.3,4.1-4.3) TF; (7.1) Hôtels et villages de vacances (Club Méditerranée); (7.3) Chambres dans HA.

NAMIBIE

(2.1-2.3) TF; (3.1) Arrivées à l'aèroport de Windhoek; (4.1-4.3) TF; (7.3) Places-lit.

MAURICE

(1.1,4.1-4.3) VF; (1.2,2.1-3.4) TF; (5.5) Grands hôtels; (7.3) Chambres; (8.2) Fonds Monétaire International.

NEPAL

(1.2) Incl arrivées en provenance de l'Inde; (3.3) Voie terrestre; (7.1,7.2) Hôtels à Kathmandou et à l'intérieur du pay; (8.2) Fonds Monétaire International.

MEXIQUE

(1.2,2.2-4.3) TF, incl nre; (1.3) Incl visiteurs frange frontalière avec les EU avec séjour inférieur à 24 h; (3.3) Incl rail; (5.1) Sélection de centres touristiques; (5.1/2000) Chiffre préliminaire; (5.6) Tourisme étranger seulement; (7.3) Chambres; (8.1) Incl recettes passagers en croisière; (8.1,8.2) Incl recettes/ dépenses visiteurs frontaliers (séjours: <de 24h, 24-72h et plus).

NICARAGUA

(1.2,2.2-4.3) TF; (5.1,5.3) Principaux établissements d'hébergement dans l'ensemble du pays (7); (5.2,5.4) Total de établissements dans l'ensemble du pays; (5.6) EC, tourisme récepteur; DMS tourisme intérieur (nuitées): 96=1,7; 97=1,5; 98=1,8; 99=1,6; 2000=2,0; (7.1,7.2) HA classés en catégories supérieures.

NOTES RELATIVES AUX INDICATEURS DE BASE

NIGER

(1.2,4.1-4.3) Arrivées par voie aérienne (aéroport de Niamey); (5.5) Jours; (7.1,7.2) Hôtels, auberges et bungalows.

NIGERIA

(1.1,2.1-2.6) VF; (1.2,4.1-4.3) TF.

NIOUE

(1.2) Arrivées par voie aérienne; Incl nationaux résidant normalement en Nouvelle-Zélande.

NORVEGE

(1.2/96/97) THA dans hôtels homologués; (1.2,2.1-2.4/98-2000) TCE, nouvelle série; (5.1) Nuitées dans les établissements classés; (5.1,7.1,7.2) A partir de 1988, les chiffres de HA se réfèrent aux établissements de 20 places-lit et plus tout au long de l'année; (6.1) Uniquement charter pour voyage à forfait; (7.3) Places-lit.

NOUVELLE-CALEDONIE

(1.2,2.1-4.3) Incl nre; (5.6) Jours, hôtels à Nouméa; (6.1) A partir de 2000, il s'agit des retours des résidents; (7.1) Source: "Nouvelle-Calédonie Tourisme"; (7.3) Chambres à Nouméa; (8.1) Dépenses effectuées dans le pays d'accueil par les visiteurs internationaux, non compris les transports internationaux; (9.1) PIB.

NOUVELLE-ZELANDE

(1.1,3.1-4.3) VF, Incl nre; (2.1-2.6) VF, Excl nre; (5.2) Estimation réalisée à partir des nuitées (pourcentage moyen des nuitées du tourisme international en janvier, avril, juillet et octobre); (5.3) hôtels/motels classés; (6.1) Départs de résidents de la NZ de courte durée (année civile); (7.1) Hôtels seulement; (7.1,7.3) Les données se réfèrent à l'année civile, fournies à travers l'Enquête dans les moyens d'hébergement (commencée en juillet 1996).

OMAN

(1.2,2.1-2.6) THA; (7.3) Chambres; (8.1) Ventes hôtelières; (8.2) Fonds Monétaire International.

OUGANDA

(7.2) Hôtels seulement; (8.1,8.2) Fonds Monétaire International.

PAKISTAN

(5.5) Jours; (8.1) Banque de l'État du Pakistan.

PALAOS

(1.2,2.2-2.4,3.1) Arrivées par voie aérienne (aéroport international de Palau).

PANAMA

(1.1) VF, aéroport international de Tocúmen (AIT), frontière de Paso Canoa (FPC), Ports de Cristóbal et Balboa (PCB) et statistiques IPAT; (2.2-2.4) VF, AIT, FPC et statistiques IPAT; (3.1-3.4) TF, AIT, FPC, PCB et statistiques IPAT; Excl arrivées à d'autres ports d'entrées (non spécifiés) (000)= 97:19; 98:23; 99:20; 2000:28; (4.1-4.3) TF, AIT et statistiques IPAT; (5.1) Hôtels de Panama-City et statistiques IPAT; (7.1,7.2) Chambres/places-lit recensées pour le tourisme internl.; (7.3) Chambres.

PAPOUASIE-NOUVELLE-GUINEE

(8.2) Fonds Monétaire International.

PARAGUAY

(1.2,2.1-4.3) Excl nre et membres des équipages; (3.4) Voie fluviale; (7.3) Places-lit; (8.1,8.2) La Banque Centrale du Paraguay a modifié sa méthodologie de calcul des recettes et dépenses touristiques, car les chiffres correspondants étaient considérés surestimés. Les données relatives aux recettes et dépenses touristiques se réfèrent seulement aux dépenses réalisées par les touristes. Les dépenses des visiteurs de la journée (excursionnistes) ne sont pas compris dans la Balance des Paiements et, par conséquent, cette information n'a plus été incorporée.

PAYS-BAS

(1.2-2.4) TEC; (5.1,5.3) Hôtels et pensions; (6.1) Départs en vacances des ressortissants nationaux; (7.2) Hôtels; (7.3) Places-lit.

PEROU

(1.2) Avec passeport et sauf-conduit; (2.1-2.5,3.1-3.4,4.1-4.3) TF, avec passeport seulement; (3.4) Incl voie fluviale; (5.5) Avec passeport et sauf-conduit; (8.1,8.2) Fonds Monétaire International.

PHILIPPINES

(1.2,3.1-4.3) TF incl nre; (2.1-2.6) TF excl nre; (4.1-4.3) arrivées par voie aérienne; (5.6,7.3) Hôtels homologués région de Manille seulement; (6.1) Incl travailleurs sous contrat en provenance d'outre-mer; (7.1,7.2) Hôtels homologués seulement.

NOTES RELATIVES AUX INDICATEURS DE BASE

POLOGNE

(1.1,2.1-3.4) VF; (4.1-4.3) TF, d'après les enquêtes de l'Institut du tourisme; (5.1,5.3/96) Chambres louées; (5.6) EC; (6.1) Voyages du tourisme émetteur enregistrés aux frontières; (7.3) Chambres; (7.3/99) Chambres, hôtels seulement; (8.1,8.2) D'après les enquêtes et les estimations de l'Institut du tourisme.

POLYNESIE FRANÇAISE

(1.2,2.2-4.3) TF, excl nre; (1.2/2000) Estimation de la fréquentation touristique réalisée par l'Institut de la Statistique (ISPF); (5.5,5.6) Jours; (7.1,7.2) Hôtels seulement; Au 31 décembre de chaque année; (7.3) Chambres dans hôtels.

PORTO RICO

(1.2) TF, arrivées par voie aérienne (année fiscale: juillet- juin); (2.2) Incl Iles Vierg- Américain et Etats-Unis seulement; (7.1) Chambres classées par la "Compañía de Turismo" de Porto Rico; (7.3) Chambres; année fiscale (juillet- juin); incl chambres occupées par résidents de Porto Rico.

PORTUGAL

(1.1,3.1-3.4) VF; (1.2,2.1-2.4,4.1-4.3) TF, excl nre; incl arrivées à Madère et Açores; (1.4) Incl passagers voie maritime en transit; (5.2) Incl nuitées dans établissements d'hébergement à Madère/ Açores; (5.6) EC; (7.1,7.2) Hôtels, motels, auberges, pensions, "pousadas" (Juillet-juin); (7.3) Places-lit (hôtels homologués).

QATAR

(1.2) Arrivées dans les hôtels; (9.1) PIB.

REPUBLIQUE ARABE SYRIENNE

(1.1,2.1-3.4) VF, excl arrivées nre; (1.2/96/97) THA; (1.2/98-2000) TEC; (1.2,5.2/98) Changement de méthodologie; (7.3) Chambres; (8.1) Fonds Monétaire International.

REPUBLIQUE CENTRAFRICAINE

(1.2) Arrivées par voie aérienne.

REPUBLIQUE DE MOLDOVA

(1.1-6.1) Visiteurs qui ont bénéficié des services des agents économiques officiellement enregistrés avec le type d'activité tourisme et des unités d'hébergement qui leur appartiennent (à l'exception des régions de la partie gauche du Dniestr et de la municipalité de Bender).

REPUBLIQUE DEMOCRATIQUE DU CONGO

(1.2/96/97) Excl nre; (1.2,4.1-4.3/98) Incl nre; (1.2-4.3/98) Arrivées aux postes de "Ndjili" et "Beach"; (2.1-2.4) Excl nre; (7.1) Hôtels homologués.

REPUBLIQUE DEM. POPULAIRE LAO

(1.2) TF; (2.2-2.5,3.1,3.3,4.1-4.3) VF; (5.5) Jours.

REPUBLIQUE DOMINICAINE

(1.2) Arrivées par voie aérienne uniquement, incl nre; (1.4) Toutes les arrivées par voie maritime; (2.2-2.4) Départs par voie aérienne, excl nre; (2.4) Japon uniquement; (7.1,7.2) Hôtels; (7.3) Chambres.

REPUBLIQUE TCHEQUE

(1.1,3.1-3.3) VF; (1.2,2.1-2.4) TEC; (1.2,2.1-2.4,5.1-5.4/2000) Données préliminaires; (6.1) Séjours à l'étranger de visiteurs (touristes et visiteurs de la journée).

REPUBLIQUE-UNIE DE TANZANIE

(8.2) Fonds Monétaire International; (9.1) Les données du PNB se réfèrent seulement à la Tanzanie continentale.

REUNION

(2.1-2.5,4.1-4.3/96-98) Arrivées par voie aérienne; (5.5) Jours.

ROUMANIE

(1.1,2.1-2.6,3.1-4.3) VF; (4.1-4.3/99) A partir de 1999 les données relatives aux arrivées internationales par motif de visite ne sont plus recensées.

ROYAUME-UNI

(1.1-4.3) VF, départs; (3.3) Tunnel; (5.5) Jours; (7.2) Hôtels; (7.3) Places-lit (Angleterre seulement).

NOTES RELATIVES AUX INDICATEURS DE BASE

SABA

(1.3) Principalement de St. Martin; (7.1) Hôtels.

SAINT-EUSTACHE

(1.1) Arrivées par voies aérienne et maritime, incl nre.

SAINT-KITTS-ET-NEVIS

(1.2) TF. arrivées par voies aérienne et maritime; (1.4) Arrivées en yacht et en bateau de croisière; (2.2,2.3) TF, arrivées par voie aérienne.

SAINT-MARIN

(1.1) Incl visiteurs Italiens; (7.1,7.2) Hôtels seulement.

SAINT-MARTIN

(1.2,2.2,2.3) Par voie aérienne, incl les arrivées à Saint-Martin (côté français de l'île); (3.1) Arrivées à l'aéroport "Juliana" (incl visiteurs à destination de Saint-Martin côté français); (7.1,7.2) Hôtels, pensions de famille et appartements; (8.1) Estimations de la Banque Centrale, incl estimations pour Saba et Saint-Eustache.

SAINT-VINCENT-ET-LES-GRENADINES

(1.2,2.2-2.3,4.1-4.3) TF; (3.4) Incl passagers en croisière et en yacht; (7.1) Hôtels, appartements, bungalows, villas et pensions de famille.

SAINTE-LUCIE

(1.2,2.2,2.3,3.1,4.1-4.3) TF, excl nre; (3.4) Incl. passagers en croisière; (7.3) Chambres.

SAMOA

(8.2) Fonds Monétaire International.

SENEGAL

(1.2,2.1-2.6) THA; (5.2-5.4) Hôtels et villages de vacances; (5.6) HA; (7.3) Places-lit; (8.2) Fonds Monétaire International.

SEYCHELLES

(1.2,2.1-4.3) TF; (5.5) Chiffres des nuitées élaborés à partir des départs; (7.1,7.2) Hôtels et pensions de famille; (7.3) Places-lit.

SIERRA LEONE

(2.1) Afrique occidentale seulement; (2.2) Amérique du Nord seulement; (2.3) France et Royaume-Uni seulement; (7.1,7.2) Hôtels seulement; (7.1,7.2/96) Réduction drastique du nombre de chambres et de places-lit enregistrées comme conséquence de l'accroissement des hostilités qui ont conduit à la destruction d'un certain nombre d'hôtels et d'établissements assimilés.

SINGAPOUR

(1.1) Excl arrivées de Malaysiens par voie terrestre mais incl visiteurs de la journée (excursionnistes); (1.3) Passagers en transit et en croisière; (5.5,5.6) Jours; (7.1) Hôtels (homologués et non-homologués); (7.3) Chambres; hôtels homologués seulement.

SLOVAQUIE

(1.1) Incl arrivées en provenance de la Rép. Tchèque; (1.2,2.1-2.4) TEC; (5.5,5.6) Tourisme récepteur dans tous types d'établissements d'hébergement touristique; (6.1) Tourisme organisé à travers l'agence de voyages slovaque; (8.1,8.2) Estimations.

SLOVENIE

(1.1) Incl toutes catégories de voyageurs, quel que soit le motif de la visite; (1.2,2.1-2.6) TEC; (2.1,2.5,2.6) Estimations; (3.1-3.4,4.1-4.3) TCE, données provenant de l'enquête (été) auprès des touristes étrangers en Slovénie portant sur 3 années; (6.1) Enquête trimestrielle des voyages de la population residente; (8.1, 8.2) Source: Banque Centrale de Slovénie: les données se réfèrent au pòste "Voyages" de la Balance des Paiements.

SOUDAN

(1.2,2.1-2.6,3.1/98-2000) Arrivées à l'aéroport de Khartoum; (7.1,7.2) Hôtels, auberges et centres touristiques; (8.1,8.2) Fonds Monétaire International.

SRI LANKA

(1.2,2.1-4.3) TF, excl nre; (7.1,7.2) Hôtels, motels, auberges, pensions de famille et apart-hôtels; (7.3) Chambres.

NOTES RELATIVES AUX INDICATEURS DE BASE

SUEDE

(1.2) TEC, excl. camping; (5.1,5.3) Hôtels seulement; (7.3) Places-lit.

SUISSE

(1.1,1.2) Estimations; (1.3) Incl personnes en transit; (2.1-2.6) THA; (5.6) THA (touristes étrangers); (7.1,7.2) Hôtels, motels et auberges homologués; (7.3) Taux d'occupation nets (places-lit disponibles).

SURINAME

(1.2,2.2-2.4,3.1,4.1-4.3) Arrivées à l'aéroport de Zanderij; (2.3) Incl personnes originaires de Suriname en provenance de Hollande; (8.1,8.2) Fonds Monétaire International.

SWAZILAND

(1.2) Arrivées dans les hôtels seulement; (7.3) Places-lit; (8.1,8.2) Fonds Monétaire International.

TAIWAN (PROVINCE DE CHINE)

(1.1) Incl. nre; (2.1-2.6) Excl. nre.

TCHAD

(1.2,3.1,3.3/96-99) THA; (1.2,3.1,3.3/2000) TF; (2.1-2.6) THA; (7.3) Chambres.

THAILANDE

(1.2,3.1-3.4) Incl arrivées nre; (2.1-2.6,4.1-4.3) Excl arrivées nre; (3.3) Incl chemin de fer; (5.5) Jours; (7.3) Dans les principales destinations touristiques seulement.

TOGO

(1.2) THA; (7.3) Chambres; (8.1) Recettes hôtelières; (8.2) Fonds Monétaire International.

TONGA

(1.2) Arrivées par voie aérienne.

TRINITE-ET-TOBAGO

(1.2) Arrivées par voie aérienne; (7.1/99/2000) Données provisoires; (8.2) Fonds Monétaire International.

TUNISIE

(1.2,2.1-3.4) TF, excl nre; (7.1,7.2) Hôtels homologués et non-homologués, pensions et villages de vacances; (7.3) Places-lit; (8.2) Fonds Monétaire International.

TURKMENISTAN

(2.2-2.6,3.1-3.4,4.1-4.3) VF; (8.2) Fonds Monétaire International.

TURQUIE

(1.1,3.1-4.3) VF; (1.3) Arrivées par mer (excl une frontière terrestre depuis 1989); (2.1-2.6) TF; (3.4) Incl passagers en croisière; (5.2) Enquête auprès des établissements d'hébergement homologués par le Ministère du Tourisme; (5.2-5.4) Incl terrains de camping; (5.5,8.1) Enquête (départ des visiteurs étrangers); (5.6,7.3) Hôtels homologués, excl terrains de camping; (7.3) Places-lit.

UKRAINE

(2.1-2.6) TF; (3.1-4.3) VF.

URUGUAY

(1.1,4.1-4.3) Inc nre; (2.2-3.4) Excl nra; (3.3) Incl chemin de fer; (5.5) Jours.

VANUATU

(3.4) Incl Passagers en croisière; (5.5) Jours; (7.3) Chambres dans la région métropolitaine de Port-Vila.

NOTES RELATIVES AUX INDICATEURS DE BASE

VENEZUELA

(1.2,2.1-4.3) TF.

VIET-NAM

(1.1) Incl nre; (1.4,3.4) Incl arrivées de passagers en croisière et par voie maritime; (2.1-4.3) VF; (5.6) Touristes non-résidents. Touristes internes: 96=1,36; 97=1,54; 98=1,54; 99=1,60; 2000=1,60.

YEMEN

(1.2,2.1-2.6) THA; (7.3) Places-lit; (8.2) . Fonds Monétaire International.

YOUGOSLAVIE

(1.2,2.2-2.4) TEC, Incl chambres, maisons et appartements loués du secteur privé; (7.1,7.2) Au 31 août de chaque année; (7.2) places-lit permanentes; (7.3) Places-lit.

ZAMBIE

(3.4) Voies fluviale et lacustre; (5.5) Jours; (7.3) Chambres.

ZIMBABWE

(2.1-2.4) TF; (3.1-3.3,4.1,4.2) VF; (7.1,7.2) Hôtels classés uniquement; (7.3) Places-lit.

NOTAS A LOS INDICADORES BÁSICOS

ALBANIA

(1.2,2.2-2.6,4.1-4.3) Llegadas en hoteles únicamente; (3.1-3.4) VF; (8.1,8.2) Fondo Monetario Internacional.

ALEMANIA

(1.2,2.1-2.6) TEC; (5.6) Turismo receptor HA; DME para turismo interior (Noches): 96=3,36; 97=3,15; 98=3,09; 99=3,07; 2000=3.05; (7.3) Plazas-cama HA; (8.1,8.2) Incluidas las transacciones de comercio de mercancías en las fronteras y las compras de los trabajadores fronterizos a la entrada y salida del país.

ANGOLA

(8.2) Fondo Monetario Internacional.

ANGUILA

(1.1,3.1-4.2) VF; (1.2,2.2-2.3) TF, excl nre; (7.1) Hoteles, casas de huéspedes y apartamentos/ villas; (7.3) Habitaciones; (9.1) PIB.

ANTIGUA AND BARBUDA

(1.2) Llegadas por vías aérea y marítima, excl nre; (1.4) Incl las llegadas en cruceros, cruceros "windjammer" y yates; (4.1-4.3) Llegadas por vía aérea; (6.1) Viajes al extranjero, incluidas salidas de residentes.

ARGELIA

(1.1) Incluidos los nacionales residentes en el extranjero; (2.1-2.6) Excluidos los nacionales residentes en el extranjero.

ARGENTINA

(1.2) Excl nre; (7.1/96) Cifras de hoteles de 1 a 5 estrellas y hoteles no categorizados.
Nota: Las llegadas y los ingresos económicos por turismo internacional receptor constituyen una nueva serie que abarca desde 1990 hasta 1999, que tiene como fuente los datos publicados por la Subsecretaría de Programación Macroeconómica dependiente del Ministerio de Economía y Obras y Servicios Públicos.

ARMENIA

(1.2,2.2-2.6) TEC.

ARUBA

(1.2,2.2-4.3) TF, (5.5) THA; (7.3) Habitaciones; (9.1) PIB.

AUSTRALIA

(1.1) Excl nre y miembros de tripulaciones; (5.5) Comercial; (5.6) Turismo receptor en alojamientos comerciales; (7.1-7.3) Hoteles, moteles y casas de huéspedes con 15 habitaciones o más; (7.3) Habitaciones.

AUSTRIA

(1.2-2.6) TEC; (5.1,5.3/96/97) Hoteles únicamente; (5.1,5.3/98/99) Incl poblados de vacaciones; (5.2,5.4) Excl alojamiento privado; (8.1,8.2) Incl transporte internacional.

AZERBAIYAN

(8.1,8.2) Fondo Monetario Internacional.

BAHAMAS

(1.2,2.2-2.4,4.1-4.3) TF; (5.2) Pernoctaciones en el conjunto de los medios comerciales de alojamiento; (7.1,7.2) Hoteles, apartamentos, bungalows y villas - Establecimientos homologados únicamente; (7.3) Habitaciones; (8.2) Fondo Monetario Internacional.

BAHREIN

(1.1,2.1-4.3) VF, Excl. nre; (3.3) Llegadas a través del King Fahad Causeway; (5.1,7.1,7.2) Unicamente hoteles clasificados; (8.1,8.2) Fondo Monetario Internacional.

BARBADOS

(1.2,2.2-4.3) TF; (7.1,7.2) Hoteles, hoteles-apartamento, apartamentos y bungalows, casas de huéspedes; (7.3) Habitaciones; (8.2) Fondo Monetario Internacional.

BELARUS

(8.1,8.2) Fondo Monetario Internacional.

NOTAS A LOS INDICADORES BÁSICOS

BELGICA

(1.2,2.1-2.4,4.1-4.3) TEC; (6.1/96) Viajes por vacaciones de 4 noches y más; (6.1/97) Viajes por vacaciones y negocios; (8.1,8.2) Fondo Monetario Internacional; Bélgica y Luxemburgo.

BELICE

(1.1,2.2-4.3) VF; (1.3,4.3) Pasajeros en tránsito y cruces de frontera; (2.2) Incl cruces de frontera y residentes en viaje de regreso; (2.4) China.

BENIN

(1.2) THA. 1998: Estimaciones.

BERMUDAS

(1.1) Excl nre; (1.2,2.2,2.7,4.1-4.3) Llegadas por vía aérea; (5.2) Incl pernoctaciones en casas particulares; (7.3) Habitaciones; (9.1) PIB.

BOLIVIA

(1.2-4.3) Datos procedentes de encuestas. A partir del año 2000 se aplicó una nueva encuesta; (1.2-4.3,8.1,8.2/99/2000) Datos preliminares; (3.4) Llegadas por vía lacustre; (5.1,5.3,7.1,7.2) Capitales de departamento únicamente; (5.6) Días, HA, turismo receptor; (7.3) Plazas-cama (hoteles).

BONAIRE

(8.1/2000) El gasto total proviene de una nueva tasa de gasto diario estimada en 2001. Esta cifra viene utilizándose por el Departamento de Economía.

BOSNIA Y HERZEGOVINA

(8.1/96) Ingresos turísticos: Mayo-Diciembre 1996.

BOTSWANA

(8.1,8.2/96-99) Fondo Monetario Internacional.

BRASIL

(3.4) Incl llegadas por vía fluvial; (5.5) Días; (7.1,7.2/96) Hoteles, hoteles-residencias, hoteles de centros de recreo y albergues del Estado ("pousadas") homologados por EMBRATUR; (7.1,7.2/97) Hoteles homologados y no homologados; (8.1) Datos obtenidos en la encuesta por muestreo realizada por EMBRATUR.
Nota 1998: Cambio de metodología.

BULGARIA

(1.1,1.2/98-2000) Se excluyen a los niños sin pasaporte propio; (3.4) Mar y ríos del interior del país; (5.1-5.6,7.2,7.3) Cubre prácticamente el antiguo alojamiento del sector público y de propiedad del Estado. Una parte considerable del sector privado (más del 70 por ciento en 1998) no está incluido en los datos; (7.2) Hoteles únicamente; (7.3) Plazas-cama en los hoteles; (8.1,8.2/98-2000) Nueva metodología elaborada por el Banco Central de Bulgaria y el Ministerio de Economía.

BURKINA FASO

(1.2,2.1-2.4) THA; (4.1-4.3) Incl turismo interno; (7.3) Habitaciones.

BURUNDI

(1.2,2.1-2.4,3.1-4.3) TF, incl nre; (3.4) Llegadas por vía lacustre; (5.6) Días; (7.1,7.2) Hoteles; (8.1,8.2) Fondo Monetario Internacional.

CABO VERDE

(1.2) Llegadas por vía aérea; (5.5) Días; (8.2) Fondo Monetario Internacional.

CAMBOYA

(1.2/96/97) Llegadas por vía aérea; (1.2/98-2000) Llegadas de turistas internacionales por todo el conjunto de medios de transporte; (1.3) Templo "Preah Vihear"; (2.2-2.6,4.1-4.3) Llegadas por vía aérea; (3.3) Llegadas por tierra y barco; (4.1/98,2000) Incl llegadas al aeropuerto de Siem Reap en vuelos directos; 1998: 10.423; 2000: 87.012; (5.5) Días; (8.2) Fondo Monetario Internacional.

CAMERUN

(1.2,2.1-2.6) THA.

CANADA

(1.1,1.3) Datos basados en la contabilidad aduanera, ajustándola en función de los resultados de las encuestas; (1.2,2.1-4.3) TF; (4.2) Incl congresos; (5.6) Turismo receptor; (6.1) Viajes-persona (una/varias noches); (8.1,8.2) Incl gastos médicos, educativos y de las tripulaciones. Excl transporte internacional.
Nota: El "Statistics Canada's Tourism Program" utiliza dos métodos para la recopilación de estadísticas relativas a los viajeros internacionales: conteos en los pasos fronterizos y recepción de cuestionarios por correo (características). Sin embargo, debido a diferencias metodológicas, ambas fuentes son la base de estimaciones diferentes del número de visitantes extranjeros del día que llegan a Canadá por vía aérea comercial o por barco.

NOTAS A LOS INDICADORES BÁSICOS

CHAD

(1.2,3.1,3.3/96-99) THA; (1.2,3.1,3.3/2000) TF; (2.1-2.6) THA; (7.3) Habitaciones.

CHINA

(1.1,3.1-3.4) Incl llegadas personas de origen étnico chino procedentes de HK, Macao, Taiwan y de ultramar (1996= 44.383.182; 1997= 50.159.917; 1998= 56.370.654; 1999= 64.363.298; 2000= 73.283.449), la mayor parte de excursionistas proceden de HK y Macao; (2.1-2.6) Excl llegadas de turistas de origen étnico chino procedentes de HK, Macao, Taiwan y de ultramar; (5.6) Turismo receptor; (6.1/98-2000) Incl miembros de las tripulaciones y otros miembros de las fuerzas armadas; (7.3) Habitaciones.

CHIPRE

(1.2,2.1-2.6) TF; (1.3) Incl pasajeros en crucero y en tránsito; (3.4) Incl. pasajeros en crucero; (7.3) Plazas-cama.

COLOMBIA

(7.3) Habitaciones.
Fuentes: Departamento Administrativo de Seguridad (DAS), Banco de la República, COTELCO.

COMORAS

(1.2,2.1-2.4,4.1-4.3) Llegadas por vía aérea.

CONGO

(1.2-2.3) THA; (7.3) Habitaciones.

COREA, REPUBLICA DE

(1.1) Incl nre y desde Junio 1988 también a los miembros de las tripulaciones; (2.1-2.6) Excl nre; (3.1,3.4) Excl nre y miembros de las tripulaciones; (7.1) Hoteles únicamente; (7.3) Habitaciones; (8.1,8.2) Excl gastos de estudiantes que realizan sus estudios fuera del país.

COSTA RICA

(4.1) Viajes de placer y visita a familiares; (5.5) En la zona central del país; (7.3) En establecimientos de "cinco categorías" en el Gran Área Metropolitana de San José (estudio por muestreo).

COTE D'IVOIRE

(1.2,2.1-3.1,4.1-4.3) Llegadas por vía aérea al aeropuerto internacional FHB de Port Bouet. No están incluidas las llegadas a las fronteras terrestres, al aeropuerto de Bouaké y al aeropuerto Air Ivoire de Abidjan; (1.2/97/98) Llegadas por vía aérea al aeropuerto internacional FHB de Port Bouet y llegadas a las fronteras terrestres; (5.1,5.3) Hoteles; (7.3) Habitaciones; (8.1,8.2) Fondo Monetario Internacional.
1998: Datos preliminares.

CROACIA

(1.2,2.2-2.6) TEC, incl llegadas a puertos de turismo náutico; (3.1-3.4) VF; (5.2,5.4) Incl pernoctaciones en puertos de turismo náutico; (5.6) Turismo interior (interno y receptor) en todos los medios de alojamiento (incl puertos de turismo náutico).

CUBA

(1.1,2.1-2.4) VF; (1.2,4.1-4.3) Llegadas por vía aérea; (1.3) Incl pasajeros en crucero; (5.1,5.3,7.1,7.2) Hoteles, moteles y aparthoteles; (5.2,5.4) Hoteles, moteles, aparthoteles, terrenos de camping/caravaning y otros; (6.1) Comprende sólo giras controladas por el Instituto del Turismo; (7.3) Habitaciones.

CURAÇAO

(1.2,2.2.2,2.3,3.1,4.1-4.3) Llegadas por vía aérea; Incl nre; (3.4) Llegadas de pasajeros en crucero; (7.1) Hoteles, casas de huéspedes y apartamentos; (7.3) Habitaciones.

DINAMARCA

(1.2,2.2-2.4) TEC; (7.1,7.2) Incl alojamientos de vacaciones; (7.3) Plazas-cama; (8.2) Incl los gastos de transporte internacional.

DOMINICA

(1.2,2.2-2.3,4.1-4.3) TF; (3.1-3.4) VF, excl pasajeros en crucero; (7.1) Hoteles, casas de huéspedes, apartamentos y bungalows.

ECUADOR

(1.1) Excl nre.

EGIPTO

(1.1,2.1-3.4) VF; (4.1-4.3) TF; (5.3) Hoteles únicamente en las principales regiones: Cairo, Giza, Sur del Sinaí, Mar Rojo, Luxor, Aswan, Alejandría; (6.1) Viajes por turismo y no-turismo (más del 50% por motivo de trabajo); (7.3) Habitaciones.

NOTAS A LOS INDICADORES BÁSICOS

EL SALVADOR

(1.2) Excl nre; (7.3) Plazas-cama; (8.2) Fondo Monetario Internacional.

ESTONIA

(1.1,2.2-4.3) VF; (4.3) Compras, tránsito, visitas a los amigos.

EMIRATOS ARABES UNIDOS

(1.2) Llegadas en los hoteles únicamente. Incl turismo interno y nre; (2.1-2.6) Llegadas en los hoteles únicamente. Excl turismo interno y nre; (5.1) Pernoctaciones en los hoteles únicamente. Incl turismo interno y nre; (7.1,7.2) Hoteles únicamente; (7.3) Habitaciones alquiladas; (8.1) Ingresos procedentes de los hoteles. Incl turismo interno y nre.

ETIOPIA

(1.2,2.1-2.6,3.1,4.1-4.3/96-99) Llegadas al aeropuerto de Bole únicamente; (1.2,2.1-2.6,3.1-3.3,4.1-4.3/2000) Llegadas a todos los puestos fronterizos; (1.2) Incl nre; (5.6) Años fiscales etíopes; (7.1,7.2/97,2000) Incl. hoteles privados y estatales; (7.3) Plazas-cama; (8.1/96-99) Incl ingresos por servicio de hoteles, operadores turísticos y agencias de viaje, tiendas exentas de impuestos, artículos de regalo y venta de recuerdos; excl moneda extranjera del informe del Banco Nacional de Etiopía e ingresos del sector privado; (8.1/2000) Incorpora una estimación de todos los ingresos del sector; (8.2) Fondo Monetario Internacional.

ERITREA

(1.1) Incl. nre; (2.1-2.6) Excl. nre.

FEDERACION DE RUSIA

(7.1,7.2) Alojamiento en hoteles y en otros establecimientos de carácter turístico.

ESLOVAQUIA

(1.1) Incl frontera con Rep. Checa; (1.2,2.1-2.4) TEC; (5.5,5.6) Turismo receptor en todo tipo de establecimientos de alojamiento turístico; (6.1) Turismo organizado a través de la Agencia de viajes eslovaca; (8.1,8.2) Estimaciones.

FIJI

(1.2,2.2-2.4,3.1-4.3) TF, excl nre; (3.4) Incl pasajeros en crucero; (5.6) Días; (7.3) Habitaciones; (8.2) Fondo Monetario Internacional.

ESLOVENIA

(1.1) Incl todas las categorías de viajeros por cualquier motivo de visita; (1.2,2.1-2.6) TEC; (2.1,2.5,2.6) Estimaciones; (3.1-3.4,4.1-4.3) TEC, datos procedentes de la encuesta sobre 3 años realizada en verano entre los turistas extranjeros llegados a Eslovenia; (6.1) Encuesta trimestral de los viajes de la población residente; (8.1,8.2) Fuente: Banco Central de Eslovenia: los datos se refieren a la partida "Viajes" de la Balanza de Pagos.

FILIPINAS

(1.2,3.1-4.3) TF incl nre; (2.1-2.6) TF excl nre; (4.1-4.3) Llegadas por vía aérea; (5.6,7.3) Hoteles homologados en Metro Manila; (6.1) Incl los trabajadores con contrato procedentes de ultramar; (7.1,7.2) Hoteles homologados únicamente.

ESPAÑA

(1.1) VF, incl nre; (2.2-4.3) TF, incl nre; (2.4) Japón únicamente; (5.1,5.3) Pernoctaciones en hoteles y hostales; (5.2,5.4/96-99) Pernoctaciones en hoteles, hostales y terrenos de camping; (5.2,5.4/2000) Pernoctaciones en hoteles, hostales, terrenos de camping y apartamentos turísticos; (7.1,7.2) Hoteles y hostales únicamente; (7.3) Plazas-cama.

FINLANDIA

1.1,3.1-3.4,4.1-4.3) VF, Encuesta en las fronteras; (1.2/96/97) TCE; (1.2/98-2000) TF, nueva serie; (2.1-2.6) VF; (5.1,5.3,7.1,7.2) Hoteles y establecimientos asimilados; (5.2,5.4) Establecimientos colectivos turísticos; (6.1) Viajes al extranjero; (7.3) Habitaciones (hoteles únicamente); (8.1,8.2) Datos compilados mediante encuestas a los viajeros.

ESTADOS UNIDOS

(1.2,2.2) Incl mexicanos que pasan 1 noche o más en EEUU; (3.1-3.4,4.1,4.2) No incluye la totalidad de mexicanos sino aquéllos que sobrepasan 40km de distancia de la frontera; (3.3) Terrestre; (3.4) Incl llegadas a puertos Great Lake y Puget Sound; (4.1,4.2) Por tipo de visado. Excl Canadá; (6.1) Incl americanos que pasan 1 o varias noches en México.

FRANCIA

(1.1-4.3/96/97) Encuestas en las fronteras; (1.1-4.3/98-2000) Estimaciones; (2.4) Incl Asia Meridional; (5.1,5.3,7.1-7.3) Hoteles únicamente; (5.2,5.4) Todo tipo de alojamiento; (5.4) Serie revisada y extrapolada retroactivamente; (5.5) DME del turismo receptor; (7.3) Tasa neta de ocupación de las habitaciones; (8.1,8.2) A partir de 1999 nueva serie, excluidos los trabajadores fronterizos pagados en divisas (véase: 5ª edición del manual del Fondo Monetario Internacional).

NOTAS A LOS INDICADORES BÁSICOS

GABON

(1.2,2.1-2.6,3.1,4.1-4.3) TF, llegadas al aeropuerto de Libreville.
Nota: 1996-1998: Estimaciones

GAMBIA

(1.2,2.1-2.3,3.1) Llegadas en vuelos fletados únicamente.

GEORGIA

(8.2) Fondo Monetario Internacional.

GHANA

(1.2) Incl nre; (2.1-2.6) Excl nre; (8.1,8.2) Fondo Monetario Internacional.

GRANADA

(1.2,2.2-4.3) TF; (7.1,7.2) Hoteles, bungalows/apartamentos y casas de huéspedes; (7.3) Habitaciones.

GRECIA

(1.1,3.1-4.3) VF; (1.2,2.1-2.6) Datos procedentes de encuestas; (3.4) Incl pasajeros en crucero; (8.1,8.2/98/99) Incluidos registros a través de nuevas metodologías; (8.1,8.2/2000) Fondo Monetario Internacional.

GUADELOUPE

(1.2) THA; (2.2,2.3,5.1/96-99) HA, llegadas y pernoctaciones en 21 establecimientos hoteleros; (2.2,2.3,5.1/2000) HA, llegadas y pernoctaciones en 83 establecimientos hoteleros; (7.1) Hoteles; (7.3) Habitaciones.

GUAM

(1.2) Llegadas por vías aérea y marítima; (2.2) Incl Hawaii; (7.3) Año fiscal al 30 de Septiembre (valor ponderado); (9.1) PIB.

GUATEMALA

(5.5) Días; (8.2) Fondo Monetario Internacional.

GUINEA

(1.2,2.1-2.6,4.1-4.3) Llegadas por vía aérea al aeropuerto de Conakry.

GUYANA

(7.1) Hoteles únicamente.

HAITI

(7.1) Hoteles, hoteles en la playa y casas de huéspedes.

HAWAII (EEUU)

(4.1) Viajes de placer; (4.2) Convenciones, reuniones corp., viajes de incentivo, otros viajes de negocios, misiones gubernamentales, estudios; (4.3) Incl. visitas a parientes y amigos; (5.2,5.5) Días.

HONDURAS

(2.2-4.3) TF; (5.5) Días; (8.2) Fondo Monetario Internacional.

HONG KONG, CHINA

(1.4) Pasajeros en crucero (incl en VF); (6.1) Excl residentes de HK viajando a Macao y China; (7.1) Hoteles (tarifas altas/medias) y albergues/ casas huéspedes; (7.3) Habitaciones; (8.1) Incl ingresos de los miembros de las fuerzas armadas, tripulaciones y pasajeros en tránsito.
Nota: A partir de 1996, las cifras incluyen las llegadas de no-macaenses vía "Macao,China".

HUNGRIA

(1.1,2.1-2.6,3.1-3.4) VF, salidas; (1.2,4.1-4.3) TF, salidas, excl nre; (3.4) Por vía fluvial; (5.2,5.4/96/97) Incl servicio organizado de habitaciones en casas particulares; (7.3) Habitaciones, Julio-Junio; (8.2) Fondo Monetario Internacional.

NOTAS A LOS INDICADORES BÁSICOS

INDIA

(1.2,2.1-4.3) TF, excl nre; (4.1-4.3) Excl llegadas de nacionales del Pakistán y de Bangladesh; (6.1) Salidas de nacionales del país únicamente, por cualquier motivo de visita; (7.1,7.2) En hoteles homologados; (7.3) Habitaciones.

INDIONESIA

(5.5) Días; (5.6,7.3) Únicamente hoteles clasificados; (7.1,7.2) Conjunto de los medios comerciales de alojamiento; (7.3) Habitaciones; (8.2) Fondo Monetario Internacional.

IRAN, REPUBLICA ISLAMICA DEL

(1.2,2.1-3.4) TF; (3.3) Incl ferrocarril; (7.1,7.2) Hoteles únicamente, 21 de Marzo-20 de Marzo; (7.3) Est. (Plazas-cama).

IRLANDA

(1.2,2.3,3.3,4.1,4.3,5.5) Incl turistas procedentes de Irlanda del Norte; (3.3) Incl ferrocarril; (5.1-5.4) Excl turistas procedentes de Irlanda del Norte; (6.1) Incl visitantes del día (excursionistas); (7.3) Habitaciones, hoteles únicamente; (8.2) Excl transporte pagado a las compañías de transporte nacionales.

ISLAS CAIMAN

(1.2,2.2-2.4,4.1-4.3) Llegadas por vía aérea; (5.5,5.6) Días; (7.1,7.2) Hoteles y apartamentos; (7.3) Hoteles (habitaciones); (8.1) Incl gastos de pasajeros en crucero; (9.1) PIB.

ISLAS COOK

(1.2,2.2-2.4,3.1,4.1-4.3) Llegadas por vías aérea y marítima; (7.3) Habitaciones.

ISLAS MARIANAS SEPTENTRIONALES

(1.1,2.2-2.4) VF; (1.2) Llegadas por vía aérea; (2.2) Incl Guam; (7.1) Cubre el 68 por ciento del total de habitaciones censadas.

ISLAS MARSHALL

(1.2,2.2,2.4,4.1-4.3) Llegadas por vía aérea; (5.5) Días.

ISLAS SALOMON

(8.1,8.2) Fondo Monetario Internacional.

ISLAS TURCAS Y CAICOS

(9.1) PIB.

ISLAS VIRGENES AMERICANAS

(2.2,2.3) THA; (3.1) Llegadas de visitantes por vía aérea excl llegadas de residentes y el tráfico entre las islas pero incl excursionistas; (3.4) Pasajeros en crucero; (5.2) Pernoctaciones incl turismo interno (cerca del 40% del total); (7.1,7.3) Hoteles y condominios o villas; (7.3) Habitaciones.

ISLAS VIRGENES BRITANICAS

(7.1) Hoteles y casas de huéspedes; (7.3) Habitaciones; (9.1) PIB.

ISRAEL

(1.1) VF, excl nre; (1.2,2.1-2.6,3.1-3.4,4.1-4.3) TF, excl nre; (3.3) Incl nueva entrada tras una visita de hasta 7 días en el Sinaí; (3.4) Incl personal de la flota EEUU en visita de cortesía; (4.3) Incl visitas a familiares y amigos y peregrinaciones; (5.1) Hoteles turísticos y apart hoteles; (5.6) Turismo receptor en hoteles turísticos; (7.3) Tasa de ocupación/camas en HA abierto.

ITALIA

(1.1,2.1-3.4,4.1,4.2) VF, excluidos los trabajadores estacionales o fronterizos; (1.1-4.2,6.1,8.18.2) A partir de 1996: nuevo sistema de recogida de datos (encuesta en fronteras del "Ufficio Italiano dei Cambi"); (1.2) TF, excluidos los trabajadores estacionales o fronterizos; (1.3) Incl pasajeros en crucero; (5.1) Hoteles únicamente; (6.1) Número de turistas residentes (visitantes que pernoctan) que viajan al extranjero; (7.3) Plazas-cama.

JAMAHIRIYA ARABE LIBIA

(1.1,2.1-2.6) Incl todos los viajeros (visitantes y otros viajeros no definidos como viajeros por la OMT); (5.1,5.2,5.4,7.3,8.2) Estimaciones.

JAMAICA

(1.2,2.1-2.4,3.1,4.1-4.3) TF, llegadas por vía aérea, incl. nre, tarjetas E/D; (5.2) Datos obtenidos multiplicando la DME por el número de escalas en cada uno de los países de origen; (5.5) Duración de estancia prevista; (5.6) Pernoctaciones en los hoteles únicamente; (7.3) Habitaciones; (8.2) Fondo Monetario Internacional.

NOTAS A LOS INDICADORES BÁSICOS

JAPON

(1.2,2.1-2.6,4.1-4.3) TF, excl nre; (3.1,3.4) VF, incl residentes extranjeros en Japón; (5.5) Días; (7.1) Hoteles homologados y no homologados así como "ryokans" (Posadas); (7.3) Tasa de ocupación de los principales hoteles gubernamentales homologados (habitaciones).

JORDANIA

(1.1,2.1-3.4) VF; (5.5) Para visitas organizadas únicamente; (7.3) Habitaciones; (8.2) Incl pagos por educación; (9.1) Margen oriental ("East Bank") únicamente.

KAZAJSTAN

(2.2-2.6) VF; (8.1,8.2) Fondo Monetario Internacional.

KENYA

(1.1-4.3) VF, excl nre, llegadas a través de todos los puestos fronterizos; (1.1,2.1-2.5) Los datos corresponden a estimaciones, cuya proyección se basa en la cuota de mercado del año 1989; (2.5) India únicamente; (5.6) Días; (7.2) Hoteles únicamente (excl los hoteles no homologados); (7.3) Plazas-cama; (8.1,8.2) Fondo Monetario Internacional.
Fuente: Encuesta económica realizada en diferentes años.

KIRGUISTAN

(8.1,8.2) Fondo Monetario Internacional.

KIRIBATI

(1.2) Llegadas por vía aérea, Tarawa e Isla Christmas; (4.1-4.3) TF.

KUWAIT

(1.1,2.1-2.6,3.1-3.4) VF; (1.2,4.1-4.3) THA; (8.1,8.2) Fondo Monetario Internacional.

MACEDONIA

(1.2,2.2-2.4) TEC; (3.1-3.3) VF.

LESOTHO

(1.1,2.1-4.3) VF; (7.1,7.2) Hoteles únicamente; (8.1,8.2) Fondo Monetario Internacional.

LETONIA

(1.1,3.1-3.4) VF, llegadas de no residentes a las fronteras. Datos procedentes de la Policía Estatal de Fronteras; (1.2-1.4,2.2-2.5,4.1-4.3,5.5) Salidas de no residentes; Encuesta realizada en los puestos fronterizos del país; (1.3) Incl pasajeros en crucero; (7.3) Plazas-cama.

LIBANO

(1.2) Excl nacionales de Siria; (8.1/99-2000) Por falta de datos sobre ingresos por turismo internacional relativo a estadísticas del turismo receptor, el Departamento "Internet y Servicio Estadístico del Ministerio de Turismo" considera que un turista gasta una media de 1.000 $EEUU.

LIECHTENSTEIN

(1.2,2.2-2.4) THA; (7.3) Plazas-cama.

LITUANIA

(2.2-2.4) TEC; (2.4) Asia/Pacífico; (3.1-3.4) VF; (4.1-4.3) TF; (5.6) EC; (7.3) Habitaciones, hoteles únicamente.

LUXEMBURGO

(1.2,2.1-2.4) TEC, incl también albergues de juventud, alojamientos turísticos privados y otros; (5.1,5.3) Pernoctaciones en hoteles, albergues y casas de huéspedes; (5.2,5.4) Incl también alojamientos turísticos privados y otros; (7.3) Habitaciones.

MACAO, CHINA

(1.1,2.1-4.3) VF; (1.1-1.3,2.4,3.1-3.4) Incl personas de origen étnico chino procedentes de Hong Kong; (1.2,1.3) Estimaciones; (3.1) Incl llegadas en helicóptero; (6.1) Viajes organizados; (7.1,7.2) Hoteles, casas de huéspedes y "pousadas"; (7.3) Habitaciones; (8.1) Incl ingresos procedentes del juego; (9.1) PIB.

MADAGASCAR

(1.2,2.1-2.4,3.1,4.1-4.3) TF. Llegadas por vía aérea; (7.3) Habitaciones.

NOTAS A LOS INDICADORES BÁSICOS

MALASIA

(1.2,2.1-2.6) TF, salida de turistas extranjeros; incl los residentes de Singapur que cruzan la frontera por la Johore Causeway; (3.1-4.3) Península de Malasia únicamente; (6.1) Salidas de malasios peninsulares, incl salidas por carretera a través de la frontera Johore Causeway; (7.1) Hoteles con 10 habitaciones y más; (7.3) Habitaciones; (8.2) Fondo Monetario Internacional.

MALAWI

(1.2-4.3) Salidas; (7.1) Incl pabellones; (7.3) Plazas-cama.
Nota: Todas las cifras de 1999 y 2000 son provisionales.

MALDIVAS

(1.2,2.1-2.6) Llegadas por vía aérea; (5.1,5.6,7.1-7.3) Centros turísticos y hoteles; (5.6) Días; (8.2) Fondo Monetario Internacional.

MALI

(1.2) Llegadas por vía aérea; (2.1-2.4) THA; (7.3) Habitaciones; (8.1,8.2/96/97) Fondo Monetario Internacional.

MALTA

(1.2-3.4/96-99) Salidas; (1.2-3.4/2000) Llegadas; (7.2) Hoteles, complejos turísticos, casas de huéspedes y apartamentos de vacaciones; (7.3) Plazas-cama en HA; (8.1,8.2/2000) Datos provisionales.

MARRUECOS

(1.2,3.1-4.3) TF, incl nre; (2.1-2.6) TF, excl nre; (5.1,5.3) Pernoctaciones en hoteles homologados y no homologados, ciudades de vacaciones y residencias turísticas; (7.3) Habitaciones (hoteles homologados).

MARTINICA

(1.2,2.2,2.3,4.1-4.3) TF; (7.1) Hoteles y ciudades de vacaciones ("Club Méditerranée"); (7.3) Habitaciones en HA.

MAURICIO

(1.1,4.1-4.3) VF; (1.2,2.1-3.4) TF; (5.5) Grandes hoteles; (7.3) Habitaciones; (8.2) Fondo Monetario Internacional.

MEXICO

(1.2,2.2-4.3) TF, incl nre; (1.3) Incl visitantes franja fronteriza EEUU y estancia inferior a 24h; (3.3) Incl ferrocarril; (5.1) Centros turísticos seleccionados; (5.1/2000) Cifra preliminar; (5.6) Turismo extranjero únicamente; (7.3) Habitaciones; (8.1) Incl ingresos pasajeros en crucero; (8.1,8.2) Incl ingresos/ gastos visitantes fronterizos (estancias: < 24h, 24-72h y más).

MICRONESIA (ESTADOS FEDERADOS DE)

(1.2,2.2,2.4) Llegadas en los Estados de Kosrae, Chuuk, Pohnpei y Yap.

MONACO

(1.2-2.6) THA.

MONGOLIA

(8.1,8.2) Fondo Monetario Internacional.

MONTSERRAT

(1.2,2.2,2.3) TF; (1.3) Llegadas de excursionistas por vía aérea únicamente; (2.2,2.3,4.1,4.2) TF, llegadas por vía aérea únicamente; (3.1,3.4) VF; (4.2) Negocios y otros motivos; (7.1) Hoteles y villas; (9.1) PIB.

MYANMAR

(1.2,2.2-2.5,3.1) Llegadas por vía aérea al aeropuerto de Yangon; (4.1-4.3) VF; (5.1,5.3,5.6) Hoteles y establecimientos asimilados administrados por el Estado únicamente; (7.1,7.2) Hoteles administrados por el Estado y casas de huéspedes privadas homologadas; (7.3) Habitaciones; (8.2) Fondo Monetario Internacional.

NAMIBIA

(2.1-2.3) TF; (3.1) Llegadas al aeropuerto de Windhoek; (4.1-4.3) TF; (7.3) Plazas-camas.

NEPAL

(1.2) Incl las llegadas procedentes de la India; (3.3) Vía terrestre; (7.1,7.2) Hoteles en Kathmandu y en el interior del país; (8.2) Fondo Monetario Internacional.

NOTAS A LOS INDICADORES BÁSICOS

NICARAGUA

(1.2,2.2-4.3) TF; (5.1,5.3) Principales establecimientos de alojamiento del país (7); (5.2,5.4) Total de establecimientos del país; (5.6) EC, turismo receptor; DME para turismo interior (Noches): 96=1,7; 97=1,5; 98=1,8; 99=1,6; 2000=2,0; (7.1,7.2) HA ubicados en categorías superiores.

NIGER

(1.2,4.1-4.3) Llegadas por vía aérea (aeropuerto de Niamey); (5.5) Días; (7.1,7.2) Hoteles, albergues y bungalows.

NIGERIA

(1.1,2.1-2.6) VF; (1.2,4.1-4.3) TF.

NIUE

(1.2) Llegadas por vía aérea, incl los nacionales de Niue que residen normalmente en Nueva Zelandia.

NORUEGA

(1.2/96/97) THA en los hoteles homologados; (1.2,2.1-2.4/98-2000) TCE, nueva serie; (5.1) Pernoctaciones en establecimientos homologados; (5.1,7.1,7.2) A partir de 1988 las cifras para HA se refieren a establecimientos con 20 camas o más durante todo el año; (6.1) Sólo viajes organizados en chárter; (7.3) Plazas-cama.

NUEVA CALEDONIA

(1.2,2.1-4.3) Incl nre; (5.6) Días, hoteles en Noumea; (6.1) A partir de 2000, esta cifra se refiere a los residentes que regresan; (7.1) Fuente: "Nouvelle Calédonie Tourisme"; (7.3) Habitaciones en Noumea; (8.1) Gastos efectuados en el país de acogida por los visitantes internacionales; excluido el transporte internacional; (9.1) PIB.

NUEVA ZELANDIA

(1.1,3.1-4.3) VF, Incl nre; (2.1-2.6) VF, Excl nre; (5.2) Estimación realizada a partir de las pernoctaciones (porcentaje medio de las pernoctaciones del turismo internacional en enero, abril, julio y octubre); (5.3) hoteles/moteles clasificados; (6.1) Salidas de residentes de NZ de corta duración (año civil); (7.1) Hoteles únicamente; (7.1,7.3) Los datos se refieren al año civil, facilitados a través de la Encuesta en los Alojamientos (que comenzó en Julio de 1996).

OMAN

(1.2,2.1-2.6) THA; (7.3) Habitaciones; (8.1) Ventas hoteleras; (8.2) Fondo Monetario Internacional.

PAISES BAJOS

(1.2-2.4) TEC; (5.1,5.3) Hoteles y pensiones; (6.1) Salidas de nacionales por vacaciones; (7.2) Hoteles; (7.3) Plazas-cama.

PAKISTAN

(5.5) Días; (8.1) Banco Estatal de Pakistán.

PALAU

(1.2,2.2-2.4,3.1) Llegadas por vía aérea (aeropuerto internacional de Palau).

PANAMA

(1.1) VF, Aeropuerto Internacional Tocúmen (AIT), frontera de Paso Canoa (FPC), puertos de Cristóbal y Balboa (PCB) y estadísticas IPAT; (2.2-2.4) VF, AIT, FPC y estad. IPAT; (3.1-3.4) TF, AIT, FPC, PCB y estad. IPAT; Excl llegadas a otros puertos de entrada (sin especificar) (000)= 97:19; 98:23; 99:20; 2000:28; (4.1-4.3) AIT y estad. IPAT; (5.1) hoteles de la Ciudad de Panamá y estadísticas IPAT; (7.1,7.2) Habitaciones/ plazas cama inventariadas para turismo internacional; (7.3) Habitaciones.

PAPUA NUEVA GUINEA

(8.2) Fondo Monetario Internacional.

PARAGUAY

(1.2,2.1-4.3) Excl nre y miembros de tripulación; (3.4) Vía fluvial; (7.3) Plazas-cama; (8.1,8.2) El Banco Central de Paraguay cambió su metodología de cálculo en los ingresos y gastos turísticos por considerarlos sobrestimados. Los datos de ingresos y gastos turísticos corresponden solamente a gastos realizados por turistas. Los gastos por excursionistas no están incluidos en la Balanza de Pagos, por tanto se excluyó esta información.

PERU

(1.2) Con pasaporte y salvoconducto; (2.1-2.5,3.1-3.4,4.1-4.3) TF, sólo con pasaporte; (3.4) Incl vía fluvial; (5.5) Con pasaporte y salvoconducto; (8.1,8.2) Fondo Monetario Internacional.

POLINESIA FRANCESA

(1.2,2.2-4.3) TF, excl nre; (1.2/2000) La cifra de 252.200 ha sido estimada por el Instituto de Estadística (ISPF); (5.5,5.6) Días; (7.1,7.2) Hoteles únicamente; al 31 de diciembre de cada año; (7.3) Habitaciones en hoteles.

NOTAS A LOS INDICADORES BÁSICOS

POLONIA

(1.1,2.1-3.4) VF; (4.1-4.3) TF, según encuestas del Instituto de Turismo; (5.1,5.3/96) Habitaciones en alquiler; (5.6) EC; (6.1) Viajes de turismo emisor registrados en las fronteras; (7.3) Habitaciones; (7.3/99) Habitaciones, hoteles únicamente; (8.1,8.2) Según encuestas y estimaciones del Instituto de Turismo.

PORTUGAL

(1.1,3.1-3.4) VF; (1.2,2.1-2.4,4.1-4.3) TF, excl nre; incl llegadas procedentes del extranjero a Madeira/Azores; (1.4) Incl pasajeros por mar en tránsito; (5.2) Incl pernoctaciones en alojamientos de Madeira y Azores.; (5.6) EC; (7.1,7.2) Hoteles, moteles, albergues, pensiones y "pousadas" (Julio-Junio); (7.3) Plazas-cama (hoteles homologados).

PUERTO RICO

(1.2) TF, llegadas por vía aérea (año fiscal: Julio-Junio); (2.2) Incl sólo Islas Vírgenes Americanas y EE.UU; (7.1) Habitaciones endosadas por la Compañía de Turismo de Puerto Rico; (7.3) Habitaciones; año fiscal (Julio-Junio); incl habitaciones ocupadas por residentes de Puerto Rico.

QATAR

(1.2) Llegadas en hoteles; (9.1) PIB.

REINO UNIDO

(1.1-4.3) VF, salidas; (3.3) Túnel; (5.5) Días; (7.2) Hoteles; (7.3) Plazas-cama (Inglaterra únicamente).

REPUBLICA ARABE SIRIA

(1.1,2.1-3.4) VF, excl las llegadas de nre; (1.2/96/97) THA; (1.2/98-2000) TEC; (1.2,5.2/98) Cambio de metodología; (7.3) Habitaciones; (8.1) Fondo Monetario Internacional.

REPUBLICA CENTROAFRICANA

(1.2) Llegadas por vía aérea.

REPUBLICA CHECA

(1.1,3.1-3.3) VF; (1.2,2.1-2.4) TEC; (1.2,2.1-2.4,5.1-5.4/2000) Datos preliminares; (6.1) Estancia en el extranjero de visitantes (turistas y excursionistas).

REPUBLICA DE MOLDOVA

(1.1-6.1) Visitantes que se beneficiaron de los servicios de los agentes económicos registrados oficialment en la actividad turística y en el alojamiento (excluidas las regiones del margen izquierdo del Dniestr y la municipalidad de Bender).

REPUBLICA DEMOCRATICA DEL CONGO

(1.2/96/97) Excl nre; (1.2,4.1-4.3/98) Incl nre; (1.2-4.3/98) Llegadas a través de los puestos fronterizos de "Ndjili" y "Beach"; (2.1-2.4) Excl nre; (7.1) Hoteles homologados.

REPUBLICA DEMOCRATICA POPULAR LAO

(1.2) TF; (2.2-2.5,3.1,3.3,4.1-4.3) VF; (5.5) Días.

REPUBLICA DOMINICANA

(1.2) Llegadas por vía aérea únicamente, incl nre; (1.4) Todas las llegadas por mar; (2.2-2.4) Salidas por vía aérea, excl nre; (2.4) Japón únicamente; (7.1,7.2) Hoteles; (7.3) Habitaciones.

REPUBLICA UNIDA DE TANZANIA

(8.2) Fondo Monetario Internacional; (9.1) Los datos del PNB se refieren a Tanzania continental únicamente.

REUNION

(2.1-2.5,4.1-4.3/96-98) Llegadas por vía aérea; (5.5) Días.

RUMANIA

(1.1,2.1-2.6,3.1-4.3) VF; (4.1-4.3/99) A partir de 1999 no se recopilan los datos relativos a las llegadas internacionales por motivo de la visita.

SABA

(1.3) Principalmente desde San Martín; (7.1) Hoteles.

NOTAS A LOS INDICADORES BÁSICOS

SAINT KITTS Y NEVIS

(1.2) TF, llegadas por vías aérea y marítima; (1.4) Llegadas en yates y cruceros; (2.2,2.3) TF, llegadas por vía aérea.

SAMOA

(8.2) Fondo Monetario Internacional.

SAN EUSTAQUIO

(1.1) Llegadas por vías aérea y marítima, incl nre.

SAN MARINO

(1.1) Incl visitantes italianos; (7.1,7.2) Hoteles únicamente.

SAN MARTIN

(1.2,2.2,2.3) Por vía aérea, incl las llegadas a San Martín (parte francesa de la isla); (3.1) Llegadas al aeropuerto "Juliana" (incl visitantes con destino a San Martín (parte francesa); (7.1,7.2) Hoteles, casas de huéspedes y apartamentos; (8.1) Estimaciones elaboradas por el Banco Central, incl estimaciones para Saba y San Eustaquio.

SAN VICENTE Y LAS GRANADINAS

(1.2,2.2-2.3,4.1-4.3) TF; (3.4) Incl pasajeros en crucero y en yate; (7.1) Hoteles, apartamentos, bungalows, villas y casas de huéspedes.

SANTA LUCIA

(1.1,2.2,2.3,3.1,4.1-4.3) TF, excl nre; (3.4) Incl. pasajeros en crucero; (7.3) Habitaciones.

SENEGAL

(1.2,2.1-2.6) THA; (5.2,5.4) Hoteles y ciudades de vacaciones; (5.6) HA; (7.3) Plazas-cama; (8.2) Fondo Monetario Internacional.

SEYCHELLES

(1.2,2.1-4.3) TF; (5.5) Pernoctaciones basadas en las salidas; (7.1,7.2) Hoteles y casas de huéspedes; (7.3) Plazas-cama.

SIERRA LEONA

(2.1) Africa Occidental únicamente; (2.2) América del Norte únicamente; (2.3) Francia y Reino Unido únicamente; (7.1,7.2) Hoteles únicamente; (7.1,7.2/96) Drástica reducción del número de habitaciones y plazas-cama registradas como consecuencia de crecientes hostilidades que dieron lugar a la destrucción de diversos hoteles y establecimientos asimilados.

SINGAPUR

(1.1) Excl llegadas de ciudadanos malasios por vía terrestre; incl visitantes del día (excursionistas); (1.3) Pasajeros en tránsito y en crucero; (5.5,5.6) Días; (7.1) Hoteles (homologados y no homologados); (7.3) Habitaciones; hoteles homologados únicamente.

SRI LANKA

(1.2,2.1-4.3) TF, excl nre; (7.1,7.2) Hoteles, moteles, albergues, casas de huéspedes y aparthoteles; (7.3) Habitaciones.

SUDAFRICA

(1.1,3.1-4.2) Excl nre; (7.1,7.2) Hoteles únicamente; (7.3) Habitaciones (hoteles); (8.1,8.2) Fondo Monetario Internacional.
Nota: Sudáfrica, incl las Repúblicas de Transkei, Bophuthatswana, Venda y Ciskei.

SUDAN

(1.2,2.1-2.6,3.1/98-2000) Llegadas al aeropuerto de Khartoum; (7.1,7.2) Hoteles, albergues y centros turísticos; (8.1,8.2) Fondo Monetario Internacional.

SUECIA

(1.2) TEC excl. camping; (5.1,5.3) Hoteles únicamente; (7.3) Plazas-cama.

SUIZA

(1.1,1.2) Estimaciones; (1.3) Incl personas en tránsito; (2.1-2.6) THA; (5.6) THA (turistas extranjeros); (7.1,7.2) Hoteles, moteles y albergues homologados; (7.3) Tasa neta de ocupación (plazas-cama disponibles).

NOTAS A LOS INDICADORES BÁSICOS

SURINAME

(1.2,2.2-2.4,3.1,4.1-4.3) Llegadas al aeropuerto de Zanderij; (2.3) Incl personas originarias de Suriname procedentes de los Países Bajos; (8.1,8.2) Fondo Monetario Internacional.

SWAZILANDIA

(1.2) Llegadas en los hoteles únicamente; (7.3) Plazas-cama; (8.1,8.2) Fondo Monetario Internacional.

TAILANDIA

(1.2,3.1-3.4) Incl las llegadas de nre; (2.1-2.6,4.1-4.3) Excl las llegadas de nre; (3.3) Incl ferrocarril; (5.5) Días; (7.3) En los principales destinos turísticos únicamente.

TAIWAN (PROVINCIA DE CHINA)

(1.1) Incl. nre; (2.1-2.6) Excl. nre.

TOGO

(1.2) THA; (7.3) Habitaciones; (8.1) Ingresos hoteleros; (8.2) Fondo Monetario Internacional.

TONGA

(1.2) Llegadas por vía aérea.

TRINIDAD Y TABAGO

(1.2) Llegadas por vía aérea; (7.1/99/2000) Datos provisionales; (8.2) Fondo Monetario Internacional.

TUNEZ

(1.2,2.1-3.4) TF, excl nre; (7.1,7.2) Hoteles homologados y no homologados, pensiones y ciudades de vacaciones; (7.3) Plazas-cama; (8.2) Fondo Monetario Internacional.

TURKMENISTAN

(2.2-2.6,3.1-3.4,4.1-4.3) VF; (8.2) Fondo Monetario Internacional.

TURQUIA

(1.1,3.1-4.3) VF; (1.3) Llegadas por mar (excl. una frontera terrestre desde 1989); (2.1-2.6) TF; (3.4) Incl pasajeros en crucero; (5.2) Encuesta en establecimientos de alojamiento homologados por el Ministerio de Turismo; (5.2,5.4) Incl terrenos de camping; (5.3,8.1) Encuesta (salidas de visitantes extranjeros); (5.6,7.3) Hoteles homologados, excl terrenos de camping; (7.3) Plazas-cama.

UCRANIA

(2.1-2.6) TF; (3.1-4.3) VF.

UGANDA

(7.2) Hoteles únicamente; (8.1,8.2) Fondo Monetario Internacional.

URUGUAY

(1.1,4.1-4.3) Incl nre; (2.2-3.4) Excl nre; (3.3) Incl ferrocarril; (5.5) Días.

VANUATU

(3.4) Incl pasajeros en crucero; (5.5) Días; (5.3) Habitaciones en la zona metropolitana de Port-Vila.

VENEZUELA

(1.2,2.1-4.3) TF.

VIET NAM

(1.1) Incl nre; (1.4,3.4) Incl llegadas de pasajeros en crucero y por vía marítima; (2.1-4.3) VF; (5.6) Turistas no residentes. Turistas internos: 96=1,36; 97=1,54; 98=1,54; 99=1,60; 2000=1,60.

NOTAS A LOS INDICADORES BÁSICOS

YEMEN

(1.2,2.1-2.6) THA; (7.3) Plazas-cama; (8.2) Fondo Monetario Internacional.

ZAMBIA

(3.4) Río o lago; (5.5) Días; (7.3) Habitaciones.

YUGOSLAVIA

(1.2,2.2-2.4) TEC, Incl habitaciones, casas y apartamentos alquilados del sector privado; (7.1,7.2) Al 31 de Agosto de cada año; (7.2) Plazas-cama permanentes; (7.3) Plazas-cama.

ZIMBABWE

(2.1-2.4) TF; (3.1-3.3,4.1,4.2) VF; (7.1,7.2) Sólo hoteles clasificados; (7.3) Plazas-cama.